SHOREHAM

SHOREHAM
A Village in Kent

MALCOLM WHITE MA
AND
JOY SAYNOR MA

THE SHOREHAM SOCIETY

British Library Cataloguing in Publication Data

White, Malcolm
    Shoreham: a village in Kent
1. Kent, Shoreham, history
I. Title II. Saynor, Joy
942.2'36
ISBN 0-9514917-0-9

© C.A.M. White and J.S. Saynor 1989

This book is copyright under the Berne Convention.
No reproduction in any form or by any means without
permission. All rights reserved.

Published by the Shoreham Society
Mill Cottage, Shoreham, Kent TN14 7RP

Designed by Michael R. Carter

Typeset in Plantin and Palatino
by The Design Team of Ascot
Printed and bound in Great Britain by
Cambridge University Press

CONTENTS

Preface and Acknowledgements		vii
Abbreviations used in text		ix
I	Beginnings	1
II	Pre-Conquest: Anglo-Saxon Kent	9
III	1066-1500	15
IV	The Tudors	47
V	Land distribution 1284-1608: The families of Tudor Shoreham	59
VI	The Seventeenth Century (1)	75
VII	The Seventeenth Century (2): Shoreham and the Civil War	85
VIII	The Eighteenth Century: The Justices, the villagers and the Church	99
IX	The Eighteenth Century: The rich and the poor	111
X	The Nineteenth Century (1)	125
XI	The Nineteenth Century (2)	137
XII	The Nineteenth Century (3)	153

XIII	The Twentieth Century (1) 1894-1918	169
XIV	The Twentieth Century (2) 1919-39	187
XV	The Twentieth Century (3) 1939-50	207
Epilogue		223
Notes		229
Appendixes		245
Index		257

PREFACE AND ACKNOWLEDGEMENTS

ANYONE who comes to Shoreham soon becomes aware of its special quality as a place and as a community, but it is only when one begins to enquire into its past that one realizes the extent of the knowledge available, and how many through the centuries have been interested in this unobtrusive village and the valley in which it nestles. William Lambarde in his *A Perambulation of Kent* noted in 1570 that the 'Town of Shoreham' paid £3 18s 0d in taxes, second only in the district to 'Sevenoak', paying £4 15s 0d. Edward Hasted in the eighteenth century and W.H. Ireland in 1830 added to the harvest of information, though Ireland sited Romney Street on the western boundary of the parish near 'Thimbling Bottom', instead of on the eastern boundary. The interest steadily increased in the nineteenth and twentieth centuries. Any writer on West Kent will be indebted to Dr Gordon Ward for his work between the wars in compiling and handing down to us his research notebooks, and to Charles Hesketh, Hubert W. Knocker and C.T. Phillips, who were working on the history of the district at that time. Much of their work as well as that of others is to be found in the West Kent branch of the Kent Archives Office, housed in the Sevenoaks Library.

It would have been hard indeed to have written the chapters of the medieval period without Professor F.R.H. Du Boulay's *The Lordship of Canterbury* providing us with the living detail complemented by Dennis Clarke's scholarly translation of the Custumal of 1284.

More recently R.G. Bennett in 1958 circulated privately his history of the ancient family, *The Kentish Polhills* — an invaluable source of information. In 1975 Dennis Clarke and Anthony Stoyel published their work *Otford in Kent – A History*. The histories of Otford and Shoreham are intimately entwined especially in the medieval period, and have only gradually taken separate paths in more recent times. This compelled us to study closely Dennis Clarke's and Anthony Stoyel's work in order to mesh in our account of Shoreham's history with theirs of neighbouring Otford and to minimize duplication. We are immensely grateful to both of them personally for the help they have given us. We are grateful too for the generous assistance given us by the Hon Helen Mildmay-White for allowing photographs to be taken from pictures in her family albums; making available to us the Shoreham estate papers of the Mildmay family covering the period from the 1830s to the 1950s and her advice on the Mildmay family's life in Shoreham during the late nineteenth and twentieth centuries.

The history of that period has been immeasurably enriched by the many contributions of those living and some now dead who gave generously of their recollections of earlier years in Shoreham. To them we give thanks and their names include: Mr W.G.G. Alexander, Mr D. Asprey, Mrs A. Ball, Mr R. Bell, Mrs E. Booker, Mr and Mrs R. Booker, Miss D. Brown, Mr R. Cornwell, Mr F.M. Crouch, Mrs A. De Decker, Mr and Mrs H. Dinnis, Mr D. Draffin, Miss D. Durrant, Mr L. Edwards, Mrs A. Gibson, Mrs G. Gillham, Mr and Mrs J. Higgins, Mr F. Hitchcock, Mr and Mrs P. Hodges, Mrs S. Horsley, Mr and Mrs P. Kingshill, Mr and Mrs H.G.F. Lambe, Mrs M. Lewis, Dr and Mrs W. Lothian, Mr and Mrs M. MacDonnell, Mr L.A. Mathias, Mr and Mrs P. Meade, Lt Col T.E. Morgan, Mr and Mrs S.A.E. Platts, Mrs H. Pollock, Mrs L. Pysden, Mrs P. Ritchie, Mr R.F. Russell, Mr P. Sharbacker, Mr E. Spurr, Mr J. Summerfield, Mrs D. Teague, Mrs Nancy Teague, Miss R. Waring, Mrs J. Waters, Mrs G. Webb, Miss Helen Wheeler, Mrs G. Franklin White, Mr and Mrs A.E. Whitworth, Mrs R.H. de B. Wilmot.

We were continually encouraged by Mrs Katharine Moore and were glad to receive her advice. She claimed to be an 'ordinary reader' who helped to bring some clarity and style to the pages. Another who wrested a clear typescript from illegible manuscript was Polly White, to whom we are immensely grateful for so much patient and hard work.

That the Shoreham Society was prepared to publish the work has been a great comfort, and the assistance of its Chairman, Nigel Britten, in the production of the book has been immeasurable. Thanks are due to David Linton for his work on the index and to Ken Wilson for his maps. For the embellishing of the book we thank Susan Platts and Herbert Morel, Ian Harper and all who have contributed to the visual record.

We recall with thanks the assistance so willingly given by the staff of all those public archive collections mentioned in the pages of the history.

Shoreham's vicar, The Revd Dr Geoffrey Simpson, has been unstinting in his assistance, always making us welcome at the vicarage to examine documents relevant to the story. Over the road at the Lodge, Edith Bracelin, a lifelong historian, gave us constant encouragement and generous help. It was her hope that having read the drafts of each chapter as they appeared she would read the history in its final form, but sadly Edith did not live to do so.

Many years ago the interviewing, searching and recording began. It has been very exciting at times, sometimes a hard grind, but always deeply satisfying. We hope that you will find as much pleasure in the reading as we did in the writing.

We dedicate the book to all the people of Shoreham.

                Malcolm White
                Joy Saynor

                Modbury and Shoreham, September 1989

ABBREVIATIONS USED IN TEXT

AC	*Archaeologia Cantiana.*
AP	*A History of the Parish Church of St Peter & St Paul, Shoreham Kent* by Augustus Payne (1930).
APM	Annual Parish Meeting, Shoreham.
Bamping	*West Kingsdown* by Lena Bamping (1983).
BGCH	*Barracuda Guide to County History* Vol.I Kent by T.A. Bushell.
DNB	*Dictionary of National Biography.*
D'ANB	Paul D'Aranda's Notebook.
Dunlop	*The Pleasant Town of Sevenoaks – A History* by Sir John Dunlop.
ER	The Electoral Register for Shoreham.
FAAG	Fawkham & Ash Archaeological Group.
GW	Dr Gordon Ward's notebooks held in Sevenoaks Library.
Hoskins	*Old Devon* by W.G. Hoskins (Pan Books 1966).
IPM	Inventory Post Mortem.
JS	*Aspects of the History of Shoreham (Kent) in the C18 and C19.* by Joy Saynor
KAS	Kent Archaeological Society.
K(C)AO	Kent (County) Archives Office.
KTGR	*The Community of Kent & the Great Rebellion 1640-1660* by Alan Everitt (Leicester University Press 1986).
L & P	Letters & Papers Foreign & Domestic Henry VIII, PRO.
LHE	*The Local Historian's Encyclopaedia* by John Richardson (Historical Publications 1974).

LPL	Lambeth Palace Library.
ODHS	Otford and District Historical Society.
OIK	*Otford in Kent – A History* by Dennis Clarke & Anthony Stoyel (ODHS 1975).
PC	Shoreham Parish Council.
PMM	The record of the Shoreham Parish Monthly Meeting (held by the Parish Clerk).
PRO	Public Record Office.
RDC	Rural District Council.
SDAH	Sevenoaks District Architectural History.
SL	Sevenoaks Library.
SP	State Papers.
SPM	Shoreham Parish Magazine.
TKP	*The Kentish Polhills, AD 1422-1958* by R.G. Bennett (Private circulation 15 Oct 1958).
VB	Vestry Book, Shoreham Parish Church.
VM	Vestry Minutes, Shoreham Parish Church.
WCM(R)	Westminster Chapter Muniment (Room).
WD	William Danks.
Youings	*Sixteenth-Century England* by Joyce Youings (Pelican 1984).

HM 1989

Shoreham and district, from the first edition of the one-inch Ordnance Survey map. (David & Charles)

I
BEGINNINGS

*'The soil of Kent is soaked in history.
Turn a stone and you start a sleeping century'*

(Richard Church, from 'The Little Kingdom')

WHEN the settlement of Kent by the English was first beginning, in the fifth century AD, a small group of Jutes or possibly Frisians called their farmstead 'the ham at the slope' or Shoreham. Their landscape provided abundant evidence of more than 2,000 years of continuous use.[1] The series of east–west boundaries crossing the Darent valley gave the inhabitants a share of the fertile riverine land as well as a portion of the less productive clay-with-flints topping of the chalk downs. Thus the Shoreham parish of later years had very early acquired its characteristic oblong shape – some four miles from east to west by two and a half miles from north to south.

But it is necessary to travel backwards through long aeons of time – at least 36,000 years, to the last Ice Age when Kent was joined to the continent by a 50-mile-wide land bridge – for evidence of early animal and human species in this part of the upper Darent valley. During a recent investigation of the river gravels of the Redland Pit, north of Sevenoaks, more than four hundred sets of identifiable animal remains from fourteen species were discovered.[2] The earliest remains were those of the woolly rhinoceros and woolly mammoth, which became extinct when the glaciers melted, although the great wild ox – the aurochs – the reindeer, the wild boar and red deer lived on into the warmer climate. Some 9,500 years ago the horse and the dog appeared. The horse remains are particularly significant: until their discovery there was no record of the animal's existence until c. 1800 BC[3] it was reintroduced as a domestic animal.

Sir Joseph Prestwich, the geologist who lived at Darent Hulme in the nineteenth century (see Chapter XII), proved that man, the hunter and gatherer, and other mammals existed together in the Old Stone Age. The flint nodules found in large quantities on the surface of the eastern and western slopes of the downs provided the raw material for the great variety of tools and weapons used by the tiny populations of the Old and New Stone Age periods. As far as man the farmer was concerned, the gravel deposits provided only evidence of his tools, not of man himself: an antler mace-head of Neolithic date (c.3500 — 1900 BC) and bronze axes from the Bronze Age (1900 — 500 BC). However, evidence of a larger type of domestic cattle than the later Iron Age animals (500 BC — AD 43) introduces man the farmer and herdsman in the third millennium BC. Man's presence in the Darent valley can now be seen to have continued unbroken from at least c.2500 BC to the present day.

Time passed, the climate became drier, the Thames Marshes and the Weald became attractive to men and the technology of working the costly bronze was perfected but there is no evidence that the Shoreham area attracted men of the Bronze Age. The activity of a thousand years is summed up in a burial urn and a bronze axe-head found to the south-east, outside the parish boundary, and a spear-head recovered from the lake in Lullingstone Park. Yet it is probable that future investigations will reveal the Bronze Age farming pattern in Shoreham, given the archaeological evidence close by in Otford. Their occupation stretched back 'Well into the early second millennium B.C.'[4]. The steep-sided Danes Trench on the lower slopes of Polhill in Otford is an indication of the land boundary of the peaceful pastoral farmers to the south of Shoreham.

The Otford tribal group seems to have looked up to the simple earthworks crowning Otford Mount for their local meeting place and for their protection in time of danger. The Shoreham tribe looked northward to Hulberry; the evidence for the division between the two territories still remains — the North Downs trackway. For a trackway cutting across grazing land was a recognized boundary at this period. Significantly, since late Anglo-Saxon times this path close to Filston has divided Shoreham parish from Otford Parish, but its importance as a trading route takes us well beyond the confines of the valley. This is the period when our communication network began. Recent analysis of the different minerals in Bronze Age polished axes and hammers points to their origin in deposits in the North and North Wales, while stone for some tools originated in the west of Britain. Goods were often traded over great distances. Early trackways crossed the country mainly on the high ground, when much of the low-lying ground was undrained and impassable. An east-west trackway can be traced to the south of Shoreham village, descending the White Hill on the east, crossing the Darent a little to the north of Filston Farm, and climbing the steep slope of the western down, passing (in pre-M25 days) Shepherds Barn. Struck flints can be found close to the river crossing.

By the first century BC the Shoreham valley was sparsely occupied by Celtic, Welsh-speaking, farmers, well skilled in Iron Age technology and the iron ore was easily mined in the Weald. West Kent was then controlled by the Catuvellaunian people from north of the Thames. It 'formed part of a larger region stretching as far north as the East Anglian rivers, west to the Chiltern ridge and south to the High Weald of Kent and Sussex'.[5] The survival of the Celtic group-name of 'Cantiaci' — transformed four hundred years later into 'Kent' — illustrates the strength of Celtic survival. (Neighbouring counties — Surrey and Sussex — have English names.) It was to be expected that river names of Kent would keep near their Celtic origins. The name Darent was no exception; the Romans latinized it to Derventio from the Welsh name Derw — meaning the river where oaks are common, an identical river name to that of the Derwent and Dart.[6]

Farming in the valley was based upon the family unit, each family occupying isolated round homesteads, protected by ditches and having stockades for animal enclosures. The nearest of these to Shoreham were two found in

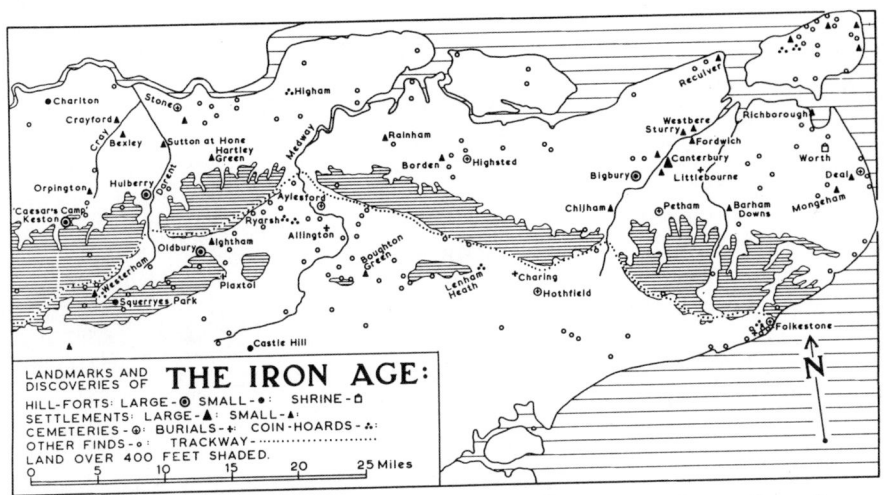

Iron Age Kent. (Map by R. R. Sellman from *Kent History Illustrated*, Kent County Council)

Lullingstone Park, one only 300 yards north of the parish boundary. Between that and the second 1,500 yards farther north there may have been one of a series of hill forts, the purpose of which was to give refuge to the peaceful population in case of attack. For Shoreham the most important hill fort was the immense construction following the contours of Oldbury Hill which unquestionably controlled the Shoreham area.[7]

Julius Caesar's two Kentish reconnaissances of 55 and 54 BC passed the Darent valley by, but he commented meticulously upon its inhabitants in his *Conquest of Gaul*.[8] He told of an aristocracy practising a druidical religion, whose priests ruled by fear and who offered human sacrifices in the woodland groves. He noted that springs and water were particularly venerated by the Celts. This may well have been the case in the Shoreham area. In the Lullingstone Roman villa 'the room below the Christian house-church had been dedicated to the worship of the triune water-spirits. '...the three spirits are shown in human form in a painting on the south wall, with a little well for the supply of water just in front of them'.[9] The later Christian terminology for Becket's Well at Otford and St Edith's Well at Kemsing may conceal earlier pagan usages.

A century was to pass before Rome added her farthest province, Britannia, to her empire. A general of great experience, Aulus Plautius, commanded the highly disciplined expeditionary force of AD 43: the result was a foregone conclusion. The Emperor Claudius came in person to finish off the campaign and to lay the foundations for a centralized government under Rome. It must, however, have been some time before the new Roman administration affected life in the countryside; probably not until Julius Agricola was appointed governor thirty-five years later. Life for the people of the Darent valley would have continued in traditional fashion, but when Agricola's agrarian policy began to take effect the traditional circular farmsteads with their ditched enclosures, like that excavated above Farningham, began to disappear. Large farming estates with centralized management took their place, the famous villa system which spread throughout lowland Britain. The tiny Iron Age fields on the valley slope at Lullingstone were merged together into one estate, with the resident farmer in a specially constructed building which survives as the Lullingstone

SHOREHAM

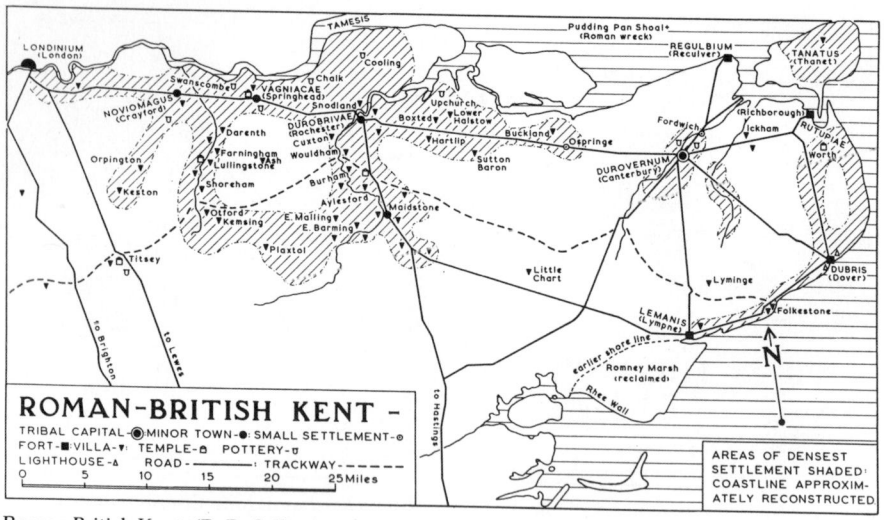

Roman British Kent. (R. R. Sellman, *op.cit.*)

Roman villa. Lullingstone was not an isolated example. The banks of the Darent and the Cray were crowded with substantial buildings constructed in the Roman style, becoming more luxurious as the years passed as bath blocks, underfloor heating and mosaic floors provided additional refinements.

To the south of Shoreham Otford provides ample evidence of the Roman way of life which the native inhabitants adopted. This includes a Romanized farmstead, an extensive corn-growing and stock-rearing site and a second-century cemetery beside the prehistoric trackway more recently named Pilgrims' Way West. Wickham Field close by suggests another Roman site, the name deriving from the Latin *vicus*, a dairy farm. So far the Roman presence at Shoreham is represented only by the recently excavated bath-house at the north end of the village close to the river. A larger building of which this structure formed a part was earlier considered to have stood some 40 yards to the north — probably because pottery and tesserae had been washed down-stream. There may, however, have been two adjacent buildings. Forty years ago G.W. Meates tested this possibility and devised 'a probing chart'.

> ...the results showed walls and floors of an extensive building ... we came down upon a finely made wall of mortared flints, one of a number encountered along the line of the test. Here seemed to be the main house, probably facing South like the great Darenth Villa. The area of ploughed-up bricks and tesserae was closely examined. The square brick pilae that once supported a floor were found intact beneath the field surface and a southward extension of the house beside the river, possibly a bath-wing strongly suggested itself. It was clear that this was a large villa which could take its place with its fellows along the valley.[10]

A first-century coin, a Dupondius in very good condition, of Vespasian's reign (AD 69-79) was found in 1949 in the Council House garden occupied by Mr Cox.[11] This is the only other evidence in Shoreham so far discovered of the four hundred years of Roman occupation.

BEGINNINGS

A Dupondius, a coin of Vespasian's reign (67–79 AD). (Maidstone Museum)

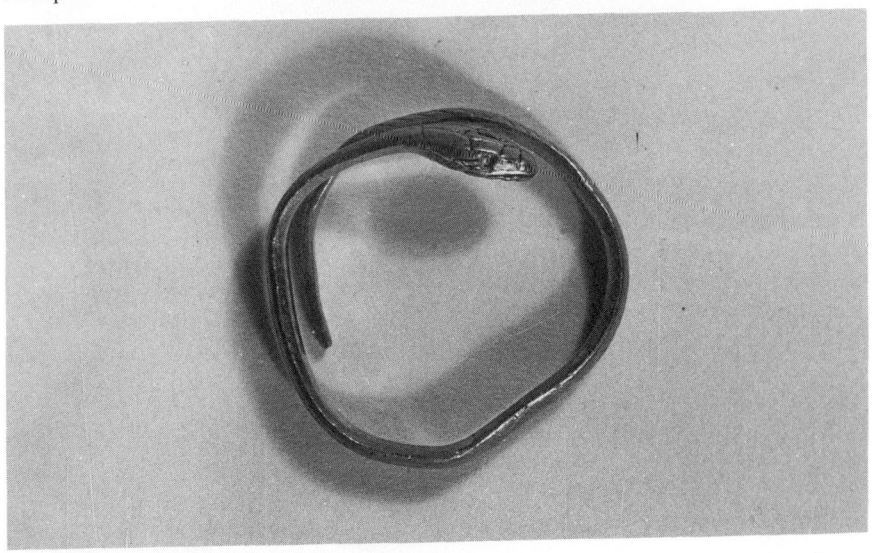

Gold Roman finger ring, its snake formation associated with healing; found at Sepham Farm, Shoreham in 1988. (Kent County Museum Service)

SHOREHAM

The greatest discovery at the Lullingstone villa was undoubtedly of the only Christian house-church ever found in a Roman domestic building. More important was its position in the villa directly above the pagan place of worship of earlier villa-owners. G.W. Meates considered that the church would have been open for neighbours from nearby settlements who wished to worship God in what was then the official faith of the Roman Empire. The Christian symbol, the CHI RHO monogram, found there was precisely similar in size and colour to the CHI RHO found at Otford. The unexcavated Shoreham villa may also have had its church and is it possible that a Christian tradition lingered in this remote valley to influence the English settlers who were to mingle with the Romano-British population in the fifth century?

For some considerable time before the Roman legions were removed in about AD 410, English mercenaries had become established in some numbers in the South-East. They even provided much-needed reinforcements for the Roman forts of the Saxon Shore in Kent, and they may have 'performed guard duties in the towns and countryside'.[12] A metal-work find at Lullingstone suggests their presence close to Shoreham.

The valley people without Roman protection probably had a poor, impoverished life devoted to mere subsistence farming. By the early fifth century the once prosperous villas fringing the Darent had been abandoned by the owners, although this was the result of the collapse of the economy rather than from the traditional picture of pillaging invaders. Almost until the end the owners of the Lullingstone villa were laying down fine mosaic floors and decorating their house-church. But by AD 455 the English had conquered Kent east of the

The CHI RHO monogram found in Lullingstone Roman villa. (The British Museum)

Medway and in West Kent the invaders found it necessary to bury their dead in a group of cemeteries, on the south bank of the Thames, on the Cray at Orpington and beside the Darent at Horton Kirby. At Lullingstone Anglo-Frisian pottery 'quite unlike anything produced in late Roman Britain' of mid fifth century date has been found 'hinting at Saxon settlement.'[13]

To the indigenous population who spoke Welsh and understood Latin, the newcomers sounded strange. In their search for permanent settlements they followed the course of the Darent from its mouth southward. To the Welsh river names they added English names for the settlements. Shoreham became a permanent settlement at an early date in the migration period; its name would appear to indicate this. It derives from the Old English word Scora which is related to *scorian*, meaning 'to project (of rock)'.[14] Shoreham thus means the 'ham or farmstead at the rock or steep slope'.[14] The latter is the better description of Shoreham's position in the valley, so 'the ham at the steep slope' can be accepted. It is likely to have become the home of individual families rather than the headquarters of a tribe; its land area was not large enough for the latter.[15] The soil of the valley floor was most suitable for crop cultivation, and the river produced water meadows of great luxuriance. The small settlement's pigs did not need to be driven far to the south to the drove 'dens' of the Weald. Before 1066 it possessed its own swine-fattening pasture at Timberden — the clearing in the woodland — reached by a drove road which curved round a steep portion of the downs on the west of the village. At that time boundaries were being delineated between settlement and settlement and between arable land and wild wood.

The boundary between Shoreham and Lullingstone remains today as a substantial bank running from Well Hill via Home Wood and across one of the fairways of the golf course. As it passes through Upper Beechen Wood it is still topped with ancient hornbeam and field maple. It then follows the old deer fence and runs outside the Park down to the Darent. An equally ancient boundary is the clearly visible plough-bank running from north to south half-way up the slope of the downs on the west of the village. It was the limit of Shoreham's cultivated land. Until 1940 above the bank an ecologically complete landscape stretched up to the woods crowning the hill. In Saxon times the wild wood came down to the bank. This was as high as the wood-cutters could clear land for cultivation, and as high as the plough could reach.

At the end of their short lives — between thirty and forty years — the village folk might well, before the seventh-century complete reconversion to Christianity, have been carried for burial to the windy cemetery on the headland above Polhill. One hundred and fifty to two hundred graves remained in the late 1960s to be excavated: they were of men, women and children, and the grave goods were of poor quality, denoting a rural community made up of the 'ceorl [or churl] class, the freemen and smaller freeholders who were the backbone of society in rural England'.[15] Although it is assumed that those buried came solely from Otford, Shoreham is almost as close and it is not possible to be dogmatic as to which community these valley forefathers relate.

II

PRE-CONQUEST:
Anglo-Saxon Kent

THE Venerable Bede, writing more than two and a half centuries later, relates that Vortigern, the Romano-British chieftain in Kent, 'called over ... from the parts beyond the sea, the Saxon nation'. Three long ships arrived commanded by Hengist and Horsa: the warriors were given land 'in the eastern part of the island' (in east Kent and Thanet).[1] Very soon they were followed by 'swarms of the aforesaid nation' who proceeded to 'turn their weapons against their confederates'. Modern archaeology has shown that this arrival was more complex and took place over a far longer period than Bede supposed. As has been described (Chapter I, p.6), English mercenaries or *foederati* had been conscripted by the Roman defenders of the Kentish coastline to assist in manning their Saxon Shore forts before the recall of the legions to Rome in AD 410. Indeed, their distinctive metal work found at Lullingstone dates from almost a century before Hengist's reputed arrival in 449. This was at the time when the villa was entering into its most luxurious phase.

However, the next stage in the English settlement of Kent as recorded in the *Anglo-Saxon Chronicle* has been accepted by historians. Hengist and Horsa, advancing westward through Kent, fought a great battle at the crossing of the Medway at Aylesford where Horsa was slain and Vortigern defeated in 455. Two years later as a result of the battle of Crayford 'the Britons then forsook Kent and fled to London in great terror'.[2] However, modern research would query any very large-scale British migration; it is more probable that a form of peaceful co-existence soon began, for most of the population in the Darent valley as elsewhere in Kent.

The present-day description of those born east or west of the Medway as Men of Kent or Kentish Men, far from being of recent antiquarian origin, enshrines the division of rule by the early Saxon kings. In order to protect the line of descent, in case of death in battle or prematurely by disease, a system of joint rule prevailed: the senior position in government going to the ruler based at Canterbury, the junior to the son or younger brother based at Rochester.[3] The creation by Augustine of the two Kentish dioceses, at Canterbury soon after 597 and at Rochester in 604, further recognized this division of the Kentish kingdom.

In spite of the endless ebb and flow of warring forces over the county of Kent during the next six hundred years, the ruthless attacks of the Mercians and West

SHOREHAM

Saxons and the even more ferocious Viking raids, constructive forces were also at work. The laws of Ethelbert, King of Kent, at the opening of the seventh century are the first instance of the social order of 'English' i.e., Anglo-Saxon society. Kent is doorstep to and from these islands, and so it is always among the first to suffer the attacks of invaders, but it also had the advantage of having the closest harbours to the Continent for the enterprising trader to use. It was natural therefore that the Mercians, an inland (Midland) people should cast envious eyes on the growing prosperity of the Kentish kingdom and about 675 decide to invade. They succeeded over the ensuing years in imposing on Kent the status of a vassal kingdom. This did not, however, prevent King Hlothhere from issuing another code of Kentish Law three years later. In 686 King Eadric considered the food trade with London sufficiently important to have a hall there with a reeve in charge, before whom cattle dealings by Kentish men were witnessed.

The very next year it was the turn of the West Saxons to invade Kent, and Mull, one of their leaders, was burnt alive by the men of Kent. As a consequence seven years later their King Wihtred agreed, — no doubt after prolonged bargaining — that they should pay 30,000 pence to Ine, the King of Wessex, as a fine for committing such an uncivilized act. A step forward to a more civilized society was the Council of Cloveshoo (Cliffe-at-Hoo) over which the King of Mercia, Ethelbald, presided in 747. Agreement was reached at the Council to end the differences in practices between the old British Church and those of the Roman Church introduced by St Augustine, and it even aimed at establishing a school in every parish.

War returned to Kent in about 774, and must have disturbed the peace of Shoreham. Offa, King of Mercia, invaded Kent. As we have already seen, a century earlier the Mercians had established some form of control over the Kentish kingdom, but Kent had over the years loosened this subjection. It was perhaps because of this that Offa decided to try to restore the earlier dominant position of Mercia. For a detailed discussion of the battle of Otford readers are recommended to study Clarke and Stoyel's *Otford in Kent — A History*. It seems possible that about the year 774 the battle took place on the rising ground near the present Otford Station where King Alric and his Kentish forces would have had greatest advantage over Offa and his men. Whether they came from the west along the Trackway (Pilgrims' Way) or from the north up the Darent Valley, passing by Shoreham, we do not know. We know little in fact of the combat but from subsequent events it seems that Offa won no outright victory over Kent, but that day-to-day contact remained between the people of Kent and the Mercians. It is known that Offa together with the Archbishop minted his coins in the city of Canterbury, just as a century later the kings of Wessex were to do.[4]

In 796 Offa died. Kent had for some time resented the Mercian attempts to subdue its people, who saw Offa's death as an opportunity to revolt, but Offa's successor soon gathered his forces together and attacked in 798. As the *Anglo-Saxon Chronicle* relates, 'Cenwulf, King of the Mercians ravaged the people of Kent and of the marshes and seized Praen their King and led him in fetters into Mercia. And they had his eyes put out and his hands cut off', and Cuthred, brother of Cenwulf, was installed as King of Kent. Cenwulf had made his ruthless and savage mark, but to make his control of the Kentish people the surer he decided to gain the support of the Church.

As the ninth century approached, those in power realized the increasing influence being exercised by the Christian Church, particularly through the establishment and activities of minsters such as Rochester, Eccles, and Minster in Sheppey, which by the eleventh century were to become mother churches around which clustered small two-cell parish churches. At the height of his power Offa had obtained the Pope's consent to create an additional Archbishopric at Lichfield, thus reducing the province of Canterbury and its standing in Christendom. Now at the second Council of Cloveshoo in 803 King and Church agreed that Lichfield should no longer be an Archbishopric, and the province of Canterbury was restored to its pre-eminence.

In 805 Wulfred became Archbishop, and was clearly resolved to take advantage of Cenwulf's friendship and need for help. He was determined to increase the Church's own power and position, not least by adding to the Archbishop's estates. Mutual self-interest therefore resulted in Cenwulf giving Wulfred in 811 'the King's little town of Fafresham.'[5] At this period more and more small churches with nave and chancel were being built on estates by the King's thegns, and rather naturally the Archbishop wished to bring them under his complete control. Equally understandable was Cenwulf's wish to retain his control and influence over these churches through his own thegns. Tension between them grew, and developed into a long-drawn-out quarrel. Only the death in 821 of Cenwulf ended it. Cenwulf was succeeded by his brother Cedwulf, who realized that he had to restore friendly relations with the Archbishop if only to ensure his consecration as King. So it was that Cedwulf, as a goodwill offering, granted Archbishop Wulfred land at a place called Milton which Professor Du Boulay considers almost certainly to have been at Shoreham.[6] Cenwulf on his death-bed had also felt the need to reconcile himself and Wulfred (and prepare to meet his Maker), and had given him land at Copton (later Westwood Court) and Greatness in Otford. Cedwulf, knowing this, complemented the gift by adding to the northern sector of the territory bounded by Shoreham and Sevenoaks, the river Darent and Kemsing which later became one of the principal manors of the Lordship of Canterbury – the Manor of Otford. It is possible that the first settlement at the site of Preston Farm may have already existed at this time, having been set up after the founding of the third episcopal minster at Rochester in 604. Certainly its Old English name 'Preosta-tun' implies a settlement worked by priests or in support of priests. Unfortunately, nothing is certain about the Church's origins in Shoreham, or the relationship of Preston to the church of St Peter and St Paul only 1,200 yards away along a straight track.

Although the story of the reconversion of Shoreham to Christianity in the seventh century will probably never be known, early evidence of the valley faith was found close to Darenth Park Hospital, Dartford, with the astonishing excavation of a fine moulded glass bowl bearing the CHI RHO monogram in an east-west aligned grave of an early fifth-century Saxon.[7] But the Christianity of the valley could not withstand the concerted paganism of the English settlers, so for the second time in 597 missionaries from Rome led by Augustine came to convert the Kentish population. Before the consecration of the present churchyard in Shoreham the villagers probably shared the large cemetery on the top of Polhill with the people of Otford. More than a hundred graves of possibly Christian men, women and children dating from the early seventh century have been excavated and examined.[8]

A church at 'Scorham' was listed in the Textus Roffensis (a document relating to the Rochester diocese) in 1122, and in 1956-8 when the wooden nave floor was being replaced by paving-stones from Shoreham Place, Anthony Stoyel discovered the footings of a Norman chancel which were coeval with the present west wall. These on the material evidence he dated 'probably around the dawn of the 12th Century'[9], but Mr Stoyel in 1988 was of the opinion — on further indirect evidence — that the development probably occurred before the end of the eleventh century.

The mention of a church in the Textus Roffensis is generally accepted as proof of a pre-Conquest origin, and that a church existing before the conquest was probably made of wood.[10] Nothing can be proved, but such conjecture is inevitable when one thinks of the pre-eminence of Shoreham as one of the four deaneries in the diocese of Rochester during the medieval period, with thirty-four benefices under its control. It is reasonable to infer that such pre-eminence arose because of the long-established settlement at Preston and the gift of land at Shoreham by Cedwulf to the Archbishop which made it inevitable that the latter should take Shoreham as his 'peculiar' (the church and parish forming part of his territorial Lordship), keeping it ecclesiastically under his own control rather than leaving it to the Bishop of Rochester to administer.

The Viking attacks on Kent began in 835 with an attack on Sheppey and were to continue with their slaughter, rape and arson throughout the ninth century. The inhabitants of Shoreham must have suffered in these persistent onslaughts, although we do not know whether they fought at Meretun (Deptford) when in 871 King Ethelred and Alfred defeated the Vikings or when Alfred in 885 returned to relieve Rochester and forced the Vikings to abandon their horses and take to their ships. They returned to the attack, and sacked Rochester in 999. Were Shoreham men in the levy that went against them? We do not know. What is more certain is that Shoreham men may well have been caught up in the second battle of Otford in 1016.

Canute, claiming the throne of England, had landed at Sandwich in that year and had attempted to seize London, held by Ethelred's widow Emma. Edmund

From the Bayeux Tapestry: Vital reporting to Duke William the approach of the Anglo-Saxon army.

Ironside in three bloody battles in Dorset, Wiltshire and Middlesex thrust back the invaders and caught up with Canute leading the Vikings, laden with booty, as they made their way east along the Pilgrims' Way just west of Otford. Taken by surprise, the raiders fled with their horses to Sheppey. Edmund might have won a complete victory had not the turncoat Earl Edric Streona of Mercia impeded his hot pursuit at Aylesford, eventually assisting Canute to final victory and the throne.[11]

The last invasion of England came in 1066. That final and permanent invasion by the Norman Duke William was recorded for all time in the Bayeux Tapestry, and in that vivid record is the picture of a Norman knight whose name is given as 'Vital' (OE Viel). The picture shows this knight reporting to the Duke the approach of the Anglo-Saxon army. There is a strong case that this same knight after the battles were over settled near Shoreham and gave his name to Vielestun — or as we know it today, Filston.[12]

III
1066-1500

ABOUT 1179 Robert Fitzneal, Treasurer of England, quoting a man whose memory went back to a generation of the great survey ordered by Duke William and known as Domesday (1086), wrote: 'When William the Conqueror had subdued the whole island and by terrible example tamed the minds of the rebels, to prevent further trouble he decided to place the government of the conquered people on a written basis and to subject them to the rule of law.'[1]

'Terrible example' was a fine example of understatement. Winston Churchill early in 1939 wrote 'William [the Conqueror] was a prime exponent of the doctrine, so well known in this civilized age as 'frightfulness' — of mass terrorism through the spectacle of bloody and merciless examples'.[2] The study of Domesday assessments of the value of land and property before and after the Conquest demonstrates clearly the fall in value resulting from the ravages that followed in the wake of the conquering army.[3] Fortunately, in his progress from Canterbury along the 'Pilgrims' Way' to Winchester the laying waste of the manor of Seal by his army does not seem to have been repeated on the neighbouring lands belonging to the Archbishop at Wrotham, Otford, Sundridge and Brasted.[4] This was possibly because William, falling sick at that time, was cared for at the Archbishop's Manor at Otford.

Having galloped through the six centuries that followed the departure of the Romans, it will be as well to pause and consider the social and administrative structure which existed at this great turning-point in English history. Commenting on the Laws of Ethelbert of Kent (mid-eighth century), Sir Frank Stenton in his volume on Anglo-Saxon England deduced that the basis of Kentish society was

> obviously the free peasant landholder, without claim to nobility, but subject to no lord below the king. He was an independent person with many rights. The laws which refers to him as head of a family show him entitled to compensation for breach of his household peace, for misconduct with his maidservant, for the slaughter of one of his 'loaf-eaters'. If he himself were killed, his slayer must pay a hundred golden shillings to his kinsfolk, and fifty to the King... If he stole from another man of his class the king might take a fine from him, or even all his goods, but he was not the man of a lord with a financial interest in his misbehaviour.

Although the feudal system was superimposed by William after the Conquest, as the centuries rolled on we shall see how this independence of spirit dealt with the hierarchical social structure, especially in the holding of land.

Kent has many special social features long predating the Conquest, but one of the most important was the custom of gavelkind by which property was inherited and held.

> The tenant in gavelkind may freely give or sell his lands to whom he wishes during his life and after his death his lands shall be equally divided between his male heirs. His widow shall receive one half of her former husband's holding as dower as long as she remains a widow. The heirs shall be in the guardianship of the PROCHEYN AMI – the nearest relative who could not inherit – all shall attain their majority for the purpose of controlling the inheritance at the age of fifteen.[5]

The customary law of gavelkind persisted into the twentieth century, and an example can be found as recently as 1859, when an indenture explained that the heirs to the property known as Record in Church Street, Shoreham, were the three sons of Susannah Margaret Fox 'in gavelkind according to the custom of gavelkind prevailing in the said county of Kent'. It certainly encouraged an individualistic attitude to land-tenure. As William Lambarde wrote of Kent in 1570, 'The Yeomanrie or common people is nowhere more free and jolly than in this shyre…the custome of gavelkind prevailing everywhere – in manner every man is a freeholder and hath some part of his own to live upon.' In more sober words, Professor Du Boulay saw the practice beginning in pre-Conquest times and developing throughout the medieval centuries of an individual moving 'from patch to patch, croft to croft, field to field'. As a local example in Shoreham, William de Dunitune gave some land to Geoffrey de Seppeham, and described it as follows:

> One acre beyond the hills in Geoffrey's rood and half an acre in Stockcumbe by the land of Henry de Twettune towards Anderdune; half an acre by the way called Dunstrete; half an acre by Stongrave; half an acre by the land of Osbert de Longo Campo; half an acre in Bekelege; half an acre by the land of Alfred de Dunitune; five virgates behind the new garden of Osbert de Longo Campo; one virgate thus in length to the land of Ralph de Timberdene; half an acre next to the land of Arnold to the way called Dunstrete on the east.

How did these independent-minded people organize themselves before the arrival of William? At the basic local level in Anglo-Saxon times the social unit above the household was the tithe, into which ten households were grouped under a tithing-man and each householder under the Anglo-Saxon law of Frankpledge was answerable for the good conduct of, or the damage done by, any one of the other members. The swearing of new members of a tithe (called 'the view of frank-pledge') usually took place in the Hundred Court, the Hundred originally consisting of ten tithes. Shoreham was in the Hundred of Codsheath, and that hundred formed part of the Lathe of Sutton-at-Hone. The lathe was a more ancient land division than the shire, with two main functions: to provide for the payment of the King's food rents as he moved around his lands; and to administer customary law.

Edward Hasted's 1797 map of the Codsheath Hundred.

At the local level the Hundred Court administered customary law in private pleas, did justice on thieves and on those who had been slack in their pursuit of thieves and provided a forum for discussion between the King's financial officers and the individual taxpayer. The Hundred Court in fact was 'a popular assembly'. It met in earliest times in the open air at intervals of four weeks. The judgements which it gave represented the deliberations of peasants learned in the law who might be guided but could not be controlled by the intervention of the King's reeve, the president of the Court.'[6]

The Codsheath Hundred Court probably met at Riverhead, where now the church of Saint Mary's stands. No documentary evidence is available from these early times, but the Hundred Courts continued their work right into the medieval period and beyond, and we get a glimpse in the Court rolls of the business there conducted. They served many functions nowadays performed by the post office as well as by the police courts. At the three-weekly court held on 14 December 1388 there were 33 pleas of debt, 14 pleas of trespass, 13 queries about changes in land-holdings, 8 fealties and reliefs following up new acquisitions of land and other payments of fines and inheritance taxes. We would not today tolerate the minor controls and the slow, tedious proceedings of these courts. All householders had to present themselves for each session of the Court, and on 12 October in 1414 in the second year of Henry V's reign (and perhaps not surprisingly) there were twenty-four defaulters from Shoreham each having to pay 2d. fine but no reason is given for so many being absent. The names of some of those defaulters send echoes down to the present – Robert Tymberden, Thomas and Robert Colegate, Henry and John Romeney. John Reeve the blacksmith was evidently the tithing-man for Shoreham then, and one of the matters dealt with was a vital one: a watercourse at Sandhurst had been diverted from its proper course. The culprit was Walter Wynker, who was fined 4d. and ordered to put it right by All Souls on pain of a much heavier fine of 20s. if he failed to do so. Geoffrey Moller the miller was fined 4d. for taking unjust dues; John Reve the butcher had been charging excessively; Peter Baker broke the assize regulations by baking white bread.

At the same session it is recorded that John Dryvere was the tithing-man for Cepham, and the tithing as a body was fined 6d. for failing 'to keep watch'. They may, of course, have failed to catch a thief. Richard Mot and Joan Oure, both brewers, 'broke the assize' and were fined 2d. each. Richard Mot was a defaulter at the Hundred Court held in Otford on 11 October 1429. At the same session another Mot, Margaret the elder, was brought to justice by Robert Smyth the beer-taster and fined 2d. Could this be Robert Smyth taking revenge on the More family, because one notes that Robert Smyth not only was Cepham's beer-taster but also the tithing-man who had recently been assaulted by Robert More? Robert Smyth had, however, defended himself and drawn blood to such good effect that Robert More 'placed himself in mercy'. Two years later, on 9 October, the Court rolls record that Margaret Mottys (Mot) was in trouble again; she brewed twice, and was fined 3d. for breaking the assize.

When William subjected England 'to the rule of law' he imposed a hierarchical structure on the land, based on the concept of the Kingdom, which took as its primary assumption that all land was owned by the King. The King then enfeoffed his tenants-in-chief with such land as he did not wish to administer directly himself, and his tenants-in-chief having been put in possession of the land had to pay the King in services and kind; and they in their turn could enfeoff others.

The degree of shock with which this 'feudal system' was received by the people of England is a subject of much discussion by historians, but it can be assumed that in the turbulent centuries leading up to the Conquest self-interest and self-protection must have led to a social structure, even in independent-minded Kent, where the weaker had tended to owe allegiance to the strong but there had been no system as such. The idea of lordship – of owing homage, service and the payment of dues in return for protection by the lord – did exist in Anglo-Saxon times, but in a variety of forms, and an untidy fashion. The Normans under their Duke insisted on 'order', and the trend was to a standardization of law and practice.

When Lanfranc became Archbishop in 1070 he was immediately required by the King to find 600 knights for royal service. This he could only manage by enfeoffing others with parts of his property, so that 1086 (*Domesday Book*) 'knightly' lands comprise 16.8 per cent of all the Canterbury lands (those of the Archbishop and those of the monks, taken together).[7]

We know from *Domesday Book* that 'the Archbishop himself holds Otefort (Otford) in demesne 8 Sulung'. But in *Domesday Book* there is no mention of Shoreham, probably because it formed part of the demesne land of Otford Manor. It is nevertheless rather surprising, considering that the deanery of Shoreham in 1081[8] had become a *peculiar* of the Archbishop of Canterbury coming under the direct jurisdiction of the Archbishop and exempt from the jurisdiction of the diocese of Rochester. By the thirteenth century it was the centre of one of the largest deaneries in the country, comprising thirty-four parishes. We know also from archaeological evidence in the foundations of the parish church of St Peter and St Paul that a church of the Norman period existed with a nave extending 37 ft 6 in from the present west wall to the tomb niche in the north wall, and a chancel of 12ft 2in extending as far as what is now the entrance to the North Chapel.[9] We can console ourselves with the thought that there were many inconsistencies in Domesday, and although churches were included for Kent, under two hundred were mentioned although it is known that there were more than twice the Domesday number in existence at that period.[10]

The Manor of Otford was very large, including the settlements of Otford, Shoreham, Dunton, Sevenoaks, Weald, Halstead, Chevening, Woodlands and Penshurst. Sepham and Filston (then known as Vielestun) and parts of Chevening and Halstead were by 1086 already sub-infeudated to Haimo, Sheriff of Kent (one of the Conqueror's most trusted vassals) and two Norman warriors, Robert the Interpreter and Geoffrey de Ros, who also held Lullingstone. We do not know, however, how these lands were divided between them. If as mentioned above (p. 13) Viel, another of the Duke's followers, gave his name to Vielestun, he must have disappeared from view during the twenty years after the battle of Hastings for one of the other three to have taken his place.

The authors of *Otford in Kent – A History* have provided us with a most thoughtful study of the details in *Domesday Book* concerning the Otford Manor in the years 1085–6, and we advise readers to turn to their Chapter 3 for those details while we limit ourselves to some general comment only.

Those living on the Archbishop's land in the Otford Manor of that time seem to have enjoyed a rather better life than elsewhere in Kent, and even on the sub-infeudated land. For instance, at the lowest level of society there were only 8 slaves (*servi*) – i.e., 6.3 per cent as against the national and Kent average of 10 per cent of the population. These were slaves of their lord in the true sense of the word, and generally they worked as ploughmen and swineherds, sleeping at night with the oxen that they drove as ploughmen during the day. In the next higher stratum of society as described by the classifiers of Domesday there were in Otford Manor 18 bordars (14.2 per cent of the manor's householders: the Kent average being 28 per cent). These held of the Lord of the Manor 8 acres each on average, compared with 5 acres elsewhere, and they supplemented the living gained from these acres by wages for work done for the lord and for those immediately above them in the social scale – the villeins, the men of the vill or village. Villeins formed the largest group of the manor's population, numbering 101 (79.5 per cent compared with 58 per cent national average). They owned the 360 oxen used to make up the forty-five 8-oxen plough teams for the Otford Manor listed in the Domesday survey, and were better off than villeins elsewhere, having on average nearly half a team each. Bordars do not appear to have owned any oxen, but on the whole the inhabitants of Otford Manor seem to have been less servile and more prosperous than most Englishmen. Expert opinion as to the total population of the whole of Otford Manor, based on figures given in *Domesday Book*, ranges from 600 to 550. David Hill (*Atlas of Anglo Saxon England*: Map 26), working from the figures given in Domesday, calculates the population of north-west Kent as between 5 and 10 persons per square mile, which would give the area of Shoreham parish a population of between 100 and 200. The census figure for 1981 was 2007.

The Manor had six mills and 50 acres of meadow and 'wood of 150 hogs'. This last phrase expresses in administrative shorthand woodland extensive enough to provide food for sufficient swine to bring in 150 hogs a year in revenue. Clarke and Stoyel think that the mills may have existed at that time at Otford, Shoreham, Greatness, Longford and Whitley, with the sixth at Otford, Shoreham or Greatness. It is tempting to claim the sixth for Shoreham, although we do not know when exactly the watermills at the north and south ends of the village were built. We read first of the mill at Home Farm (south of the village) in 1190, but not of the one at the bottom of Mill Lane until 1323. A point to remember is that all mills played a vital part in the medieval community. From the conquest of 1066 they were made the property of the lord of the manor, and under feudal law all in the community had to use the lord's mill for grinding their corn. Over the years a feeling of resentment and even hostility grew up between the inhabitants and the lord's miller who held the monopoly.

Sadly, little is known of the life of the Shoreham community in 1086, and we must leap forward another two hundred years to get a glimpse of everyday life in medieval Shoreham. The church at Shoreham by 1272 was the centre of a Deanery comprising thirty-four parishes, extending from Erith and Northfleet in the north to Chiddingstone and Penshurst in the south, and from Keston in the west to Wrotham in the east. Territorially, however, Shoreham formed part of the manor of Otford which in turn formed part of the extensive lordship of Canterbury.

In 1284 Henry Lovel, steward of all Archbishop Pecham's lands, drew up a custumal[11] giving details of the customs and services of the Manor of Otford; the yokes into which the Manor was divided; the tenants of the yokes and the cottars; and the duties both owed to the Archbishop as lord of the manor. These duties did not in Kent as elsewhere in the country include so many days a week working for the lord of the manor (which was easily arranged in 'open-field' country where the tenants' own holdings lay close to the lord's demesne land). Kentish services consisted rather of special tasks or a day's work to be done at a particular time of the year.[12]

Before we describe in detail the contents of this document some explanation is needed of the word 'yoke'. The authors of *Domesday Book* used the *sulung* as the unit for measuring the land area of an estate. Sulung was derived from the old English *sulh* meaning plough, and one sulung was considered the area of land which could be ploughed in a year by one plough and eight oxen. Four yokes were used for coupling the eight oxen, and so the word yoke came to mean, as a

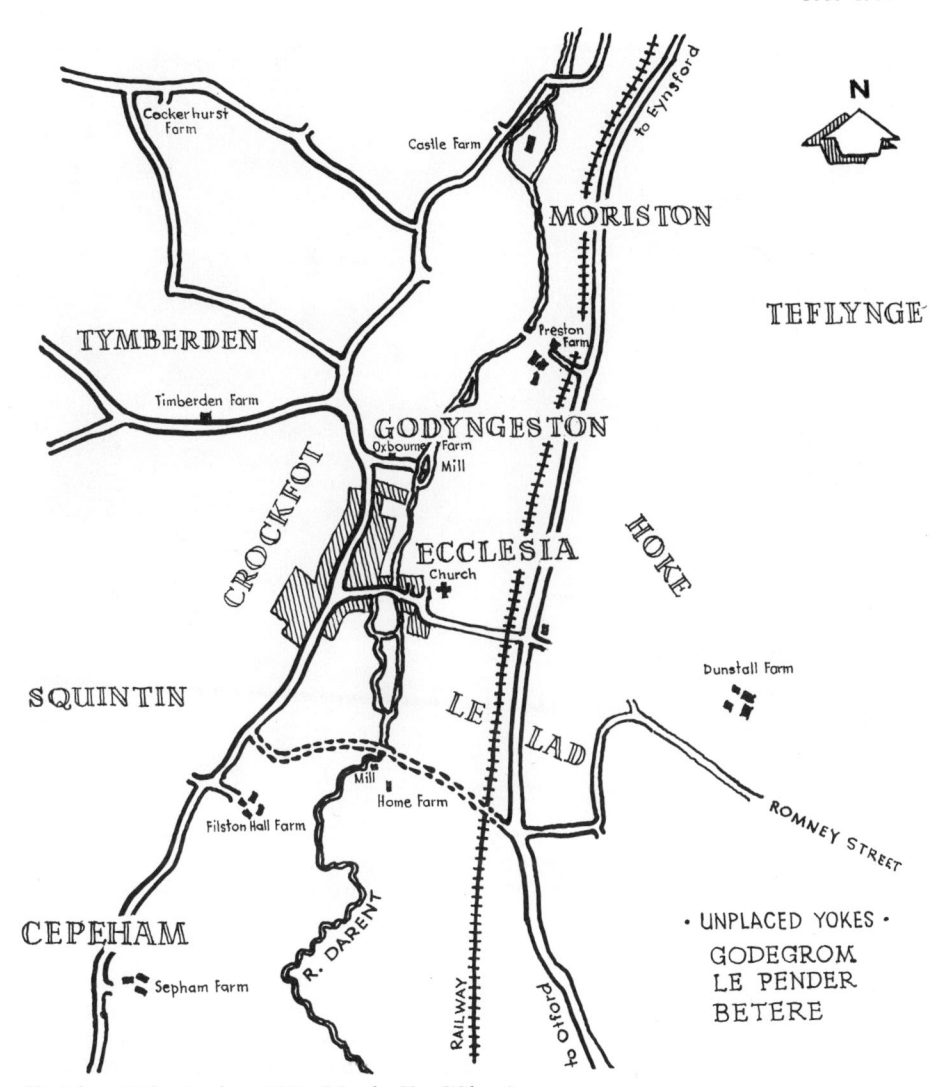

Shoreham Yokes in about 1284. (Map by Ken Wilson)

unit of measurement, a quarter of a sulung, which is usually reckoned as 200 acres. The size of each yoke varies greatly, depending usually on the quality of the land, but in the custumal of 1284 the yoke on average seems to equal 120 acres. The yoke by 1284 had become a means of dividing up the land in a way convenient to administrators and could not be directly related to the boundaries of fields, although some even to this day do coincide.

In Shoreham the custumal lists 13 yokes:

Teflynge	Squintin	Le Lad	Le Pender and Betere
Godegrom	Ecclesia	Moriston	Godyngeston
Tymberden	Cepeham (1) & (2)	Crokfot	Hoke

SHOREHAM

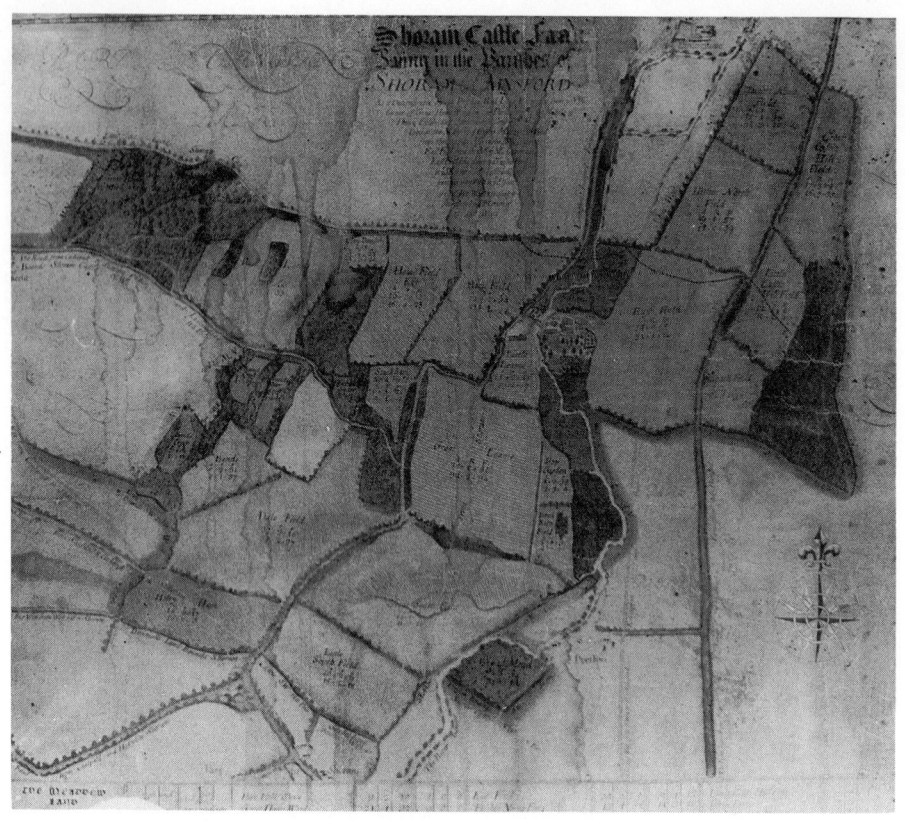

'Shoram Castle Farm', a map drawn by a surveyor, Richard Adams, in c.1720 showing field names and acreages and a detailed description of the parish boundary. (Mr and Mrs W. Alexander)

Although Cepeham is divided into two, each being described as ¾ yokes, there is no mention of Filston, and only obliquely are Preston and Planas mentioned in the document. As will be seen on the sketch map (p. 21), some yoke names have come through to the present day, but we have been able to locate only some of those yokes whose names have disappeared from our modern maps. A field map of Castle Farm dated 1720[13] shows Great Murry Mead and Little Murry Mead, confirming other evidence (see p. 40) that Moriston Yoke was in the area of that farmstead. The tithe map of 1840 shows two fields, Great and Little Goddestone (Godyngeston), as north-east of Oxbourne farmstead; another field known as Crookfoot in 1840 lies west of Filston Lane and south of Mesne Way and it is probable that Crokfot Yoke extended from the southern boundary of this field, running parallel to the High Street as far as Oxbourne House. In 1840 Squinton field (Squintin) was high on the hill next to the southern boundary of Meanfield Wood. Hook Bank and Little Hookland are names given to fields between Dunstall Priory and the A 225, and seem to be related to Hoke Yoke; Ecclesia Yoke must have been near the church. One of the most difficult to identify was Teflynge Yoke. The first element of that name – Tefl – may be derived from *taefl* meaning 'chess-board' in Old English, and in this context meaning a plateau.[14] Thus the name could mean 'the people living on the plateau', and there is some evidence that the Teflynge Yoke was located in the area we now know as Romney Street.[15] The three yokes Le Lad, Le Pender and Betere, and Godegrom must remain unidentified for the present, although Dr Ward suggested that Le Lad Yoke may have been in the area now occupied by Shoreham Place and Home Farm.

According to the custumal, there were 59 tenants of the Archbishop's land in Shoreham, the number varying greatly from yoke to yoke. Nine tenants held Teflynge, and nine also the half-yoke of Godegrom. On the other hand, Hugo de Poynz, the lord of Lullingstone Manor, also held the yoke of Moriston as sole tenant; and William de Chelefeld held Godyngeston similarly. Tymberden was exceptionally large, consisting of three ¾ yokes, and was held by Richard and Robert de Tymberden, who shared Crokfot with eight others. They included William and Thomas Pender who occupied all the quarter-yoke of Le Lad and who shared the quarter-yoke of Le Pendere and Betere with Thomas Le Betere. John son of Martin de Cepeham, occupied the three-quarter yoke of Cepeham (1) and seven others occupied the other three-quarter yoke of Cepeham (2). Thus the tenancies display a complex pattern, and illustrate well the point made by Professor Du Boulay (p. 16) that the individual in Kent over the centuries tended to move 'from patch to patch, croft to croft, field to field'. The tenancies of Crokfot also show the effect of inheritance under gavelkind: among the ten tenants of the yoke are William, John and Richard, sons of Adam Huitegos (Whitegoose), and Alicia, widow of the same Adam. It seems probable from this that Adam had only recently died and his share of Crokfot was inherited by his three sons and his widow. Under gavelkind even at this early date there was sufficient freedom to buy and sell tenancies, and it is possible that given time the two youngest Whitegoose sons might have sold their share of the inheritance to the eldest and thus provided him with a holding of reasonable size. Although the majority of tenants (or gavelmen, as they are sometimes called) must have had as their ancestors the villeins of Domesday, clearly those like Richard and Robert de Tymberden, William and Thomas Le Pender and John de Cepeham were on the way to becoming considerable landholders. Tenants' possessions, however, varied greatly at this time; some might have a full plough team, others a beast or two and others none.

What of the bordars mentioned in Domesday? The 1284 Custumal refers only to cottars — each cottar having a smallholding (cotary) of eight acres. Of these smallholdings there were seven in Shoreham and eleven (plus fractions) in Otford, a total of eighteen (plus) — a figure which corresponds closely with the 18 bordars recorded in *Domesday Book*. It may be presumed, therefore, that both terms refer to the same social group. By the thirteenth century the *servi* or slaves had achieved a certain measure of freedom, and we find below the cottars on the social ladder the *famuli* or paid labourers receiving a wage of 1*d*. a day.

By 1284 the Archbishop was depending less on the feudal services of his tenants than on his paid labourers for the cultivation of his land, and it is probable that the cottars — with only their eight acres on which to subsist — were also taking paid work with those above them, as well as performing the customary services for the lord of the manor. This shows up clearly in the custumal: of the 38¼ acres of hay in the lord's demesne meadows, the cottars had to mow 14 acres, leaving 24¼ to be mown by the *famuli*. A similar situation seemed to exist in the arable land, though it cannot be so easily illustrated.

At Appendix 1 (p. 245) we give in Dennis Clarke's translation the full text of the customary services to be rendered by the tenants of Teflynge Yoke and by the cottar Adam Haymund. Both are given in detail in the custumal as standard services, to be followed by the tenants of other yokes and by other cottars, and give a valuable insight into the life of thirteenth-century Shoreham.

The cultivation of the demesne arable acres is prominent in the customary services. The task of carrying and spreading manure is given to the cottar if he has a horse to transport it. If not he must help with the loading. Tenants are given the ploughing, sowing and harrowing, but only for 32½ acres, which is little more than a third of the arable available for sowing each year if one assumes that one-third of the total 139 acres in Shoreham is fallow. Thus two-thirds of the sowing must be left to the paid labourers of the manor. The cottars join the tenants in reaping the corn and oats, but again they appear to leave a third to be harvested by the paid labour. Tenants and cottars gather about half the hay crop from the meadows.

The Archbishop spent a great deal of his time touring his estates, and this meant not only transporting clothes and creature comforts for a large retinue but also the bulky collection of the medieval equivalent of a modern office filing system. Thus most of the yoke tenants of Shoreham had to provide four carrying services when the lord was present at Otford Manor: carrying to his establishments at Lambeth, Croydon, Bexley, Northfleet, Wrotham or Penshurst. Such carrying duties must have been a heavy and wearisome labour given the frightful state of the roads, especially in winter. The collection and carrying of firewood from the lord's woods (mainly from Whitley Forest, west of Sevenoaks) to his court at Otford was a regular service for tenants between Hokeday (second Tuesday after Easter) and the day of St Peter ad Vincula. They had also to see to the fencing of the burghyard at Shoreham when this was required. They had to pay rent for pasturing their pigs of 2*d*. per pig (1*d*. for a young pig) if pannage (acorns and beech-mast in the lord's forests) was available; if not the rent was halved. The Yoke tenants had to make four seams (packhorse loads) of malt, and to do this they were provided with four loads of wood to dry it and if they brewed beer to sell they had to pay 2*d*. 'gavelsister' (an excise tax) on the first, second and third brewing in a year 'but not beyond'.

The cottar had to make only one seam of malt and received one load of wood for drying, but he had to bake one seam of wheat for the lord's alms, receiving one load of wood for baking. From his household he had to find one man to do guard duty at night in the fields when the lord's corn was reaped and stooked and awaiting carting. Cottars had the onerous task of helping the beadle to arrest people within the Hundred, guarding prisoners taken within the Otford 'curia' (the Otford court district) and were responsible at their peril and that of other cottars for the safe custody of the prisoners until the court was held and a verdict reached. In 1286 Archbishop Pecham ordered the dean of Shoreham to excommunicate those who had allowed prisoners awaiting trial for homicide to escape. On occasion a cottar might have to find a man from his household to work the lord's plough for one whole year, but he would be rewarded by being quit of all rent and services during that year, and would have the lord's plough to plough his land on the third Saturday during the ploughing season as well as receiving a 'cop' of corn, one of barley and one of oats as a perquisite. Again, he might be required to spend the whole autumn at the curia at Otford to help bring in the corn. As a recompense for his being prevented from working his own eight acres 'he shall be at table and for each day he carries he shall have one sheaf of corn that he carries and have a seed-cot full of corn. Then on Shrove Tuesday with the Smith and other servants he shall have one salted hog.'

The prerequisite for carting manure gives us some idea of the cottar's diet; he received food three times a day, at Prime and Vespers a whole loaf, a whole cheese and drink; at the ninth hour a wheat loaf, pottage, cheese and drink. For reaping, binding and stooking two acres he received sixteen loaves. It sounds an excessive amount of bread to our ears, accustomed as we are to a more balanced diet, but at that period bread made up nearly 50 per cent of the peasant's food.[16]

The custumal of 1284 tells us of the tenants' and cottars' obligations to the lord of the manor. The manor accounts give us more detail of what it meant to administer a large medieval manor. During the years 1316-23 John Stuket was serjeant of Otford manor and was responsible for keeping, in considerable detail, the accounts of revenue from rents, feudal dues and sales of wheat, barley, oats and livestock, and of expenditure on demesne buildings, repairs to the mills and bridges, hedges and ditches; on the stipends and wages of permanent staff and casual labourers; on the purchase of livestock and seed corn. The accounts for 1316-17 contain only a brief mention of Shoreham; 37s. 1d. was spent on plastering the walls of the ox-house, stable, grange and the sheep-house in Shoreham and Otford. Excessive rain in 1316-17, we know, had caused extensive flooding, and no doubt had started leaks in the roofs of buildings, because 8,000 singles had to be bought from William Sweyneslond for 48s. to repair the manor-house at Otford.

The serjeant and his colleague the parker (who was responsible for the upkeep of the two parks of the manor) both received a stipend of 10s. a year, the bedell 4s., a carter 5s. 6d.; a ploughman 7s. 1d.; a swineherd 3s. The shepherd at Shoreham received 4s., as did also the bailiff of the demesne farm at Shoreham, but the bailiff earned a further 8s. for harvest work, as did the reaper at Shoreham. The 1323 accounts show what appears at first sight to be a remarkably high annual stipend for a smith of 77s., but for this sum he had to find iron and steel, make the ploughshares and shoe the draught horses and oxen: a considerable task when the estate had some 290 horses for plough and harrow work and 400 draught oxen. Skilled labourers were brought in to do special work, and so a carpenter and his help were paid 6d. a day, a thatcher and his help 5d. a day, a tiler and his help working 16 days at 7d. a day mending the leaks in the roof of the Esquire's Chamber and the stable at the manor made 9s. 4d., a plumber and his mate working 16 days at 10d. a day made 13s. 4d. At first sight it might seem as if the skilled outside craftsman could earn more than his equal on the permanent payroll, but an accurate comparison is not possible because we cannot assess accurately the value of the food 'at table', or the livery received by the manor servants and labourers, nor do we know the annual earnings of the outside craftsman. In the second half of the fourteenth century, however, the disparities grew and became obvious, and led to discontent among the manor employees.

At the opening of the century weather conditions deteriorated and affected agriculture. In 1315-16 the severe floods already mentioned brought terrible famine to England, and those 'at table' and living within the secure confines of the manor must have considered themselves very fortunate when the price of food was rocketing. Wheat had risen steadily in price from 10s. a quarter on 1 November to 24s. at midsummer,[17] and so desperate were some that sixteen men from the villages around Otford were taken with stolen goods and led off to Maidstone gaol. Despite that, the manor in 1323 (only six years later) bought 7 quarters of wheat for seed at 9s. a quarter. Perhaps that had been time enough for the price to have settled back, or perhaps since the manor was the centre of power locally it was able to buy at very favourable rates. In the 1323 accounts there is mention of 'the watermill of Shoreham which belonged to William de Cheliffield'. This almost certainly refers to the mill at Godyngeston Yoke held by William de Cheliffield, and thus to the mill which continued to operate into the twentieth century at the bottom of Mill Lane. Of this only the Mill House remains.

In 1318 the bridge over the Darent in the centre of the village — known then as Longebregge — was broken down, and the Archbishop's bailiff ordered it to be repaired at the expense of all the tenants. Hamon de Morton refused to pay the five shillings at which he was assessed by the tithing-man, so the bailiff ordered the jurymen to seize Hamon's horse, much to his annoyance.[18]

Throughout the land, and in spite of bad weather and poor harvests, the first half of the fourteenth century was a time of much church-building, and at Shoreham probably between 1300 and 1320 the present north wall of the nave was rebuilt and extended farther than its predecessor, up to and including the tomb niche. This must have meant the considerable rebuilding of the church, except for the twelfth-century tower. As elsewhere, this rebuilding was the responsibility not of the Archbishop but of the parishioners.[19] It is interesting to speculate therefore on the source of the funds found for such extensive building in a period of dearth and famine. Perhaps those paid who benefited from the rocketing prices of wheat and other farm produce, but more probably the contributors were those who had been gradually building up their wealth in land holdings, such as the Tymberdens and the Cepehams, and those who had been providing material services within the manorial structure, such as the suppliers of chalk, lime, tiles and shingles for building, and the brewers.

It is appropriate to introduce here a poet writing at the beginning of the fourteenth century, a generation earlier than Chaucer, not in Latin but in the local Kentish dialect of English. He was undoubtedly a native of Shoreham, William de Shoreham by name, a zealous and learned preacher who saw the need to convey the doctrines of the Church to those around him who were only capable of understanding them in a popular form and language. William de Shoreham was a monk of the priory of Leeds (Kent), and when Archbishop Walter (1313-27) impropriated the rectory of Chart Sutton to the prior and convent of Leeds and it became a vicarage, William de Shoreham was chosen as the first vicar. Seven of his poems were published by the Percy Society in 1849, transcribed by Thomas Wright Esq., MA, FSA. There are four didactic poems which lay down what his parishioners should believe, what they should do, what they should not do and where to find means of grace. The remaining three poems are devotional and lyrical, possibly translations from lost Latin originals. We are indebted to Helen Wheeler MA for translating some of William's poems into modern English. In her unpublished paper Helen Wheeler writes: 'what frequently resonates behind these verses is a vivid impression of the questions he must have been asked by his worried parishioners: what happened to an unbaptised child who died; why did God wait so long after the fall of Adam to send a Redeemer. William does his best to answer these pertinent questions:

> "And here mankind laboured and dug
> Five thousand winters and a half
> And yet some more,
> Before the time of living came...."

Some of the questions he tackles sound ageless:

> "Some men may ask where God was
> When nothing of the world existed
> Neither great nor small?...."

and the answer is equally elusive:

> "Where the world is now, was he
> And yet he is and ever shall be
> Whole over all."

Of the age for marriage his prescription sounds strange to our ears:

> "Of them that would be wedded
> Here the age you can learn,
> The boy child fourteen years must have
> And just twelve the girl.
> Betrothals
> May at seven years be made
> But not a proper wedding.'"

William spoke in a simple language that his listeners could understand. There was a William who was a tenant of the Church Yoke in Shoreham in 1294. The son who lived with him was called John — the dating could allow the poet William to be his elder brother, carrying his father's name.[20]

Barbara Tuchman gave to her book *A Distant Mirror* the sub-title 'The Calamitous 14th Century'. It is an accurate epithet to apply. As already mentioned, there was a marked increase in rainfall from 1300 which naturally affected agriculture — in 1311 there was a poor harvest, and that was followed thoughout Europe by the heavy floods in 1315-17 which immediately resulted in famine. Unusually heavy flooding recurred in Kent in the 1320s and 1330s, accompanied by inevitable food shortages. It was as if God was preparing for the *coup de grâce* by weakening the people's physical resistance to disease. Genoese trading ships put in to Messina during the autumn of 1347 with sick and dying sailors on board. They had developed strange black swellings in armpits and groins: foul-smelling when the skin broke. The Black Death had arrived in Europe and spread its horrible contagion with awful speed throughout the continent. It reached Southern England late in 1348 (just before Edward III celebrated Christmas at Otford Manor), and spread to the rest of the country in 1349. It struck when the resources of the country were stretched to the limit. The wars against the Welsh and Scots were ending but the long intermittent war against France was only beginning, so that the people of Kent not only had to suffer flood and famine and the bubonic plague but ever-increasing demands from King and government for men and money to carry on the wars. We know from Poll Tax figures that the population of the whole country in 1377 was just over 2,000,000. About a third of the population of England perished in the first bout of the plague, and attacks followed until the end of the century, by which time nearly 50% of the population had succumbed.

No record of the plague in Shoreham is available, but it may be significant that there is a gap in the list of rectors provided in Chapter IX of his history of the parish by Augustus Payne. Edmund de London became rector in 1331 but died the following year, and there is no record of any priest in the parish until Thomas de Bradewell came in 1355. It is possible, therefore, that the parish was without a rector during the first attacks of the plague. Many priests died attending their parishioners; others with less courage abandoned their flock. We do not know the fate of those at Shoreham.

The villagers as they prayed in the newly rebuilt church for their loved ones lost and for their own salvation must have felt in their hearts what William Langland expressed in his poem *Piers Plowman*, that England was a country out of joint, corruption ruling Court, Church and law, that the end of the world was approaching, that God in his anger was punishing them for their sins and no man on earth could prevent the devastation caused by the plague. Yet it does not seem that those in Otford manor suffered as much as elsewhere. Wrotham manor was ruined: neither men nor resources could be found to restore and maintain it following the plague.

The devastating loss of life left the government and land-owners desperate, and they reacted ruthlessly to restore the pre-1348 situation. They tried to halt the rise in wages by the harsh application of the Statute of Labourers, compelling labourers without means of subsistence to accept whatever work was given to them at 1347 rates. But the economic reality was against a return to pre-plague conditions. Conflict increased, craftsmen and labourers realized their increased power, and changes in the feudal system began to emerge. Lords of the manor had to face up to inevitable change. It seems that manorial policy at Otford was modified to ensure that production from demesne land was sufficient for the upkeep and use of the household while the renting of land was increasingly relied on to provide the larger part of the lord's income. At the same time those in charge accepted the changed situation and gave increasing rewards to the *famuli* to encourage them to work.

Yet discontent increased and finally erupted. The poll taxes imposed on all classes to finance the war were the last straw. The Peasants' Revolt in Kent began in the Dartford area in June 1381. Richard II had as his Lord Chancellor the 'capable and conscientious'[21] Archbishop of Canterbury, Simon Sudbury, who was rather naturally seen by the rebels as responsible for the excessive taxation. Hearing that the rebels were marching into London from Kent and Essex, Sudbury and others took refuge in the Tower, but at the heart of rebellion the garrison let in the rebels, who dragged out the Archbishop and executed him. His houses at Lambeth, Croydon and Harrow were burnt down. Although it is not mentioned by name, the Archbishop's house at Otford must be included among the other unnamed residences which were also attacked because of the evidence of abnormal expenditure on repairs and reconstruction recorded in the accounts for 1382/3 following the rising. For example, there were extra costs for smithery 'on account of the great carriage this year of stone and timber'. Another entry is 'in wages of 3 men felling timber in Whyteclyf (Whitley Forest) for posts and palings and rails about the mote — 12d. and on 6 carts for 6 days carrying timber to Otford 6s.'

It is not difficult to imagine in the first days of June 1381 the growing excitement in Shoreham as news came up the valley from Dartford, of the growing numbers of the discontented gathering there, of the taking of Rochester by the rebels and the subsequent taking of Maidstone and Canterbury, and then the appearance of rebel bands in the village encouraging the people of Shoreham in an attack on the manor-house. The authors of *Otford in Kent — A History* have suggested the possible sequence of events at the manor (p. 81). Entry was forced and damage done externally and internally; there is no doubt that we would today know more about the Shoreham and Otford of those times had not great numbers of manor records been destroyed by those wishing to obliterate official records of taxes, feudal dues and obligations. The revolt collapsed with the death of the rebel leader Wat Tyler, and the King's Council regained control in London.

Only gradually did the rebellious feelings against the government cool. With the murder of Archbishop Sudbury, Otford manor had reverted temporarily to the Crown, and so unwilling were the yoke tenants and cottars of Shoreham and Otford to do their reaping services for the manor that autumn that a royal commission was appointed to compel them to do so.

There was a reduction in farming activity on Otford demesne land. Whereas in 1316 there were some 300 acres of ploughed land (not counting fallow), after the plague there were rarely more than 200 acres put to the plough.[22] This suggests that the fall of a third in cultivation may have been caused partly by the reduction in the population but was also due to the increased leasing of land to tenants. For instance, in 1402 the demesne land and pasture with 9 acres of meadow in Shoreham was 'demised' (leased) to Thomas Brownswayn for a term of 7 years for 66s. 8d. (Incidentally, in that same year the manor accounts show that no revenue was received from the brewing of beer (gavelsister) 'for want of barley'.)

Although feudal services in the limited form existing in the Otford manor lasted longer than elsewhere, at the end of the fourteenth century and the opening of the fifteenth century not only did discontent with the old feudal order show itself in the burning of custumals and rentals — of which the destruction at Otford in 1381 was one example among many — but there was a more general reluctance to toe the line. We have already instanced the absence of twenty-four tenants of Shoreham from the Codsheath Hundred Court on 12 October 1414, but several other examples are to be found at that time[23]

On 2 November 1406 the Court at Otford fined the tenants of the Castle of Lullingstone 12d. and Robert Tymberden for the yoke of Tymberden 6d for 'default of suit of court' — i.e., for failing to attend their lord's court. In the previous August the tenants of the yoke of Tymberden had been distrained for not carrying wood for the lord on the day assigned in the custumal. Four years later on the death of Hamon Tymberden, Thomas Tymberden his son and heir very conscientiously came to the court to do fealty to the lord, and because Hamon 'had no animal' paid 3s. 6d. as heriot (death duty). At the same time he cleaned his slate personally by paying 'relief' for his own property, in Hamon's croft which he was inheriting, as well for other lands, tenements, rents and services which he had purchased of Hamon by a charter dated at Shoreham 1 December 1405.

With Thomas in their hands the court seized the opportunity to distrain another Tymberden, Robert, to attend the next court for relief and fealty for his share of the property purchased of Hamon. He failed to attend court the following June, and some years later he was still apparently in default. Thomas also was in trouble, being fined 4d. for not attending court. The Tymberdens do not seem to have been exceptional in their behaviour, for the same court in 1419 fined the tenants of Cepeham 4d. also. Eight years later Robert Tymberden did attend the court and 'put himself in mercy for default of common suit of court of Northeld in Tymberden'. He was fined 8d. — the equivalent of a labourer's

SHOREHAM

wages for four days' work. This was a very mild fine, suggesting that the manor authorities — shaken by the discontents of recent years and realizing that the medieval framework was cracking — were treating the sentence handed down as a formality. This impression is reinforced in February 1429 when John Cepeham gave the lord as fine 12*d*. 'for his release from suit of court until Michaelmas next' for the Cepehams' property of Planas, (of which more anon). This does suggest that tenants were now able to buy their freedom from court attendance. This might have been an exceptional case, because John Cepcham could have been ill. In fact he died a few months later, and his heirs had to pay an addition as 'relief and fealty to the lord' on taking over the property of Planas.

Meanwhile the courts were also dealing with the minor irritations of human behaviour. In 1388 William Okebourne in the Otford Manor Court complained against John Cepeham that 'on Saturday next before the feast of St Dunstan he, John Cepeham, came to Shoreham to the place called Godyzok (God's Oak) and there took 100 sheep because they were on his own ground doing damage.' And so began the painfully slow process of writing down the plaintiff's case, of the appointment of a jury to look into the truth of the matter and the return of the jury's verdict. That same court dealt with 33 pleas of debt, 13 pleas of trespass in addition to the one mentioned, 24 land tenure cases, 6 pleas of covenant, 3 of unlawful detention and one fine for default of court.[24] A crowded agenda indeed.

At the Hundred Court held in 1406 on Wednesday next after Michaelmas the jury reported that the highway leading 'from Danestronche to Halsted' (old Polhill) was 'noisome for want of repair'. The tithing of Shoreham was fined 3*d*. and had to repair it by the next court on pain of a 10*s*. fine, and in addition because the tithing concealed the poor state of the road they were fined an extra 6*d*. This case is of special interest to us now with the near-obliteration of Old Polhill by the building of the M25 motorway.

One John Pemyll found himself in trouble when William Cadelok complained against him in the manor court held on 10 January 1429 that he trampled and destroyed two acres of barley of his at the 'castell' in Shoreham (Castle Farm) with his cattle. John naturally denied the charge. Again at the same court Alan Tymberden complained that John Pemyll at the feast of St Peter ad Vincula 1428 at Shoreham in the place called Holehame, came and trampled his pasture with his pigs. John denied the charge and 'put himself upon the country', and so yet another jury was set up to decide upon the truth of the matter. (Incidentally, the place called Holehame was almost certainly the same field on Castle Farm called Holey Ham on the 1720 map owned by Mr William Alexander.) So it looks as if Alan Tymberden and William Cadelok got together in an attempt to put a stop to John Pemyll and his casual grazing habits. Could this John Pemyll have been an ancestor of Peter Pemell, the member of the select vestry in 1828 whose memorial hangs on the north wall of the nave in Shoreham church?

The Hundred of Codsheath belonged to the Lordship of Canterbury, and so for administrative convenience at this time both Manor Court and Hundred Court were held at Otford. The cumbersome machinery of justice that had evolved during the medieval period must have been extremely costly, and emphasizes the importance of maintaining the revenue of the lordship.

The 1404/5 accounts drawn up by Richard at Forde, the manor reeve, illustrate in meticulous detail of what elements the manor's revenue consisted.

From 309 hens received as Christmas Rent, sold at 3d per hen — 77s 3d

From 1850 eggs received as Easter Rent 850 sold at 6d a hundred — 9s 3d

From 15 pullets received as Michaelmas Rent sold at 1d per head — 15d

From 17 Plough Shares Rent at 12d each — 17s

From a Sparrow hawk sold — 2s etc etc.

There are items in the accounts showing that Sevenoaks was becoming increasingly important locally as a market. One example among several reads 'a new rent of 4d. of John Depeden and Richard Dryvere for a plot of land 13 ft long and 12 ft wide in the Market of Sevenoaks'.

From 1422 the great majority of the Archbishop's demesnes were leased out, but at Otford things went more slowly. In 1437/8 only 23 acres of the demesne could be let, and only on an annual basis, and in that year Shoreham demesne land was given over to grazing the Archbishop's sheep, which suggests a shortage of ploughmen to cultivate the arable land. However, by 1444 the whole of Otford demesne was permanently leased. An entry in the accounts of John More, Serjeant and Keeper in 1447, points to one of the reasons for this development — 'on a labourer brought in for digging loam for one day — 4d.'.[25] In 1290 the labourer's wage was 1d. a day.[26] Whereas wages had quadrupled, prices had only doubled in the intervening years.

In the 1440s the yokelands were still unchanged since 1284 apart from minor alterations. It is true that in some greater parcelling of the land had taken place, so that a quarter of the holdings were only one or two acres in extent while a handful of tenants held 100 acres or more: among these was John de Sepham, whose family had continued to prosper since before 1284. The number of eight-acre cottaries had remained as before. From the mid-fifteenth century the manor of Otford was split up into separate accounting units, so that we find Shoreham — now called a 'borgha' — had its own collector of taxes (usually styled a 'reeve').[27] This was another sign of change in the manorial structure — a loosening of the bonds tying Shoreham to Otford.

The discontents which erupted in 1381, and in which some from Shoreham must have been involved, did not disappear with the death of Wat Tyler. Although the feudal controls were gradually being loosened and abandoned, rebellion remained in the air, especially among the independently minded of Kent. The war dragged on against the French, wasting the country's money and its manhood, and although the hearts of the people of Shoreham must have been lifted by the daring and brilliant victories of first Crécy and then Agincourt they must also have been depressed by the tales told by soldiers turned adrift in the country after the loss of the provinces in France. Henry V provided a short inspiring interlude in the sad story of dynastic intrigue and strife which led eventually to the War of the Roses. Henry VI could provide no inspiration, and his councillors were distrusted; distrust of some turning to hatred. Following violent elections to the Commons in 1430 Parliament passed an Act restricting the country vote to 40s. freeholders. This deprived many of the right to vote for Knights of the Shire. It was an Act especially resented in Kent, where from the thirteenth century the legal freedom of Kentish men had been fairly well established, and in 1430 gavelkind tenure within the lordship of Canterbury was treated as free tenure.

It is not surprising, therefore, that when another eruption of general discontent with government took place the two thousand taking part in 'Jack

Cade's Rebellion' were not as suggested by Shakespeare 'the filth and scum of Kent', but included 1 knight, 18 esquires, 74 gentlemen, merchants, shopkeepers, yeomen and craftsmen; even twenty-four constables from the hundreds as well as priests.

At Easter 1450 Parliament was at Leicester, and the Commons in angry mood demanded that those responsible for the loss of Anjou and Maine should be punished. They named particularly William de la Pole, first Duke of Suffolk, and James Fiennes, Lord Saye and Sele, at that time the King's much-hated Lord Lieutenant of Kent who resided at Knole. Suffolk was banished to France, but was intercepted in the Channel by one of his rivals, brought ashore and beheaded on the beach at Dover. Lord Saye and Sele was furious at the loss of his friend and threatened vengeance upon the people of Kent. It was his threat that probably inspired the first of the fifteen grievances drawn up by the rebels for presentation to the King which read: 'It is openly noysed that Kent should be destroyed with royall power and made a wild forest, for the death of the Earl of Suffolk, of which the commons were never guilty.' Anger increased, and risings started at Whitsun all over Kent. On the 5th of June the rebels concentrated on Blackheath with their list of grievances, which was prefaced with an assurance to the King of their loyalty, and advising him to change his councillors. The points of grievance were discussed with some sympathy at Westminster and in the City, as the King moved slowly towards London from the Midlands, gathering his forces as he came.

He reached London with some 15,000 men. His council, now feeling more secure, advised him against listening to the rebels' grievances. He accepted their advice and rejected the Kentish petition, and about the 17th of June marched out of London to attack them at Blackheath. Before reaching the Heath, however, news came that the birds had flown, so returning to London Henry VI ordered Sir Humphrey Stafford and his kinsman William Stafford Esq. with a light force to hunt them down. So on June 1450, following up reports that the Kentishmen had fled the night before the King's coming, 'into the wood countrie neere unto Sennocke',[28] Sir Humphrey and his men met up with rebels at Solefields and 'fought with them a long time, but in the end both Staffords were slaine with many others of their people', and according to unrecorded local tradition the last Lancastrian was slain in the doorway of the Dorset Arms or rather of the inn then standing on the site.

The news of the rebels' success sent a shudder down the spines of those in London, and the King's large force seems to have dwindled away. Jack Cade through the Hundred constables, including the constable of Codsheath Hundred, called on the men of the villages to reassemble at Blackheath. A well-organized camp was set up there during the next two weeks where the forces of Kent and Sussex came together. On the 2nd of July Cade moved down to Southwark, and on the 3rd he forced his way over London Bridge and into the city. The next day the rebels found William Crowner, the Sheriff of Kent, who was also a son-in-law of Lord Saye and Sele and who had been captured by the Essex rebels. He was handed over and beheaded. After that Cade returned to the Tower and persuaded the guard to hand over Lord Saye and Sele himself. The much-hated extortioner was taken and executed 'at the Standard in the Cheppe'. The citizens of London were now desperate to defend themselves and their property, and having obtained arms from the Governor of the Tower joined with the garrison in attacking the rebels. All Sunday evening and night the fight went on, and so serious had the situation become that on Monday morning as mediators from the King came the three leading prelates of the realm, the Archbishops of Canterbury and York and the Bishop of Winchester, and sat down with the rebel leaders at the church of St Margaret in Southwark. We do not know whether they made promises of reform, but what they did bring for the Kentishmen were guarantees of safety from any royal revenge. Pardons were given and sealed, some on Monday afternoon and others on Tuesday. How many is uncertain, but some two thousand persons were covered, not all by name.

One name did not appear in the lists – 'Jack Cade'. Those pardoned soon dispersed, and the King on the 10th of July denounced 'Cade' as a traitor, offering 1,000 marks for his capture. He fled into Sussex and was eventually wounded and seized at Heathfield. He died in the cart taking him back to London. The exact identity of Cade must remain a mystery.

But another mystery yet unsolved lies closer to our story of Shoreham. In the long list of those who received pardons from King Henry VI, the names appear of people from Orpington, St Mary Cray, Chevening, Brasted, Sundridge, Westerham, Wrotham and elsewhere, but there is no mention of anyone from Shoreham or Otford. Were the inhabitants of those villages so law-abiding and contented with their lot? Were they so cowed by the nearness of Knole and that power behind the throne, James Fiennes and his extortioners? Did they all feel unshakable loyalty to the Lord of the Manor? These do not seem adequate explanations of the total absence of local names in the lists of those obtaining pardons, especially when the Codsheath Hundred Constable had called out the men of the tithings, giving quasi-legal authority to the reassembly of the rebels after the Solefields victory. A more attractive explanation is one put forward by Sir John Dunlop,[29] that as the Archbishop was personally involved in delivering the King's pardons he may well have made special arrangements for his own people from Shoreham and Otford.

In the autumn of 1450 royal justices heard accusations in Canterbury, Maidstone, Rochester and Dartford against a number of gentlemen of the King's household who had committed atrocities and plundered in the course of military operations against the Cade rebels during the uprising of that year at St Paul's Cray, Eynsford, Otford, Chipstead and elsewhere. Shoreham seems to have escaped these troubles.

Whoever was involved of the inhabitants of Shoreham in those dramatic events, we know that about the same year 1450 one yeoman farmer decided that the time had come when he could afford to build himself a house. He chose a site just above the flood-level on the east bank of the river Darent by the Shoreham Bridge and ford. It was an ordinary small timber-framed house having a central hall open from ground to soot-encrusted crown-post roof, where his wife could make her fire safely in the centre of the packed-earth floor. The north end was jettied along its west front and north side and consisted of two service rooms with a single room above them, probably the solar, its tie-beam being simply but well decorated with chamfering of the period. This hall-house is today part of Chapel Alley Cottages, and has been much changed over the past five hundred years. The original main frame remains except at the south end of the hall, which was totally rebuilt in the eighteenth century.

In Shoreham today there remain two other houses from the years 1450-1530. They were a sign of the growing wealth of the period. At a safe distance above the flood-level to the west of the river is Reedbeds. K.W.E. Gravett FSA after visits in 1987 and 1988 described Reedbeds as a four-bay timber-frame building which included a two-bay open central hall with crown-post roofs. His most interesting discovery was that the apparent cottage at the rear of the main building could be identified as a detached medieval kitchen. It possessed a smoke-blackened crown-post roof and was of fifteenth or possibly fourteenth-century date. The fire risk from cooking in a timber building was great, and insufficient heat was generated for thorough cooking at the central open fire in the main house; hence the need to detach the kitchen from the main building. A little to the north of Reedbeds was a house built c. 1480–1500, of which the double-storeyed north end with its handsome bargeboards remains as part of Holly Place. The present main stem of that house parallel with the High Street was rebuilt in c. 1600-30.[30]

Before leaving the Middle Ages we need to add further important details to the picture of Shoreham. Today when we think of Shoreham we think first of the village and then of the farms, especially those in the valley: Castle, Preston, Oxbourne, Filston and also Sepham. We shall describe the one closest to the heart of the village and close to the river, but the one which few know about, and about which little was known even at the end of the eighteenth century — Planers.

These now consist of the farmer's family dwelling, a cluster of farm buildings and a cottage or two; all set trimly among the efficiently cultivated fields. The view of them in the period we have been considering must have been very different. Even up to the end of the eighteenth century and well into the nineteenth century farming was a labour-intensive occupation. Now it is capital-intensive, with maximum mechanization and minimum labour. Since the roads and lanes were little more than rough tracks, and they had to rely on their own feet to get to work, the agricultural labourers tended to settle around the farmstead for which they worked. The farms were the centres of their own communities to a much larger extent before 1500 than they are today. This is particularly so in the case of those that were sub-manors, such as Filston.

Immediately after the Conquest, with the danger of another Viking invasion always present in King William's mind, it was natural for him to place trusted henchmen in possession of strategically important places throughout the south-east of England. He had created his half-brother Odo, Bishop of Bayeux, to be Earl of Kent in 1067. One such follower was Richard, the son of Count Gilbert de Brionne, who was the founder of the Clare family and honoured later as the Earl of Gloucester. Richard was given Tonbridge and its castle to defend and other lands including Brasted and later Filston (then known as Vielestun) possibly in 1130 or 1207 for services to the Archbishop. Certainly in 1258 an agreement was drawn up between Archbishop Boniface of Savoy and Earl Richard de Clare which covered not only Tonbridge but also the Earl's demesne manor of Brasted and fees in Filston and elsewhere, which he held of the Archbishop in return for suit of court and the service of butler at the Archbishop's enthronement feast.[31]

According to Edward Hasted,[32] about this period in Henry III's reign (1216-72) Filston was occupied as tenant of the Clares by Hamon de Vielestun and his family, and in the next century by John de Vielestun, who from 1343 to 1347 was Sheriff of Kent. But in 1314 the Earl of Gloucester was killed at

The detached medieval kitchen of Balsattes (Reedbeds), the oldest domestic building in Shoreham. (Photo by Ian Harper)

Holly Place, a late fifteenth-century hall house. The cross wing at the northern (left-hand) end is original but the hall was reconstructed in about 1600. (Drawing by Richard Reid)

Bannockburn and the tenancy must have reverted to the Crown because in 1327 Sir Reginald de Cobham was charged with one knight's fee for the estate held by grant direct from the King. For a while Robert Blague held Filston, until in the second half of the fourteenth century it passed to William Petley, whose family had during the early medieval period spread its branches over the district from Downe, where the Petley family had its roots. The small manor of Hewitt's in Chelsfield (now well known as a pick-your-own farm) was held by members of the Petley family in the thirteenth century. Other members appear in Riverhead, Halstead and Chipstead as well as Shoreham.

In the fifteenth century one John Roos acquired Filston and became lord of the manor, and in his will drawn up in 1473 he instructed that 'his feofees and executors should sell the said manor and premises, lands called Andrews and Skypps [alias Colgates] in the parish and with the money coming thereof should edify and build three Almshouses within the said parish'.[33] This instruction was carried out on John Roos's death, and the three almshouses were built by the purchaser of Filston, Richard Page, to the benefit of the parish – a benefit enduring to this day.

At the end of the fifteenth century William Petley brought Filston back into his family and continued to pay the pension of 7d. per week to the three 'poor alms folk' which Richard Page had begun. It was a Thomas Petley at the end of the seventeenth century who sold Filston to Sir John Borrett, of whom we shall write later.

Sepham today consists of five families. How many families were there in the fourteenth and fifteenth centuries? We can't say exactly, but in 1284 in addition to John Cepeham and his family, there was Martin Stibard; Margery, widow of Simon Clerk; John, Geoffrey and Henry, sons of John Clerk; Walter and William, sons of Roger Bitersmyth. All were tenants of land in Sepham, and as they do not appear to have held land in any other yokes (from evidence in the custumal of 1284) it is reasonable to suppose that they were living in Sepham

Yoke. Each one of them was probably mentioned in the custumal because he or she was head of a household making eight families in all. There may in addition have been one or two cottars' and labourers' families, giving a community of a dozen households and possibly between forty and fifty people.

In the Codsheath Hundred court records for the fourteenth and fifteenth centuries there is periodic mention of the Tithing of Sepham, which suggests a community in earlier times of at least ten households. There is also mention in 1388 of trouble with the water-supply in 'Wellestret [Well Street] Sepham', which suggests at least a lane with dwellings along it. In the early Tudor period Sepham was described as the 'Half-Burgh of Upsepham', suggesting steady increase in size and importance. But enough of these conjectures. Let us return to the Sepham family, living there throughout the thirteenth and fourteenth centuries, steadily improving their position in the world until at the beginning of the reign of Henry VI (1422-61) they found themselves rich enough to acquire the estate of Planers. From this time forward Sepham and Planers remained linked, and at some point the Sepham family went to live at Planers and remained there until the end of the century, when in Hasted's words 'Mr. John Sepham who in the 5th year of that reign [Henry VII's] had rendered his services for them to the archbishop passed away Sepham to William Martin and Planers, the name of which is now [in 1797] almost unknown, to Cobbe.'

What do we know of Planers, the name being 'almost unknown' at the end of the eighteenth century? We must go back to the twelfth century for the first sight of it. In 1189 the Third Crusade was launched against Saladin, who had just seized Jerusalem from its Christian defenders. Shortly before King Richard I departed for the Holy Land his Vice-Chancellor John De Alençon, Archdeacon of Lisieux, had drawn up for him a charter confirming the gift made by Richard, formerly Archbishop of Canterbury (1174-85) to Ralph de Planers 'our butler' of

The Almshouses, Filston Lane, built in 1473 under the will of John Roos. (Photo by Ian Harper)

all the land belonging to Pagan de Otheford at Sorham (Shoreham). According to the charter, this handsome gift consisted of 'a messuage with a mill next to the messuage with land and all appertaining to the mill and the yoke of Godiva and half the yoke of land of Chepman and half the yokeland of Sepeham which Edward Long held and Elldone and a field of 28 acres at Aldeleg which is the land of Preston'. Ralph de Planers held this estate by service of $\frac{1}{8}$th of a knight's fee and by rendering 20 shillings at the court of Othefort (Otford) for all customs and services.

The estate must have been carved out of land between Preston and Sepham, but it has not been possible to identify the yokes of Godiva or Chepman to provide fuller details of its extent.

The Charter was witnessed by Pagan de Rocheford, Seneschal of Anjou and others whose names are a reminder of the close ties at that time between this country (and particularly Kent) and the Norman and Angevin territories across the Channel. Conditioned as we are to 'our butlers' giving service 'upstairs and downstairs', it strikes us as strange that a butler (even an Archbishop's butler) was worthy of such a gift, but in the early medieval period the office of butler was an exalted one. This was brought home to us when we referred earlier (p 34) to Richard, Earl of Gloucester holding his demesne manor of Brasted and feudal fees at Filston in return for suit of court and service of butler at the Archbishop of Canterbury's enthronement feast.[34]

In a Rental of 1280 for 'the district or borough of Shoreham in the manor of Otford' it is noted that 'among the holders of 'inland [land within the domain] is John de Planas'. Professor Du Boulay, writing of the same period, mentions a John de Planaz who died in 1293 as holding a messuage of 43 acres of arable, 8½ acres of meadow, 70 acres of pasture, 16 acres of underwood and a water-mill in Shoreham, of the Archbishop for $\frac{1}{8}$th fee. The conclusion one is bound to draw is that both sources refer to the same man and the same estate, and that the 'inland' being sub-infeudated to Ralph de Planers had been part of the demesne farm of the Otford manor in Shoreham.

The de Planers family continued to hold the estate until the fourteenth century, when it passed to the Passele family of Palstre in the Isle of Oxney and from that time Palsters became an alternative name for the estate.

As already mentioned, early in the fifteenth century the Sepham family, which had been steadily enlarging its property, acquired Planers, and in 1477 it negotiated a new lease from the Archbishop of the broken-down fulling-mill in order to build a new mill there.

Towards the end of John Sepham senior's life we get a glimpse of life at Planers in 1480. John senior (now a grandfather) and John his son drew up an agreement clearly defining the old man's rights when he decided to hand over the property to his son. They agreed that he should have four rooms to himself, two on the ground floor at the west end of the hall and two others — one over those on the ground floor and one over the larder. As head of the family he was to have access on high days and holidays to the dais in the hall and of course to the kitchens, so that he could 'ley his table and make fire to sit and have his pleasur with his neighbours and gests suche as be to hym dayly comyin atte all tyme of the year'. He was to have to himself a garden on the south side of the house where there was a vine, and also the part of the garden in front of his two rooms on the west side. He would, however, allow his daughter-in-law and grandchildren to fish in the moat when he felt like it. The middle yard at the foot of the bridge over the moat was to be his, as also the 'frute of a costarde [apple] tree in the long Grascrofte growyng'. Although the dovehouse was to be his, the son had to 'cherish' the doves, and for his pains would receive one dove in ten for the pot.[35] By the time this agreement was signed John Sepham the son was already a successful fishmonger in London, so he could look on the old man's arrangements with a certain detachment and one suspects with a certain amount of amusement.

R.G. Bennett in his unpublished history of the Kentish Polhills described Planers probably at the time when John, son of David (I) Polhill, inherited it from his grandfather, Francis Sandbach, in 1580. It then comprised a manor house with stables, barns, dovehouses, orchard and gardens covering two acres; 15 acres of meadow and pasture, 40 acres of arable land, 20 acres of 'jenoper and gorseground with coneyborough'; a fulling mill with buildings; a tenter close (for the stretching of the cloth after fulling); and land 3 acres. Although the acreage is smaller in this description than those of 1190 and 1280, the basic characteristics of the estate are similar. It is interesting to see that in the sixteenth century they were using the mill for the fulling of cloth.

Where was the 'manor' house of Planers? Dr Gordon Ward suggested that Home Farm was the site, but with the very definite mention in documents of a moat and a drawbridge, although the mill probably stood where the converted mill now stands to the south of the village, the house and garden must have been at river-level. More likely, therefore, is R.G. Bennett's suggestion when he writes that Sir John Borrett built New House 'on the right bank of the Darent opposite to Great House Mead, the site of the earliest mansion in this area'.[36] It must be significant that the name Great House Mead has remained, and that through Great House Mead runs the Manor Drain. One hopes that archaeology will confirm that Great House Mead is the site of Planers, and that Shoreham during the Middle Ages had a mansion close to its centre, with the humbler dwellings clustering between it and the church.

The church at Shoreham is linked to Preston by a cart-track running 1,200 yards north from the churchyard, but that is not the only link. The name Preston (Preosta-tun in Old English) means priests' estate or enclosure, and takes us back to Saxon times when there may well have been a settlement of priests established there to spread the Christian message in the area even before the church existed. Possibly it was the priests inhabiting Preston who decided on the location of the church at a safe distance from the flood-levels of the river and near the track leading up from the ford to the cutting in the eastern escarpment of the downs.

We have noted in the Planers Charter (1189) that the description of the gift to the Archbishop's butler included 'a field of 28 acres at Aldeleg which is the land of Preston'. Again, there is a brief mention in the custumal of 1284, where in describing the Archbishop's demesne lands in Shoreham it lists 58 acres 'in the field next to Preston'. Hasted points out that Preston formed part of the Manor of Chelsfield and was held by William de Chelsfield, who in 1284 also held the yoke of Godyngestone, which was neighbouring land to Preston. About 1377 Preston became the estate of Sir Thomas Buckland, who also decided to live there in spite of holding 'good estates elsewhere in the country'.[37] He and his wife clearly became very attached to Shoreham and built their own chapel in the Church of St Peter and St Paul which has been called the Polhill or Lady Chapel.

There is an interesting brief entry in the Otford manor accounts for 1391-2[38] which reads '4½d from a horse of John Preston agisted [grazed] there (in the manor park) for 3 weeks'. One wonders whether this refers to the grazing fee paid by a member of the Buckland family for his horse during his feudal service at the manor.

Another Thomas Buckland died about 1460 leaving his only daughter, Alice, as his heir. Alice shortly afterwards married John Polley (otherwise known as Polhill) whose family lived in Detling. Once more Preston cast its spell, and the newly married couple settled there. In fact, for over two hundred years Preston became the residence of no fewer than seven generations of the senior line of the Polhill family until one of them, John Polhill, sold it to Paul D'Aranda before he died in 1689.

Shoreham Castle — 'formerly called Lullingstone, alias "Shoreham Castle" — is situated close to the river Darent, on the western side of it and adjoining the southern pales of Lullingstone park'. Edward Hasted wrote that rather puzzling sentence at the end of the eighteenth century. It appears from contemporary maps that the ruins of 'Shoreham Castle' did in fact lie on the western side of the river, and an earlier map (by John Seller) shows the river running both west and east of the castle, providing it with an island site. Now, of course, Castle Farm built on the ruins stands to the east of the river.

The castle was described by W.H. Ireland in 1830 as 'a battlemented building which in 1224 was held by a family called Aldham of St Cleres in Kemsing' but it was already in ruins in the time of Henry VIII and no one knows when it was built. Sir John Dunlop in conversation with Mr and Mrs Alexander of Castle Farm suggested that it might have been used as an assembly point for knights gathering before departure on Crusades but there seems to be no hard evidence for this suggestion. Like Eynsford Castle, it might have been built in Henry II's time in the twelfth century. We do not know.

We have already suggested (p 22) the probable link between the names of Great and Little Murry Mead, lying just north of Castle Farm given in the field map of 1720, with the name Moriston Yoke listed in the custumal of 1284. We also know from that document that Moriston Yoke was held by 'The Lord Hugo Poynz', and from Hasted that Hugo de Poyntz 'died possessed of it' (the castle) in 1307. Thus the identification of Moriston Yoke with Castle Farm is firmly established. From our study of the subject there is, it seems, no connection except proximity between Shoreham Castle and the mansion built by Sir John Peche at Lullingstone in Henry VII's reign (1485-1509), and which later was called Lullingstone Castle.

William Cadelok was farming the 'castell' land in 1429 (p. 30), although some time during that century John de Neuburgh appears to have been the tenant. A descendant of his, John Newborough, was to sell the property to Thomas Polhill in Elizabeth I's reign, adding yet another piece to the jigsaw picture of the Polhill family acquisitions in Shoreham.

The farmstead close to the northern boundary of the village is now known as Oxbourne, but in the medieval period the name that echoes through the years is Okebourne. It is possible that Okebourne was one of the settlements mentioned as being 'held of the manor of Otford by one of three thegns by various services'.[39] The reasons for thinking that Oxbourne was sub-infeudated to a thegn in the eleventh century are both negative and positive. First, there is no mention of Oxbourne or Okebourne in the custumal of 1284, which sets out the customary obligations of tenants within his manor to the Archbishop, and one can deduce from this that as with Preston, Planers and Filston, Okebourne enjoyed a different (feudal) relationship with the Archbishop. That Okebourne existed we know because nine years before the custumal was written, on 31

March 1275, Henry de Okebourne and others witnessed a deed of grant from Thomas Le Bete to John de Ceppeham,[40] William Okebourne witnessed a deed of gift from Geoffrey Shrop to William Ewrere[41] in 1367. Earlier Henry de Oxebourne contributed 5 shillings to the Kent lay subsidy to Edward III in 1334-5. More positive evidence occurred in 1356 when Henry de Okebourne died. His heir was then a minor, and because he held his land under feudal tenure his knightly tenements and the wardship and marriage of his heir was granted to Master John Cayly, the Archbishop's cook, presumably as a reward for good service,[42] until such time as Henry's heir came of age. We have already quoted on page 30 the complaint brought by William Okebourne against John Cepeham in 1388, and that case, brought to court at Otford, may give us a clue to the location of the land held by the Okebourne family because William's sheep had strayed on to John's land. The Okebournes and Cepehams must therefore have shared a common boundary to the south-west of the village. In spite of our searches we have to date found no reference to the Okebournes during the fifteenth century, so there their story must end for the moment.

The element that linked these valley farms was water, the all-important river Darent, but there were other settlements existing during the medieval period which must be mentioned, although at present we have little lively detail with which to clothe the bare bones of historic fact. These three settlements are all high on the downs: to the west, Colgates lies on the earlier boundary of the parish although now just outside it, while to the north-west is Great Cockerhurst, and to the east Paine's Farm. All must have depended on well-water, since they were far out of reach of the Darent.

The first mention that we have of the name Colgate occurs in 1226-7 in the eleventh year of Henry III's reign, when Godelef de Colgate of Shoreham was involved as a tenant in a claim by Gilbert de Helles against Ralph de Planas.[43] There were other brief mentions in the thirteenth and fourteenth centuries. It was not, however, until 1410 that we have evidence of the Colgate family whose descendants live today both in the Sevenoaks area and in the USA. In that year Willaim Petley of Chelsfield witnessed a deed of John 'Coldigate' of Coldigate Farm.[44] Four years later we find Thomas and Robert Colgate fined 2d. each for failing to attend the Coddisheathe Hundred Court, and in 1478 Alice Colegate was brought to the Court by the Halsted 'tester', possibly because her brewing was not up to the required standard. About this time the prospering Sephams come into the picture when John Sepham senior gave Colgates to John Sepham junior as a gift to compensate him, it appears, for the trouble and cost of renovating their fulling-mill, which had fallen into decay (see p 38). From this it would seem that the Colgate family left Colgates Farm at the end of the fifteenth century. By 1525 Robert Colgate was renting '4 acres of land lying in ye yoke of Tymberden' – i.e. away from Colgates – and in 1528 William Petley was clearly the owner of Colgates, leaving it in his will to his wife Alice. By that date the Colgate family had moved away from Colgates Farm, but not far, because as we shall see in the eighteenth and nineteenth centuries they are still active in the parish.

In the Ordnance Survey maps of 1801 and 1819 Great Cockerhurst appears as Great Cockerice – an interesting spelling which is very close to the local pronunciation of the name as it exists today – but in 1208-9 it was written Cokerherst.[45] In that year Thomas de Cokerherst agreed at a hearing in Canterbury that William son of Waldin had a right to eighteen acres of land in 'Lullingeston' and they agreed that Thomas de Cokerherst should rent the land from William and his heirs for 6*d*. yearly payable at Michaelmas, during his life. Kokerhurst is mentioned in 1315 in a claim for rent brought at Westminster by Walter and Isabella de Rokesle against William le Mareschial, parson of St Mary of Wolnoth of London, but unfortunately details are lacking as Kokerhurst lumped together in the claim with property and land in Shoreham, Eynsford, Dartford, Otham and Lullingstone.

One gets the impression from these brief glimpses in official records that Cockerhurst from the late medieval period on did not enjoy an independent existence, but was linked with Lullingstone, possibly providing the agricultural needs of the estate as a complementary element to the deer park. In addition to holding Lullingstone Rosse and Lullingstone Payfrere, a close Roll issued by Henry IV in 1410 describes the Peche family as holding in Shoreham 195 acres of arable land, two acres of meadow, nine acres of pasture and fifteen acres of wood.[46] This could well have been Cockerhurst, because Sir William Peche, Sheriff of Kent in 1463-4, on his death in 1487 passed to his son Sir John (soon to be a close companion of the future Henry VIII) 'the manor of Lullingstone Rosse, Lullingstone Payfrere and Cockerhurst.'[47] Moreover, the acreage of the fifteenth-century farm shows certain interesting similarities to Cockerhurst Farm, up for sale in 1939, which comprised 216 acres of arable and market-garden land, 15 acres of pasture and 48 acres of fruit plantation.

Taxation of the Fifteenth and Tenth was granted to King Edward III in the eighth year of his reign (1334-5) by the Abbot of St Augustine Canterbury, and Sir Thomas Baconn. Among those named as contributors to this lay subsidy from the Codsheath Hundred were

Richard de Preston	5s 0d
William Belsote	1s 4d
Hamon de Morstone (Moriston)	2s 6d
Robert de Tymberdenne	4s 0d
John de Ceppeham	10s 0d
John de Vielestone	6s 8d
Henry de Oxebourne	5s 0d
Adam Payn	1s 0d
Thomas Payn	1s 2d
John Payn	1s 2d

It is reasonable to surmise that in that company the Payns may have been early tenants of land near Highfield which we know today as 'Paine's Farm'. Their name had appeared in 1327 in a Subsidy Roll, and in 1313 Richard Payn appeared in an Assize Roll. Later, in 1391-2 William Payn was charged 6*d*. for grazing two oxen in the Manor Park at Otford. From these details we can take it that the Payn family were active in the fourteenth century, though the name beyond the fifteenth century only endures in the name of the farm, as far as we know.

The readers of this chapter may well have noted the gradual loosening of the feudal hold of the Archbishop's manor over those who lived and laboured in Shoreham parish, and we have tried to show how the social and economic forces loosened these ties, enabling the energetic and the resourceful — such as the Sephams — to enlarge their land-holdings, freeing themselves from feudal services. We are reminded of this historic trend in a note on the back of the last folio of the 1284 custumal. This was added in English, not Latin, in the fourth year of Edward IV's reign (1464-5), giving details of the rents payable in lieu of services:

> Those holding a yoke of land and plough, sow and reap wheat, barley and oats should pay 10*d*. (an acre).
>
> They that should mow an acre of grass to pay 10*d*.
>
> They that hold Cotland shall pay for reaping an acre — 10*d*.
>
> For gathering and cocking an acre — 4*d*. A yoke of land for carriage of wood to the Lord — 2½*d*.

So the feudal ties were loosening, and although it had been a century of war both foreign and civil a labourer's earnings (which had doubled since the mid-fourteenth century) could buy plenty of the available foodstuffs, and there was even a bit over for buying better clothes. Over a long period from 1300 to 1500 the price of foodstuffs varied little, especially the basic necessities: if one looks at average wheat prices taken for a whole decade those in 1451-60 were almost exactly the same as those in 1301-10, and those in 1491-1500 were even a little cheaper.[48] Striking local examples can be taken from the Manor accounts. Richard at Forde, the manor reeve in 1404-5, sold 309 hens (received as Christmas rent) at 3*d*. per hen, and 1,850 eggs (received as Easter Rent) at 6*d*. per 100. John Polhill, deputy reeve for Shoreham, in 1533 sold 41 hens at 3*d*. per hen and 175 eggs at 6*d*. per 100: the same rates as 129 years earlier. That situation was to change in the next hundred years under the Tudors. Moreover, Shoreham with the whole of north-west Kent, was benefiting from London, the ever-growing market for its produce.

In 1018 Shoreham had become the peculiar of the Archbishop of Canterbury, and in 1241 the Rural Deanery of Shoreham (comprising thirty-four parishes) had as its first recorded dean Master Henry de Chaumbray, then Rector of Sevenoaks. The first recorded appointment of a rector to Shoreham came shortly afterwards, on 17 October 1242, and he was given responsibility late in the thirteenth century for the chapel at Otford. Thus Shoreham was as it were superior to Otford in the matter of the 'cure of souls' and the administration of the parishes of the area, and yet its position in the hierarchy of the feudal manor of Otford was reversed, and Otford was clearly the seat of power and preferment. What more natural, therefore, than that the Rectors should prefer to live at Otford close to the manor house and the Archbishop (when he was present) rather than at Shoreham? The Valor Ecclesiasticus of 1535 tells us that a chaplain at that time celebrated divine service at Shoreham, and the vicar (appointed for the first time in 1531) celebrated at Otford, and it is probable that in the fourteenth and fifteenth centuries a similar practice pertained, with the rectors living at Otford at the rectory house (now known as the Old Parsonage). This seems especially likely because during those two centuries three rectors were buried at Otford and none at Shoreham.[49]

One of the evils suffered by parishioners during the medieval period was the practice of incumbents holding two or even more benefices at the same time and absenting themselves from the parishes. Shoreham did not escape this evil. Hugh (Hugo Wickins), appointed rector in 1293, was a pluralist, being also chaplain and secretary to Francis, Cardinal of St Lucy. He must have spent some of his time in Shoreham soon after his appointment because it is recorded that in 1293

> John, son of Peter Butiller and his brethren, complained to the Justices itinerant against Hugh, Parson of this Parish, for detaining from him a part of a messuage and 50 acres of arable land in Shoreham which of right did belong to them. But Hugh appearing answered that the Archbishop of Canterbury, for the time being was his Patron and Diocesan and therefore he ought not to answer till the See was filled again, for John Peckham was then newly dead. And the Court agreed to it.[50]

A clever move by the Rector, and unfortunately we do not know whether the Butiller brothers brought the matter before the Court again when in September 1294 Robert Winchelsea was consecrated Archbishop.

Four years later Winchelsea, visiting his diocese of Canterbury, discovered that Hugh was not only Rector of Shoreham with the chapel at Otford and Chaplain to the Cardinal of St Lucy but had also for a long time held the benefice of Castelion Aretin. The Archbishop in a letter to Cardinal Francis expressed his wish to discipline Hugh as an absentee pluralist, especially as he had given none of the 'fruits of the church' for distribution among the needy parishioners, but the Archbishop failed to persuade the Cardinal on that occasion. Hugh was, however, dismissed as a pluralist later in 1298. The rector in 1316, William de Testa, was another pluralist, since he was Cardinal Priest of St Ciriac in Ternis, papal legate, Archdeacon of Ely, and Precentor of St Mary, Lincoln, as well as parson of Shoreham. Moreover, Archbishop Reynolds had accepted the 'favour' done by Pope John XXII in making William parson of Shoreham by 'admitting him in the person (as proxy) of Henry de Goldingh', clerk to the aforesaid church'[51] thus assuming that it would in any case be impossible for William de Testa to find the time to appear in Shoreham in person.

One of the rectors — who was buried at Otford in 1366 — Thomas de Bradewelle, was not a pluralist or a rogue but an honest residential priest who served his parishioners to the best of his ability. He[52] came to Shoreham probably in 1355, and it seems possible that he filled a vacancy that had lasted twenty years following the death of Edmund de London in 1332. During that time Shoreham and Otford had suffered the trauma of the Black Death, and Thomas de Bradewelle's arrival must have been particularly welcome. He established himself at the 'Rectorial Manse' in Otford, and was resident there for ten years. He was looked after indoors by his cook Radulph, who had 'little boys' to help him in the kitchen, and John his keg-bearer. Robert his groom looked after the outdoor establishment, assisted by John, the keeper of his horse, Ade his carter and a stable boy.

When Thomas de Bradewelle died all his servants benefited in his will. Robert his senior servant received twenty shillings and the chestnut horse 'which he used to ride', with saddle and bridle, two caps, a cloak and tunic with 'best hood' and also his girdle with its purse, tablet and other things (though not his seal and chain). Even the kitchen boys received two shillings each.

Of his relations a nephew, Thomas Le Wayte, and a niece, Isabella, must have been brother and sister because he chose their bequests with great care. To be fair to each he gave a bed complete with blankets, linen, 'tester' (canopy) covers; each received a silver cup and six spoons 'of medium weight', one laver (washing bowl), one horse for a cart and forty shillings. But in addition Isabella received a 'great carpet'. To another nephew, Master John (probably a priest), he left similar gifts, but instead of a horse his 'better girdle of black silk barred with silver' and his diary 'that I may be specially remembered in masses and his other devotions'. Master John's brother Thomas received twenty shillings. A William Kerl received a small nut with silver foot and cover and his wife Alice a ring with a sapphire stone. Another friend, Master John Severlee, received 'my smaller cup of silver with cover', and Master Richard Wodeland 'my better nut with silver foot and cover'.

As Rector of Shoreham and Otford he wished to be buried in the Chapel of Otford at the high altar in front of the image of St Thomas with but five wax candles round his body. He bequeathed for the repair of the southern part of his church of Shoreham forty shillings. To his two parish priests at Shoreham and Otford he bequeathed two best robes and ten shillings, and to the poor of the parishes he left money and 'winter or Lent Barley'.

His quite substantial library of religious and legal volumes he decided to divide into two gifts. One collection he left to the 'Religious men, the Prior and Convent of the Cathedral Church of Rochester with forty shillings for pittance', on condition that every year on his anniversary they celebrate one mass for his soul and the souls of his relations and benefactors. He may have had some doubts about the religious men of Rochester, for he added 'and if they shall not have taken heed to fulfil the foregoing I will that by my executors the aforesaid books one and all be sold and the money distributed to the poor'. He did not make any conditions for his bequest of the other collection of books to the Prior and Convent of 'Tonebregge', and in addition he gave him the best horse he had at the time of his death and even 'one summer house' which he had received as a legacy from his master John Leck, and one cloth called a 'dorsorium' containing the pictures of Christ and the Twelve Apostles and twenty shillings for pittance on the day of his death 'that I may be a sharer in the masses, prayers and devotions of the same as one of the same for ever'.

Although he had 'caused the whole Rectorial Manse to be built anew', he took the precaution of leaving sixty shillings to his successor' if he do not impeach my executors about the repair of the defects of the houses'. Master Thomas de Bradewelle leaves to us a glimpse of a much-loved and respected rector who cared well for his parishioners at Shoreham and Otford and had their support.

This seems to be confirmed when he found himself in dispute with the vicar of Sevenoaks, Sir Geoffrey de Haryngworth, over their respective claims for the tithes of pannage and pasturage coming from the two parks of Otford Manor. They appeared before Simon Islip, the Archbishop, in September 1353 at Otford, and were able to make an agreed statement to the effect that

> it had been attested by the parishioners worthy of credence that there belonged to the said rector in the name of his church the reception of all the tithes of pannage and of the two parts of the tithes of pasturage and that the third part of the tithes of pasturage only belonged to the vicar of Sevenoaks.[53]

In 1425 Richard Clerk became rector of Shoreham-with-Otford, and was also appointed the titular bishop of Ross in far-off Scotland so that he could attend to the duties of coadjutor-bishop in the Canterbury diocese (just as others were ordained to a see in some remote part of the world in order to perform duties at the right ecclesiastical levels in this country). It was to him that the Archbishop in 1444 leased all the demesne lands in Otford as a rent farmer for eight years at £15 6s. 8d. Clerk also farmed the manor of Filston and possibly lived there, but he fell foul of the lord of the manor, John Roos (who was later to endow and have built the alms houses in Shoreham). John Roos' complaints against Richard Clerk were recorded in some detail. The Rector's herd of goats had eaten the bark off the Filston apple-trees, causing £20 worth of damage. The elms around the manor house and other trees had also suffered. His hogs had caused 20s. worth of damage 'subvertyn' the meadow. He had also removed door locks, a ladder and even the lead off the dove-house roof, as well as other objects. Nor had he paid his rent.[54]

It is unfortunate that often it is the records of people's misdemeanours that survive the passage of time, and the good they do goes unrecorded. However great were the problems of absenteeism and plurality of benefices, one thing is certain — the church of St Peter and St Paul must have remained the centre of the spiritual life of Shoreham. Whoever took mass and confession, whoever baptized the children, married and buried the parishioners — whether conscientious rector or preaching friar on his rounds — the church itself (then a simple nave, chancel and tower) sustained the labourers when they came in from the fields. Those labourers can have had only a hazy understanding of the Latin repeated Sunday after Sunday at Mass but they saw clearly enough the large crucifix ('the High Rood') over the entrance to the chancel, and the figures of St Mary and St John standing on either side. Familiar to them within the chancel were the features of the blessed Virgin Mary, and probably those of St Peter and St Paul as well.[55] There may well have been Bible stories told in paintings on the walls, while other pictures that set their imaginations working shone from the stained-glass windows. One small picture in stained glass remains from this time — the pelican perched high in the westernmost window on the north wall of the nave. Who put it there? Could it have been a rector with a sense of humour? Major Charles Hesketh in a list of rectors transcribed at Lambeth c. 1930 includes against the date 1431 the name Sir Thomas Pellican. In 1485 Katheryn Mason, then a widow living in London, left in her will 'to the Church werks of Shoreham 6s. 8d'.[56] One who would probably have had memories of Shoreham in his youth was at this period rising in the hierarchy of the Church: Thomas de Shoreham in 1429 was Abbot of Bayham Abbey, but unfortunately we know nothing further about his life, and we cannot identify his family — Thomas was a very common name at that time.[57]

Great changes were to come in the next century. The seeds of change were already sown. Between 1380 and 1384 Wyclif's followers under his guidance made the first complete English translation of the Bible since the Conquest. His secretary John Purvey completed another in 1396. Wyclif's influence continued to grow throughout the fifteenth century. Another seed of change was sown when about 1422 William Caxton was born. For the rest of the century Caxton's printing press, and those of the other early printers, was gradually creating a standard English speech from the many dialects that existed. It all prepared the way for the time when one of Wyclif's ideas would be realized — the Bible in English, and in the hands of everyone.

IV
THE TUDORS

UNLIKE the civil war that divided the country in the seventeenth century, the Wars of the Roses in the second half of the fifteenth was a war between the contenders for the crown of England with little ravaging of the countryside, little involvement of whole communities. The armies were small. There may or may not have been any from Shoreham fighting with the Kentish archers at the battle of Northampton in 1460. It was the nobility and their immediate followers who died in battle, murder or other sudden death. When, therefore, Henry VII seized power in 1485 the country was ready to accept this new ruler, who compared with some of his predecessors appeared civilized and businesslike: more interested in developing trade than waging wars. Above all he was determined to restore order and control the barons and their private armies.

Maintenance of public order was indeed the policy ever present in the minds of the Tudor kings and queens during the sixteenth century. That the people of north-west Kent were unwilling to rebel was clearly shown when 16,000 Cornishmen marched in arms against the Government tax demands for the Scottish war in 1497, but failed to persuade the Kentish folk to rise and join their revolt.

The 'bastard feudalism'[1] prevalent in the second half of the fifteenth century, of local barons who indentured large numbers of knights and squires as their liveried servants in peace and war, was a factor in the eruption of the Wars of the Roses and one which Shoreham was spared, for it was part of the Archbishop's manor. Henry VII determined to reduce this lawless element by issuing the Statute of Livery in 1504. He also determined through other legislation to establish respect for the law, to make the law open to all, to enable private persons if they felt it necessary to accuse Justices of the Peace before Assize Judges, and to enable the poor to obtain writs without payment.

These beginnings as they developed throughout the Tudor century provided early elements in the structure of the modern state, and we find the medieval manor and hundred courts gradually giving way to the King's justice in the King's courts, central government taking over from the lords of the manor. In a century when violence was part of everyday life brutal crimes led to brutal punishment (branding, flogging and hanging), and the maintenance of public order was always at the forefront of the Government's thoughts.

Henry VII provided a measure of order and prosperity, and during his reign

SHOREHAM

John Sepham — active in London as citizen and fishmonger with other members of his family — was still adding a wood here, a field there to his holdings centred on the Sepham and Planers estates. So also did Thomas and John Polhill and other up-and-coming yeomen add to their holdings. They were no doubt feeling the benefits of Henry VII's policing of England, and his encouragement of commercial prosperity, and were enjoying the knowledge that London only twenty miles away was growing in size and making greater and greater demands for food which they could provide. Inflation — which had been almost unknown for a century — had not yet begun its destructive rise.

Then in 1509 a young king, Henry VIII, came to the throne magnificent in mind and body, newly married to Catherine of Aragon. In these opening decades of the century the optimism of the times expressed itself in building. Archbishop Warham was demolishing his house at Otford[2] with plans drawn up to build in its place a splendid palace, and during the period benefactors were to express their piety and no doubt some self-glorification in enlarging and embellishing their parish churches. There is ample evidence of this in the Sevenoaks area.

Here at Shoreham the Rector and his Parishioners decided to add a south aisle to the church with an arcade of fine chalk pillars, linking it to the nave with a chapel at its east end next the chancel. It is probable that the magnificent south porch was also added at this time. These additions were a very considerable enterprise, the financing of which was the responsibility of the parishioners, and therefore indicates a time of some prosperity and devotion as well as optimism.

What will always stand, we hope, in Shoreham church to the glory of God and the nameless early Tudor workers in wood is the rood-screen, which has survived the Reformation and the Civil War. Which master-craftsman designed and carved its beautiful fan-vaulting and decorated this near-perfect screen with the vine and more especially the rose and pomegranate (symbols that bring together the Tudors and Catherine of Aragon) we do not know. The rose and the pomegranate are carved again in the stone spandrels of the arch over the door which leads up the winding stair to the rood-loft. Augustus Payne in his history of Shoreham church in 1930 wrote of the screen 'it is clearly C15 work and most probably constructed in the reign of King Henry VII'. We, however, support the opinion expressed by Anthony Stoyel[3] in 1959 that the rood-screen was built at the same time as the south aisle and chapel were constructed in the early years of Henry VIII's reign. It is possible that the rose and pomegranate were included in the design to celebrate the marriage of Arthur, Prince of Wales, with Catherine of Aragon but as the marriage lasted only a few months, cut short by Prince Arthur's premature death in 1502, it is much more probable that they celebrated Catherine's marriage to Henry VIII. Besides, the screen could not have been built before the south aisle and chapel as it spans the whole width of the church. Alternatively it could have been added later to celebrate the visit in 1520 of Henry VIII and Catherine to Archbishop Warham's newly completed palace on their way to meet Francis I of France at the Field of the Cloth of Gold.

The royal visit must have been the talk of the Shoreham beer-houses for weeks. The vast retinue participating in that royal progress must have looked to the surrounding estates for accommodation. The Petleys at Filston, the Martyns at Planers, the Polhills at Dypdens and Preston could well have entertained some of the hundreds attending upon the royal party, inviting them into their 'fields where there be great plentye of partryges, feasants and other fowles with fox and hare very comodious for huntynge and hawkynge' and even fish in the 'ryver

The entrance to the south porch made from the trunk of a single oak. (Photo by H.N. Crawshaw, ARPS)

runninge thorowe the said towne [Shoreham] wherein is trowtes and other ffyshe'.[4]

Five years earlier one individual with fond memories of Shoreham church, a widow named Maryone Pawley, died in London and left money 'to the parish church of Shoreham in Kent towards the buying of an antyphoner [a book of anthems] that the service of God may be better maynteyned'.[5] There is no doubt that the parishioners as pious Catholics took it for granted that on the new screen over the chancel steps would be placed a large crucifix, the 'High Rood' with the figures of St Mary and St John on either side, and they took comfort from seeing

The rood-screen in Shoreham church, possibly the finest in Kent. (Photo by H.N. Crawshaw, ARPS)

through the screen the figures of the Blessed Virgin and possibly the images of St Peter and St Paul standing beside the altar.[6]

The religious storm that was to rage throughout the land could not have been imagined by the inhabitants of Shoreham in those early days of Henry VIII, but no one doubts that a growing cynicism existed over the attitudes and behaviour of many within the Church. Changes were taking place. The English language in the printed word was entering the churches. John Frith, born in Westerham and a pupil at Sevenoaks School, helped Tyndale in the translation into English of the New Testament. In 1539 the Great Bible in English was printed and published in London, and authorized for use in churches in the 1530s. But John Frith was not only a scholar but a keen and committed writer in favour of the Reformation. He was accused of heresy in 1533 and burned at the stake at Smithfield in July of the same year. His death was a sign of the times. Henry VIII may have broken with the Pope in Rome over his wish to divorce Catherine, but he remained a devout Catholic except that he insisted on being head of the Church in England. Following Parliament's approval of Henry's stand and the passing of the Act of Supremacy the Dean of Shoreham with others in 1534 signed the declaration required of the clergy that no Bishop of Rome had any jurisdiction whatsoever in England.[7]

During the opening years of Henry VIII's reign his own ambition led him into ever-increasing expenditure on war with France, and he found in Cardinal Wolsey a first minister who could govern according to his wishes and raise the funds required. Archbishop Warham, overshadowed towards the end of his life by the Cardinal, found himself appointed in 1524 Chief Commissioner in Kent for the collection of Wolsey's latest fund-raising demand, an 'amicable grant' due from the laity and clergy. To find these taxes people had been digging deeper and deeper into their pockets, and the 'amicable grant' hit all levels of income, touching even the poorest peasant farmers. Archbishop Warham on calling a meeting of his own peculiars and deaneries including Shoreham found that none of his clergy were willing to pay. Neither were the hundred unhappy yeomen and husbandmen whom he met at Knole in April 1525. Following these encounters Warham, Lord Cobham and Sir Thomas Boleyn wrote in May to the King

> There is great poverty especially of money in Kent. At several fairs men having wares and cattle to sell have departed without selling anything unless they would have sold them at less than half their values. Landed men can get nothing or little from their farmers who say they can get no money for their corn and cattle.[8]

Following the meeting a reluctant scribe was found to write a petition, but no record exists of his ultimate fate. Such was the fear of the King's anger and the long arm of his power that the 'amicable grant' was eventually paid.

It must have been with some relief that Warham turned to the affairs of his 'peculiar' — Shoreham. John Waren, the Rector of Shoreham from 1527 to 1531 who also acted as Reeve of the Manor, formally suggested that the Archbishop of Canterbury as Patron of the Benefice of Shoreham with the chapel should institute a perpetual vicarage at Shoreham with Otford. John Waren claimed that 'not seeking his own but the things that are Christ's, the fruits and oblations of the benefice of Shoreham with the chapel of Otford annexed are sufficient for a rector vicar and other priests and ministers'.[9] The 'fruits and oblations' may have seemed adequate to John Waren in 1530 but were to look very different in the 1550s and later, when inflation had really taken hold of the economy. The Archbishop adopted the suggestion. All tithes were to go to the rector. The vicar was to have a stipend of £20 per annum (somewhat above the national average at that time for parochial benefices[10]) and he was to receive in addition twenty shillings for collecting the tithes for the rectory. John Waren undertook to build a vicarage house with a garden at his own expense, although the maintenance of the house was to be the responsibility of the vicar. Part of the original building, the northern half of the area between the two nineteenth-century wings, remains to this day.[11] The first vicar was Robert Clements, who had previously been priest of St Mary's Chantry, Sevenoaks.

On the national stage Cardinal Wolsey, having failed to persuade Pope Clement VII to allow Henry's divorce of Catherine, his policies a failure and his standing with the King destroyed by his greed and lust for power, had died in 1530. Archbishop Warham died in 1532, just as the vicarage house in Shoreham was being built beside the church.

One who had been outspoken in Parliament against the ruinous policies of Wolsey was Thomas Cromwell, who even in 1528 must have seen his opportunity approaching of becoming Wolsey's successor as Henry's first minister. An intelligent self-made man who admired Machiavelli, he had worked with Wolsey in the dissolution of certain monasteries, and knew the driving forces at work in Henry VIII and his insatiable need of funds. By an interesting coincidence, in the very year of Wolsey's failure with the Pope (1529) Thomas Cromwell took a £12 per annum lease for sixty years of Filston Manor in Shoreham, at that time held by Stephen Petley.[12] One is bound to speculate on his reasons for this choice of country property. Was it proximity to the Archbishop's palace at Otford, or to Knole, which he knew Henry preferred? He must have appreciated, in spite of the poor roads, the closeness of Filston to London and the good farm land, hunting and fishing. His father has variously been 'described as a fuller, a smith and a brewer'.[13] so he may have felt the homely attractions of the Planers fulling mill and the tenter close (for the stretching of the cloth after fulling) between Filston and the village.

Thomas Cranmer, who had been chaplain to the Boleyn family, succeeded Warham as Archbishop of Canterbury in 1533, and in that same year the struggle between Pope and Henry over his divorce from Catherine reached its climax. Convocation, increasingly anti-papal, recognized the King as supreme head of the Church in England. Parliament, also anti-papal and anti-clerical, supported the King and expressed the growing strength of nationalist feeling in an Act of Appeals which declared that England was 'an empire' which could settle all cases in its own courts. The way was clear for Cranmer to pronounce the marriage with Catherine void, enabling Henry to make public his secret marriage to Anne Boleyn.

Henry was now relying fully on Thomas Cromwell as his first minister to provide him with funds. Cromwell met the King's needs by dissolving religious houses and seizing for the Crown their lands and wealth on an ever-increasing scale. In this he was assisted by one Thomas Mildmay, a Commissioner responsible for receiving the surrender of the monasteries, abbeys and priories at their dissolution, and who was rewarded by being granted the manor of Moulsham near Chelmsford. Thomas Mildmay's son Sir Walter Mildmay was to reach greater prominence under Queen Elizabeth I as Chancellor of the Exchequer, but three hundred years were to pass before the Mildmay family was to become linked by marriage to Shoreham.

In his search for ever more sources of income for the King one can imagine Cromwell letting his eyes wander over the fields of Shoreham and Otford and suggesting to Cranmer that he might like to offer his manor of Otford and his demesne lands in Shoreham as a gift to the King. As an admirer of Machiavelli, he may well have put his suggestion to Cranmer in 1536 at a particularly embarrassing moment for the Archbishop when he was summoned from Otford to Lambeth for the trial of Queen Anne Boleyn. We know that Cranmer made the offer and Henry VIII gladly accepted the gift. The Great Transfer Deed was signed in 1537 and the Otford Manor with Shoreham became Crown property and was to remain so until the nineteenth century (except for a break during the Commonwealth). The link with the Archbishop of Canterbury was broken after seven hundred years.

Although in the Great Transfer Deed Shoreham was described as the 'Manor of Shoreham', this is not strictly speaking so in the full medieval meaning of the word 'manor': an organization having demesne lands, services from its tenants and a court baron. It is possible that at Shoreham as elsewhere in the post-medieval period the title of manor was used loosely. Professor Du Boulay describes the administrative position:

> since 1450 the large manor at Otford was broken up into a number of separate accounting collectorates — the borgha of Otford under its reeve and the borgha of Shoreham and the once dependent settlements at Chevening, Sevenoaks and Weald were placed each under its collector (usually styled reeve).'[14]

Major Charles Hesketh, the local historian, also points out that in the extensive and careful rent roll of 1547 Shoreham is not shown as a manor but only as a town like Sevenoaks. The only sub-manors that were created in the thirteenth century or before were Planers, Filston, Preston (of Halstead) and Cockerhurst (of Lullingstone), and none could have been created subsequent to the passing of the statute Quia Emptores in 1290 which prohibited such creations. This did not prevent freeholders in Shoreham and elsewhere throughout the country getting together and organizing themselves into manors without any crown grant.[15]

We have an example of this in 1550 at Shoreham, when the first court was held of Edmund Cobbe and Isabelle his wife as lords of the manor of Planers and Sepham 'on Monday next after the feast of St. Luke the Evangelist [October 18] in the fourth year of the reign of Edward VI by the grace of God, King of England, France and Ireland, defender of the faith and supreme head of the church in the lands of England and Ireland'. There were no absentees, and to the court came Thomas Polhyll, gentleman, George Gylman, John Crytyan and John Beverley tenants of the manor. 'And each of them for himself acknowledges the said Edmund and Isabelle his wife as lords of this manor in full court, namely by paying for each one penny by name of an acknowledgement. And each of them does fealty to the lord . . .'

This document from which we have quoted, which was translated from the Latin by Dr Gordon Ward,[16] has an archaic ring to it considering that it was written in the middle of the century which ushered in the modern world. It was, however, a time of drastic change and uncertainty. Isabelle Cobbe must have been a very well-known figure in Shoreham in her day. A statement of rents in 1550, and those due earlier in 1536, were signed in her own hand, reminding us that she was the daughter of one owner of the 'manor', the wife of another and the mother of a third — viz, William Martin, Edmund Cobbe and Martin Cobbe.

One of the first acts of King Edward VI on the death of his father Henry VIII in 1547 was to carry out the many bequests contained in his will. He granted to

SHOREHAM

Sir Anthony Denny, Gentleman of the Bedchamber and Remembrancer to Henry VIII, various properties including 'the advowson, gift, free disposal and right of patronage of the Rectory of the church of Shoreham with the chapel of Otford'.[17] Sir Anthony's other properties were mainly in Hertfordshire, and he decided to consolidate his holding by offering Shoreham to the Dean and Chapter of Westminster in exchange for the Rectory of Cheshunt, both rectories being valued at £40 per annum. Thus in 1547 Westminster Abbey became the patron of Shoreham, and has remained so until this day.

So even if the inhabitants of Shoreham were not greatly moved by the high politics of the Reformation, they must have been aware that Archbishop Cranmer had handed over his Otford manor (including Shoreham) to Henry VIII, and that Henry VIII had handed over Shoreham Rectory to one of his favourites, Sir Anthony Denny, who in his turn had handed the parish and church to Westminster Abbey. Thus Shoreham reverted to the Church.

In such a time of turbulence and change it was perhaps natural for those who were experiencing the break-up of the medieval order to seek a substitute, and the Cobbes of Sepham and Planers seem to have provided such a substitute for some. There was likewise the tendency to think of Shoreham itself as a separate manor, although in strict administrative terms it was now a collectorate of medieval dues levied on the manor of Otford by the Crown.

Many like John Frith were to pay with their lives for their religious beliefs during the birth-pangs of the Reformation in England, but there were many who found themselves able to bend to the prevailing wind. An outstanding example of one who survived was rector and vicar of Shoreham. Born in London about 1501, Nicholas Heath became a doctor of divinity at Cambridge and vicar of Bishopsbourne in 1535. Three years later he became vicar and dean of Shoreham, and in 1539 he was elected Bishop of Rochester, holding all three posts at the same time. That he was trusted by Henry VIII is clear from the inscription on the title-page of the English translation of the Bible, known as the 'Great Bible' published in that same year, which read 'overseen and perused at Henry VIII's command by Heath and Cuthbert Tunstall (Bishop of Durham)'. He appeared outwardly to be in favour of the reforming movement, but was in fact constantly in touch with Reginald Pole and Princess Mary on the possible return of papal influence to England. His real beliefs were tested in 1550 when he was appointed as one of the bishops to prepare a new form of ordination. The other commissioners accepted a form already arranged by Cranmer, but Heath refused to sign it and even when brought before the Council of State he still refused, saying he would never consent to take down altars and set up tables in churches. He was deprived of his see.

When Queen Mary came to the throne in 1553 he was immediately restored as bishop and two years later found himself confirmed as Archbishop of York by Pope Paul IV in time to receive Cardinal Pole at Westminster Abbey when he returned from exile that year. It is interesting that he was given various estates, including Shoreham, by King Philip and Queen Mary.[18]

In 1556 the Queen made Heath Lord Chancellor, and while he held the Great Seal not only did he issue the writ for the execution of his old friend Archbishop Cranmer, but 217 other persons were executed as supporters of the reformed church. Nicholas Heath himself died of old age at the end of 1578. His survival into the reign of Elizabeth I illustrates the tolerance shown by the Queen to those who had done her service. On Mary's death Heath as Archbishop and Lord Chancellor immediately proclaimed Elizabeth's accession — 'the next and undisputed heir to the crown'. Elizabeth never forgot this service performed by Heath at the most crucial moment in her life. Heath, though, refused to take the oath imposed by the Act of Uniformity whereby the Queen like her father was made supreme head of the Church in England. Elizabeth deprived him of office and his see and sent him to the Tower, but in a short while allowed him to retire to his estate at Chobham in Surrey, where she visited him on two occasions.[19]

In the opening years of her reign, in the aftermath of Mary's 'counter-Reformation', Elizabeth was determined to restore her father's reforms of the Church in England while attempting to placate the Catholics. The Act of Uniformity in 1559 compelled everyone, including the inhabitants of Shoreham, to attend their parish church on Sundays, but the changes it contained to the 1552 prayer book did not satisfy the Catholic clergy and the Justices of the Peace had to enforce the provisions of the Act. Then in 1563 Convocation authorized the 39 Articles. They did not please everyone, and neither did an Act extending the taking of the supremacy oath to members of the House of Commons and teachers. It was a testing time for the Queen and her government, fighting for reformation of the Church against the conservative elements. The tensions existing between Church and Crown may well be reflected in events at Shoreham.

William Lambarde in 1570 pointed out that 'the town of Shoreham pays £3 18s.0' in tax and only Sevenoaks was greater with £4 15s. (Otford paid £1 2s. 2d., Eynsford £1 17s.11d, Lullingstone £2 4s.2½d. and Farningham 5s. 5½d.). We have already seen something of the hostility of the parishioners to the payment of tithes and subsidies to Henry VIII and there is evidence of the periodic build-up of arrears in their payment to the Crown throughout the century.

When the vicarage of Shoreham was first established in 1530 the vicar's stipend was set at £20 per year, with an extra 20s. for collecting the tithes. This was an above-average salary. In 1600 Lewes Kyffyn, as vicar, received only £17 6s.8d. a year. The assistant clergy in Shoreham and Otford in the 1550s were receiving £10 yearly, but in 1572 they received only £8.13s.4d.[20] This reduction in salary must be seen against the persistent inflation of the period. If one takes a base-line 100 in 1475, inflation had moved to 370 by 1556 and to 685 by 1597.[21] Clearly all parishioners in the second half of the sixteenth century must have suffered, and the clergy on a fixed wage were serving the parishes in increasingly straitened circumstances and reluctant or unable to meet the regular demands for subsidies and tithes due to the Queen's exchequer.

It is possible that this difficult situation was aggravated by the administrative arrangement introduced by the Dean and Chapter of Westminster at the end of Nicholas Heath's rectorate, when instead of making a further appointment the Abbey 'farmed out' the rectory. That is to say, the Dean and Chapter contracted with laymen for a fixed payment to collect the financial proceeds of the customs, tithes and taxes due from the rectory. One of the earliest 'farmers' was John Dudley, who as Earl of Warwick had presented himself with Otford manor after he had taken over as King's protector from Somerset in 1551.[22] By 1553 he had become the Duke of Northumberland, and was owing to Westminster Abbey £110, as two years' rent of Otford and Shoreham rectory.

The following year Thomas Polhill took over the 'farm' at a rent of £30 yearly and it remained with him, his son and grandson, Sir Thomas Polhill, well into Charles I's reign, except for 1589-90 when Thomas Petley took over on Thomas Polhill senior's death and for 1605-7 when George Causten held it.[23] From the proceeds of the rectory the 'farmers' had to pay the salaries of the vicars and curates, and this they did sometimes half-yearly, sometimes quarterly, sometimes monthly, probably depending on the availability of cash. They also had on the Dean's instructions to pay for the repairs to the church, the tithe barn and vicar's house. It cannot always have been easy to pay, and there must have been 'cash-flow' problems at a time of inflation when one's possessions consisted very largely of land, stock and corn in the barn. In 1566 Thomas Polhill received a letter signed by the Dean and no fewer than six prebendaries instructing him to pay to John Baker, the vicar, 'his due stipend' and to repair his house. Was Thomas at that moment short of cash or had he fallen out with John Baker? We do not know.

In these circumstances it is not surprising to find Shoreham falling behind in paying the tithes and subsidies due to the Queen, to the extent that the Bishop of Rochester was forced to sequestrate the living, ordering the vicar to appear at Rochester. The first occasion came following some years of arrears on the 12th of February, 1564.[24] Shoreham was not alone in not compounding 'with the Queen's Majesty for the first fruits of their benefices'. There were ten other rectories and vicarages in Kent which were sequestrated. The second sequestration after four years' failure to pay the Queen her dues came in January 1574. It was a time when nationally and locally there was much concern with the poor and unemployment, and since 1572 all in the parish had had to contribute to poor relief. On this occasion it was Sir Thomas Williamson the vicar who had to appear at Rochester, and it is recorded that three years' arrears of tithes from Shoreham vicarage amounting to £4 6s. were paid in June 1574.[25] We do not know if or when the subsidies to the Queen which were outstanding were paid, but it is possible that the Westminster Chapter may have settled the debt with the Exchequer. This appears to have happened on other occasions towards the end of the century in times of greater hardship and scarcity, although it is recorded that Thomas Polley paid 24s. for the second payment of the third subsidy due to the Queen on 2 October 1600.

One of the more colourful vicars of Elizabeth's reign was a Welshman. Cadwallader Lewis came to Shoreham just two years after the last sequestration in 1576, and soon discovered the vicar's house to be in a thoroughly dilapidated state. On 6 July he wrote a strong letter to Dr Gabriel Goodman, the Dean of Westminster, threatening to leave Shoreham and live at Otford if the house were not soon repaired. He ended his letter – 'I love my health better than wealth, thus fare ye well.'[26] The Dean was sufficiently perturbed to decide to ride down to Shoreham with Mr Burden the Deputy Receiver, to put the repairs in train and probably to have a word with Thomas Polhill – who would be responsible for them, considering the diminishing value of the vicar's salary. Cadwallader Lewis settled down and served Shoreham and Otford until 1582 except for one year. Just before Christmas 1579 he was roused to action once more against paying tithes to the Queen, and wrote to Mr Burden at Westminster to say he would not pay. We can only presume that he was immediately removed from his vicarage because we find the Deputy Collector at Westminster accepting in February 1580 from the Dean of Westminster 'as incumbent of Shoreham' the sum of 28s.8d. for his tenth due to the Queen at Christmas last. The Bishop of Rochester was approached, and it was evidently decided to reinstate Mr Lewis in Shoreham. In a letter to him dated Bromley 27 Sept 1581 the Bishop gave him a warning that he must pay to him or his deputy in Bromley parish church on 9 October next the first payment of the subsidy due to the Queen on 1 October

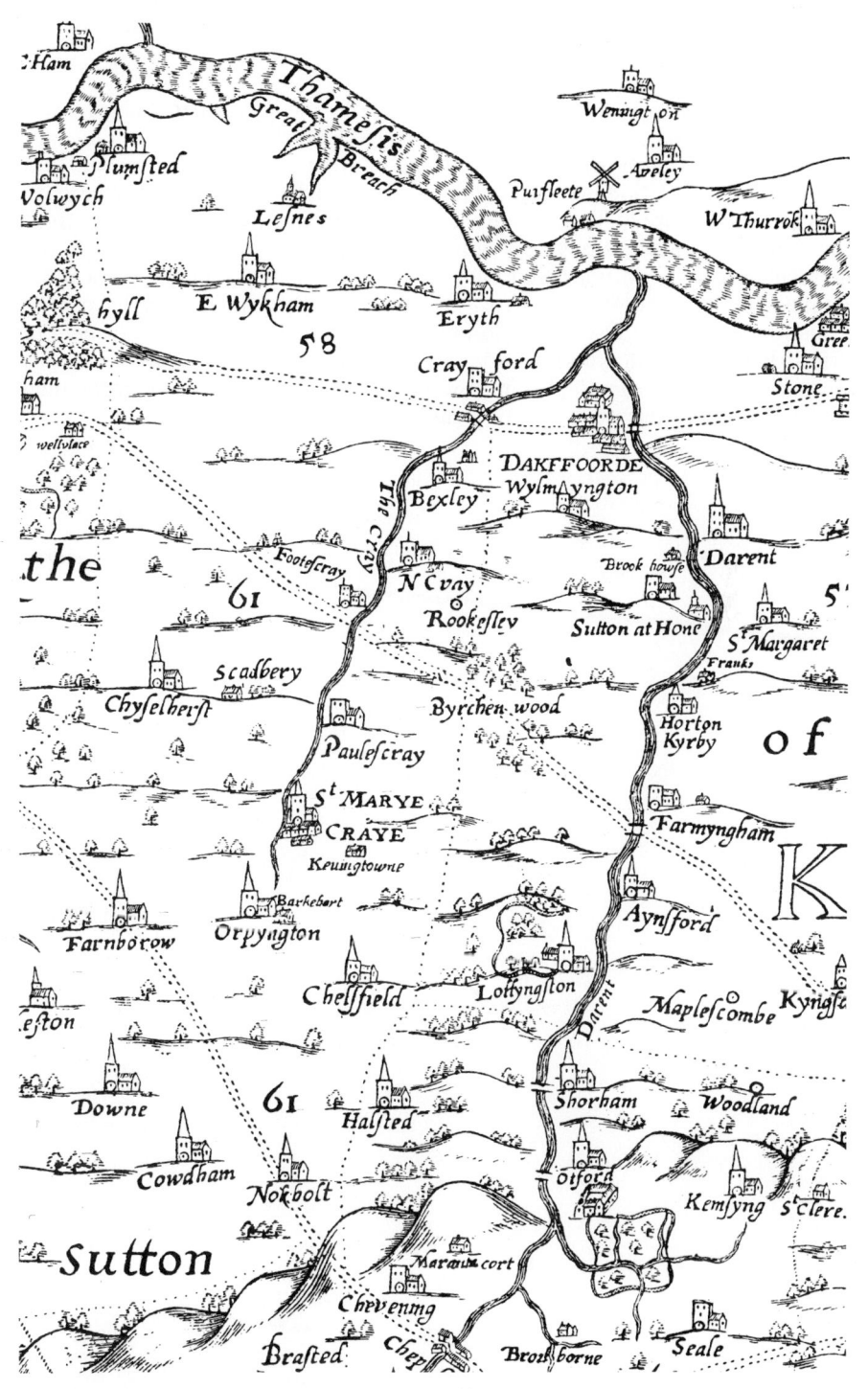

A detail from the first map of Kent, drawn by Philip Symondson in 1596. (Ordnance Survey)

next. Cadwallader Lewis paid without further argument the 24s. as ordered, and moreover paid the 24s. for the second payment of the subsidy in 1582.[27]

Earlier in this chapter we mentioned John Frith, the Westerham scholar who was burnt at the stake at Smithfield for heresy in 1533. Before going to Eton and King's College, Cambridge, he most probably went to Sevenoaks School. In a century when education had become a passion it would have been satisfactory to complete the picture of Tudor Shoreham with some mention of those boys from the village who must surely have attended that school, but unfortunately the attendance records do not reach back that far. No doubt some of the leading families employed tutors to instruct their children, and there may have been school dames in the village. We do know, however, that there was a school in Otford Palace early in Tudor times, and Shoreham pupils may have gone over the fields to the palace and also in 1586 to the school run at Otford by the then minister William Marcrofte with Henry Jedder.[28]

V
LAND DISTRIBUTION 1284–1608:
The Families of Tudor Shoreham

AT this halfway stage, as it were, in the history of Shoreham it is interesting to see the changes in land-tenure over the period 1284 to 1608 but before doing so it is worth noting that the 'Reformation' parliament in 1540 and its successors were beginning to regard the buying and selling of land between private persons as a normal part of everyday life'.[1] Henry VIII by the statutes of Uses and Enrolments in 1536 had hoped to maximize his revenues from his feudal tenants but the Statute of Wills in 1540 lifted the ban on the devising (giving by will) of land, and for the first time landowners could provide at Common Law for their younger sons instead of using more devious means.

No very accurate analysis is possible of the changes in land-tenure in Shoreham because we must depend on documents of varying quality, produced for different purposes. It is worth, however, comparing information given in the custumal of 1284 with the rent-roll of about 1410, in spite of the fact that some of the entries at the beginning of the latter document involving the rents in the yoke of Godegrome are missing. The first impression one receives is a marked increase in the number of tenants in 1410 compared with 1284 — for example:

Godingston Yoke in 1284 had 1 tenant, and in 1410 it had 19

Godegrome Yoke in 1284 had 9 tenants and in 1410 it had 18

SHOREHAM

Timberden Yoke in 1284 had 2 tenants and in 1410 it had 17

Lad Yoke in 1284 had 2 tenants and in 1410 it had 6

In only one yoke, Teflynge, were there fewer in 1410 (7) than in 1284 (9). Further study shows, however, that there was no appreciable increase in land under cultivation and only a limited increase in tenants — i.e., 47 in 1284 and 58 in 1410. Of the 47 only 8 held more than one parcel of land, but of the 58 tenants 27 held more than one parcel. This points to the likelihood that those tenants who prospered acquired more land wherever it became available, some having land in three or four or more different yokes.

For a comparison with the position a century later, in the early sixteenth century, it would have been illuminating to have had available the list for Shoreham's contribution to Wolsey's 'amicable grant' of 1524, which would have given details of the amounts demanded of the highest and humblest of tenants, but it has alas been lost. We can, however, compare the 1410 rent-roll with that of 1608 and note changes taking place between those years: years of great change from the medieval to the modern world and in Shoreham from life on the demesne lands of the Archbishop's manor to life in the incipient modern parish.

Opposite we compare the acreage in these two years held by individuals, but a word of explanation is needed. The 1608 rent-roll included 274 acres in the Filston estate, 74 acres in Colgates, 83 acres in Planers, 40 acres in Sepham and 19 acres in Hewets estate which were not included in the 1410 roll. These have been excluded from the table, in order that a true comparison can be made of the remaining acreage.

What conclusions can be drawn from these figures? There was a fall of a third in the number of landholders, and the most marked fall was in those holding 4 acres and under. The most marked increase in acreage goes to those holding 51 acres or more. This reflects a trend throughout England in the sixteenth century when smallholders, who were increasingly dependent on wages rather than subsistence farming, ran into financial difficulties in the periods of inflation and famine and sold their land to the large owners who prospered as producers and sellers.

In 1589 Queen Elizabeth I made it illegal to build a cottage with less than four acres of land to go with it. This law was passed to thwart a practice of husbandmen splitting up their modest holdings into units too small to provide for their sons. There seems no evidence in the figures available that the law had any effect in Shoreham, where the population was increasing.

Who were those holding the rich acres of Shoreham? The great majority of them were themselves working the land, or were providing a service to those doing so. One family we can follow through the Tudor years (already mentioned on p. 42) was called Belsote in 1334, when William Belsote paid 1*s*. 4*d*. tax to King Edward III. Early in the fifteenth century Thomas Bellisot held 24 acres spread over Godegrome, Better, Ladde, Timberden and Godeston yokes, and Ralph Bellisot had a house. By 1490 John Balsote (or Balsattes) only had 17 acres and a house and garden (which is a property now called Reedbeds, see Chapter X, p. 133). However, after that the family disappeared, and in 1620 Balsattes had become only the name of a property: in the list of those parishioners responsible for the repair of the churchyard fence is the entry 'William Petley for Balsattes — makes 5 feet'.

LAND DISTRIBUTION 1284–1608

Land-holdings in Shoreham Parish, 1410 and 1608

		4 acres and under	5-10 acres	11-30 acres	31-50 acres	51-100 acres	101 plus	Totals
About 1410	Acres	37	55	118½	137½	190	586	1124
	Land-holders	28	8	10	3	3	4	56
	Average acres per holder	1·32	6·88	11·85	45·83	63·3	146·5	19·38
1608	Acres	15 (−12)	37 (−18)	90 (−28½)	118 (−19½)	332 (+142)	709 (+123)	1198 (+74)
	Land-holders	15 (−13)	6 (−2)	5 (−5)	3 (no change)	5 (+2)	4 (no change)	38 (−18)
	Average acres pre holder	1 (−·32)	6·17 (−·71)	18 (+6·15)	39·3 (−6·53)	66·4 (+3·1)	177·25 (+30·75)	31·53 (+10·67)

In the rent-roll of 1410 there were six tenants all having the name Reve. From the little we know of them they give the impression of being a lively group of artisans and smallholders belonging to the same family. One John Reve was a smith farming 5½ acres. He must have been a person of consequence in Shoreham as he was also tithing-man. Another John Reve had 6½ acres. He was the butcher who the hundred court noted had been charging excessive prices for his meat, and was fined 2 pence for failing to attend the court. So also was William Reve, the carpenter who had 6 acres of land. Another William Reve was sexton with 5½ acres. Thomas Reve, a shepherd, had only one acre to look after, and lastly another Thomas Reve was a labourer who had just over 3 acres. Ninety years later there is only one Reve called John, holding 44½ acres and one of the mills, but it seems that other Reves no longer held any land. In the record of sale of two of his acres to neighbours in 1501 he is described as 'John Reve, senior, of Shoreham, yeoman'. He appears to have been a good example of the English farmer praised by historians and eulogized in song, who striving hard

61

from small beginnings had improved his position in the community. In 1608 Adry, the widow of Thomas Reve, had a house, stables and 14 acres, while another Thomas Reve had ten acres.

In 1284 two tenants Richard and Robert of Timberden farmed the yoke of that name. The family lived on in the 1400s. A Robert Timberden and probably his widow, Alicia, continued to farm the Timberden and Crokfot yokes, but sharing Timberden with John Newborough whose main holding was in the Shoreham Castle area. John and then William Timberden continued to farm in the sixteenth century, but by 1608 all trace of the family was lost, and from then on Timberden reverted to being only the name of the farmstead and the land surrounding it.

Sepham we saw belonging to a lively and vigorous family of the thirteenth and fourteenth centuries who in Shoreham history ended with John Sepham. John was the fishmonger and citizen of London who by 1500 had passed most of his property (at that time Sepham was known as Upsepham) to William Martin, and in 1528 surrendered what appear to have been his last holdings, including the fulling mill, to the lord of the manor.

No other family name recorded in the custumal of 1284 seems to have survived into the Tudor period except as the name of a house or parcel of land. Thomas Reve in 1608 lived in a 'mansion' called Whitegoose — a name which could well have descended from the family of Huitegos living in 1284 in the yoke of Crokfot.

Thomas Depeden had been tithing-man in Shoreham in 1388 whose namesake and probable relation John Depeden was serjeant at Otford Manor during the same period. Thomas's descendant, John Depeden, was one of the four largest land-holders in the first half of the fifteenth century (other than those holding sub-manors), with 115 acres scattered over the parish but centred on land in Church Yoke and his hall. His hall was situated on the right bank of the Darent just south of the bridge opposite Great House Meadow and Planers, and on the site where Sir John Borrett was to build his 'New House' some three hundred years later. In a grant dated 1439 he describes the property being conveyed thus:

> a half-hall of my dwelling called Dependennys in the said parish, with the arched chamber on the North side annexed to the same hall with a barn standing beside the water with a garden adjacent to the barn . . . I give also a kitchen with four acres of meadow there lying between two rivers as far as the lands of John Reve, butcher, on the North side and lands of John Sepham South.[2]

It may sound strange to us, but because of the danger of fire it was advisable in the time of wood-framed buildings and thatch to have the kitchen a safe distance from the house. However, it will be seen from the map[3] — probably drawn in the seventeenth century — of Dibden (see opposite) that the kitchen is linked to the hall by a bridge. The name Dibden disappeared when Sir John Borrett built New House in 1715.

One of the most frequently encountered names in this period is Romney. In 1414 Henry and John Romney held between them 74 acres to the north and east of the parish in the Moriston and Teflynge yokes. By 1533 there was John Romney established at Cockerhurst; a John senior and John junior near East Hill held land which by then seems to have acquired through long association

LAND DISTRIBUTION 1284–1608

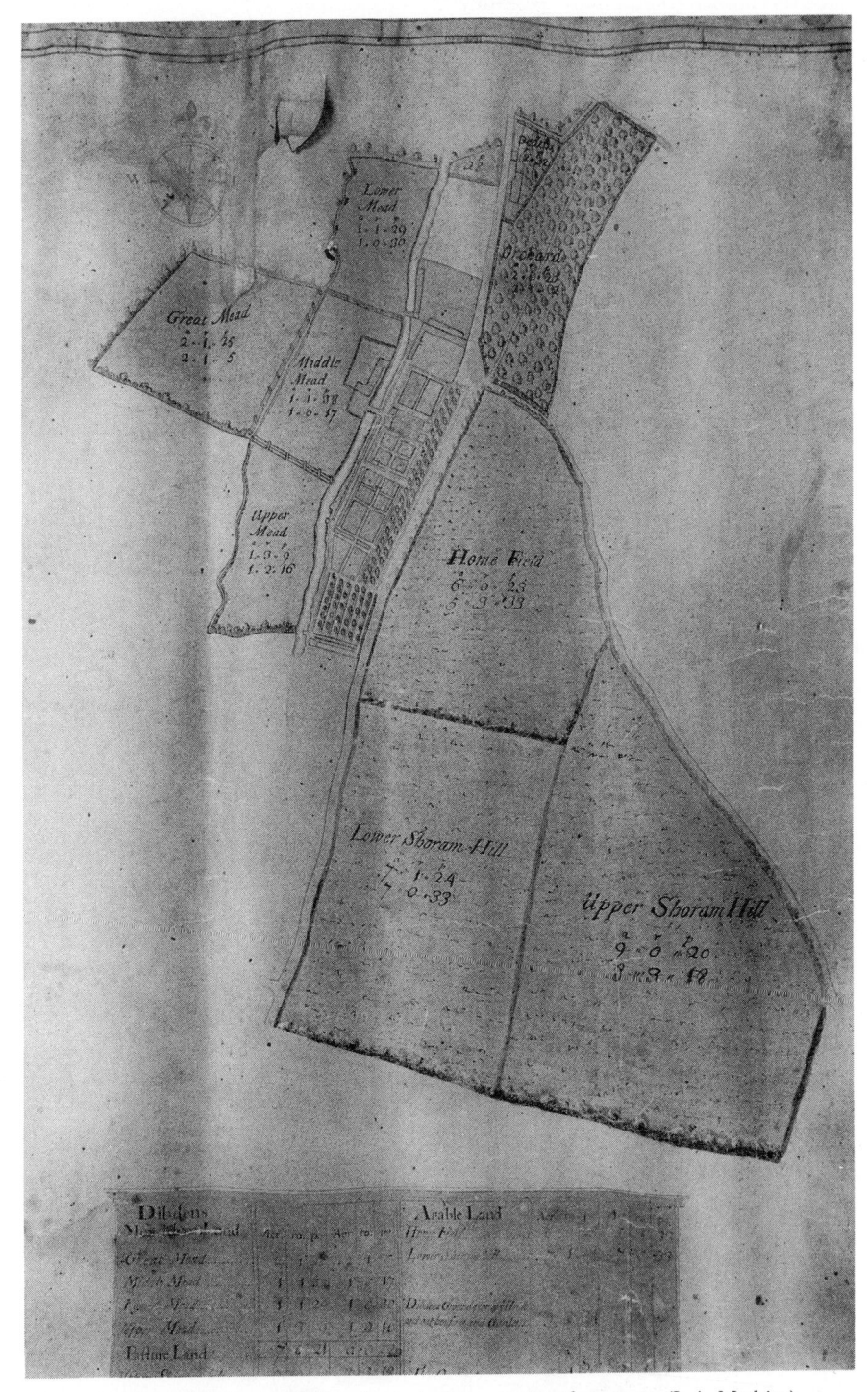

The ground plan of Dibden, probably drawn in the seventeenth century. (L.A. Mathias)

with the family the name of Romney Street; William Romney had just died in his house called Hameneks. There was moreover Thomas Romney, whose main holdings were in Otford but who owned 'Record' in Church Street before Christopher Rackard moved in and gave the house its name. The Romneys continued to flourish throughout the reigns of the Tudors, and we find in 1608 a John senior and a John junior (who was a butcher) farming 60 acres each at Romney Street.

William Petley, though living in Halstead, had bought Filston back into the family at the end of the fifteenth century. Thomas and Stephen Petley were adding to their property in Shoreham during the sixteenth century. Thomas, probably living at what we now know as the George Inn, took over land from the Balsattes family. Stephen with his base at the manor of Hewets acquired the mill and its land at the north end of the village. By 1608 Thomas Petley, son of William Petley – christened on 22 December 1560 near the commencement of Elizabeth I's reign – had gathered to himself by the beginning of the next reign not only the sub-manor of Filston but also Hewets, Andrews Wood and other land all amounting to 349 acres, the largest holding in Shoreham.

The second largest holding belonged to Thomas Polhill junior with 308 acres, and next to him came his cousin John of Otford, who held 114 acres in Shoreham. These two Polhills had reached this position during the turbulent fifteenth century, through careful management, well-chosen marriages and hard work. The first Polhill (or Polley as they were sometimes called) to settle in Shoreham was John Polley (see p. 40) when he married the heiress of Preston, Alice Buckland, in 1461. John's branch of the family, the senior branch, was to own Preston until another John Polhill sold it to Paul D'Aranda in 1689. Although Preston was in the possession of the senior branch for 228 years, they did not live there continuously. In a letter to Dr Gordon Ward in 1950 A.V. Polhill wrote: 'My own, the senior branch of the Polhill family left Shoreham to go to Burwash in Sussex about 1590 and then via Southwark to Bedford where the head of the family is now C.C. Polhill of Howbery Hall.'[4] Although from 1590 their Burwash estate attracted many of the family, others were attracted to Shoreham. John, who made the move to Burwash, died there in 1613 but his son

Probably the home of Thomas Petley in the sixteenth century, now The George Inn. (Drawing by Richard Reid)

John had married Anne, daughter of Sir Edward Gilbourne, who lived at Planers and they settled at Preston near his wife's family. Their Kent cousins sometimes made use of Frenches, their house at Burwash.

It was John Polley's second son Thomas who 'founded' the Kent branch of the family. Fortunately, he left a will[5] dated 21 December 1528 which allows us a glimpse of the man and the extent of his property. As was customary, his will opened with his instructions for his burial. He wished to be buried in Our Lady Chapel in the church of Shoreham 'under the stone where as my mother was buried', and he made gifts to various churches, including 30 shillings to Shoreham and 3*s*. 4*d*. towards the keeping of a young child found in the church porch of Eynsford. This last was a characteristic act for a Polhill, several of whom stood as godparents for children of the village, and occasionally for children of wandering beggers. Thomas made careful provision for Joane, his wife, and divided his property among his five sons. To his daughter Agnes he bequeathed £20 on her marriage, which turned out to be a good one — to George Multon of St Cleres, Kemsing. To each of his children he bequeathed 20 ewes on reaching the age of twenty. 'My son John [the eldest] to have my tenement at the churchyard gate of Shoreham and my lands lying at the east side of the common water unto the top of the hill except a meadow called Harde Mead.' John also received Orkisden (now called Upper Austin Lodge[6]). Thomas his second son received Hiltesbury in the Wrotham area; Robert was to receive the rents of his mother's family lands in Chelsfield and the use of the corn-mill; William received lands bought from the Lese family (probably in the East Hill area) and his tenements at Detling; David was to have his tenements in 'Nokolt, Brasted, Sundrishe and Orpyngton'. Thus did Thomas Polhill dispose of his considerable estate.

Later in the century John, with Orkisden to farm, evidently decided to consolidate his holdings by acquiring the Shoreham Castle estate from John Newborough, and it appears that his children like those of John of Preston became increasingly attached to Frenches at Burwash, although one of his sons, Abraham, settled at Goddingston in a house which may have been where Oxbourne Farm now stands.

It was Thomas, the second son, and his descendants who remained firmly attached to Shoreham and probably acquired Dibden from John. Certainly both he and his wife Anne were buried in Shoreham church, and two generations later Sir Thomas Polhill and his wife Elizabeth ended their days in Shoreham.

Thomas's youngest son, David, and his descendants proved to the most vigorous branch of the family. He was the first of the four Polhills to bear that name. His line inspired R.G. Bennett in his (unpublished) history of the Polhills to write:

> The Polhills proved strong and loyal supporters of King and Country, Church and State and provided the country with stout yeomen, landed gentry, members of Parliament, Justices of the Peace, soldiers, lawyers, clergy, authors, doctors, artists, mayors and philanthropists and with at least one port admiral, one banker, one theatre lessee and one school master.

David, as we have seen, began well with a good spread of property in the district around Shoreham and then married Alice, the sister and heiress of Francis Sandbach of the Inner Temple and King's Bench. David purchased Broughtons in Otford in 1554, and his son John received Planers from Francis Sandbach in 1580 two years after his father David had died. By well-chosen wives (he married three times), skilful purchases and management John is said to have held all the land on both sides of the road from Otford Mount to Halstead.[7] With the gift of Planers to John the connection with Shoreham of the 'David' line of Polhills is broken. Their activities in the political life of county and country and their investment in property has been woven into the history of Otford by Dennis Clarke and Anthony Stoyel, and we must return to Shoreham.

In October 1574 John Gilman, a carpenter of Shoreham, sold half an acre in a field called Shoreham Field[8] to Thomas, David's brother. This is a small example of the way in which increasingly over the centuries to come families like the Polhills invested in land. But while Thomas was increasing his acres he was also playing his part in the community. In 1555 he wrote[9] 'Laid out by me, Thomas Polhill for the glazing of the chancell wyndows there [Shoreham church] by Mr. Dean's commandment, forty shillings in the month of March in the first and second years of the reign of our Sovereign Lord and Lady Phylyppe and Mary.' This payment and others already described he was obliged to make as farmer of the Shoreham rectory. Papers in the Westminster Abbey Muniment Room refer to three further occasions in 1567, 1575 and 1581 when Thomas paid the glazier for 'making up and glazing the windows of Shoreham church'.

On 4 March 1582 John Polhill, Thomas' nephew, went with William Brown and Edward Stonynge to Pilots Wood and marked 390 oaks to be reserved for future felling. Edward Stonynge had previously carried out a survey of the wood with a Mr White, who was buying the remainder of the timber that was above twenty years old.[10] This careful accounting by the owner and tenant farmer pinpoints the importance attached throughout the country at that time to the efficient management of the nation's woods and forests. The oaks were needed for the steady upsurge in house-building and improvement beginning at this period and continuing well into the next century. The south range of Holly Place was added early in the seventeenth century to the late fifteenth-century north wing, and some of the timber from the oaks marked on that day quite possibly is today to be found in Holly Place and in several houses and cottages in Shoreham dating from the sixteenth and seventeenth centuries. The oaks were also needed for the building of the Queen's fleet. It was a time of increasing population and increasing prosperity for those producing the nation's food, and also a time of national peril with the threat of invasion by the Spanish.

Someone who might well have been called up with the local muster from Shoreham during the Armada crisis was Thomas Causten, a friend of the Polhills. In fact John Polhill of Planers and Otford with William Hill and Thomas Pearche 'made and praysed' an inventory of Thomas Causten's possessions in accordance with the law, after he had died in September 1596.[11] The inventory gives us a sight of a household of the late Elizabethan period in Shoreham. Thomas Causten farmed Shoreham Castle land rented from Thomas Polhill.[12] His son Robert lived at and farmed Sepham. Thomas when he died was farming in a modest way with 5 cattle, 37 sheep and lambs, 5 hogs, 2 pigs, 2 'weyners' (weaners) and one old gelding and £20 worth of corn in the barn. (The price of wheat in 1596, following five disastrous harvests, was 50 shillings a quarter — eight times the price a century earlier[13]). Thomas had, however, acquired during his life 2 silver cups, 2 silver 'salts' (salt cellars), 11 silver spoons, a 'maser' cup (a double-handled loving-cup), 12 platters, 20 pewter dishes, 12 'sawcers' and 6 porringers. His furniture, household linen and kitchen equipment were comfortably adequate for his family and the farm workers who were part of his household. Although he possessed a 'liverie cupbord', there is no record of it containing any servants' livery. It is also to be noted that he left 'all munition of warr', which means that he had the weapons and equipment required under the still existing Statute of Winchester (1285) of him and all able-bodied men between sixteen and sixty. 'All munitions' quite probably for him meant a coat of armour, a helmet and a longbow[14]. The puzzling item in the inventory was the last — the debt of £240 owing to him by John Polhill of Otford (one of those making the inventory), about which we are given no clues. It was possibly some informal arrangement between friends. John's second wife was Friswith, the daughter of Robert Causten of Orpington, and the two families must have been quite close. At a future date (1624) David Polhill witnessed the will of Robert Causten of Sepham, and in the same year Robert witnessed Abraham Polhill's will.

His inventory gives the impression that Thomas Causten was farming in a traditional way for he does not appear to have included in his range of produce any of the new crops introduced into Kent during the Tudor era.[15]

In 1532 various statutes ordered occupiers of over 60 acres of land to provide a proportion of their land to flax and hemp for making linen, ropes and canvas. Later their oil was used for soap-making and lighting. In Elizabeth's reign coleseed and rape were also introduced. Hops, which we inevitably associate with Filston and Castle farms, were introduced for commercial cultivation in Kent and England about 1524 but there is no indication of their reaching the Darent valley in Tudor times. Perhaps the farmers were deterred by the decree that was immediately issued forbidding their use in flavouring beer because 'they tend to make the people melancholy'.[16]

About the year 1580 a tithe list for Shoreham showed that 18 farmers paid tithes for a total of 328 lambs of 43*s*. 10*d*; 24 farmers paid tithes for 965 lb of wool of 65*s*. and about 5 farmers paid the tithes of 68*s*. 10*d*. for unspecified quantities of grass, a mill, cattle and conyes (rabbits) — a total for Shoreham of £8 15*s*. As mentioned by Dennis Clarke and Anthony Stoyel, it is clear from this list that Shoreham had a markedly larger flock of sheep than Otford at this time.

The Romans were attracted by the quality of the agricultural land in the Darent valley and the adjacent downs and planted their villas at regular intervals along the valley, so that it is not surprising to find other outsiders also acquiring land in the Shoreham parish, placed as it was and always had been close to an ever-growing capital city requiring more and more food. This was especially so in Elizabeth's reign — for instance in 1500 there were 3,000 alien craftsmen in London, while by 1571 with Government encouragement there were more than 7000. William Lambarde, the Sevenoaks landowner and Kent historian, wrote in 1570:

> The people of this countrie [Kent] consisteth chiefly (as in Other Countries also) of the gentrie and yeomanrie. The gentlemen be not heere (throughout) of so ancient stockes as elsewhere, especially in the partes neerer to London from which citie . . . courtiers, lawyers and merchants be continually translated and do become new plants amongst them.

Sir Francis Sandbach already mentioned was just such a new plant. But there were others established in north-west Kent who wanted to invest in Shoreham land: for example Sir Samuel Leonard, whose family had been living at Knole and were to build the mansion at Chevening, held 100 acres in Shoreham in 1608 – acres which had previously been held by Lord Burrough. Sir Percival Hart of Lullingstone had a modest 35 acres. One branch of the Lovelace family (related to the future Cavalier and poet Richard Lovelace) lived at West Kingsdown and held some 30 acres in Shoreham. There was also William Rowe, a successful citizen of London who in 1575 bought Woodlands and Leese Court from John Pett of Sevenoaks, and who by 1593 was an Alderman and in that year had become Sir William Rowe and Lord Mayor of the City of London.[17]

But what of the great majority of the population, those whose ancestors had been cottars and villeins? We have shown how a few by careful husbandry had joined the yeomanry, but an ever-growing number were losing their land and becoming dependent on selling their labour to others. It is not always realized that the bubonic plague had reduced the population in England of some six million in the fourteenth century to about four million in 1500, so that in Henry VII's reign England was short of people and the wage-earning labourer was at an advantage. So much was this the case that anxiety was expressed in Parliament that the lower classes were breaking the sumptuary laws and were spending more than the law allowed on food and clothes. There was a mood of optimism, and the parishioners expressed that optimism, in the enlarging and embellishing of their churches, which were the centres of village life with their festivals, church ales and revels. Why then did an anonymous poet in the late 1530s cry out:

> That from pillar unto post
> The poor man he was tost;
> I mean the labouring man
> I mean the husbandman
> I mean the ploughman
> I mean the plain true man
> I mean the handcraftman
> I mean the victualling man
> Also the good yeoman
> That sometime in this realm
> Had plenty of kye [cows] and cream
> But now alack alack
> All these men go to wrack
> That are the body and stay
> of your grace's realm alway.[18]

Unfortunately, his Grace King Henry VIII was needing and was demanding more and more funds for his wars and his spendthrift policies. He was debasing the value of the coinage, and his first minister, Wolsey, was making heavier and heavier demands in subsidies from even the humblest householders. Inflation took hold. Although a labourer's wage in 1560 had risen on average to 7*d*. a day when it had been 4*d* a day in 1447 (see p. 31), inflation had increased fourfold.

Towards the end of the century widespread concern for the poor was to become the responsibility of the Justices of the Peace, and under their direction of the parish vestry.

The harshness of life was added to by the periodic outbreaks of disease, particularly the bubonic plague, which tended to coincide with widespread harvest failure and the consequent lowering of people's vitality. In 1557-8, at the end of Queen Mary's reign and following the famine of 1556, a 'new sickness' appeared, a virus disease causing a hot, burning fever called later the 'marian flu'. The result was a temporary decrease in the country's population (which had been rising), but the gradual upward trend was restored by the late 1560s. This was due in part to improved agricultural methods producing greater quantities of food, and in part to earlier marriages and increased fertility. The church registers which begin for Shoreham in 1558 tell us something of the degree to which Shoreham was affected by these epidemics and population fluctuations. Around the year 1590 the plague was active, and it may have suffered an attack in 1589, when 18 deaths are recorded compared with an average for the decade 1585–94 of 9.4. This cannot be considered a heavy attack when compared with attacks elsewhere. In Devon, for example, in 1590 in three of the poorest parishes 559 died, compared with a normal 96.[19] Shoreham, being a rich farming parish, may well have been better-fed and better able to resist infection and disease. The death-rate in 1602 was 17, against the average for the decade (1598−1607) of 10.6, which could have resulted from another mild epidemic. In spite of these epidemics a gradual increase in the country's population was maintained, and Shoreham seems to have played its part in this trend, births persistently exceeding deaths:

(annual averages)
1568–1577 baptisms 12·6 marriages 2·8 deaths 6·3

Tudor Cottage, probably built at the same time as The George Inn. (Etching by Harold Copping; Mrs J Saynor)

SHOREHAM

1578–1587 baptisms 13·2 marriages 3·2 deaths 5·9

1588–1597 baptisms 11·7 marriages 3·2 deaths 9·2

1598–1607 baptisms 13·4 marriages 3·3 deaths 10·6

When the Spanish Armada sailed up the Channel in 1588 there were some 3,800,000 inhabitants of England, and for some years Queen Elizabeth had been mobilizing ships and men to meet the challenge. We have been unable to discover any muster roll of those who from Shoreham were called to defend the country, but in 1572 the four Justices of the Peace for the lower division of the Lathe of Sutton-at-Hone – an administrative district extending from Shoreham to Cowden and Penshurst – confirmed the existence of a force under James Austyn, Gentleman, of:

Gunners	104
Archers	153
Pikemen	79
Billmen	400
Total	736

with the following arms:

Harquebusses	20
Bows	130
Sheaths of arrows	129
Bills	350
Swords	66
Daggers	100
Total	795[20]

The four Justices who signed the document were William Irton, Thomas Willoughby, Thomas Potter and Ralph Bosseville, the latter a gentleman of Lincoln's Inn who in 1555 had purchased the Bradbourne estate from the Crown.[21]

As the external threat increased, so within the Lathe of Sutton-at-Hone certain gentlemen were identified by the Queen's government who were 'thought meet to be charged with demi-lances and light horse'.[22] In the final count in June 1580 there were twenty-four identified as rich enough to provide demi-lances and 33 light horse fully equipped: the list included the Justices mentioned above, but also John Lennard, George and Francis Hart and Lennard Lovelace. It should be noted that the Militia Act of 1558 – sounding more like a sumptuary law than a tax assessment – laid down that gentlemen whose wives wore velvet kirtles or silk petticoats were required to provide a light horse apiece.

At the beginning of this chapter we stressed the need as seen by Henry VII for firmly established law and order – a need which persisted through a century of drastic change – and to meet it the Tudors made increasing use of the Justices of the Peace in the Shires, and particularly the parishes. It was fortunate that

Richard I in the twelfth century appointed as his Chief Officer Herbert Walter, who decided to trust and use the knights settling down on their manors as unpaid instruments of government. This started a valuable tradition, and two centuries later we find these knights and smaller gentry as Justices of the Peace, taking over more and more work for central government previously done by the Sheriff or by judges on circuit.[23] Dependence on them increased during Henry VIII's reign as the dissolution of religious houses gathered momentum and the authority and organization of the Church diminished, depriving those in need of the support that they previously received from that quarter. For Shoreham the transfer of the Archbishop's manor to the Crown in 1537 exposed the need for some new authority, even some new paternal presence to take the place of the Archbishop and his manor, and although the manor structure with its court was to continue it continued with diminishing importance while the local gentry as Justices were taking on more and more varied responsibilities and powers.

Informally the Petleys and Polhills were beginning to provide the father-figures needed by the community, but as G.M. Trevelyan wrote of the Justices: 'When Elizabeth died, hardly anything in the countryside was alien to their province. They kept up roads and bridges and prisons . . . they licensed ale-houses, they arrested criminals'[24] (with the aid of the local constables). They also watched over the churchwardens who collected the one shilling fines from parishioners who failed to attend Sunday service, and over the parish overseers in vestry who cared for the poor and the administration of the compulsory rate under the 1563 and 1598 Poor Laws. The Labour Act of 1531 had savagely proclaimed the work ethic — 'idleness is the root of all vice; the able bodied should be whipped "Till his body be bloody and returned to his native place" to labour like as true man oweth to do', and the Justices of the Peace saw that it was done. We shall see later how this harsh and brutal attitude persisted in the seventeenth and eighteenth centuries. Inevitably the Statute of Artificers (1563) closely involved the Justices in regulating local levels of wages and contracts of service in directing labour to agricultural priorities and two entirely new tasks: deciding hours of work and local breaks and penalties for absence (1*d.* per hour late, even when the labourer's daily wage was only 7*d.*), and the introduction into the agricultural communities of seven-year apprenticeships.

Queen Elizabeth I was most successful in developing her grandfather Henry VII's plan to increase the use of the King's courts instead of those of local barons. In 1500 two thousand civil cases came before the court of King's Bench and Court of Common Pleas. By 1600 that figure had increased to 22,000. But what kind of cases were brought before the conscientious and hard-working Justices of the Peace locally at the turn of the century? One such was William Lambarde the historian, who lived in Sevenoaks, and whose *Perambulation of Kent* went to the printers in 1576, and another was Sir Edward Gilbourne, who lived at Planers in Shoreham and whose daughter Anne was to marry John Polhill of Preston in 1646.

At Easter 1595 Edmond Halfpenny, the miller of Shoreham, was accused of 'engrossing' 54 quarters of wheat.[25] Millers were always unpopular because for centuries they held the monopoly under the lord of the manor of grinding the villagers' corn. Edmond Halfpenny was evidently suspected of buying up the wheat in order to sell it again locally at a substantial profit. Those indicting him were two Shoreham husbandmen, Thomas Danyell and John Cripps, and a glover, John Homewood, with his wife Elizabeth. Among those supporting them were John Lawrence the wheelwright and William Gates and William

Brooker, husbandmen. 1595 was a difficult year of food shortages and rising prices (in 1558 one penny had bought a wheaten loaf of 57 oz. but in 1597 a penny loaf only weighed 8 oz).[26] It is perhaps significant, therefore, that it was the small farmers and craftsmen that levelled the accusation. The justices having listened to the case decided that Edmond Halfpenny be bound over to be of good behaviour. They were supported in their decision by a certificate of good behaviour on Halfpenny's behalf by the vicar of Shoreham, Lewes Kyffin, and twenty-two parishioners, including Thomas Pearch the tailor, no fewer than five Polhills, two Petleys and other yeomen of the parish.

Five months later John Homewood and John Lawrence found themselves in prison for having 'uttered seditious words', but fortunately three yeomen, William Collins, John Romney and Robert Brown, came to their defence and bailed them for £10 each to be of good behaviour.

At the Michaelmas sessions of 1597 John Brewer was accused of taking from the house of Thomas Fletcher at Shoreham

- a cloak worth 20s
- a coat worth 6s
- a pair of 'tibialium' (shin armour) worth 12d
- 3 neckingers worth 20s.

This was a serious case of grand larceny.[27] A thin line was drawn in Elizabethan times between petty larceny (for which the punishment was whipping) and grand larceny (for which the punishment was hanging). If the goods stolen were valued at less than 12d. the case was one of petty larceny; if they were valued at 12d. or more the case was one of grand larceny. So John Brewer faced the prospect of hanging. However, when he came before the justices he claimed 'benefit of clergy', a privilege granted originally to clergy, allowing them to be tried by an ecclesiastical court. The privilege was extended later to all who could read. So John was discharged by the justices, probably with only a branding on the thumb to identify him as a first offender, and was passed to the ecclesiastical court where punishments were less severe. Goods stolen were sometimes deliberately undervalued when the person bringing the charge — possibly with encouragement from the justices (who were also responsible for the care of the poor and destitute) — did not wish to see the accused hanged but only whipped. This may have been the intention of John Jarman, who charged James Warren, a blacksmith, with stealing a coulter, a 'tight' and a spindle all worth 10d.[28]

William Mills junior in 1597 farmed Oxbourne and lived at the farmstead (where now stands the school dining-hall and No 1 High Street). It seems that he must have fallen foul of the sheriff, Moile Finch, who sent his bailiff, John Bowle, to distrain one of William's cows or a gelding (the record is ambiguous). William was having none of it, and attacked Bowle with four of his farm hands and 'rescued' the animal. The court having studied the indictment decided not to bring William to trial.

A substantial amount of the justices' time was spent acting as peace-makers in quarrels between neighbours — living up to their titles of justices of the peace. On one occasion in 1595 even a Polhill family quarrel was brought to court, when William Hills a yeoman was involved with his friend Thomas Polhill in providing sureties of £10 each that Agnes, Thomas's wife, should keep the peace towards Thomas Polhill senior.[29] Alas, we are denied the details.

A rather more serious situation faced Abraham Polhill in 1609,[30] who lived

The Polhill coat of arms at the time of John Polhill's marriage to Alice Buckland in 1461. (R.G. Bennett, AR Hist S)

and farmed Goddingston (now Oxbourne). He was charged by William Giles, a yeoman of Shoreham, with keeping and retaining 'in his possession Jane Polhill his daughter and covenant servant to the said William Giles without pryvity [knowledge] or consent of the said William Giles'. One can imagine Abraham Polhill's problem — he had made a contract for his daughter to go as servant to William Giles. Jane, unhappy with the arrangement, runs home and refuses to return to Mr Giles. It is tantalizing that we do not have fuller details, or the outcome of this charge.

The limited records of cases involving the inhabitants of Shoreham that survive from this period may give the reader the impression that the courts were quite lenient in the punishments handed down. However, the Gaol Delivery Roll covering both Maidstone and Canterbury gaols for the years 1596-1605 corrects that impression. For instance in fourteen cases of burglary 8 of the accused were acquitted but 21 were hanged; in thirteen cases of petty larceny 2 were acquitted, 10 were whipped, one was hanged and one was 'to be kept in prison until his death'. In eight cases of horse-stealing 4 were acquitted but 7 were hanged. Out of a total of some 50 punished, 15 were whipped, 31 hanged and only 3 imprisoned. This underlines the fact that except in the case of political offenders, at this time (and indeed up to the end of the eighteenth century) prisons were used primarily as places of safe custody for those awaiting trial or punishment, or until fines, debts or sureties were found.[31]

This is perhaps a suitable point at which to mention the Cage. In November 1924 Mr Loveland wrote in the parish magazine 'At the corner of the street next to the Alms houses was the Cage, a quaint little stone building with an iron gate where prisoners could be kept in safety pending their removal to the nearest prison.' When it was put up or when it was removed we do not know, but as it was of stone it might well have been built before bricks became the popular material in Tudor times. Certainly another cage of Kentish ragstone in Ashford was probably built in the fourteenth century.[32] With its iron gate it gave villagers the opportunity of seeing who was locked up, and even of throwing abuse or bad eggs at the prisoner.

VI

THE SEVENTEENTH CENTURY (1)

WHEN James I came to the throne in 1603 Shoreham was still an isolated village. The nearest road was a quarter of a mile to the east of the church, running from Farningham through Eynsford to Otford and Sevenoaks. Its chalk and stone surface made rough going for travellers in wet weather — rather like the track which runs today past the vicarage and churchyard to Preston Farm. To the west there was the 'Old Polhill' lane from Otford to Halstead. There was still no A21, and the main road from the important Channel port of Rye to London went through Sevenoaks and Knockholt. As mentioned in Chapter III (p. 26), the repair of Shoreham bridge had been the responsibility of the Archbishop's tenants, but then later, in 1485, Katheryn Mason of London had left in her will 8 shillings and 4 pence 'to the works of the Brigge of Shoreham', suggesting the continuing parish responsibility for its repair. In 1645 the justices adjudged that the bridge 'for footmen, horsemen and carriages' should be a county charge.[1] This is particularly puzzling, as the bridge over the Darent at Longford on the more important London to Rye road was still repaired at the expense of the parishes of Sevenoaks, Otford and Chevening. It is difficult to understand why Shoreham parish was favoured in this way unless the traffic over the Shoreham bridge to the Farningham/Sevenoaks road or up Whitehill to Romney Street was much heavier than we can imagine it to have been, and more than Hasted at the end of the eighteenth century considered it to be.

Compared to the growing market town of Sevenoaks with its 1,436 inhabitants, Shoreham was a small community, with 409 in 1664; but it was larger than Otford, Eynsford and Orpington.

The heart of the village nestled between the church with its tithe-barn and the bridge, and apart from the George Inn (still a private house), the dwellings on both sides of the lane leading down to the bridge were almost all single-storied thatched cottages, although the owner of the hall house (now called Chapel Alley Cottages) had a floor built to make an upper room in the central hall section, probably about 1600.[2] To the south of this intimate cluster of cottages was Dibden on the east bank of the Darent, where New House and Shoreham Place were to stand in later centuries. To the west of the bridge beyond the strongly flowing Darent the rough road ran through water meadows, and just beyond the flood-levels was a group of buildings; on the right the hall house probably called Balsattes (now Reedbeds) on the left a row of cottages. Across the winding lane

SHOREHAM

Friars and Pilgrims, a timber-framed building encased in brick in the seventeenth century. (Photo by Ian Harper)

which leads from Filston to Castle Farm was the farmstead of Oxbourne. A little to the left towards Filston the Almshouses stood as they stand today. On the corner was the Cage, ever ready for the next prisoner. As the traveller made his way north he would notice building activity at Holly Place where the front wing we know today was being added to the older north wing.[3] Next to Holly Place was the three-bay timber-framed house which at the end of the seventeenth century was to be clad in brick with a chimney, and a century later as the population increased was to be divided into three dwellings now called Friars and Pilgrims.[4] There was also the Walnut Tree Cottage complex and Winslade cottages opposite and others on the lane before the traveller reached Goddingston House at the top of the lane leading down to the mill on the river, past April Cottage.

James I brought a limited relaxation of Elizabeth's controls on manufactured goods and materials, and this resulted among other things in an increase of weaving throughout the country, practised as a cottage industry. Shoreham had its weavers, but as far as the evidence goes only a few families participated. The fulling-mill and the tenter close at Planers had been worked certainly since 1477, making use of the fuller's earth available in the Darent Valley. Fuller's earth was used for cleaning and thickening the woven cloth, which was then stretched for drying on the wooden frames provided in the tenter close. The fulling-mill must have been a valuable asset in the fifteenth century when we recall that John Sepham senior gave Colgates and its land to his son to compensate for the break-down of the mill and the cost of rebuilding it. It is possible that the fulling-mill attracted business from the weavers of the Weald in the earlier period, as well as from Eynsford and Otford.[5]

In 1568 Roger Taylor was a shearman (clothier) in Shoreham, and in 1618

THE SEVENTEENTH CENTURY (1)

Arthur Gates was weaving in the village, while in 1654 Thomas Lewen, a clothworker, leased the fulling-mill from David Polhill. Michael Elks – who proudly called himself a 'fuller of cloth' – took over from Thomas Lewen. At the time of his death in 1667 he had a load of fuller's earth in the mill and tools for keeping the mill in working order. In his 'shop' there were 8 pairs of clothier's sheers, 9 pairs of barling irons, 2 leaden weights, 2 sheer boards, a hot press and 'a stage of handles'. In the dyeing house and close he kept a pair of 'tainters', an 'iron furnace with a leaden curb to dye withall and a dyeing vault [vat?]'. Beside the tools of his trade he possessed three acres of arable land where he grew a little maslin (probably a mixture of wheat and rye), barley and hay for his mule.

Evidence of weaving continues into the eighteenth century with John Homewood. Another John Homewood in Elizabeth's time had practised the craft of glover.

Other craftsmen and artisans living in Shoreham in the seventeenth century were John Allen and Daniell Perritt, blacksmiths; John Rumney the butcher; Robert Wyllis, a carpenter; and Richard Gesling, the miller working the mill at the north end of the village. There were two tailors – William Brewett and Thomas Pearch – and a sawyer called John Munke. Thomas Chillmaid was a successful bricklayer. Robert and John Dallin were wheelwrights. Strangely, with the predominance of sheep on the farms of Shoreham, we have no names of shepherds though they must have existed.

We have studied a sample of eleven probate inventories of Shoreham farmers from the period of 1666 to 1707 which gives a limited picture of the livestock raised and crops grown in the parish. Generally speaking, the supply of food in relation to demand in England improved during the century, although there were some bad harvests in the 1620s and 1630s. Improved efficiency of production had to wait until the eighteenth century.[6] Although clover and sainfoin were introduced into England in the second half of the century, there is reference to clover and sainfoin in only two inventories. Hop gardens became widely established in Kent in the opening years of the century, but the first sight we have of them was in John Rawlin's barn in 1679 – '2 baggs new hopps, 3 baggs and a pockett of old hopps – £8' and 'one old oast haire' (the hair mat on which hops were spread for drying). Seven years later there is mention of 'one oast haire' at Filston when Thomas Petley junior died, though no hops are listed (probably because they had already been marketed).

Sheep far outnumbered other livestock: horses 34, cattle 63, pigs 80 and sheep 323. With the export of wool prohibited between 1600 and 1675 the price of wool had dropped by half,[7] so it is likely that the numbers of sheep in Shoreham point to breeding for mutton rather than wool, to feed the top and middle classes in the county and London. The export of grain was being encouraged, and Shoreham farmers were growing substantial quantities (concentration on grain-production may well have encouraged the building of Shepherds Barn with its threshing floor in the latter half of the seventeenth century[8]): wheat and barley head the probate inventory lists in terms of a cash value of £315, followed closely by maslin, £130. Hay totalled £100, oats £25 and sainfoin seed £6. Peas and tares were valued at £65, malt £24 and hops £8. There was no sign yet in these inventories of the potato or the turnip having arrived in Shoreham fields, although they were introduced into England in mid-century.

In spite of civil war, war against the Dutch and war against the French, inflation had levelled off and the price of corn had decreased slightly, but the

SHOREHAM

April Cottage in Mill Lane is an example of a Wealden hall house. (Photo by Ian Harper)

farm labourer's wage in 1620 was 1s. a day, and in 1700 had only reached 1s. 3d. a day.[9] This was, however, higher than in other parts of England.

The spiritual forces released by the Reformation continued during the seventeenth century to spread turbulence throughout the land. Catholics and Protestants were struggling for position; access to the Bible in English was giving to increasing numbers of the literate the opportunity to form and express their own interpretation of its message. The decade 1640-50 became the great age of pamphleteers as well as of civil war (the British Library preserves 17,000 pamphlets from those years). Church-going was compulsory in the only legal Church — the established Church of England — and as a consequence dissent increased. Quakers were well entrenched in Kent, and Kent being nearest to the Continent, 'separatists' (who wanted the Church to be disestablished) in the county were in touch with 'separatists' in Holland. The Puritans took up the sword for religious and parliamentary freedom.

In spite of what lay ahead of them, it is safe to assume that in the reign of James I the inhabitants of Shoreham continued to enjoy their medieval folk festivals — the visiting mummers, masques, May Day, even Sunday sports and the occasional bell-ringing contest, with the church of St Peter and St Paul at the heart of village life.

The church vestry provided, as in Elizabeth's reign, the natural meeting-place for the parish government consisting of the vicar and churchwardens with some ten others including those voluntary officers the surveyor of the highways, the overseer of the poor, constables and borsholders (petty constables), all of whom had to be recommended to and approved by the local justices. Looking after the records of their deliberations in Shoreham (alas, no longer available to us) was Henry Bostock, the Parish Clerk for sixty-eight years from 1603.

One who was close to the hearts of the villagers was John Emerson, vicar from 1615 to 1645. During the difficult period leading up to the civil war a study of the wills of parishioners shows that whereas among the yeomen it was a fairly common practice to bequeath sums between 10s. and 40s. to the poor of the village, either in money or in bread, it was only John Emerson among the ministers who received bequests from parishioners (as for example from Marie Rose, see p. 85).

But there is more substantial evidence of the esteem in which he was held.

In 1640 Parliament set up a committee to study religious matters, and immediately complaints poured into it from all over the country, including a petition from Shoreham and Otford signed by thirty inhabitants.

They pointed out that Shoreham and Otford were different parishes, their churches about a mile from each other. Shoreham had at least 80 families, and Otford 60. Secondly, the tithe and glebe income of Shoreham was £160 a year, and of Otford worth 200 marks (£133) yearly 'both which spirituall livings are annexed to ye colledge of Westminster' which provided less than £24 a year for one minister only (roughly equivalent to a labourer's wage). So the inhabitants of both parishes have had from time to time to provide, beside the 'small benevolence' to Mr Emerson, for the maintenance of another minister (Thomas Browne) to assist him. They most humbly beseeched Parliament that Mr Emerson, who had remained in Shoreham for twenty-five years, preaching in one or other of the churches every Sabbath day and 'further gained our love by his honest and peaceable life and vocation' may have such adequate maintenance

Shepherds Barn, associated with Samuel Palmer. Its site (NGR TQ50596097) is now buried beneath the M25 motorway. (Photo by Ian Harper)

settled on him and his successors and this for the work of the ministry in Shoreham only'. They then went on to ask for a separate 'honest and able minister' to take charge of Otford only, so that they might be relieved of the burden long time and 'voluntarily undergone over and above the paying of the tithes by lawe required'.[10]

It is difficult to see how Emerson and Browne could have survived on the stipend originally approved in Archbishop Warham's time (1530), now only a fifth of its value, without private means or donations from the parishes. Thomas Browne had received £10 a year from Sir Robert Heath, a former attorney-general who, although he lived at Brasted, held the lease of the rectorial benefice of Otford.[11]

The petition was submitted at the wrong moment. In 1642 civil war broke out. Not until 1645 did a parliamentary report state: 'The vicar of Shoreham, Mr. Emerson is a good man, but the services of the two parishes are too heavy for him. Both livings [Shoreham and Otford] are too poor to be separated.' The conclusion one must draw from these laconic words is that Parliament was not prepared to release any more of the Rectorial revenue now under its control when every penny was needed to prosecute the war against Charles I.

John Emerson in 1626–7 had suffered grievous losses – first of a son in December and of another son on 3 January following. Finally, on the 11th of that same month, his wife Joan died. The years 1624-7 saw an unusual number die in the parish, possibly because of the bad harvests, and even the much-loved minister was not spared his portion of grief. John Emerson made his last entry in the church register in 1642, and finally stood down as minister in 1644.

Once again Shoreham petitioned 'the most honourable and high court of

Parliament' that 'a pious and painful [painstaking] preacher may be established'. In fact Thomas Browne, who had leanings towards Puritanism, was put in by Parliament and served as the one minister for both parishes until 1661 after the restoration of the monarchy. Otford had to wait until 1878 for their first vicar. There is no sign of any assistant or curate on record[12] until Theophilus Beck joined the vicar William Wall in 1708.

In studying 31 of the 56 seventeenth-century wills in the Lambeth Palace Library made by Shoreham parishioners we found that all were happy to commit their souls simply into the hands of God and of His Son Jesus Christ: Catholic terminology had disappeared. Husbandman William Batte expressed a simple faith: 'I give and bequeath my soul unto God my maker and Jesus Christ my Saviour and Redeemer and my body to the earth there to rest till God by his mighty power shall raise it upward at the last day.' It seems that only those who had reached the social standing of gentleman or yeoman asked to be buried in the church. Henry Sone, a yeoman, was specific. He wished to be buried in the church of Shoreham 'in the space against the seate where I used to sytt in safe and certain hope of a joyful resurrection'. Most asked to be buried in the churchyard or like Thomas Pearch the tailor left the decision to the discretion of their executors. John Munke the sawyer quite simply wished his body to be consigned to the 'earth from which it was taken'.

The ways in which the people of Shoreham disposed of their worldly goods were as varied as their characters. John Vaughan, a labourer, in 1625 did not have much to leave. He arranged for his wife Anne to have all his worldly goods and chattels. After her death his sons Thomas and William were to receive each £11, and Thomas was to have his father's iron pot, bedstead and a cupboard while William received a cupboard, a table and a kettle. John Munke the sawyer, being a craftsman, did have a modest property to dispose of. He gave his grandson John his barn, orchard and the 1½ acres of coppice adjoining it. His two grand-daughters Ann and Elen received 40s. each at twenty, his two other grandchildren James and Mary Haric only 12 pence each and Jems Palmer got his iron pot. The growing importance in the seventeenth century of brick as a building material is seen in the field names, 'brick kiln mead' and 'brick kiln field' at Filston, Colgates and Castle Farm, and the much-prized skills of the bricklayer are brought home to us in the will (1692) of Thomas Chillmaid, a most successful bricklayer. He had four sons, and he arranged to give his wife Joan an annuity of £5 by his son Thomas and an annuity of £3 by his son Robert. Thomas himself was bequeathed 'Stone House', Shoreham, and 16½ acres; Robert received his father's clothes, a clock and £40 (via Thomas) and 'New House' (not Sir John Borrett's) with a field and curtilage. Jeremiah received £20 by Thomas and £20 by Robert, a messuage and tenement called 'The Castle' and a cottage, both in Kemsing. Thomas Chillmaid senior had evidently invested most of his quite considerable savings in property, because his goods and chattels found in the house after his death were only valued at £12 0s. 4d.

The timing of bequests is interesting. Joseph Nash, yeoman, decided in 1640 that his son Joseph in addition to certain houses and land in Shoreham should receive £100 at 14 years, and his daughter Mary likewise £100 at the same tender age. It was, however, quite general practice throughout the century to leave any rather precious object such as a clock to children on their reaching 21 or 22 years. Exceptionally, John Round in 1674 took special precautions by bequeathing his 'clock standing in my house' to John Round (grandson) 'when he attains 24 years and not before'. Meanwhile the clock was to be left in the care of Francis Everest, who with Joseph Nash was overseer of John Round's somewhat complex will and guardian of his grandchildren — John and Jane. 'For their paines' in carrying out these duties he bequeathed to them 'one suite each of silver buttons' and 20 shillings in money.

Robert Dallin, husbandman, must have had a clear and 'ingeniose' mind. He had five sons and two daughters. Thomas, his eldest son, received the 'house and backside' and the cupboard in the loft; Thomas's wife received a pair of hempen sheets. The other four sons received 40 shillings each, but staggered over a number of years: William in the second and sixth year after his father's death, John in the third and seventh year, Robert in the fourth and eighth year and Richard in the fifth and ninth year. It was an ingenious way of easing the burden on Thomas, who had to pay these bequests. It was fortunate that the inflation that had afflicted the Tudor century had levelled off by 1631. Dallin's daughter had married into the Round family and received only some pieces of brass and pewter, since she had already received a dowry, but Elizabeth her unmarried sister seems to have taken on her mother's responsibilities after she died, because her father made her his executor, leaving his unbequeathed goods to her. Moreover, he added: 'my will is that my daughter Elizabeth should have her dwelling in my house after my death and she should have the chamber wherein she now lyeth for three years after my decease'.

The differing treatment of their wives demonstrates the contrasting characters of two Shoreham yeomen, John Goldsmith, and John Baker, both of whom died in 1634. John Goldsmith after bequeathing his two daughters £20 each on reaching the age of twenty-four, gave the rest of his goods and chattels to Alice his wife and James his son 'to be used jointly by them during both their lives or to be divided and distributed between them when either of them require', and he made them joint executors. John Baker, on the other hand, bequeathed

> unto Alice Baker my beloved wife twenty shillings . . . yearly so long as she shall keep herself a widow to be paid unto her in quarterly payments by Thomas Baker my youngest sonne, but if she shall after my decease, marry to another man then my will is that the said annuity will immediately cease to be paid unto her.

Neither Goldsmith nor Baker were isolated examples of such contrasting marital attitudes. Robert Hilles, another yeoman, who died the following year treated his wife Agnes rather more generously. If widow Hilles married again her annuity was to be reduced from £6 to £4. He does not appear to have reduced the other bequests to her, which were in kind, and which he instructed his executor (his eldest son Robert) to deliver to his mother's house annually — 'eight bushells of good sweet and well dryed barley malt . . . and four loads of fire wood of the best', nor was there any mention of her having to give up the long list of furniture and 'household stuffe' which he left to her.

Robert Oliver, wealthy yeoman and relation of Edward Oliver the vicar, arranged a careful and considerate schedule of payments for his widow: annuities of £30 per annum to be paid quarterly, but also £5 to be paid within one month of his death and £50 within one year.

Anthony Rose in his will (1626) described himself as a yeoman, although eight years earlier he had called himself a victualler and in the record of a case before the Justices as a gardener. In his will having bequeathed 10s. to Mr Emerson, the vicar, and 5s. in money and 5s. in bread for the poor, he arranged that 'my wife shall dispence 3 pounds for the solemnizing of my burial' and then quite simply bequeathed all his goods and chattels to Marie his wife. Marie was an outward-looking and sociable person. She had first married into an old-established Shoreham family, the Campes (Letitia Campe had been elected a Reeve for Shoreham in Henry VIII's reign). By her first marriage Marie had a son John Campe and daughter Marie who married a David Polhill (though not of Otford), then in 1608 Marie married Edward Petley and by him had a son George and a daughter Jane. Marie in her busy life finally married Anthony Rose but had no children by him. Marie (now a widow) enjoyed drawing up her will in 1631 — 'My desire is that the minister of Shoreham whoever he be at the time of my decease shall preach at the time of my burial', for which he was to be rewarded with 10s. She could not mention Mr Emerson by name as he was present to witness her will. The poor of Shoreham were also to have ten shillings on the day of her burial. She then bequeathed modest sums to her son John and his two children; gave a generous portion of her bed linen, 'the feather bed and feather bolster where on I lie' and furniture to Marie and to her two Polhill daughters. She bequeathed to 'My daughter Jane Petley one chest of linnen. I mean both the chest and all the linnen therein contained which was sometimes of Mrs. Petley her grandmother, deceased.' Her two daughters Jane and Marie shared her wearing apparel. Before making George and Jane Petley her residual legatees and joint executors she added 'my will is that 40s. shall be layed out for provision of entertainment unto those who shall be present at my burial', and one can imagine a cheerful gathering taking place of all her many and varied relations and friends.

A third of those whose wills we examined bequeathed sums to the poor of Shoreham, but that was not the only form of charity provided. Between 1500 and 1600 the population of England and Wales had increased by about 40 per cent, and between 1600 and 1630 by a further 30 per cent, and it went on steadily increasing in spite of epidemics, 100,000 deaths in the civil war and the casualties of the foreign wars.[13] Shoreham was no exception to this steady growth, and found itself almost certainly with a labour surplus. To an extent not seen before it fell to private donors with social conscience or acting through self-interest to care for the poor. Donations in Kent by 1640 had risen to a total of £8,500, and according to Professor W.K. Jordan the first of these donations in 1628 was also the largest, consisting of real property with a capital value of £410.[14] The donor was Thomas Terry, a yeoman who in Shoreham owned a property called Roffes which his father had owned before him. He created by will and deed four separate trusts for the relief of the poor of Sutton-at-Hone, Shoreham, Horton Kirby and Eynsford. The most valuable of the properties incorporated in the trust was that for Shoreham. In the list of benefactors on the north wall of the parish church an entry reads '1628 Thomas Terry, Yeoman gave to the poor £7 per annum for ever'. In fact the property went on increasing in value, and a generation later was yielding a rental of £10 1s. per annum. It is still bearing fruit today. There were many other acts of charity less formal and unrecorded — for instance, from members of the Polhill family and others.

VII
THE SEVENTEENTH CENTURY (2): Shoreham and the Civil War

DURING the latter part of the seventeenth century the senior branch of the Polhill family preferred to live at Burwash in Sussex rather than at Preston, as did the descendants of John Polhill of Shoreham Castle. An exception was Abraham, who remained at 'Goddingston' House (possibly the Oxbourne farmhouse of today), where he farmed on a modest scale. At times he was known as a husbandman, at times as a yeoman. His four daughters married within the parish into the Johnson, Hilles and Eversfield families, and his one son Edward inherited Goddingston and married Agnes, the daughter of Thomas Pearch, the tailor. John Polhill of Otford died in 1614, handing on Planers and Sepham to his son David II, who was appointed Sheriff of Kent in 1640.

The Thomas Polhills of Shoreham had steadily enhanced their position, owning land in Lullingstone, Eynsford and Otford as well as Shoreham. On the front step leading to the chancel of Shoreham church is a brass plate which reads 'Here lyeth Thomas Polhyll who deceased the XXth day of February 1588 and Anne his wife daughter of William Plumly of Otford . . . '. Although a space was provided on the plate to record Anne's death, sadly no one thought to inscribe the date. His son continued to farm the Shoreham rectorial revenues, and his grandson (also called Thomas) was knighted in 1619. We have failed to discover the reason for his being singled out for this distinction. It is possible that he may have helped James I when the King was short of funds. We do know that Sir Thomas owned a number of manor houses, though not their location.[1] He may well have lived at Wrotham after marrying Elizabeth, daughter of Sir George Byng, who also lived there. Nevertheless, he and all his family were buried in Shoreham church.

Sir Thomas was involved personally as a defendant in an unusual case which incidentally illustrates the unbiased attitude of the justices towards their peers and the compassion which they exercised towards the poor and 'impotent' (destitute). In this case a poor widow, Margaret Churchman, petitioned the Quarter Sessions in 1631, complaining that she was unable to maintain herself, being lame. Although she had been born and had lived in West Peckham, the parish overseer of the poor there refused to accept her as a responsibility of the parish under the Poor Laws. Under pressure from the justices and the assize judge it came to light that Sir Thomas Polhill was Margaret's brother. Three justices, including Sir Edward Gilbourne who lived at Planers in Shoreham and whose daughter Anne was to marry John Polhill of Preston, examined Sir Thomas, and eventually it was found that widow Churchman was legally entitled to receive an annuity of £7 from her brother. There was a reckoning for Sir Thomas, for he had misled the court which 'conceiveth itselfe to some sorte abused'. He was therefore ordered to appear in six months' time to explain himself, being bound over by Sir Percival Hart and Sir Thomas Walsingham. We do not know the outcome of that subsequent appearance, and there does not seem to be any trace of Margaret Churchman in the very full family tree drawn up by R.G. Bennett.

On a previous occasion in 1630 Sir Thomas was presented at quarter sessions for stopping up the highway 'between Shoreham and Whitehill in Romney Street'. (To make sense of that phrase in the court report it should probably read 'between Shoreham and Romney Street in Whitehill.')

It is unfortunate that the only details of Sir Thomas's life come from court records, but if his children are any reflection of the man there must have been a sunnier side to his nature. Their stories are engraved in black marble beneath the choir stalls of Shoreham church. On the north side of the chancel a Latin inscription which Mr Bennett translated tells us that Sir George, the eldest son who took the title after his father's death in 1636, was

> a man born of an ancient house, a house built on honest endeavour. Given to moderation and courtesy, an eminent soldier, very learned in the knowledge of God, zealous in liberality to the poor, a very lovable person. Weary of abundance yet seeking renown (he yearned to benefit all men) he exchanged a life of trouble for one of fame and died 19th October 1678 aged 66. Readers make him your example.

His wife, Margaret, died in 1682. They were childless.

Thomas, Sir Thomas's second son, is described as 'being politely learned, affable and a bachelor'. He died in 1667 aged fifty-four, and lies on the north side of the chancel beside his sister Elizabeth who was 'pious and to this church munificent, who died a virgin 29th July 1686 aged 72'. What form her munificence took we do not know, but since Elizabeth had given a bell to Otford church it is possible that she may also have given the bell hung in Shoreham belfry that was dated 1675.

Sir Thomas had two other daughters, Jane and Martha, and a son William, but none survived infancy. Thus this branch of the Polhill family – which Hasted called the Wrotham branch, but which we prefer to call the Shoreham branch – became extinct.

Although the Otford Polhills held land in Shoreham into the nineteenth century, the only other Polhill to continue living in Shoreham parish was John of the senior branch, who married as mentioned above Anne, daughter of Sir Edward Gilbourne. They continued to live at Preston with their children John, Edward and Elizabeth. John senior was buried on the 16th of May 1651, and

THE SEVENTEENTH CENTURY (2)

commemorated by a tablet on the west wall of the Buckland chapel in Shoreham church. John his son sold Preston to Paul D'Aranda in 1689 and went to live at Burwash.

Petleys had been living in the North Downs, Darent Valley and Homesdale area from the thirteenth century (see p. 36), and Thomas at the beginning of James I's reign, with Filston as his base, was the largest land-owner in Shoreham, holding also Andrews Wood, Chelsfield and the Manor of Hewets. His grandson, another Thomas, maintained and increased the standing of the family. In 1646, in the midst of the Civil War, he was married in Shoreham church to Elizabeth Perrwere.

When Francis Sandback and his wife Joan were living at Planers it is possible that they may have invited to stay with them another member of the Inner Temple, Edward Gilbourne Esquire (admitted a member in 1595), because after they died Edward Gilbourne made Planers his home, leasing it from the Otford Polhills. He probably had been living with his elder brother Nicholas at Charing, but decided that Shoreham would be more convenient for his legal work in London. He had also recently married Anne Purefoy, and wanted a place of his own. His son William was baptized in Shoreham church in 1609, and his daughter Anne was baptized two years later. In that same year as a justice of the peace he signed the victualler's recognizance (licence) for William Hill, the husbandman, who also ran an ale house 'at the sign of the Black Eagle' in Shoreham.[2]

By 1625 Edward Gilbourne was clearly accepted in the county as a man of influence. In the April of that year he wrote to David Polhill:[3]

Filston Hall, a moated medieval manor house which was rebuilt in about 1690 following a fire. (Mr and Mrs H. Dinnis)

> Good Mr. Polhill, I received a letter yesternight from Sir Thomas Wallsingham and Sir Percyvall Hart: intimating unto mee their resolutions to concur . . . . in the nomination of Lord Burghersh, the sonn of Sir Francis Fane now Earle of Westmoreland and Sir Albertas Mourton principall secretary to the King's Majestie to be our Knights for the shire, and withall intreatinge mee to request the gentlemen and other Free holders my neighbours, to joyne with them in the said nomination. The day appointed for the election is the second day of May being Munday, the hour seven in the morning . . . Sir I heartily intreate . . . that you will not fail to make one yourself at this meeting and to carry along with you as many of your neighbour Free holders as you can procure. For the which I assure myself both Sir Thomas Wallsingham and Sir Percyvall will acknowledge themselves much beholding unto you and myself shall be ever ready to deserve your kindnes herin as often as you shall have any occasion to use.
>
> Your veary lovinge friend
> Edward Gilbourne

It is interesting to note that members of senior knightly families of Kent in canvassing for their chosen candidates in the election considered Edward Gilbourne Esquire to be a key person to approach in rallying to their cause others, such as the Otford Polhills. For Charles I's subsidy levied in 1629 we find that one of the Commissioners was Sir Edward Gilbourne, now a knight himself, and heading the list of those in Shoreham contributing to the subsidy.[4] At some stage in his career, and possibly following his work as a commissioner, he became a King's pensioner.[5]

As a justice in 1631 he and five others were desired to examine and resolve a dispute over the maintenance of decayed bridges in the parishes of Penshurst, Leigh, Speldhurst, Cowden and Chiddingstone. Another of the many tasks of justices which seemed to have been neglected of late was given to him and two colleagues: to rate the wages of labourers, servants and artificers for the lower division of Sutton-at-Hone which includes Shoreham.[6]

His first wife Anne died in 1634, and two years later he married Elizabeth Whatman in Shoreham church. In spite of all the troubles of the Civil War which we shall narrate later, the Gilbournes remained firmly settled in Shoreham and as already mentioned his daughter Anne married John Polhill of Preston.

In the middle of Elizabeth I's reign a family came to Shoreham who were to play a lively part in the village well into the nineteenth century – the Rounds. It is probable that the family had been in the district long before, though not in Shoreham, but by 1580 John Round was farming in Shoreham, and Thomas (possibly his brother) was farming with him.[7] Thomas had four sons baptized in Shoreham church, and in 1604 he was described as a yeoman when he supported William Hills in his application for the licence of the Black Eagle. The following year John also was so described when he went surety for Thomas, who had quarrelled with a neighbour John Shepster and was ordered to pay £20 into the court and keep the peace.

They were a family who became closely woven into the fabric of the village. Several married members of Shoreham families such as the Hilles, Dallins, Fleets and Medhursts, and were ready to take on tasks for the vestry: John Round for instance in the years 1666-9 'taking and appraising' the probate inventories of Robert Oliver, Michael Elks and Edward Everest. They set a tradition of service to the community which was to continue into future centuries, farming on a modest scale as respected yeomen.

The Powcys were another seventeenth-century Shoreham family. When Thomas Powcy, a husbandman, died in April 1625 he left his house and land to his son Thomas. To each of his daughters Andrian and Marie he left £20 when they reached 21 years as well as 4 pairs each of sheets (2 hemp and 2 flax), his 'small linnen' and 'to either of them a chest to keep their linnen in'. What was unique in his will was provision for Marie's education: he gave £3 yearly to his sister Elizabeth Fielder to pay for that 'until she come to the age of fourteen years'. Who educated Marie? Was it John Emerson the vicar, to supplement his meagre income, or the school at Otford? We do not know. The Powcy family went on its quiet way through the seventeenth and into the eighteenth century.

The Nashes first appeared in Shoreham in 1619, when Joseph Nash married Joan of the Milles family, who were yeomen farming Oxbourne in the west of the parish. They were probably neighbours, as Joseph owned land in Halstead at that time. His son (also a Joseph) owned part of Oxbourne Farm, probably through the family connection. We shall see the Nashes from time to time in eighteenth- and nineteenth-century Shoreham.

As these and other parishioners of Shoreham worked in the fields or at their anvils they must have become increasingly anxious when regiments were mustered and orders for swords superseded orders for coulters. As the crisis developed between King and Parliament so the old-established families, particularly of east and central Kent, became politically active. The leading families of the Darent Valley were also to become involved, for Parliament was in control of London and Members knew that control of Kent, the county closest to the Continent, was of vital importance to their winning the struggle against the King.

The majority of the Kentish gentry were moderates, either mild parliamentarians or mild royalists, most believing in a moderate Anglican church, reform rather than rebellion. As the tensions increased with the misrule of Charles I's government, so extreme groups formed.

Sir Edward Gilbourne in Shoreham became involved early in the crisis when he supported Sir Edward Dering as a candidate in the election of the Short Parliament, and again in the Long Parliament. In the following two years even the moderates lost their moderation; Sir Edward Dering's anger increased against King Charles and Archbishop Laud. He and Sir Roger Twysden his cousin were arrested by Parliament for helping in the preparation of the Kentish petition to it in favour of county autonomy, and as a result the Commons found that more extreme elements – Cavaliers such as Sir Thomas Bosvile of Eynsford – took over the petition.

In August 1642 King Charles raised his standard at Nottingham, and in the same month Parliament realized from a captured bundle of royalist letters that a local Cavalier coup in Kent was imminent. With tactical brilliance they sent Colonel Edwyn Sandys, a Kentish puritan, with troops to Sevenoaks. Colonel Sandys arrested Sir John Sackville (the leading Cavalier there) and seized five wagon-loads of arms from Knole. Going well beyond his commission, he plundered the house for money and supplies. He was sent on a second sortie into Kent five days later expressly to seek out malignants and recusants (Catholics) and to gather in stores and arms. His troops left a trail of ruthless and brutish destruction in Homesdale and elsewhere, but in the end he had subdued

SHOREHAM

Rochester, Maidstone, Canterbury and Dover, and Parliament was firmly in control of Kent.

An oral tradition in Shoreham has it that during the Civil War all ancient stained glass in the windows of the church was destroyed except for the 'Pelican' in the north-west window of the nave and that the rood-screen was carefully dismantled and hidden from the parliamentary forces. This might have been so. A number of villagers were involved, and armed action came close to the village. It is possible, on the other hand, that Shoreham may have escaped the punitive raids of the Puritans. There is no evidence of Shoreham sheltering papists or having well-known Catholic families living in the parish who were the main targets of Colonel Sandys's troops; John Emerson the vicar was a moderate Anglican whom Parliament considered to be 'a good man' (see p. 80), and Thomas Browne his curate had leanings towards Puritanism so it is probable that Shoreham church and its ministers were left in peace as sometimes happened elsewhere, and avoided the devastation suffered by Canterbury cathedral.

Parliament now (1642) set up a County Committee for Kent under Sir Anthony Weldon, a ruthless and power-seeking parliamentarian who gathered round him other extremists. They met at Knole and became in fact the government of Kent. An uneasy equilibrium followed that was shattered in 1643, when the Committee was ordered by John Pym, leader of the Long Parliament, to administer through parish churches a 'sacred Vow and Covenant' to every person of age in the county, a covenant which included the words 'I will . . . assist the forces raised and continued by both houses of parliament against the forces raised by the King without their consent . . .'[8] Moderates could no longer ignore the choice to be made. The minister at Ightham who refused to administer the vow and covenant was arrested. Immediately the whole district rose in revolt. The Polhills at Otford, the Gilbournes of Shoreham, the Harts of Lullingstone were all involved, and possibly the Petleys, Everests, Rounds and Hills. The rebels were essentially moderates.

The four thousand that gathered at the Vine in Sevenoaks presented a motley crowd. Parliament sent a force to Reigate to prevent the King's troops joining the rebels, and others to Rochester and Faversham, while against the heart of the revolt Colonel Browne brought a regiment towards Sevenoaks. Negotiations with the rebels failed, but by the time his troops reached Sevenoaks, and after forty-eight hours of continuous rain, all but five or six hundred of them had gone back home. Colonel Browne's regiment took three hundred prisoners and arms for six hundred men. The scattered groups in the Darent Valley were rounded up by a Captain Twistleton. The leading rebels (including David Polhill of Broughtons, Otford and Sir Edward Gilbourne of Planers) were fined, others were imprisoned and had their estates sequestered. Nevertheless, in Kent the covenant was forgotten for the moment, and the continued use of the prayer book was overlooked, except where ministers were extreme royalists. Royalists continued to elaborate high-flown plans centred upon the seizure of Dover Castle, but as on previous occasions their plans were betrayed and the conspiracy failed. They next decided to attack the hated County Committee, which had moved from Knole to Aylesford Friary. The Harts of Lullingstone Castle led this conspiracy in April 1645. Lullingstone Castle was fortified and garrisoned with 500 soldiers who had mutinied after being impressed for Sir Thomas Fairfax's armies. The parishioners of Shoreham could not have escaped involvement, their horses, arms and other supplies were seized if not given

THE SEVENTEENTH CENTURY (2)

willingly; the Black Eagle, the Rose and Crown and their other ale-houses invaded by the motley crowd of rogues and vagabonds bent on drinking and whoring while Royalist pay lasted.

Hearing of this new threat, the two Houses of Parliament took immediate action. Fairfax sent a party of his cavalry into Kent. Sir Anthony Weldon and the County Committee called out their trained bands. At the approach of these troops the royalists at Lullingstone found themselves unable to discipline their force; some were caught in their beds, others fled into the surrounding hills and woods. A group set off for Rochester but were easily defeated by the trained bands. Fresh sequestrations followed this rising. Taxes on the county rose to unprecedented heights to finance the New Model Army. In 1643 Pym had introduced a new type of tax which with the Land Tax was to become the principal source of government revenue down to the Napoleonic Wars. He imposed an excise duty on ale, beer, cider, spirits, meat, victuals, salt, alum, hops, starch, hats, caps, saffron. It roused immense hostility because it fell on people's necessities. There was more trouble for Sir Anthony in the offing. With the defeated Cavaliers of the King's army returning home, the people of Kent suffering under his oppressive rule were roused again.

The Great Rebellion of 1648 was mainly a rising against the hated County Committee and its Chairman rather than a rising in support of the King. As Professor Alan Everitt wrote, 'it was a rising of thousands of countrymen spurred on by lingering legends of Cade and Wyatt . . . it was in fact the last of the great local insurrections of English history'.[9]

The confrontations of the rebel forces with Fairfax's New Model Army took place in central and east Kent and do not concern Shoreham directly, though several of its inhabitants may have been involved. After its collapse the people of Shoreham must have suffered from eleven years of repressive rule by the County Committee, followed by the military government of Major-General Kelsey.

The reason why we can presume involvement by some from Shoreham in the 1648 and possibly the Cavalier conspiracy of 1655 is that nine of their names appear in the Cromwellian Commission's lists (1655-7) of 'those required to bring in particulars of their estates or security for their peaceable demeanour'. Their names were sent to London and their future movements reported.[10] From Shoreham were:

William Artnope
Edward Everest
Robert Hills
Thomas Petley (Filston)
William Small

Thomas Lewin
Joseph Nash
Richard Petley
John Round

These nine represent a high concentration of suspects compared with other communities in the district. Bromley had most with 13, then came Shoreham with 9, Orpington 7, Westerham 4, Sevenoaks 3, Otford 3, Eynsford 1 and Farningham 1. Generally speaking, those included in the lists ranged widely in political persuasion: uncompromising royalists; those previously favouring Parliament but who rebelled in 1648; those who tried to steer a middle course, and even those inclined to the Parliament side and who were able to prove their service to it.[11]

William 'Artnope' may be a misspelling of William 'Hartnup'. He, with John Round and Robert Hills, was summoned to appear before the Cromwellian

Commissioners on 3 June 1656, and after examination all three were 'respited' (had their sentence delayed) while the witness who deposed against them was ordered to be further examined. William Artnope does not seem to have suffered further, as he was able to buy the tannery business in Otford in 1659.[12]

Edward Everest may well have been penalized for royalist sentiments. He was the first of the Everest family to appear in Shoreham (paying the subsidy to King Charles in 1620). Over the next forty years he became a well-known and well-liked yeoman and mercer, though when he died in 1669 his worldly goods were valued at a very modest £28 2s. 8d. (those of John Rawlins in 1679 were valued at £389, and Thomas Petley's in 1686 at £358). Everest was living modestly with his wife, son Francis and his family in a four-roomed dwelling and paying tax on only two hearths, so he may well have been fined by Parliament during the Civil War. His son Francis continued to play a lively part in the village and added modestly to his property, including part of Oxbourne Farm. Their descendants continued living in Shoreham into the nineteenth century.

Certainly Robert Hills, yeoman farmer and maltmaker, did not suffer during the Civil War. On the contrary, he prospered and was able to leave £386 to his family, marriage portions to three daughters and property, including one house, one forge and thirteen acres left to a grandson. His father's bequests had been on a more modest scale.

There is no positive evidence that any of the others named by the Cromwellian Commission suffered sequestration of property or fines. The Petleys, who from later evidence appear to have had royalist sympathies, must have played a careful waiting game and did not suffer loss. As mentioned earlier, a Thomas Petley had married in the middle of the Civil War, and three years later according to Ireland he acquired the Vane family estate of Hadlow Place.[13] He was later to become a justice of the peace. His second son, Thomas, inherited Filston, and on his death was described as a gentleman. His probate inventory testifies to the continuing prosperity of the Petley family. However, he died a bachelor, bequeathing Filston and all his property and worldly goods to his brother James, whose marriage appears[14] to have been childless. Shortly after Thomas's death Filston was badly damaged by fire, but was rebuilt in 1690.

Although his young cousin Henry Gilbourne in 1651 was fined £160 for his 'delinquency'[15] we have been unable to discover the fate of Sir Edward following the rising of 1645. In 1661 he died, and in his will asked to be buried 'in the chappell belonging to Shoreham church as near as conveniently may be to the place where my two wives doe lye interned'. His will gives no evidence of great wealth: he left property in Farnborough and Shoreham 'and elsewhere in Kent' to his eldest son William; to his son George he bequeathed £50 (to be paid by William) and his son Percivall only received his 'chafing-dish' and a share of his father's goods, chattels and household stuffs which were to be divided between the three sons. Each of his six grandchildren received 20 shillings each, and the poor of Shoreham £3. It was not the will of a wealthy justice of the peace, and one can only conclude that the County Committee and its autocratic chairman got their revenge.

It would be wrong to leave the reader with the impression from the few examples of the Petleys' and Hills' continuing prosperity that Shoreham had not suffered during the Civil War —'. . . that bloody difference between the King and Parliament', as John Evelyn described it. Increasing purchase taxes were

THE SEVENTEENTH CENTURY (2)

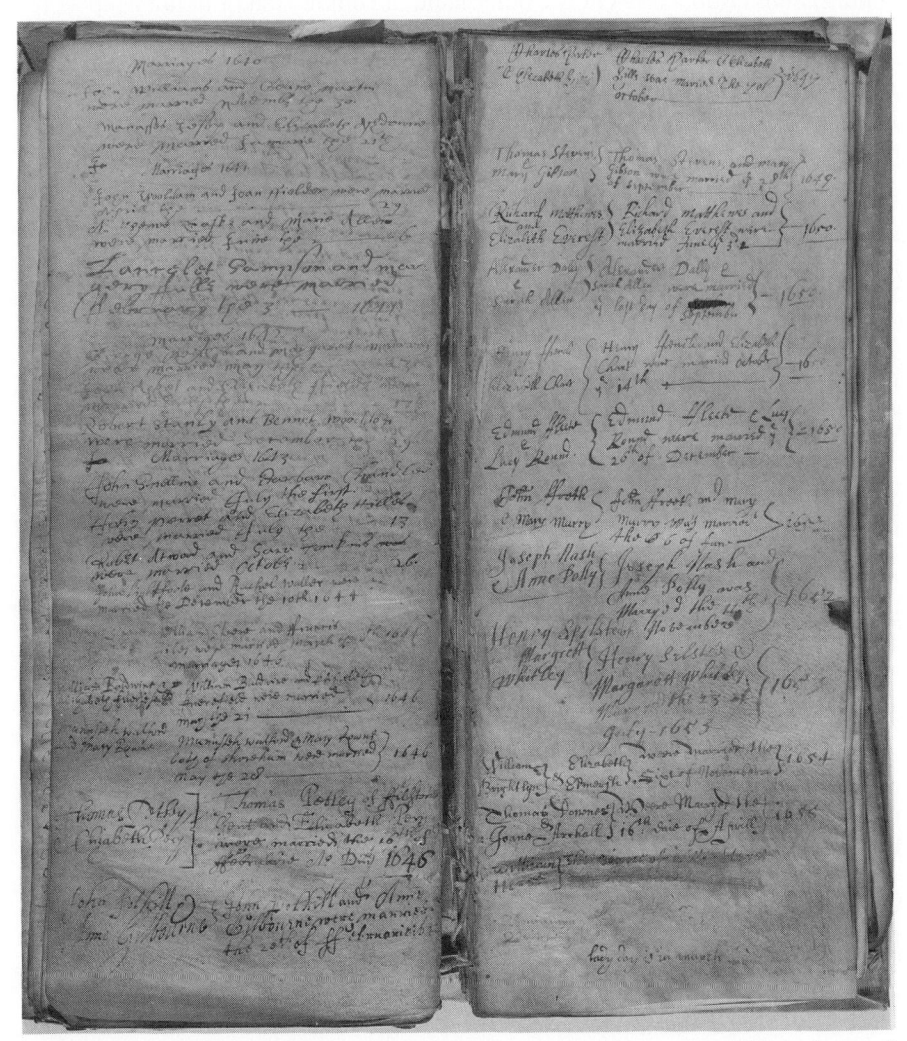

Several different hands making entries in the church register reflect, perhaps, the confusion of the times. (Kent Archives Office)

imposed. Depression and uncertainty deepened as the republican interregnum continued, and again to quote John Evelyn: 'All is confusion — we have no government in the Nation.' One even senses this confusion in the several hands that wrote the Shoreham church registers: a striking contrast to the ordered entries made over the years by Mr Emerson. Yet in spite of the drastic reforming legislation of the Cromwellian period, the weeding out of the unfit and ignorant from the Church elsewhere, Thomas Browne served both Shoreham and Otford painstakingly as vicar until 1661; after, the monarchy was restored, Edward Oliver took over.

According to Ireland, on the death of Charles I Parliament sold Shoreham rectory ('to supply the necessities of the state') to John Singleton, with whom it remained till the restoration of the monarchy. We have failed to find

93

confirmation of this sale. On the other hand, a commission of inquiry report in 1650 stated that Shoreham parish was 'all in the hands of Erasmus Moyce' and valued the parish, its land and buildings at over £100 per annum. Moreover, a note in the Westminster Chapter Muniments confirms Erasmus Moyce and Jane his wife as 'farmers of Shoreham Impropriate Rectory' who were plaintiffs against Christopher Haywood, a Shoreham landowner who had failed to pay to them the 'tithe coneys' (rabbits) in 1656. Again twenty-nine years later Shoreham Rectory was leased to a Susan Moyce, 'widow of Totenham Hycross, county Middlesex.'[16] Parishioners paying their tithes must have sighed for the distant times past when the Archbishop's reeve they knew as a neighbour pestered them for their dues.

The penury of the vicars continued after the Restoration, and is revealed in Edward Oliver's probate inventory. He left to his widow Margery his worldly goods, worth £38 18s. 10d, almost exactly a tenth the value of those of John Rawlins, yeoman, who died five years later, and a twentieth of those of his wealthy relation Robert Oliver (£752).

Edward Oliver, with his wife and daughter, lived his simple life in the vicarage. Nineteenth-century north and south wings of the building that we know today did not yet exist. It was a timber-framed house with two floors facing towards the church. The parlour — or as it was called then 'the hall' — was at the east end, and at the west end was the kitchen with a passage and staircase between them. There was a small room beyond the kitchen. These were the ground-floor rooms of the original 'vicarage house' built about 1531: a cross-wing to the south had been added early in the seventeenth century, and repairs carried out by the 'governors of Westminster College' in 1649.[17]

Mr Oliver kept his desk in the hall, where there was a fireplace with andirons. The hall must have been the family living-room as it was furnished with two tables, a form, five chairs and two stools. His books were in the 'studdy' (presumably the room next the hall in the south cross-wing) which was furnished 'with a table and chair, and old chest and other old things'. Beyond the kitchen to the west were the 'little butteries', a cellar (not necessarily underground) and the brew house with the usual 'furnace'. He and Mrs Oliver probably slept in the room over the hall, and their daughter over the 'studdy'. There were three beds in the rooms over the kitchen, possibly for servants, and another in the room over the butteries. To us the Olivers' home would seem bleakly furnished indeed. Edward Oliver was buried in Shoreham on 7 June 1674, and his name was inscribed on one of the church bells dated 1672. When William Wall, Doctor of Divinity, arrived in Shoreham to take over from Edward Oliver as the new incumbent in 1674, no-one could have imagined that he would remain vicar until 1727, the year George II was crowned. After the turmoil of the Civil War and then the Revolution of 1688 Dr Wall and his successor the Revd Vincent Perronet seemed to bring (at least locally) a new stability. In succession they served Shoreham for 111 years — an extraordinary record of devotion, of which more later.

With fears of a return to the traumas of the Civil War very much in people's minds, the Church must have drawn parishioners to itself. This seems confirmed by a census organized by Bishop Compton of London in 1676, which showed that in the Shoreham deanery there were only 46 recorded papists, representing 0.6 per cent of the total population, and 174 non-conformists, or 2.2 per cent. With the exception of Wrotham, over 90 per cent of the population were conformist.[18] Of course the authorities of Church and State were determined that no one should rock the boat. The public, between the death of Charles I and the return of Charles II, had grown used to the multitude of regulations that controlled their lives. Fear of conspiracies and uprisings forced authority to forbid public gatherings even for cricket, bowling and horse-racing, and the regulation of life in Charles II's time was accepted by the majority. Evidence of this regulation is a submission to the justices in 1664 by William Edwards and Percivall Smith, the constables of the Hundred of Codsheath, who had to report periodically on a wide range of matters of interest to government. In this particular 'Bill of Presentation' the constables stated that:

> They know of noe Recusants (particularly catholics) but such as they presented to the last assizes;
>
> they know of noe unlicensed ale houses within their hundred;
>
> they found noe person drunk within their hundred;
>
> they know of noe unlawfull weights and measures;
>
> they have executed all hue and cries to them directed;
>
> they know of noe highways or bridges unrepaired;
>
> they know of noe cottage latelie erected.
>
> They saie that they took Richard Deane a tall big bodied person black haired and about fifty years of age at Otford the XVII of April, who was openly whipped and sent from officer to officer to Southwark according to the law;
>
> they know of noe cursers or swearers;
>
> they saie that poor children are provided for at the monthly meeting of the vestry. . . .'[19]

The harsh treatment of Richard Deane (who had evidently strayed from his parish of Southwark) and the report on cottage-building show that the fear of persons moving and settling unlawfully in parishes of the hundred was as lively in Charles II's reign as in Elizabeth's, especially since the Act of Settlement was passed in 1662.

No doubt too as in Elizabeth's reign, Alexander Hill, Thomas Carpenter and their wives of Shoreham were fined one shilling each for every Sunday they had failed to attend church service when they were brought in 1682 by Edward Hill, the borsholder of Shoreham, before the justices at Riverhead.[20] (The year 1689 was approaching, with the reign of William and Mary — when non-conformists — though not Catholics, would obtain the legal right to opt out of worship of the established Anglican Church.) There was also the case in 1668 which sounds strange in our tolerant times brought against four youngsters of the village: John Seamarke, John Boteler, William Rackett (possibly an odd spelling of Rackard or Record) and Baldock who were accused of 'profaninge the Lord's day on September 20 last past by playinge at Crickett and strokebase' in Shoreham.[21]

SHOREHAM

A man who was to be closely involved in this regulation of Shoreham life in the first decade of the eighteenth century was baptized on 25 October 1652 at Patcham. The service was probably conducted by his father, who was minister of the French protestant church at Patcham and Mayfield, Sussex. Paul D'Aranda was a Huguenot whose ancestors were originally Spanish and who for their religious beliefs had been driven out of Flanders by the persecutions of the Duke of Alva.[22] A member of the D'Aranda family had been known in Amsterdam as 'the merchant prince' and Paul seems to have followed his ancestor's rather than his father's calling because he became established as a merchant in London, marrying Mary Barker of St Mary Aldermary when he was thirty.[23] It must have been shortly after their marriage that with increasing prosperity, and following the example of many London merchants, Paul decided to have a place in the country. He discovered that John Polhill was about to sell his Preston estate in Shoreham: a convenient distance from the city. So Paul D'Aranda decided to buy Preston, and over the years added other Shoreham property to his estate, including Dibden. After some twenty years in Kent his worth and standing were recognized by the county when he was sworn in as Justice. We will say more about his activities on the bench in the next chapter.

One of the ways that Charles II raised revenue was by placing a tax of 1s. (sometimes 2s.) on each hearth in the homes of his subjects. It was a most unpopular tax. The return of the 1662 tax tells us that in Shoreham there were 91 dwellings, an increase of eleven over the 80 families given in the petition to

An early sketch of the paper-mill including the late seventeenth-century Mill House. (*Unknown Kent*, John Lane, The Bodley Head, 1921)

Parliament in 1641. The owners of 63 of these paid the hearth tax, but the owners of 28 of the dwellings were considered too poor to pay. Gregory King, the seventeenth-century demographer, suggested that an owner could be considered to be a 'gentleman' if his house had five or more hearths taxed. By this definition there were five 'gentlemen' in Shoreham: George Polhill who had 12; John Whitehead (8); Henry Gilbourne (7); Thomas Petley (6); and Robert Hills (5). Twenty-three dwellings had two hearths and 20 one hearth only. The Earl of Dorset at Knole had 85 hearths.[24]

Towards the close of the century the first indications of the way in which modern industry in England was to develop began to appear, and it was then that Shoreham itself experienced its industrial development. As early as 1648 it had been discovered that the water of the Darent was perfectly suited to the making of paper, and flowed with sufficient strength to power the machines. In that year a small body of paper-makers — some of whom may have been skilled Huguenots — set up a vat in the corn mill at Eynsford. Queen Elizabeth I fifty-nine years earlier had given the monopoly for paper-making and collecting rags to John Spilman, her German jeweller, who was the first maker of paper on a large scale in Britain at his mills at Dartford.[25] It was not until the 1670s that the number of paper-mills in England increased appreciably, and it was probably between that date and 1690 that Alexander Russell was one of fourteen native-born 'ancient paper makers' who petitioned against the parliamentary act confirming and extending the monopoly of the Company of White Paper Makers. Evidently Mr Russell was planning or had already started to make fine-quality white paper. The Shoreham paper mill was to continue for 250 years providing the inhabitants of the village with an alternative to work in the fields and we shall follow its development in future chapters.

VIII

THE EIGHTEENTH CENTURY:
The Justices, the villagers and the Church

ENGLAND and even isolated Shoreham was now faced with 110 years of almost continuous war. Louis XIV of France was once again making war inevitable by accepting the empty throne of Spain on his grandson's behalf, and in Kent 'people were saying that they had sown their corn only for the French to reap it'.[1]

It came as no surprise, therefore, in 1705 for some 38 freeholders in Shoreham along with those elsewhere in the district that they were charged according to the size of their property for the cost of Captain Robert Watson's Militia Company of Foot in the Regiment of Sir Stephen Lennard. They were charged for twenty-two Musketeers and their arms,[2] and as the century progressed other such charges may have been made.

War intruded in other ways. Two years later warrants were issued by the justices to all constables and borsholders 'to search for Persons lyable to be impressed into her Majestys land service'. At first James Hibbin, the Shoreham borsholder, could not find any man for the service, 'but two days later he brought in John Sinyard as a person fit to be listed as a soldier'. However, the justices rejected Sinyard 'for several reasons'. He had a bad record, and Paul D'Aranda only ten days later was to fine him eleven shillings for stealing conies in Homewood on the borders of Lullingstone Park (six shillings for the owner of the conies, William Haswell, and five shillings for the use of the parish).[3]

Almost a hundred years later William Danks, resting from work on his Eastdown farm, wrote in his diary in February 1806 'the papers were issued out for raising the Army-in-Mass about the time Buonaparte conquered Germany. Age from 17 to 55 years old for the army' and a little later he noted that there was an army camp for volunteers on the Vine at Sevenoaks — 'they had a strict adjatant' and on a visit down the hill to Shoreham William Danks paid to Mr. Coxon his one-guinea subscription to the Militia Club.[4] It was possibly at this time that volunteers from Shoreham used to go to collect the Queen's shilling from a grill in the kitchen of the house now known as Reedbeds, wearing out the floor tiles in the process.[5]

The Church was playing its part in those troubled times. 17 April 1793 was appointed as a fast day when a collection was made at the church door 'for the French Emigrants, Refugees in the British Dominions which amounted to the sum of two pounds three shillings'[6] and during three years at the turn of the century among those getting married in Shoreham church were four girls married to four men in the Royal Artillery, all of Shoreham parish. So it is probable that there was an artillery regiment stationed nearby. In the eighteenth century as in the twentieth Shoreham was very conscious of wars in Europe.

Paul D'Aranda had lived in Shoreham since buying Preston from John Polhill in 1693 and on 12 March 1706 was sworn in as justice. We are fortunate in having available the note book in which he wrote in his neat, legible hand the details of the Commission – the writ of Dedimus Potestatem (We have given power) given to him, the oaths he took and the declaration he was obliged to make on that occasion.[7] They give a distillation of the ideals of justice, of the fears of the Established Church in Queen Anne's reign, of the fears of her government of counter-revolution and her government's attempts to ensure the Protestant Succession.

The Queen's Commission directed him to 'do equal Right to the Poor and to the rich after your cunning, wit and Power and after all ye laws and customs of the Realm and statutes there made' and that he take 'nothing for your office of Justice of the Peace to be done but of the Queen and fees accustomed and costs limited by statute'. He was given authority to bring before him

> those threatening to cause harm to persons or their property. Enquire into all manner of felonies, witchcrafts, inchantments, sorceries, magick-art, trespasses, Forestallings, Regratings, Ingrossings and Extorsions whatsoever . . . and of all those who . . shall presume to go and ride in companies with armed force against ye Peace to ye disturbance of ye People . . . or who . . ly in wait to maim or kill our people, or Inn holders and others who . . may offend in the abuse of weights and measures.

He then took two oaths: the first swearing true allegiance to her Majesty Queen Anne, while in the second he swore

> that I do from my heart abhor, detest and abjure, as impious and heretical, that damnable Doctrine and Position, that Princes Excommunicated or deprived by the Pope or any Authority of the See of Rome, may be deposed by their subjects . . . and I do declare that no foreign Person, Prince, Prelate, State or Potentate hath or ought to have any Jurisdiction, Power, Superiority, Preeminence or authority Ecclesiastical or Spiritual with this Realm.

Yet more – he signed a declaration 'that I do believe that there is not any transubstantiation in the sacrament of the Lord's Supper or in the elements of Bread and wine.' He took an oath acknowledging Queen Anne as the lawful and rightful Queen of the realm, and solemnly declared that 'I do believe in my conscience that the Person pretended to be Prince of Wales, during the time of

A page from Paul D'Aranda's notebook of 1707–08 describing his encounter with Joast Didley. (Kent Archives Office)

King James and since his Decease, pretending to be and taking upon himself the stile and title of King of England by the name of James ye third, hath not any right or title whatsoever to the crown of this Realm'. He would also support the succession to the throne of the Queen's 'heirs of her body' or if the Queen had no issue, the succession of the issue of Princess Sophia, Electress and Duchess Dowager of Hanover, and the heirs of her body being Protestant. In 1707 Paul D'Aranda was one of eighteen members of the grand jury in Maidstone who sent

101

an address to the Queen congratulating her Majesty on frustrating the Pretender's design on Scotland.

On 6 April 1707 as a test of his declarations of belief in the tenets of the Established Church he received a Sacrament at St Anthony's Church in London, and received a certificate duly witnessed. Then, on a second occasion he notes 'I received the sacrament of ye Lords Supper of Mr. Wall at Shoreham and obtained a certificate signed by Mr. Wall and Thomas Peryer church warden.' Subsequently John Wood, Yeoman, and William Natt, both of Shoreham, swore that they knew Paul D'Aranda and confirmed the certificate at the Quarter Session at Maidstone on 22 April.

From that date and for the next five years Preston by the powers vested in Paul D'Aranda must have witnessed a regular flow of parishioners to its doors to put their problems to the Justice or to further the government of the parish.

A study of his notebook, which covers the years 1707-8, shows that the great majority of matters with which he dealt concerned the 'settlement' of parishioners and poor relief. Since the Acts of Settlement had been introduced in Elizabeth's reign, extended and clarified in the 1662 Law of Settlement and Removal, the officers of the parish spurred on by those who had to pay the Poor Rates were ever on the lookout for anyone who had no right to be living in the parish. They were liable to become a charge on parish funds, and had to be sent back to where they legally belonged. No fewer than twenty-three persons had to be examined by D'Aranda during those two years. Some, like the 'honest, sober and laborious hoopshaver Edward Francis', and Henry Carpenter the shoemaker, had to be given certificates to work at their crafts not only in Shoreham but elsewhere.

The case of Robert Broomfield junior was more complicated. He was born in Shoreham but four years past had gone to (West) Kingsdown, where he worked for Mr Chapman as a servant for just under the regulation twelve months required to secure his settlement there. Because of this Kingsdown refused to accept him as their responsibility, and a special session of the Justices at Sevenoaks was convened which ordered him to be settled at Kingsdown. The Kingsdown officers then appealed and the case went to the Maidstone Easter Sessions, where the original settlement was confirmed. Broomfield's worries did not end there. Paul D'Aranda was forced to order the constable of Kingsdown to summon the parish officers before him at the Bull Inn, Sevenoaks, as they had failed to find lodging for Broomfield and his family. D'Aranda added in his notebook 'NB Burroughs, Church warden of Kingsdown appeared before me with others of that parish and proved in ye presence of Broomfield and his father that he might have a convenient dwelling in their parish, tho' not so cheap by £5 a year as he bid for it not quite so good as desired'.

In December 1708 William Hilles, yeoman, overseer of the poor and surveyor of the highways in Shoreham, complained to D'Aranda against William Corbut, a vagrant who with his family had been given relief by him and others, including D'Aranda himself. Corbut was born at Cockermouth in Cumberland and had gone to sea at the age of sixteen. D'Aranda ordered William Everest, the Shoreham constable, to convey Corbut and his family to his birthplace, for settlement. William Everest thereupon started them on their journey as far as Croydon, where he presumably handed them on to the local constable, and for that received 11 shillings and 6 pence.

Of the twenty-three settlement cases brought D'Aranda found six to be perfectly bona-fide parishioners of Shoreham. Nine cases were settled quite simply by the production of certificates or by an agreed removal to another parish. It was the minority of cases which were time-consuming.

Before Christmas 1708 D'Aranda was faced with a troublesome and persistent problem. Goodwife Curtis and the wife of Edward Francis had come for a 'Christmas gooding' (Christmas box) but had failed to wear the hated Poor Law PS badge on the shoulder of the right sleeve of their outer garments when in public, to show that they were in receipt of Poor Relief from Shoreham parish. They pleaded with him that they could not survive if he ordered their poor relief allowance to be cut by six pence. 'Both of them seemed to promise' to wear the hated letters in future, and D'Aranda warned them of severe punishment for failure. 'Notwithstanding all this', added the justice, 'I, the very next day, Wednesday 22 December saw them both abroad without the badge or mark on'.

There were only a few cases of theft in those two years. One of D'Aranda's first cases was brought to him by Timothy Wells, the maltster, who had had at least two quarters of malt stolen from his house. D'Aranda ordered the constable and borsholders of Shoreham to search the houses adjoining the Wells's property, but no malt was found. Later in the year James Yowart, a travelling seller of lace and linen, had visited the paper-mill house in the hope of selling his wares to Elizabeth, Alexander Russell's wife. Susan Causten and Susan Francis were with her when he called. James Yowart declared on oath that he lost one piece of lace which he had shown them. He could not charge any one of them with having taken it, but said he would be satisfied if they would all swear that they had *not* taken it. They were brought before D'Aranda, and each on oath said 'that she had not taken the said piece of lace or know what became of it' and D'Aranda discharged them.

Nowadays district councils, the Inland Revenue, the DSS and other branches of central government carry the administrative burdens which the justice of the peace in a voluntary capacity, assisted by the local vestry, undertook in 1707-8. D'Aranda and his fellow-justices appointed parish officers, fixed rates and taxes and approved the parish accounts of monies spent on poor relief, roads and bridges.

Apart from disputes between individuals and criminal cases dealt with at the petty sessions, there were some tasks then not required of any authority today: for instance, a warrant was sent to Westerham by the justices to levy ten pence of William Underhill for profanely swearing ten oaths. Such was the power of the clothiers in 1662 that the Government passed the Burial in Wool Act in that year, so that whenever a parishioner was buried a friend or relation would visit Preston for a certificate that the deceased was buried in wool. If he was buried illegally in linen the family had to pay a fine, half of which went to the poor of the parish and half to the informant. In the case of Benjamin Porter, maltster, the certificate was witnessed by D'Aranda's wife Mary and his cousin Rebeckah Straynern who was visiting them at the time.[8]

On another occasion Paul D'Aranda copied into his notebook the statement provided by Robert Russell, a coachman of Shoreham, made upon oath before him — following a 'cricketting' at Richmore Hill when Robert Russell and Thomas Capon after a late carousal tried to prevent William Hammond from seeing Anne Willicks home through a wood. William Hammond, fortunately for him, avoided future trouble by giving Robert 'a shilling into his hand to be forfeited if he did not return to them within half an hour at farthest'. Robert and Thomas 'sate down on a bank by ye said gate of ye wood (which is standing in the great road to London) and waited there, without hearing any crying out, screaming or calling ... till the said William Hammond returned so certainly within the appointed half hour.' As if these multifarious tasks were not enough, Paul D'Aranda offered himself and was appointed with John Capon in January 1708 as a surveyor of the highways for the coming year.

He continued his busy life until at the age of sixty he died, on 27 October 1712. On his gravestone of black marble in the chancel of Shoreham church was written

> Here under lyeth the body of Paul D'Aranda of Shoreham in the County of Kent, Esquire who having acted during the whole of his life with the utmost piety to God and probity, honour and steadfast, immovable justice to mankind in every station dyed much lamented by his friends.

The war against Louis XIV involved all western Europe, and the French devastation of the German Palatinate resulted in a flood of Protestant refugees, several thousand of whom looked to England for shelter. They were dumped down on Blackheath, and the only provision for their survival was a thousand tents sent by the Government from the Tower of London.

An attempt was made to settle some of them in the villages of west Kent. In view of all the 'settlement' problems, it is not surprising that this request had a frosty reception. When Cowden turned down the appeal to help them it expressed a view repeated by other parishes: 'We have more of our own poor than we can employ, neither have we any housing to put them in.' Only one parish gave a positive answer: 'John Capon and William Beardsworth, Church warden and overseer of the Parish of Shoreham, appeared (August 13 1709) and say they are willing to take a protestant family that are labourers and not exceeding four in family.'[9] There is no certain evidence that Shoreham actually received a family, but on 25 April 1714 Esther, daughter of Peter and Mary Johannet, was baptized in Shoreham Church. The family's unusual name might suggest that they had originally fled from Germany.

D'Aranda had been given authority to bring before him those 'who go and ride in companies with armed force and lie in wait to maim and kill our people'. Among such undesirable elements were the smugglers, Owlers or Free Traders (no matter how they described themselves), who were an increasing menace. They had always flourished whenever authority tried to control or prohibit their business. Eighteenth-century governments found the excise tax imposed by Pym during the Civil War increasingly useful as a revenue-raiser. This tax and the restrictions of war made smuggling a lucrative business for high and low alike. There were 20,000 smugglers active in Kent alone. Faced with highly organized gangs, Government had set up not only coastal patrols but a network of 'riding officers' inland. There were also the excisemen, the most unpopular people in the community. One such exciseman was John Baltern,[10] living at Shoreham in 1747. In his enthusiasm for his work he tried to seize contraband goods being 'run' through Shoreham by a notorious gang based on Hawkhurst forty miles away. The gang overwhelmed John Baltern and his three assistants, trussed them up and rode them back to Hawkhurst. Unluckily for Baltern and his men, Thomas Kingsmill – the particularly ruthless leader of the gang – discovered that two of Baltern's men were renegade smugglers. They were tied to trees and flogged almost to death. A reward was offered for information about this brutal act, but was never paid. The last report of Baltern and his men was that they were all put on a smuggler's boat for France.[11]

In his history of the eighteenth century, J.H. Plumb wrote 'life had a taut neurotic quality: fantastic gambling and drinking, riots, brutality and violence and everywhere and always a constant sense of death'.[12] The response of the Church to this situation did not come early in the century, and at Shoreham an intellectual and a scholar, William Wall, took over from Edward Oliver as vicar in 1674. He was born at Morants Court Farm, Chevening, in 1647 and obtained his MA degree at Cambridge in 1676. For the next thirty years he worked on his magnum opus, the *History of Infant Baptism*[13], which set out in the first part 'an impartial collection of all such passages in the writers of the four first centuries as do make FOR or AGAINST IT. The second part containing several things that do illustrate the said history.' This book was published in 1705, and its importance was at once recognized, while it generated considerable discussion and debate. Wall was accepted as a leading authority on the subject. Oxford University in appreciation of his work conferred on him a Doctorate of Divinity in 1720.[14]

He was a scholar and a High Churchman but he lived in and cared for his parish on a modest £45 a year until with increasing family responsibilities he accepted the additional living of Milton-next-Gravesend twelve miles away, which provided an extra £60. His conscience had prevented him previously accepting the living of Chelsfield, valued at £300. William Wall died in 1728, and was buried in his church at Shoreham.

William Wall's successor, Vincent Perronet (1693-1785), although like him a scholar, was a warmer and more likeable character. He had a frank, generous and cheerful temper, gentle and affectionate, and interested in all the men, women and children in the parish. He believed that God had many times directly intervened in his long life, and he describes these interventions in one of his eleven published works, entitled *Some Remarkable Facts in The Life of a Person We Shall Call Eusebius*. He followed Wall in writing *A Defence of Infant Baptism*, and his other works included studies of the philosophers Locke and Hobbes.[15] He also wrote an *Ernest Exhortation to his Parishioners* on the strict practice of Christianity, speaking strongly against Sabbath-breaking, swearing and drunkenness and denouncing the number of public houses in the village — those 'temptations in the way of idle people'.[16] In an *Essay On Recreations* he discussed dancing, but thought it unsuitable for the lower orders of his time. One can understand his concern, especially during the 1770s. Although illegitimate births in Shoreham averaged about one per year during the eighteenth century, there was a period from 1775 to 1779 when there was a total of twenty-one, with a peak of six in 1778. Although Richard Price the Rational Dissenter was doubtless thinking of the cities, his strictures may have applied to Shoreham when he wrote in 1776 'we are running wild after pleasure and forgetting everything serious and decent, in Masquerades'.[17]

Vincent Perronet's father David was a native of Switzerland, of French Huguenot stock who had come over to England in about 1680. He died in 1717, the year before Vincent obtained his BA degree at Oxford and married his wife Charity. In view of his upbringing in a Protestant family from Calvinist Switzerland, it was natural that when in 1744 he met John and Charles Wesley for the first time a relationship of deep sympathy and understanding began

The Rev.d VINCENT PERRONET, A. M

Late Vicar of SHOREHAM in KENT.

Obiit Maij 9. 1785. Æt. suæ 92.

Vincent Perronet, vicar from 1728 to 1785, was the son of a French Calvinist from Switzerland.

which was to develop and endure for the rest of his long life. It was a relationship of immense importance to him and to the Wesley brothers. Fortunately, Shoreham lay near one of the routes on the 'Rye circuit' radiating out from London that John Wesley used for preaching, counselling and organizing.[18] John and Charles were able to drop in to seek Perronet's advice, whether on the rules governing itinerant preachers or on such personal questions as marriage or the resolution of a quarrel between John and Charles. Vincent Perronet became over the years a source of strength and advice, to the extent that the Wesleys called him the Archbishop of Methodism.

In replying to Archbishop Secker's Questionnaire in 1758[19] he stated that there were no dissenters, no Quakers and only one Baptist in the parish; he firmly placed Methodism within the Church itself. He set an extremely high standard for his parish to follow: 'the meanest from any place is welcome to join at my house in family devotion' and in the church itself

> public service is duly performed twice every Lord's Day . . . and a sermon preached. There are prayers on all holidays: twice a week in Lent and every day in Passion week and a sermon on Good Friday . . . The sacrament of the Lord's Supper is administered twelve times a year

(a remarkable number considering the general neglect of Communion in the eighteenth century), with about forty communicants. He was quite prepared to confront the higher ranks: 'One gentleman that comes down to his house in the sporting seasons seldom makes his appearance at church and though I have told him how unbecoming and fatal his example is, my remonstrancies have had no good effect.'

What more natural for this Anglican clergyman who believed in the Evangelical Revival than to invite the Wesley brothers to preach in church on Sunday, and occasionally in his kitchen on Friday evenings? On the first occasion in 1744 when Charles Wesley began preaching in the church a riot broke out amid members of the congregation –

> the wild beasts [as Charles described them] began roaring and storming, blaspheming, ringing the bells and turning the church into a bear garden. I spoke for half-an-hour . . . the rioters followed us to Mr. Perronet's house raging . . . Charles Perronet hung over me to intercept the blows.

That 'taut neurotic quality' described by Professor Plumb must have been latent in Shoreham, and the half-hour of Charles Wesley's powerful, emotional sermon unleashed the villagers' pent-up feelings. A further comment by Plumb is significant – 'It was when Wesley preached of death and hell that his roughest audiences were most prone to convulsions and hysterics'.[20]

The Wesleys broke the peace of Shoreham, and it took some time for their message to be understood and accepted. A year after the first 'riot' John Wesley had to admit 'the season of fruit is not yet'.[21] Perronet himself in 1758 reported to the Archbishop 'As to Methodists there are 5 or 6 serious people of low rank who together with my family are distinguished by that name.' However, by 5 December 1763 the tide seemed about to turn:

> I [John Wesley] preaching in the evening to a more than usually serious company. The next evening they were considerably increased. The small-pox, just broke out in the town, has made many of them thoughtful. Oh! let not the impression pass away as the morning dew![22] [Twenty-six parishioners were buried in 1763, compared with the average for the period 1761–90 of eighteen].

John Wesley, the founder of Methodism, who preached in Shoreham.

In 1776 Wesley wrote 'No society in the country grows so fast as this either in grace or numbers. A chief instrument of this glorious work is Miss Perronet, a burning and shining light.' Damaris, Perronet's 'bold, masculine minded' eldest daughter, was indeed the leader of the Methodist society in Shoreham. Two of Perronet's sons, Edward and Charles, became itinerant preachers with the Wesleys for a time, but went their separate ways because John Wesley would not tolerate their independent attitudes. Edward was the author of the hymn *All Hail the Power of Jesus' Name*.

Vincent Perronet was indeed fortunate in possessing a steadfast and dynamic faith, for of his twelve children ten died before him, and he was long a widower, Charity dying in 1763. He was fortunate too in owning a farm near Canterbury, and was able to live in easy circumstances. Near the end of his long life yet another great test of his faith awaited him. His only grand-daughter, who alone was left to care for him in his old age, died in tragic circumstances. According to John Wesley,[23] Miss Briggs was engaged to a Mr H.:

> The time of the marriage was fixed, the ring bought; the wedding clothes were sent to her . . . He came . . . on the Wednesday, sat down carelessly on a chair and told her with great composure that he did not love her at all, therefore could not think of marrying her . . . Three or four days after, she felt a pain in her breast and in four minutes died. One of the ventricles of her heart burst — she literally died of a broken heart. When old Mr. Perronet heard that his favourite child, the stay of his old age, was dead he broke into praise and thanksgiving to God who had 'taken another of his children out of this evil world'.

Vincent Perronet lived for three years after this tragedy, dying at the age of ninety-two on 9 May 1785. Unlike some eighteenth-century parish priests who took to learning, or fox-hunting or just drink, he was an original and a radical, making an inestimable contribution to the religious life of the eighteenth and nineteenth centuries through the inspiration and guidance he gave to the Wesleys.

It was probably a deliberate decision of the Dean and Chapter of Westminster that Perronet's two successors, Charles Wake (1785-96) and William Cole DD (1796-1806), were both prebendaries of Westminster, and therefore intended to bring greater orthodoxy to the parish after the turbulence of Perronet's fifty-seven years. Charles Wake followed his example of residing 'constantly upon my cure in the vicarage house till misfortune drove me from it. My present residence (is) at Corpus Christi in Oxford'.[24] (We are spared knowledge of his 'misfortune'.) William Cole was an absentee vicar 'resident on my Cure of Croydon'.[25] Richard W. Wood, the curate who was also responsible for Otford, lived in Shoreham vicarage.

Charles Wake complained to Archbishop Moore: 'The Methodist Sect had much increased of late years by the great countenance given to them by my late predecessor'. Its members were 'chiefly all the parish of the lower class'. Wake held no Sunday School — 'no children sent to me at all but chiefly instructed by the Methodist teacher'. This Methodist teacher was Samson Staniforth, who held meetings in his rooms. He was assisted in his teaching by the cobbler, William Hider. Charles Wake earnestly appealed to the Archbishop: 'I should most heartily wish your grace would put a stop to this Mr. Staniford's creeping into the habitations of the sick and with the assistance of an ignorant cobbler named Hyder (who on these occasions as well as others, passes for his clerk), praying and singing with them . . .'

Vincent Perronet had reported that there was only one Baptist in Shoreham in 1758 (p. 107). Whom he was referring to we do not know. It might have been a member of the Colgate family. Even before the Baptist Chapel at Bessels Green was built in 1716[26] meetings of Baptists had been held at John Colgate's house,

Quarnden in Brasted, and throughout the eighteenth century the Colgate family was closely involved with the Baptist Chapel at Bessels Green. In the Chapel records on 23 September 1792 and 8 May 1704 the births of Harriett and George are registered, the children of David and Mary Colgate. They were born at Shoreham Mill, where they were probably living with David's brother Robert and his family.

William Draffin, when owner of Colgates Farm, in his unpublished notes (1932), kindly shown to us by his son Desmond, records this story told to him by John Dinnis, then living at Filston. A very pious family named Colgate were farming the land surrounding Filston. They became politically involved in the stormy days of Pitt by a 'too ardent advocacy of the French Revolution' according to the *Dictionary of American Biography* and discovered that the elder brother (Robert Colgate) was about to be arrested. He journeyed with his family to Gravesend, and embarked on a sailing-ship and reached America. There were three in the family, the father, mother and son, and in the country of their adoption they started to farm, only to find after a few years that there was a flaw in the title of the land they had acquired. This meant the struggle of beginning life on another farm for the third time. The son rather than face that prospect became an apprentice in a firm of soap-makers, but soon dissatisfied with his progress he decided to find a better opening. The proprietor of the firm was so alarmed at losing such an able man that he offered him a partnership which he accepted. Thus was laid the foundation of the great commercial enterprise of the Colgates in the USA. The descendants of this young man (who still control the firm) never fail to visit Filston when they are in England. It was from one of these that Mr Dinnis obtained the story of their connection with the old place.

We know that Robert and David Colgate were occupying a property of Thomas Borrett which could well have been the mill to the south of the village in 1792 [27] and that both their names had disappeared from the land tax list for 1793. David and his family moved to Chevening to look after his ageing father,[28] and Robert and his family could indeed have left for America in 1791 or 1792.

IX
THE EIGHTEENTH CENTURY:
The rich and the poor

MENTION of Thomas Borrett must bring us back to the beginning of the century when the Borrett family came to Shoreham. Ever since he was a 23-year-old law student in 1680 John Borrett had remained close to the Honourable Society of the Inner Temple. He became an Associate in 1704 on being appointed a Protonotary of the Court of Common Pleas, and having become a Master of the Bench he was appointed a Reader within the Inn and its Treasurer in 1714. Thus in 1715 at the peak of his career he decided as did many successful men of his period to acquire a place in the country suitably close to the City of London, and he chose Shoreham. It was a happy choice, for his elder daughter Elizabeth married David Polhill four years later and came to live at Chipstead. David Polhill had by then been a Whig member of Parliament (1708-10) and High Sheriff of Kent in 1715.

In that same year John Borrett purchased from Paul D'Aranda's son the 'manors [sic] of Shoreham, Castle Farm, Preston and Filston alias Violeston' and having replaced Paul D'Aranda as the local squire he entered into the life of the village without delay. As a member of the vestry he volunteered to become with William Round a surveyor of the highways just as D'Aranda had done before him, and in 1716 he became a justice of the peace.

John Borrett evidently felt the need to dwell nearer to the heart of the village and to allow Preston to become thenceforth a rented farm. According to Hasted,[1] he set about building 'a handsome seat close to the river at the South end of the village . . . which he called New House where he was living at the time of his death on January 29 1739'. The site chosen for New House must have been that of Dibden (p 62). New House has been variously referred to as Otford Court, Shoreham Court and even, it seems, Simmers in 1781.[2] For some reason this 'elegant palladian villa' was never completed; it came to suffer from dry rot and was demolished a hundred years later.

A month before his death John Borrett drew up his will,[3] which showed him to have been a very wealthy lawyer and landowner, very conscious of his obligations to his family and those dependent on him. John, his eldest son, died

111

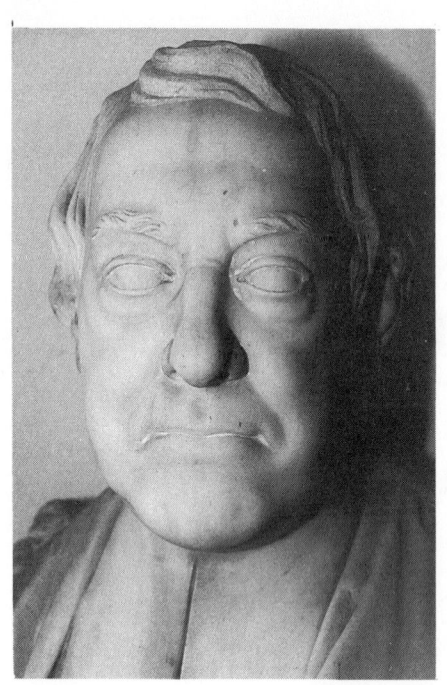

John Borrett, the builder of New House, and his wife.

before him, so his second son Thomas became his heir. He had assigned to him on his marriage the Shoreham Castle, Preston and Filston estates, and as heir he received manors and lands in Lancashire, Westmorland and Wales and a copyhold estate at Epsom. Trever, John Borrett's third son, received £2,000 (£2,000 having already been advanced to him 'in the purchase of a place of employment for him which he now enjoys'). His youngest son, Edward, inherited manors and lordships in Lancashire with £2,500 (£1,500 had already been advanced to him).

Although he left New House and its contents to Thomas, he made generous provision for his wife in monetary terms as well as property and land in London and Croydon and 'my coach with a pair of my best coach-horses, harness and furniture'. His daughters Mary and Ruth received £7,000 each (Ruth having married Sir Abraham Shard, whose elaborate memorial is to be found on the south wall of the chancel in Shoreham church). The 'maintenance and education' of David and Elizabeth Polhill's sons were well taken care of, and so were several other relations.

John Borrett had been interested in the education of poor children in Shoreham, bequeathing five pounds to be given to the schoolmaster of the Charity school on Christmas Day each year, 'so long as the Charity School shall continue', and on the same day each year five shillings was to be given to 'twelve of the poorest and most ancient men and women as do not receive Alms of the said parish'. He also increased from 2s. 4d. per month the dole paid to the three inhabitants of the almshouse in Shoreham. He finally left £100 to the vicar, Vincent 'Parron' (Perronet). He desired his body 'may be buried in the Chancell or New Vault belonging to my house at Shoreham', and today his fine Latin memorial is to be found in the Buckland Chapel.

Evidently Thomas continued his father's interest in New House and Shoreham. He bought from Charles Polhill in 1741[4] various small parcels of land already rented from him: one such 'lying at the South West end of the mansion house' the Borretts had already 'converted into a wilderness'. This was near what was called 'the lower kitchen garden', which was also close to the Borretts' 'cold bath' or bathing place. These details suggest an early development of what were to become significant elements of the Shoreham Place grounds a hundred years later. A final clause in the indenture of this sale sets out certain exceptions and reservations. As well as the not uncommon one of reserving Charles Polhill's right to fish in the river, the clause included:

> All money coin or Treasure Trove that may hereafter be found or discovered under or in all or any part of the hereby granted and released ground, land and premises, there being a tradition that one of the ancestors of the said Charles Polhill laid or concealed money or coin within or near adjoining some part of the ground . . . with free liberty and lycense for him or them to digg and seek the same . . . .

One's imagination races back to the time of the Civil War or an earlier time of civil strife when such treasure may have been buried. As far as we know that treasure, if it existed at all, has remained in the ground.

Like his father, Thomas Borrett became a justice of the peace and continued to share in the prosperity of the early eighteenth century. In 1744 he leased from Charles Polhill Esquire for 21 years with other properties 'all that messuage or farm house called . . . Pastures or Plainers together with the barns, stables' etc. etc. and its lands amounting in all to 110 acres. This is the last detailed mention we have found of Planers — the twelfth-century sub-manor given by Richard, Archbishop of Canterbury, to Ralph de Planers in 1190. Hasted, writing at the end of the century, refers to Planers as but a memory — 'the name of which is now almost unknown'.[5] It had disappeared and its site left with only the name Great House Meadow.

In that same year (1744) Thomas Borrett showed himself much concerned, as did the vicar, Vincent Perronet, and the churchwardens, for the fabric of the church which was 'much decayed and in a very ruinous condition'. A plan was drawn to pull down part and rebuild it, 'making it much more regular and hansome and convenient'. Thomas Borrett was willing to pay 'at his own proper costs' for this considerable renovation, which although approved by a commission of five local clergy and five gentlemen of the district and licensed by Archbishop John does not appear to have been implemented, as the dimensions of the church today remain as they were before 1744.[6]

Thomas Borrett died in 1751, and since he did not have a male heir his estate after his wife's death devolved upon their daughter, who had married her cousin (another Thomas Borrett, son of Trever Borrett). This second Thomas did not have the social conscience or the financial skills of his father-in-law or his grandfather, and soon found himself in financial difficulties. As early as 1788 hints of these appeared. Mr Wake reported to the Archbishop[7] — 'upon there being large arrears due from the late Thomas Borrett Esquire, the [Charity] School was not carried on' and in 1792 the schoolmaster William Pinnock retired because his salary was no longer being paid.[8]

On 13 February 1796 an indenture for the sale of the estate was drawn up as a result of the pressing demands of no less than thirty-two creditors.[9] There are no further records of the sale, so with this document the Borrett family disappear from the history of Shoreham.

Certainly landowners flourished in the eighteenth century, and so did the farmers, benefiting from the scientific advances in agriculture made by such people as Coke in soil-improvement and Bakewell in breeding cattle and sheep. At Smithfield market the average weights in 1710 and 1795 respectively were:-

Oxen 370 lb. and 800 lb.[10]
Calves 50 lb. and 150 lb.
Sheep 38 lb. and 80 lb.

With improved soil-management wheat could be grown almost anywhere in England. William Wall in Shoreham noticed at the turn of the century that farmers were grubbing up woods to the east of the river Darent in order to increase the land available for arable crops such as corn, turnips, peas and beans. Mr Wall drew the attention of the Westminster Abbey authorities to this development, and in order to compensate the vicar for his tithes on the woodland lost to tillage, the Dean and Chapter reached an agreement with the lessee of the rectory, George Ballard of the Inner Temple,[11] to pay a compensatory sum at the rate of one shilling per acre yearly for woodland thus converted. The grubbing up of woodland may have continued throughout the century because of the greater food needs of the country's increasing population and the greater demand for corn and meat for the Army. In 1726 Mr Wall reported to Westminster a further 60 acres grubbed up by five farmers.[12] There is evidence also in an agreement dated 1796 between the Dean and Chapter and Charles Polhill for the payment of a similar yearly rent of £10 to the vicar, compensating for loss of woodland tithes.

No close comparative study is possible of the late seventeenth-century parish survey with that of 1777 and that of 1806[13] but they do show that the acreage under corn remained about the same over the whole period, and likewise for peas and beans. The 1806 survey also gave the following:

312 ¾ acres of Turnips and Rape
1707¼ acres of Rye Grass, Clover and Tares
56½ acres of Hops
30 acres of Orchard

But it should be added that we have already shown the existence of hops and the grasses in the seventeenth century, and we know that at Castle Farm a map dated about 1720[14] showed two fields named 'Great Damsen Lay' and 'Little Damsen Lay'. This suggests that their 12 acres were used for damson-growing. The map also showed hops growing in the same gardens as in the 1980s. Turnips as a fodder crop were introduced about the same time, but the 30 acres of orchard/gardens points to the future development of fruit-growing in the parish.

It was a century of prosperity for the farmers and landowners. In Shoreham the surveys just mentioned show that the value of corn in 1777 had increased by 89 per cent since the late seventeenth century, and likewise the value of peas and

THE EIGHTEENTH CENTURY (2)

William Pinnocke's shop at Record, named after a previous owner in the seventeenth century. (Photo by Ian Harper)

beans had risen by 70 per cent, while that of coppice wood had more than doubled. But we shall see that corn prices at the beginning of the nineteenth century were to tumble disastrously. Meanwhile such prosperity was reflected in the lives of the shopkeepers in the village.

To meet the needs of the inhabitants of Shoreham and the surrounding district William Pinnocke ran a successful business as a mercer, keeping a well-stocked shop, almost certainly at 'Record' in Church Street. His stock in 1732 consisted of:

> 575 yards of broadcloth, Druggetts, Linseys, shalloons and sagathy; whole pieces of Fustians and dimitys; 461 ells of Dowlass; 188 yards of blue and white ruchia; 250 yards of printed linnen, printed and striped cotton and cheques; 14 ells of bagg holland; 95 yards of Irish and Scotch Cloth; brown canvass, buckram and ticken; worsted and yarn hose; men's and women's hankerchiefs, gloves and hatts and all manner of haberdashery.

In another part of the shop he sold butter and cheese and other groceries, tobacco, hops and 'sillary goods' (which may well have been high-class wine from the village of Sillary in the Champagne district of France[15]). Finally, in his hardware department there were candles, tallow and implements for making candles, turners' goods, 'hard wavelin ware' and white earthenware.

William Pinnocke was already a widower when he died in 1732[16] and he named John Russell, the papermaker at the mill, and his servant Thomas Lovell as his executors. His two young children he left 'during their minority' in the care of Elizabeth Homewood. To his son William he gave one silver cup, one silver salver, six silver spoons, four salts, one silver mug, his mother's gold wedding ring and two gold Jacobuses. To Sarah his daughter he left two large silver spoons, seven silver teaspoons and tongs, two silver salts, one small silver cup, a silver strainer and a trunk of linen and 'all her mother's things'. He arranged for his children's maintenance and education by the sale of his stock and household possessions valued at £505.

It seems probable[17] that after his death Thomas Lovell his servant remained at Record with the Pinnocke children in the care of Elizabeth Homewood.

Another shopkeeper who had prospered was William Beardsworth, whose son William Denham Beardsworth was to take over 'Record' from Thomas Lovell, and who ran a chandler's business there with his wife from 1777. The father William Beardsworth on his death in 1751 was able to leave three properties in Sevenoaks to his sister and two of his daughters, and £100 to another daughter. A satisfactory end to a profitable life.

Although landowners and farmers prospered along with lawyers, surveyors, shopkeepers and craftsmen whose services were in demand, the unskilled labourer did not. As the century wore on with advances in food-production and medicine, the population increased more and more rapidly: Shoreham in 1700 had some 400 inhabitants and in 1801 it had 828.[18] At the same time the demands for agricultural workers were decreasing because of developments in farm-management and machinery, such as the four-wheel drill plough. It was the parish vestry under the benign supervision of the justices who still had to provide relief for the increasing numbers of those in need. In the opening years of the century D'Aranda showed us the disproportionate time then spent on 'settlement' cases in Shoreham. In the closing years settlement cases were rare, and with the passing of the Gilbert Act in 1782 a new spirit of humanitarianism was introduced into Poor Relief. The Shoreham vestry conscientiously provided housing, medical attention and general care for the poor.

With parliamentary encouragement Otford and other communities had established a workhouse for the homeless in 1730-1 which during the years 1727 to 1757 effected a reduction in the poor-rate assessment of about 20 per cent.[19] and in 1756 a large workhouse had been set up at Farnborough sheltering the poor of 10 parishes including Eynsford.[20] There is some indirect evidence that earlier than 1741 the churchwardens and the overseers of the poor of the parish of Shoreham owned a house called Hunts or Tainter House which probably was used for housing the poor.[21] The absence of early vestry records prevents us from knowing the true situation. However, in the earliest extant Vestry Book the entry for 29 December 1782 reads:

> It is this day decided at a Vestry now held that the poor of this parish shall be placed as soon as conveniently can be in a house hired for that purpose of Charles Broomfield and that from henceforward no person shall be

allowed any provision out of the said house exceeding the sum of one shilling per week or on some extraordinary occasion as of infectious disorder or such like.

Two weeks later the vestry drew up the rules for the running of the workhouse under its master Charles Broomfield.[22]

The master was allowed 2s. 6d. per head per week for six months in the year and 2s. 3d. per head for the other six months, and the parish was to pay him '10 guineas per year for the use of the houses he now rents under Mr. Willmott [the mill owner].' The parish was to provide clothing and bedding for all the poor sent to the care of Charles Broomfield, who was to allow them good and sufficient meat, drink, washing and mending. The poor were to be allowed 2 pence out of every shilling they earned by their labour, the parish 2 pence more out of every shilling earned and 'Charles Broomfield shall have the full residue of the money earned'. Yarn and worsted were provided for the inmates to knit and spin. If at any time any of the poor had occasion for wine by order of the doctor it was to be paid by the parish.

Charles Broomfield was to keep proper account books, and the overseers of the parish were to inspect the workhouse once a week 'to see they have all things necessary',[23] and it appears from the absence of complaints that Charles Broomfield was a good master.

Some measure of relief outside the workhouse did continue. In October 1785, for instance, Edward Swan's boy was given a 'round frock, shoes and waistcoat.[24] Elizabeth Powsey was to have a pair of shoes and some 'linsey woolsoy'. John Piper was allowed 5s. per week during his illness.

The conditions of the poor deteriorated, and during the winter of 1787 the vestry decided they had to prosecute certain parishioners for 'pulling hedges, stealing wood, turnips and hop 'powls' '.[25] The same meeting heard complaints against the parish officers, and agreed that they should provide sufficient wood for those in real need. It was on such occasions that the vestry when the weather was cold decided to 'adjourn to the George' to continue their deliberations. In April 1797 as a temporary measure for six years another small house was rented (again from Mr Willmott of the paper-mill) to accommodate those needing care under Charles Broomfield, but in 1802[26] it was decided to bring all the accommodation together by purchasing three 'tenements and premises . . at the sum of £110' from William Jordon. These houses (now replaced by others) stood on the corner of the junction of Shoreham Street (now called the High Street) with Church Street, opposite the Cage and the row of cottages now called The Terrace.

The vestry provided medical attention for the poor both in and outside the workhouse. The first agreement recorded for a parish doctor was noted in the Vestry Book in March 1783:

> Between us the parishioners of Shoreham and Thomas Waring. To attend the poor of the parish (in and outside the workhouse) as Apothecary and Surgeon . . . for one year at £4 3s 9½d. To supply . . . with attendance and medisens [sic] all the poor . . . if thought fit objects by the church wardens and overseers of Shoreham including all sickness and lameness, natural small-pox and all exidents [sic] of all kinds.

By 1815 the fees for the doctors' services had increased more than five times, viz:

George Edwardes of Farningham should attend the poor . . . and to find them in medicine including all kinds of — small pox and venereal complaints for the sum of £23 per year . . . If sent for in cases of midwifery to charge £1 1s 0 each including all medical attendance.

The Charity School was almost certainly established in the eighteenth century. The Charity Commissioners in 1839 reported that it had been 'erected upon subscription; some subscribers of ability give 20s, some 40s per annum those that have children give more than their teaching would come to, so that the poor may be taught gratis, who are generally about 25'[27] Charles Seymour in 1776 referred to the school teaching 'what is needful to qualify them [the children] for trade and service.'[28] At that date this probably meant reading, writing and arithmetic. Mr Borrett appears to have been the main subscriber, and as already mentioned he directed his heirs to continue paying the schoolmaster £5 per annum (which unfortunately Thomas his grandson failed to do). The Charity Commissioners added that there had been 'no free school since Pinnocke gave up the situation'. Charles Wake the vicar in 1788 added 'Tho' we have 5 or 6 little schools [dame schools, presumably]; yet we have not had, for some years, a voluntary Charity School. What we formerly had — the perverseness of some and the weakness of others brought to nothing.'[29]

Because no rate books survive, no evaluation of the actual cost to the parish of Poor Relief is possible, although the Vestry Book does give the estimate of the cost at any given time and their poor-rate assessment. These represent the hoped-for levy. What was actually collected remains unknown. Assessments were made generally twice in the year, and to begin with in 1783 averaged 3s. in the pound, increasing to 6s. in 1810 but with an exceptional peak in 1801 of an 8s. 6d. assessment made three times in the year. Only in 1833 and 1834 was 8s. reached again, after which there was a steady falling off. This decrease probably resulted in part from setting up the new Union Workhouse at Sevenoaks (about which more will be said later) and in part as a result of the Poor Law Reform Act, which abolished the subsidizing of low wages from the rates and compelled farmers to pay an adequate wage.

The condition of the unskilled labourers and their families might have been worse in Shoreham had not the paper-mill existed to provide alternative employment to work on the farms.

The paper-mill under its founder Alexander Russell continued production successfully throughout the century. Alexander handed over to his brother John in 1728. Nine years later, in 1737, the only other family to own and manage it during its 250-year history took over when William Willmott bought the firm. His son William handed on the mill to Thomas Willmott towards the end of the century.

Thomas was already well established in the village and a member of the vestry by 1783, when he was able to provide houses for the workhouse. The paper-mill and its owner were prospering. Thomas was described as a master paper-maker at a meeting of paper-makers of Kent and Surrey in 1801, and in that same year he was awarded a 20 guinea prize by the Society of Arts for some paper made from jute. One gets the impression that Thomas Willmott was a very busy man, always in a hurry. On one occasion he drove his chaise into the bridge and removed a large corner-stone.[30]

In 1804 when he was one of the Surveyors of the Shoreham highways, having repaired 'the footpath through his meadow leading from the town to his mill' he appears to have confused parish funds with his own, because the vestry was required to mediate between the parishioners in general and the surveyors and 'Mr. Thomas Willmott in particular'. George Brooker, one of the major landowners at the time, and Richard Squib were deputed to tell him that 'if he will deduct the expense incurred . . . the parishioners will drop all proceedings, if not, they are determined to settle the business by due course of law'. Fortunately, Mr Willmott evidently put matters to right and no proceedings followed.[31]

One imaginative son of Shoreham was baptized in the church on 11 February 1759. There were several branches of the Medhurst family in the district; George was the son of George and Anne Medhurst, whose family had been in Shoreham for a century and were close friends of the Rounds. George had an inventive mind that had been fired by the Industrial Revolution, and he was fascinated by the possibilities of using compressed air as a source of motive power. He was brought up as a clockmaker, but his business in Clerkenwell was ruined by a duty imposed on clocks in 1797. He then started as an engineer, and two years later patented a wind mill for compressing air. Within a year he had developed his ideas further, describing in the patent of his 'Aeolian engine' (1800) how carriages could be driven by compressed air contained in a reservoir underneath the vehicle. He next patented a 'compound crank' for converting rotary into rectilinear motion.

By this time he was established as a machinist and ironfounder in Denmark Street, Soho, and turned his attention to weighing machines and scales, inventing the 'equal balance weighing machine' and those scales used for the next 150 years or more in retail shops.

Meanwhile his preoccupation with the use of compressed air continued, and he was the first to suggest 'A New Method of Conveying letters and Goods with great certainty and Rapidity': small parcels and letters to go in tubes by compressed air and heavy goods up to a ton and a half, through brick tunnels which the carriage just fitted. He worked on and in 1812 published *Calculations and Remarks tending to prove the Practicability, Effects and Advantages of a Plan for the Rapid Conveyance of Passengers upon an Iron Railway, through a tube of Thirty Feet in Area*' — average speeds of fifty miles an hour might be achieved, and the cost of conveying passengers might be a farthing a mile and goods a penny per ton per mile. He even hinted at the possibility of driving a carriage on rails in the open air by means of a piston in a continuous tube between the rails. This was long afterwards known as the Atmospheric Railway. Although he had a very clear conception of the conditions required for atmospheric propulsion, he does not appear to have had the opportunity of putting any of his schemes into practice. The first steam railway between Stockton and Darlington was run in 1825, and George Medhurst was still developing his ideas when he died in 1827 and was buried in Shoreham.[32]

Let us end this chapter with a picture of life in the parish as seen through the diary of William Danks, a farmer in his forties who worked some 50 to 60 acres at Eastdown above Magpie Bottom with his brother Thomas who was two years younger. His mother Henrietta Danks owned the farm which was valued at '£10½' for tax purposes.[33] All three lived there from 1800 to 1811.

He recorded in detail the taxes, rates and tithes paid. Down in Shoreham one day he called at the George Inn and gave to John Day the innkeeper's son 'two one pound notes one (Bank of) Tonbridge and one (Bank of) England' to pass on to George Brooker the church-warden in payment of his tithe. 'He gave me change five shillings, a half crown piece and 2 shillings and sixpence.' Two months later he handed to Mr Relph from Kemsing (where they also owned some land) 10s. poor rate and 2s. which appears to have been late payment of a tithe. A month later Mr Relph appeared again when William was working in the corner of their wheat-field and 'asked about the hop-poles that I had sold to Mr Taylor'. So William took the opportunity of paying him a further 10s. poor rate. Two days passed and William 'paid Russell (for Shoreham parish) £1 4s. 7½d. for the land and cess rate tax' and on the same day he paid Thomas Bennett £1 for land tax 'for Kemsing'. This was in April, a favourite time for tax-gathering. After that he had some respite until in December he paid John Martin 2s. 6d. for Highways 'when he came to ask about the turnips'. No one liked paying taxes, and there is a veiled criticism of the parish authorities when he wrote — 'in the year 1805 Shoreham Parish desired us to brush our hedges as far as they went by the road side and afterwards came in the same year and demanded twelve shillings for the Highway money — Thomas Kebble surveyor.' He does not mention the church rate of nine pence in the pound levied in that year to repay the £100 borrowed to repair the steeple and other repairs to Shoreham Church[34].

The main crops raised on the Danks' farm were wheat, barley, oats, grasses (sanfoin and trayfoin) and clover. There were also peas, broad beans (long pod), turnips and potatoes. Fruit grown by them included apples (Flanders pippins and Bolton greens), blackcurrants, damsons and Round Margate plums. They also grew hops down at Kemsing (a crop of 137 bushels in 1806).

Apart from their horses, livestock was limited to keeping lambs. They did a regular 'keeping of lambs' for Mr Love, who since about 1785 had been farming Filston with his two daughters: the practice being for the Danks to receive in August '60 lambs to keep at 4 shillings a score a week' grazing and caring for them until February or March of the following year when they were returned to Filston — they 'went away the 12th day of February 1810 Kept them 26 weeks — money £15. 12. 0.' They probably did the same for a Mr Kinnard of Offham — 'we started with the lambs a little before 8 o'clock a Thursday morning April 16 1807 from our house and got to Ofham (sic) about a quarter past 12 o'clock, so we was about 4 hours and a half a going with the lambs.'

They rotated their crops conscientiously—

> memorandum of the time our sanfoin lays was broken: Bottomfield was broke up in 1803 and sow'd with peas that year and had a good price and fallowed in 1804. February 1804 Hatry fro (another field) broke up and sow'd Barnfield with Black Oats, sow'd a sack on an acre, 14 bushells of seed . . . the first Black Oats we ever sow'd.

Having 'sturred Barnfield sufficiently', William notes 'one days work Dung cart in Barnfield 4 horses and 36 or 37 loads' in preparation for the turnip crop. Just as carefully he records the harvesting of their crops.

Unfortunately, during the harvesting he had an accident: 'I cutt my hand very much a Riping [reaping] in Redcroft. Mr Richards at Seal doctored it. I went to him to and fro for 3 weeks'. The same Mr Richards had been contracted by the vestry to attend the poor of the parish as Surgeon and Apothecary in 1789.

They sold most crops locally. For example, Richard Venner the baker at Shoreham bought 'Eight Quarters at 84 shillings a quarter'. Thomas Luck their neighbour at Romney Street bought a 'load and a half of sanfoin and trayfoin Hay – £8. 12. 6' and on 20 April 1810 William 'received of Mr. Glover at Asten [now Austin] Lodge the sum of five pounds on account of turnips in Great Harebush (field) – the purchase was 5 guineas so there is 5 shillings to come to Mrs Danks'. Only on one occasion did Mrs Danks take a crop of Longpod beans to Dartford. A valuable crop was timber, mainly elm and oak. In January 1806 Mr Martin of Kemsing bought 5 elms at one pound a piece 'by the lump'. Mr Martin was a prompt payer, and William on receiving the five pounds writes regretfully 'forc'd to deduct 2s 6d to him for ready money and a pot of beer'.

Shopping expeditions to Sevenoaks are recorded: 14.5.1806 'Bought a flannell waistcoat for Thos. Danks'; 14.1.1809 'I had a waistcoat of Mr. Turner, taylor at Sevenoaks price eleven shillings'. Satisfied with the quality, he 'bought Thos. a coat and waistcoat from Thos. Turners, Sevenoaks Price £4. 2. 6 superfine I suppose.' Two months later 'I bought a watch for Thos at £3. 3. 0 . . . the makers name Northey, Spitalfields No. 1123'. After that economies followed: on 16 October 1810 'I bought a second hand pair of leather briches at Mrs Cronks at Sevenoaks, price 14 shillings.'

Their boots, half-boots, shoes and slippers they took to William Hider the cobbler for mending, and new ones they bought from John Hartrup the shoemaker, both in Shoreham.

A big event occurred in the winter of 1806: the parliamentary election. 'Mr. Dyke [probably Thomas Dyke Esquire] came to us as we were cleaning some wheat and asked for our votes in interest of Sir Edward Knatchbull. Mr. Honeywood, Sir Edward Knatchbull and Sir William Gary putts up.' The election was the occasion for a real outing –

> 11.11.1806 We went to Maidstone to pole in interest of Capt. Honeywood. I went in Waterses caryvan and Thos. in Everest's cart and both came back in cart again . . . nine of us dinnered at the Bell Maidstone and we had three bottles of wine and the Reconing came to £2. 9. 6. Mr. Everest paid expenses and so forth.

The election result got a very brief mention – 'Gary soon throwd up, so Sir Edward and Honeywood came in'.

On 23 November 1806 there must have been a west wind blowing because William noticed 'they were Chiming at Shoreham for churching about half past 10 o'clock in the morning', and although he did not on that occasion feel called to prayer, he was interested in reading and showed real enthusiasm for one particular book – 'a fine book the title The Christian Mans Calling by George Swinnock'. He mentioned a day when the curate, Mr Hood, called with six books for the family – 'short sermons, Bristol in Taxham, two Prayer Books, a prayer for each day, one morning and one evening, 3 blew covered ones, one is Husbandry Improved, the other is the Farmers Guide and the other is Pastoral Advice'.

At the beginning of Chapter VIII we quoted William's entries about the militia and the war against 'Buonaparte'. It was a time of violent discontent against the Government and its repressive measures. William clearly followed events in the newspapers with interest, because on 6.4.1810 he notes – 'Sir Francis Burdett put in Tower for putting his speach (made in parliament) in the paper which was thought against the Government I suppose'. Sir Francis Burdett, fighting for parliamentary reform, individual freedom and freedom of

SHOREHAM

Riverside House, built in 1774–75 by Robert Streatfield, saddler and collarmaker. (Drawing by Richard Reid)

publicity and printing, stirred many a heart, including that of William Danks when with London guarded by the Brigade of Guards and artillery he was imprisoned for several weeks.[35]

Before leaving the eighteenth century and the opening years of the nineteenth the traveller through time should note changes in the visual scene at Shoreham, where brick and tile were taking over from timber and thatch. Some of the earliest building or rebuilding of this period was on the dwellings close to the churchyard gate and opposite the George Inn (now known as Nos 1 and 2 Church Street); a street, by the way, which was then called Shoreham Street that wound right through the village and included the present High Street. Those semi-detached cottages were built some time before 1710 and No 3[36] was added at the end of the eighteenth century.

The sharp-eyed traveller coming down 'Shoreham Street' from the church might notice a brick incised TR 1738 on the wall above the imposing shop-front of the house — even then probably known as Record after an earlier owner of the property called Christopher Rackard or Rickord. The house was built on the site of an older dwelling.[37]

There is a close similarity in its eighteenth-century construction to that of the rather more elegant Riverside House. It was built in 1774-5, and its Georgian style was a marked contrast to the humble cottages clustering near the bridge. The house was built by Robert Streatfield, a saddler and collarmaker who had his workshop on the right side of the ground floor with his living quarters on the left side and on the first floor.[38] The horses when brought for fittings of collars and other harness came round to the yard beside the workshop, possibly after calling at the blacksmith who still worked at his smithy where now stand the door to Pentangle and the gate to The Eyot.

Between the smithy and the George Inn there was still a row of cottages opposite Record, and looking between them one could glimpse New House, the Palladian villa on the river's edge built early in the eighteenth century by John Borrett, with one or two other cottages nearby.

Beyond Riverside House and standing back from the river behind the cottages near the bridge the mid-fifteenth-century hall house now known as Nos 1-5 Chapel Alley Cottages underwent considerable changes in the eighteenth century. Although No 1 was still showing its timber frame, today's Nos 2 and 3 were given a wholly mid-eighteenth-century brick front (one of its bricks was incised 1764). The southern section of No 3 was in fact totally rebuilt in the eighteenth century, with further building about 1859.[39]

A brick near the back door of Water House has incised upon it WH 1704, which has generally been accepted as the possible date of its construction. Water House was a humbler-looking dwelling then, with no late Georgian façade, only single windows to each room and no windows at all on the west and east walls. Water House in 1800 was bought by a carpenter, Benjamin Russell, who altered it extensively and divided it into two separate dwellings, in one of which he lived.[40]

Over the bridge to the west of the Darent ancient Balsattes (now Reedbeds) was given a new look — an eighteenth-century brick façade with typical dentilling under the eves, its eastern corner clearly showing the jettying of its timber frame.

Farther along 'Shoreham Street' there are late eighteenth-century or early nineteenth-century alterations: Friars and Pilgrims was converted to three dwellings. Extensive brick cladding was applied to Walnut Tree Cottages, and probably to Winslade. Beyond Winslade on the same side of Shoreham Street, Forge Cottage may have been built early in the eighteenth century, although we have as yet found no authoritative dating of the building.

Lack of church records prevents us from giving details of the disastrous fire which destroyed the Shoreham church tower in 1774, but it seems firmly established that the building of the present tower in flint and brick was completed in 1775.[41]

X

THE NINETEENTH CENTURY (1)

WITH the break-up of the Borretts' estate one of their distant relations, Sir Walter Stirling, was attracted by the properties available in Shoreham, and in September 1805 he and his wife Suzannah decided to make the cottages (now known as Shoreham House) behind the George Inn their home rather than New House, which he had already acquired but never occupied. Sir Walter's plan was to extend the garden around these cottages. First he purchased the four cottages on the south side of Shoreham Street facing Record between the George and the bridge, removed the buildings and made their sites part of his 'cottage' garden. He then acquired what were called the Malthouse Cottages and other premises in Malthouse meadow which lay to the west, beyond the man-made stream that flows past Shoreham House, once more removing all the buildings. Thus what may have been thought of in ancient times as the heart of the village between the George Inn and New House was enclosed to become Sir Walter's 'pleasure garden' (to use a contemporary description).[1] It was the Gregory family who bought the property from Sir Walter and developed the Stirlings' cottages to become Shoreham House as we know it today.

Who was Sir Walter? Born in 1758 of an American mother in Philadelphia, he never forgot that his father had been offered a baronetcy at the end of a distinguished career in the Navy. The Duke of Gordon writing to a friend described him even in 1796 as 'a gentleman of independent fortune . . . whose sole ambition is to be created a baronet', and this he achieved by giving positive support to Pitt and his government as member for the pocket borough of Gatton, even inviting Pitt and the speaker of the House to dine with him in Queen Square, London. Having applied first to Pitt in 1791, he was honoured with a baronetcy in December 1800, when George Canning reported to his wife 'The fool with whom I dined yesterday gave us bad wine and a bad dinner. He is Sir Walter Stirling for whom I believe Dundas negotiated a seat in Parliament and whom Pitt had made a baronet just now and who revenges himself for both by asking me to dinner.'[2]

Having gained his baronetcy, he next became High Sheriff of Kent in 1804, and still striving for a place in Society he bought the Honor of Otford from the

Crown for £3,156.[3] With it he acquired the shadow of ancient power and eight manors including Shoreham. As 'a gentleman of independent fortune,' a partner in the bank of Hodsoll and Stirling in the Strand and Director of the Globe Insurance Co., he had no need of any manorial dues (which had in any case long fallen into disuse).[4]

Almost immediately after this purchase he suffered a grievous loss: to quote from her memorial which he erected in the Buckland Chapel of Shoreham Church 'Susannah Lady Stirling of Faskine, Lanarkshire, Shoreham Castle and the Honor of Otford, Kent . . . died 8th June 1806 in childbed in the 37th year of her age.' This tragedy did not deter Sir Walter from continuing to buy property in Shoreham, and by the following year John Ireland, the vicar, was able to report to Archbishop Manners Sutton that he was 'the principal person of the parish'. He appears to have been so distracted by his wife's death or so absorbed in buying property that he may have neglected his responsibilities as 'principal person of the parish' if one accepts the plaintive tone of his father-in-law, G.T. Goodenough, writing to Mr Claridge of Sevenoaks:

> Every time I have come to this place [Shoreham] I am attacked on the subject of the Bridge, having it is true, undertaken to obtain an order for its repair at the session in October last . . . .
> I find Sir J. Dyke has been in the habit of taking the management of this business, but he like myself is old and probably supposes it is now a duty more properly belonging to Sir W. Stirling . . .[5]

However, Sir Walter showed every sign of settling into the village when he forwarded a letter to the Dean and Chapter of Westminster. This was a message received from Mrs Polhill, giving him leave to occupy 'the vacant space left in the gallery of Shoreham Church in Kent' and asking for the Dean and Chapters' agreement to him and his family fitting it up and using it — 'at present it is totally useless to anyone'[6] was his comment. The gallery referred to must at this time have been the converted rood loft. Over the years the loft had been used for storing parish bows and arrows, ladders, or housing a small organ and providing space for the choir. It had then been made into an 'eastern gallery'[7] and used as a family pew, and the worshippers there were said to be 'going up to their rooms'.[8]

About the time of Lady Stirling's death Sir Walter was approached by one of his tenants, Richard Frederic Thompson, whose London address was 109 Pall Mall. Thompson suggested that a turnpike road running straight down from the Otford-Eynsford road over Shoreham Bridge through the village and on to Green Street Green, Farnborough, Bromley and the west would benefit the parish and those travelling from Kemsing and places farther east.

W.H. Ireland's comment in his *History of the County of Kent* is relevant here:

> The high road from Dartford through Farningham and Eynsford towards Sevenoaks runs along the hill on the Eastern side of this parish about a ¼ mile from the village of Shoreham, which having no high road of any public description, is but little frequented by travellers and the Turnpike road being wholly chalk and stones is by no means pleasant for travelling.

Sir Walter at first was not impressed by Thompson's suggestion. There was some local support from Benjamin Russell, the owner of Water House; from William Round, Stirling's tenant farmer of Holly Place; from Michael Coxon, another tenant, and from Henry Wilmot of the paper-mill, who used the road through Green Street Green to Bromley and London for bringing his wagon-loads of rags to the mill for pulping, and for taking the finished paper back to the capital. He knew well that the road was narrow and twisting, 'flinty and clayey'[9] and terrible in winter.

Two years later Sir Walter — now MP for St Ives — decided to support the project, and contributed £1,000, while R.F. Thompson acted as agent to see the Shoreham Turnpike Bill through Parliament. The Act received the Royal Assent on 21 March 1810. Two months later at the King's Head (now the King's Arms) on 14 May 1810 a meeting was held of the thirty trustees of the Turnpike Road, who apart from twelve friends of Sir Walter were mainly country gentlemen of Kent. After a statement by George Polhill Esquire and Sir Walter's reply the trustees were 'unanimously of the opinion that application should be made to Parliament for the repeal of the bill'.[10] What happened to cause this sudden turn-about?

The plan (see overleaf) was to make a 60-foot-wide cut straight from the Otford-Eynsford road to the bridge over the Darent. This cut through Mrs Nash's[11] land (between the new vicarage and the station), the tithe barn yard and the gardens of James Martin's house (now Church House), and of Barbara Beardsworth (running Record as a chandlers). These three had reluctantly agreed to Sir Walter's proposals, but the Verrells of Riverside House decided not to sell the piece of their garden required. However, the critical point in the plan for Sir Walter was to obtain possession of the three small cottages immediately to the east of the bridge owned by the small free-holders William Ashdown (No 7), George Gilbert (No 8) and James Martin (No 9).

Thompson and William Round (acting for Sir Walter) tried to persuade William Ashdown to support the new road, assuring him that it 'would not meddle' with his house. When later he learned that it would in fact run right through his garden and house he agreed to the house being pulled down, provided Sir Walter 'build me one upon a spot of land that I would pitch upon'. Sir Walter turned that down and offered him £126 for his freehold cottage. However, Ashdown and his wife thought Sir Walter was 'rather imposing' and decided not to sell. James Martin, although reluctantly prepared to sell some of his garden and orchard, was not prepared to sell his cottage by the bridge because Mrs Martin was planning to have it as her 'dower house' when the time came. Meanwhile it was occupied by Thomas Booker, Martin's son-in-law (a day labourer) and his wife, who kept a shop there selling 'a little tea, sugar, sweetmeats, gingerbred and apples'. George Gilbert owned and occupied the middle cottage, and on 20 February 1810 (only a month before the Turnpike Bill received the Royal Assent) put his mark to an agreement drafted by William Round for Sir Walter 'to take it down and build it up for me at another convenient place' with a little more garden. Benjamin Russell drew a plan of the old cottage and then pulled it down, leaving Martin's and Ashdown's cottages 'open to the weather'. Gilbert, however, after making the agreement discussed it with his employer William Everest and his friend Thomas Selby (one of the leading farmers of Otford), and they were on their way up Shoreham Street 'to make terms for Gilbert with Sir Walter' when they met George Polhill. He was astonished to learn their purpose.

Why such astonishment? At a private meeting on 27 February 1810 held at Sir Edward Knatchbull's house in Wimpole Street, London (Sir Edward was one of the MPs for Kent) George Polhill produced a plan of the 'new cut' and said 'the

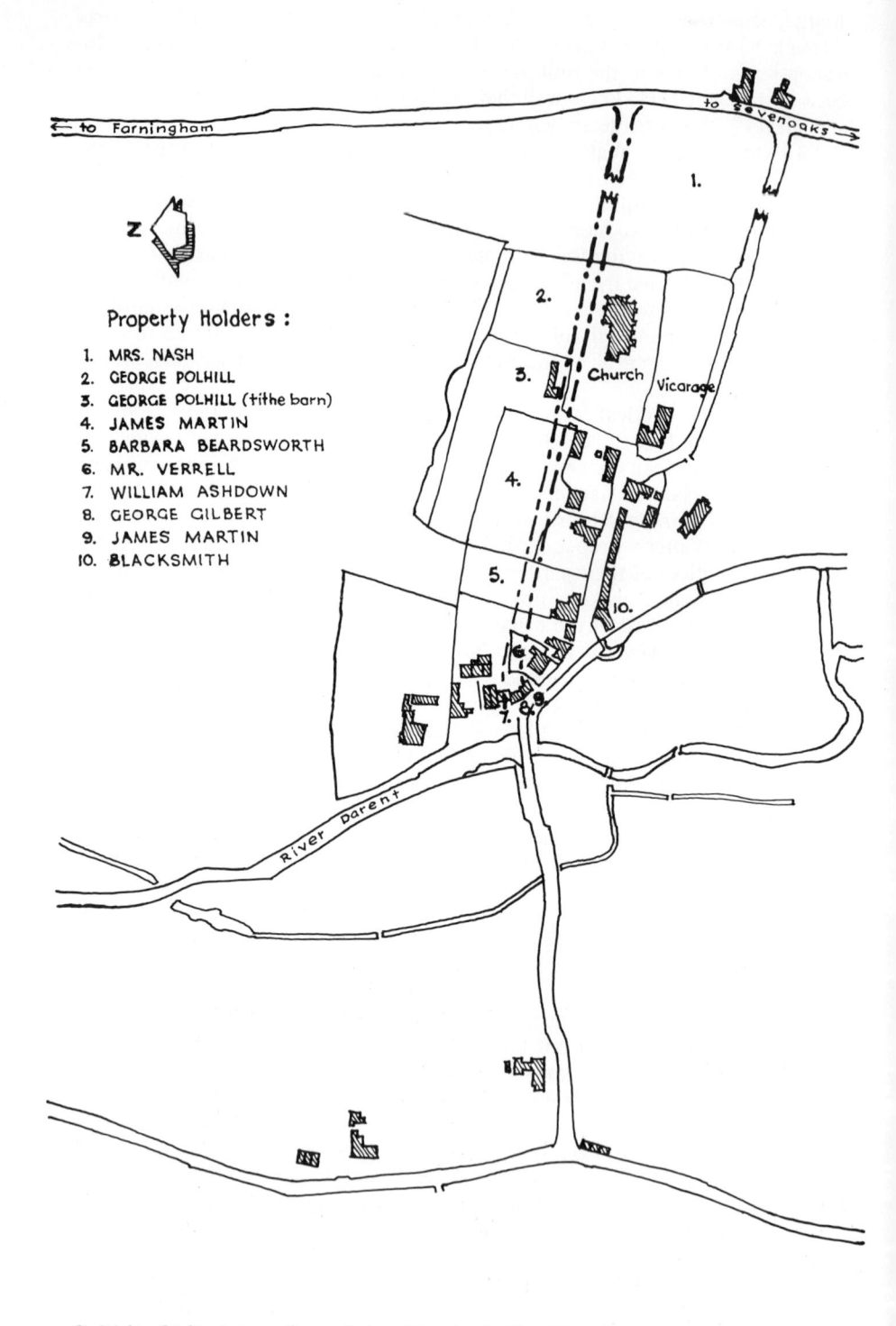

SHOREHAM

Property Holders:
1. MRS. NASH
2. GEORGE POLHILL
3. GEORGE POLHILL (tithe barn)
4. JAMES MARTIN
5. BARBARA BEARDSWORTH
6. MR. VERRELL
7. WILLIAM ASHDOWN
8. GEORGE GILBERT
9. JAMES MARTIN
10. BLACKSMITH

Sir Walter Stirling's turnpike road plan. (Drawing by Ken Wilson) first grounds of objection (to the turnpike scheme) were three cottages belonging to persons of the name of Ashdown, Gilbert and Martin'. Questioned by Sir Edward, 'Sir Walter (who was present) directly put his hand upon the spot on the plan and said "they are mine now, Sir Edward"'. Admittedly he had received Gilbert's agreement a week earlier, but he certainly did not own Ashdown's or Martin's cottage.

When George Polhill (an independent-minded magistrate) met Everest, Gilbert and Selby and learned the situation he joined them and found Sir Walter standing by the river near New House. When challenged on his ownership of the three cottages he flew into a temper and attacked Polhill for 'interfering in matters that did not concern him'. In his anger he had overlooked Polhill's interest as lessee of the Shoreham Rectory and owner of over 500 acres in Shoreham. He later apologized and admitted the truth.

George Polhill, following the long tradition of his family in looking after the interests of the 'small free-holders', had joined the Turnpike Trustees when he believed that Sir Walter had gained control of the situation in order to obtain the best possible conditions for those affected by the 'new cut'. On realizing the true situation he immediately set about arranging for the repeal of the Act. A House of Commons inquiry was set up under Sir Edward Knatchbull which found that Thompson had not given proper notice of the scheme to the gentlemen of the county, the property-owners or the parish authorities, and established that the great majority of those concerned saw 'no utility' to the district in the scheme. The Act was repealed in 1811, leaving the village scarred but not irremediably.

Today the roof-line of the houses facing the bridge is a broken one because Gilbert's cottage was removed while Ashdown's and Martin's remained standing.[12]

In 1834 the extreme western portion of the parish was surveyed for 'The proposed diversion of the Sevenoaks Turnpike Road',[13] and in due course this section of the modern A21 Hastings Road was constructed. George Polhill owned part of the land through which it passed, and because of this the hill down the escarpment was given the name Polhill. The old route had run through Knockholt and down the notoriously difficult Star Hill to Dunton Green. The new section was not necessarily shorter but avoided Star Hill. For Shoreham it provided much easier access to the London Road; the old route through Chelsfield was no longer needed.

Although by his actions and deceptions Sir Walter lost the respect of the gentlemen of the county and the affections of the inhabitants of Shoreham, he continued to add properties to his estates in the parish, and was still the leading landowner in 1824.[14] In that year Alexander Baring, a banker in the City of London, had already acquired Filston and eight other properties and continued to buy up property when Sir Walter decided to withdraw from Shoreham. By 1835 Alexander Baring (now Lord Ashburton) had acquired twenty-four properties.[15] Sir Walter died in 1832.

How very different was another person who came to live in Shoreham for a while! In 1824 a young lad of nineteen, Samuel Palmer, came to Shoreham from London, since he needed fresh country air to recover from illness. He came with his cousin Frederick Tatham, who (like him) was an art student. They were followed shortly afterwards by his father, young brother William and Mary Ward, their old nurse. His father may have known Shoreham when his relation Charles Wake was vicar in 1785/6. Samuel Palmer was showing great promise as an artist; already at the age of thirteen he had had three pictures accepted for exhibition at the Royal Academy and two at the British Institution. As a student at the Royal Academy School in 1823 he met John Linnell, an artist older than himself and who compared with Palmer had his feet firmly on the ground. Palmer accepted him as his mentor.

Soon after they had met John Linnell introduced Palmer to William Blake, who was much impressed by the young student, and for Palmer it was an awe-inspiring moment in his life.

Palmer had been educated at home by his father, a devout Baptist and a bookseller, keener on reading his books than selling them. Blake personified all that Palmer was searching after in art, literature and religion.

At the Royal Academy School he found himself one of a group of friends revelling in the flood-tide of youthful enthusiasm for new ideas and experience who were creating an idyllic vision of a new world. It was a world in which art and religion were fused, to bring a new order and perception into the lives of men. They dubbed themselves 'The Ancients' because of the frequency with which they referred to ancient philosophers, artists and musicians.

The fertile abundance of Shoreham's fields, woods, orchards and flocks, the dramatic perspectives in its surrounding hills and valleys, the constant variety and at times astonishing brilliance of colour and light seen in and around the village fired Palmer's imagination, and induced the most creative period in his career. It was a career, moreover, which in the twentieth century was to be recognized as that of a genius. Shoreham for Palmer had become a valley of vision, where *The Pear Tree, The Shoreham Garden, The Yellow Twilight* and *The Magic Apple Tree* were to be created over a period of eight years. In later life he recalled 'there [in Shoreham] sometimes by ourselves and some time with friends of congenial taste in literature and art and ancient music, (we) wiled away the hours and a small independence made me heedless for the time of further gain . . .'.[16] The small independence came from a legacy from his grandfather William Giles [a banker] of £3,000. With part of this Palmer bought 5 cottages and gardens, one of which was on the site of the present Myrtle Cottage in Church Street. The rents for each of these averaging £1 5s. per annum[17] gave him a tiny income for meeting his simple needs. He once asserted 'a person living as an epic poet should be able to exist on 5s. 2d. per week.'[18]

The Palmer family and friends probably lived in 1826 in what is now known as Ivy Cottage in Church Street. William Blake visited them there shortly before he died, and Samuel Palmer had to sleep out nearby at Mr Gregory's the baker's (possibly at Chapel Alley Cottages). George Richmond, one of the 'ancients', in later life suggested that the encounter with this youthful group may have inspired Blake to write the lines:

> And by came an angel with a bright key
> He opened the coffins and set them all free
> And down the green plains leaping they run
> And washed in the river and shine in the sun.[19]

The 'ancients' did indeed swim in the Darent, especially after the Palmers moved late in 1827 into part of Water House, which at that time had no high wall separating it from the river.

The inhabitants of Shoreham were understandably puzzled by this group of ebullient youths singing together in a deserted chalk-pit in the stillness of the

Self-portrait by Samuel Palmer, 1828. (Ashmolean Museum)

evening; improvising a tragic drama in a dark lane, or striding the hills to some distant village at night to see the dawn. Because of their night wanderings the villagers thought they must be 'extologers' or 'astrologers'. Yet Palmer and his friends got to know their neighbours such as Arthur Tooth, the small tenant farmer with whom Frederick Tatham and he first lodged. George Richmond lodged at times with Mr and Mrs Barham, and thought Mr Barham 'a nice old labourer who had a bright and busy wife with two daughters' (one of whom became a teacher) –

Water House, Samuel Palmer's home in the 1830s. (Drawing by Richard Reid)

> my rent was two shillings a week including service. My room a spacious one with a fine bed in it . . . everything was blamelessly clean and the white curtains of the bed and at the windows gave a bright and cheerful aspect to the room, the walls of which were newly white-washed. It was believed that John Wesley had once held a little meeting in these rooms.

Richmond summed up the situation 'In time they grew to know us and we to love them'.[20]

Samuel Palmer became a very practical adviser on lodgings for his friends. He writes in haste to Richmond

> Mr. Brewer the tailor between Mr. Tooth's and the bridge has a front bedroom 3s. per week . . . Mr. Yates on the terrace road where the Clerk and Mrs. Broomfield live (fine open view) has a little front room through which he and his wife must pass to go upstairs. He has a bedstead but no bed, terms 2s. per week.

He added 'his wife goes to the mill at 7 in the morning and returns at one o'clock for an hour . . . . you might use their kitchen for cooking your breakfast'. To John Linnell he passed on information about hops from Mr Love at Filston, 'one of the best farmers hereabouts and a large grower . . . he says they will be about a shilling per pound. . . . If Mr. Frederick Tatham calls . . . in answer to a question about potatoes (tell him) that we always give 2 shillings a bushel.'[21] (the same price as William Danks at Eastdown was asking twenty years earlier). On another occasion when Linnell was planning to bring his family to stay in Shoreham he asked Palmer whether there was a suitable girl 'to attend upon our children and do other little jobs such as you have seen our Eliza do'. Palmer thought that Clarissa Tooth, aged seventeen, would be suitable, but Mr Tooth was cautious in negotiation and did not want her 'to wash dishes and be under the cook or do scullary work'. He also asked for particulars. Clarissa's last wages had been 8 guineas a year. All was satisfactorily arranged, and Palmer added the useful information that the Tonbridge coach left Charing Cross at 9 a.m. and reached Morants Court at 12 noon.

All too soon time brought changes to the 'ancients', each treading a different path. In 1829 Samuel Palmer senior was forced to return to London to seek a career opening for William, leaving Samuel at Water House with old Mary Ward to care for him. He was depressed, earning little from his paintings. He had fallen in love, possibly with one of Frederick Tatham's sisters, but his love had not been reciprocated. He may also gradually have become aware of the suffering around him, especially of the farm labourers. Famine in the Weald had forced fifty-six men and their families to emigrate to America in 1827. The harvest in 1828 was bad, and in 1829 even worse. In March 1830 George Polhill was one of fifty freeholders who called a meeting in Maidstone to petition the King on the distress in the county. In spite of — or perhaps because of — the uncertainties of the times, in that same month Palmer made a further investment in Shoreham. He leased a property called Balsatts, which by one of history's outstanding ironies was to become a century later the home of 'The Samuel Palmer School of Fine Art' founded by the Australian artist Franklin White. Balsatts, the fourteenth-century property, was to remain in the possession of Palmer, his wife and son until the end of the nineteenth century.[22]

With fighting in the streets of Paris being reported in the English radical press, the general election in 1830 created an unheard-of disturbance, with opposition candidates calling for parliamentary reform, cheap bread and the abolition of slavery. On 7 September four hundred agricultural labourers rioted at Hardres in East Kent and destroyed threshing-machines there. Threshing-machines had become for the unskilled agricultural labourer the solid symbol of the advance of the machine, and the consequent loss of work. In that same week Samuel Palmer from Water House saw fires blazing across the meadows to the west. The stacks newly harvested on Mr Love's farm at Filston had been set on fire. More stacks and outbuildings in Brasted were burnt the following week, and other fires followed in Orpington. At the same time threatening letters (signed quite often 'Captain Swing') reached the homes of unpopular people, particularly those administering the poor law, the tithes and wage levels. This violent revolt was largely spontaneous, not centrally organized, and spread through Kent to other counties. Rewards by the 'Association for the detection of Incendiaries' hastily set up by the farmers of the district at the Crown Inn, Sevenoaks, on 11 September were offered: £100 for information leading to the arrest and conviction of the incendiaries and £10 for information on the writers of threatening letters. In spite of the rewards, it was never discovered that a 'Captain Swing' existed and the collective *nom-de-guerre* appears to have been spontaneously adopted by those in revolt.[23]

The unrest continued, and Samuel Palmer, his sentimental illusions of country life broken, became actively involved in politics. In 1832, the year when the Great Reform Bill was at last passed, Palmer wrote and had printed and circulated *An Address to the Electors of West Kent* attacking the radical reforms.

'Already the fires have begun,' he wrote.

> Do you wish them to blaze once more over the Kingdom? If you do send Radicals into Parliament, make Radicals of the Poor . . . now is the time

for your last struggle! The ensuing Election is not a question of party politics much less a paltry squabble of family interest; but Existence or Annihilation to good old England.

Given the mood for change in the country, such heady rhetoric did not help the Tory candidate for West Kent, Sir William Geary, who came bottom of the poll.

In spite of the political turmoil and uncertainty about his creative powers, Palmer was producing some of his greatest work. He and John Linnell's daughter Hannah had fallen in love, but he saw that isolated in Shoreham he would never be able financially to offer her a home and a secure future, so in 1832 (drawing on his inheritance once more) he returned to London to a house near his friend Frederick Tatham, where he could increase his income by teaching art. Samuel and Hannah were married at The Court House, Marylebone, on 30 September 1837.

The Maidstone Gaol Calendar for 1833-51[24] provides a grim footnote: 'B. Skinner 44 and S. Iggledon 30 were charged on suspicion of setting fire to a certain corn stack whereby the same was burnt and destroyed at Shoreham also having conspired feloniously to set fire to certain stacks of corn belonging to S. Love the Younger (at Castle Farm) and others at Shoreham'. Skinner was also charged with stealing a purse containing 16s. 6d. from T. Wickenden, and receiving a quantity of mutton from James Atkins Esquire at Shoreham. Both were transported, Iggledon for fourteen years and Skinner for life. George Blundell was accused of having conspired to set fire to certain stacks of corn in Shoreham, but he was discharged.

It was the smallholders who ultimately had frustrated Sir Walter Stirling's plans to drive a turnpike road through the village, and even a generation later, in spite of the hard post war times they had come through, smallholders were still a group to be reckoned with in Shoreham. On Wednesday 22 July 1835 the rate-payers at a meeting at the George Inn agreed to have a general valuation of the Parish 'for the purpose of equalising the Rates . . . as many alterations and improvements have taken place' since the last valuation in April 1824. Richard Bowles, who ran the corn mill and was 'treasurer' of the vestry, proposed and the vicar Mr Robert Price seconded his proposal, to invite two competent and disinterested persons living over fifteen miles from the parish to make the survey. Mr Joseph Nash of Reigate and Mr William Taylor of Gillingham were proposed by John Tooth, and they agreed to make the assessment between September and December 1835.[25] Their survey and the census schedule for 1841[26] provide an interesting picture of the parish at the start of Queen Victoria's reign.

There had been an increase in population since 1801 of 193, Shoreham's 1,021 inhabitants lived on 5,021 acres of the parish[27] in 206 dwellings, though it was noted that some of the 645 agricultural labourers were sleeping in barns and sheds (possibly at Shepherds Barn). There were those servicing the workers of the land such as the seven blacksmiths (including Willis at Well Hill), four shoemakers, nine carpenters, wheelwrights and sawyers; Streatfield Verrells the harness-maker and Bowles the miller and his two assistants at the corn-mill; one gamekeeper responsible for pheasant-rearing in the woods on the downs west of the village. There were those whose trade depended on agriculture: Richard Squib operating the malthouse between Water House and the paper-mill; Mary

Mills and her sons running the butcher's shop at Walnut Tree Cottages and Robert Foreman the carrier. Others were serving the community as a whole. There were four bricklayers, John Griffiths the painter and glazier, Wood and Martin the two bakers, three shopkeepers, Mary Booker at the Post Office, the schoolmaster Robert Barton and the schoolmistress Sarah Barham, five publicans[28] and five beer-house keepers. A group that might be described as industrial workers were the twelve paper-makers and paper-pickers working with George Wilmot at the paper-mill and living in the parish. There were but eight persons of independent means and two old paupers.

Several of those mentioned above were also working smallholdings. George Wilmot and his wife farmed 33 acres as well as running the paper-mill, John Day ran the George Inn and farmed 13 acres; James Griffiths, who ran his paintshop probably at Balsatts, rented Timberden Field (8 acres) from Peter Pemell Ricketts. There were therefore 29 smallholdings of up to 50 acres (totalling 431 acres), only three of which were farmed by the owners.

The survey records that there were 137 'cottages', assessed at an average value of £2 14s. 8d. each. Of these 36 were owned by 17 smallholders, artisans and tradesmen. One family was outstanding for their numbers and their active lives in the parish — the Sakers, of whom we have already mentioned David senior. They provided four of the five blacksmiths in the parish, one of whom, James, married Martha the widow of Benjamin Russell, who owned and shared Water House with the Palmers. Three other Sakers were bricklayers. One of them, Robert, rented a cottage with a lime shed in his garden from George Jessup the lime burner at Otford, whose stacks like those of Love at Filston had been burned in the troubles of 1830. (This was not because he was rich and powerful but probably because he personified authority: he was borsholder for Dunton Green[29]). William Saker owned six cottages, one of which Thomas Saker ran as a beer-house. David Saker senior not only was a smith and a farmer but he played an active part in the vestry, as an overseer of the poor and for a time churchwarden. David junior was to be nominated constable in 1845. With David senior there were eight other smallholders who were members of the vestry. For example, Edward Crowhurst of Magpie Bottom was surveyor of the Highways and paid a salary of £12 per annum; James Squib, the publican of the Crown Inn and farming 13 acres, was an assessor of taxes — not an enviable position. The tenant farmers of the largest farms were in a minority on the vestry with seven members (see Appendix, Shoreham Farms 1835).

There were six holdings of between 83 and 175 acres (total 735 acres) all tenanted except for Weeks Farm, owned and farmed by John Vincent, and at the top of the pile there were 9 holdings of 250 acres and over (total 2,837 acres) of which the largest was Cockerhurst (481 acres). Only one, Colgates, was farmed by its owner Peter Pemell Ricketts. The Appendix on p. 252 gives details of the 15 holdings over 83 acres. Two landowners head the 1835 list, Lord Ashburton and Sir Percyval Hart Dyke. Lord Ashburton had stepped in to buy the larger farms when Sir Walter Stirling withdrew, while Sir Percyval's only large property was Cockerhurst, which he must have considered an appendage to Lullingstone. George Polhill of Chipstead still owned 550 acres, mainly woodland to the east and west of the valley. There was one landowner new to the parish at this time, Captain (later Admiral) James Ryder Burton, who was the maternal grandfather of a much-loved resident in the twentieth century — Lord Dunsany. Captain Burton had already acquired the Dunstall and Romney Street farms and more recently Dunstall Priory,[30] built earlier in the century to designs by Robert Lugar,[31] on land given in the fourteenth century to the Prior and Convent of Charterhouse, London. This accounts for its name, although it was never itself a priory.[32] At one time Captain Burton had tried to buy all Samuel Palmer's cottages, but had been thwarted by John Linnell.

There was no mention in the valuation of 1835 of Otford Court or Shoreham Court — the name by which Shoreham Place was known in earlier years — and it is probable that the rotting remains of New House were in that year being cleared away in preparation for the building of the new mansion farther away from the river and to the east of the old site. (The odd pieces of statuary built into the façade of Flint Cottage and the rear wall of the Old Vicarage were probably rescued at this time from the rubble of New House.) On the other hand, the 1835 valuation listed J.S. Gregory Esqre as the owner-occupier of a 'house, coach house, garden, stabling, 2 cottages and 2 meadows' in the village. The Gregory family had acquired Shoreham Cottage on 17 September 1831 from Sir Walter Stirling, who by then had withdrawn from Shoreham to the Albany, Piccadilly, London.[33] John Swarbreck Gregory's occupation of Shoreham Cottage began the association with Shoreham of three generations of a family of lawyers, all three generations providing Presidents of the Law Society. John became President in 1851, his son George Burrow Gregory followed him as President in 1875 and George's second son John Roger Burrow Gregory became President in 1930, all fully justifying that distinction by their contributions to the work of the Society and their profession. John Gregory's father Dr Gregory, Rector of West Ham, became a governor of the famous Thomas Coram's Foundling Hospital in Coram's Field, Bloomsbury, in 1801 and over the next 170 years the Gregory family provided three Treasurers for this foundation: George Burrow Gregory and his two sons George and Roger.[34] John seems to have spent an active life in Shoreham as a member of the vestry and as a vice-president of the Shoreham Amicable Benefit Society.

It was not until 28 June 1838 that the vestry decided that 'Mr. Samuel Green of Sevenoaks should be employed to value the improvements in the parish for the purpose of rating (viz) the new house in the paddock . . .' and in that year C. Greenwood included this entry in his history of Kent:[35]

> Otford Court in the parish of Shoreham, the seat of Humphrey St. John Mildmay Esq., is situated on the banks of the River Darent adjoining Shoreham Southward. This mansion has within these few years been rebuilt in the Elizabethan style and is now a very elegant residence.

XI

THE NINETEENTH CENTURY (2)

THUS began a new chapter in the history of Shoreham – a new house and a new family. A family new to Shoreham but ancient in the history of England. A member of the Mildmay family answered the call of King Stephen (1135-54) to join the Second Crusade, and from that time the family adopted its motto ALLA TA HARA which translated from the Arabic means 'God with Us'. Four hundred years later Thomas Mildmay was chosen by Henry VIII to be auditor of the Court of Augmentation, responsible for the dissolution of the monasteries, and was granted as a reward for his labours the Manor of Moulsham near Chelmsford. His son, Sir Walter Mildmay, was probably the outstanding member of the family. He was a skilful financier, who in spite of being a convinced Calvinist (but fortunately not a prominent politician) survived Queen Mary's reign and became Queen Elizabeth I's Chancellor of the Exchequer.

Sir Henry Mildmay in the seventeeth century, a very different character, ran all the risks of political prominence, and according to Clarendon was 'a great flatterer of all in authority'. He became Master of the King's Jewel House, but eventually deserted Charles I. He was appointed one of the Committee of the Commons, and as a much-esteemed convert from the royal party was allowed to retain his salary as Master of the Jewel House. His brother Anthony was governor of Carisbrooke Castle, and it was Henry – now a member of the Council of State and a commissioner of revenue – who suggested that Charles I's three younger children be kept in custody at the Castle when Charles II landed in Scotland in 1650. Henry's and Anthony's careers in national politics ended disastrously and ignominiously when at the restoration of the monarchy Henry was ordered to attend the committee set up to plan Charles II's reception. He was unable to account for the whereabouts of the Crown Plate.[1]

The Mildmays in the eighteenth century do not appear to have achieved prominence in national politics (Sir William Mildmay Bt. was Sheriff of Essex in mid-century), but the financial and administrative skills evidently remained with the family, for in September 1823 when Humphrey St John Mildmay married Anne Eugenia Baring, daughter of Alexander Baring (created Lord Ashburton in 1835), he became a partner in the financial house of Baring

Brothers. As a wedding gift her father gave them the estate in Shoreham which was described in the marriage settlement[2] as 'all land and grounds in Shoreham formerly belonging to Thomas Borrett Esq.'. The estate was to remain in the hands of the Mildmay family until 1950. The newly married couple lived to begin with in their London house in Berkeley Square, only occupying the new mansion when it was ready to receive them in 1838. Built in yellow stock brick with a purplish slated roof, it was described by the Hon. Mrs Helen Mildmay-White as 'ugly but very comfortable'. Humphrey St John Mildmay Esquire had to pay £33 18s. 3d. tax on its 122 windows (William Round at Holly Place paid £2 4s. 9d. on 12 windows).[3] The buildings now (1989) called The Farm House and The Old Dairy to the left of the drive between the Lodge and the mansion housed the carriages and the horses. The Ice House built next to it was a very necessary amenity in those days. In it was stored ice taken in winter from the pond between the river and the leat for use during the summer months. Sadly, Anne Eugenia was only able to enjoy Shoreham Place for one year, as she died in 1839.

Humphrey Mildmay soon took up the traditional responsibilities of the 'principal person' of the parish with the same enthusiasm as the Polhills, D'Aranda and the Borretts had shown. He became an active member of the vestry, and one of his first positive acts was to assist substantially in founding and building up the village school. Soon after this Humphrey Mildmay took his place on the bench as a Justice of the Peace.

In 1843 Humphrey married Marianne, daughter of Granville Harcourt Vernon MP. The land brought by the second Mrs Mildmay extended the estate from Oxbourne farm at the north end of Shoreham Street (the present High Street) to Halstead parish on the west with the addition of Colgates. Other lands mentioned in the marriage settlement[4] filled in gaps in the estate: water meadows in the village and farther south up the river towards Otford, taking in land

Shoreham Place, built in 1838 for Humphrey St J. Mildmay and his wife Anne Eugenia. (The Mildmay Collection)

previously held by the Polhills and woodland on the downs; land in Otford parish with shops and cottages in Otford village; finally land in Berkeley Square, London, was brought into the estate. Of the nineteenth century as well as of the eighteenth H.J. Habakkuk could have said 'of all the factors which contributed to the increase in the size of estates marriage was the most important'.[5] When Humphrey died in 1853 his elder son Humphrey Francis inherited the estate and in his turn became a justice.

The decision of a half-empty House of Commons in mid-1833 to vote a sum 'not exceeding £20,000 . . . for the Erection of School Houses for the education of the Poorer Classes' attracted little contemporary enthusiasm. Yet this small beginning of State interest in education together with future legislation has been described as 'the central feature of the age of reform'. The 1833 grant was made in equal parts, to the Church of England for their 'National' schools and to the Nonconformists for their 'British' schools.[6] Generally 'National' schools were built in the countryside where parson and squire held sway while British Schools were to be found in the new industrial towns. Eynsford's British School was an exception to prove the rule, and reflected the strength of the Baptist persuasion in the village.

Humphrey Mildmay's strong adherence to the Established Church ensured that Shoreham should have a National School, and he can be credited with subscribing at least half the estimated cost of the school-house and class-room (still the larger part of the present Shoreham school), for no grant was payable until this sum could be raised.[7] Mr Mildmay declared himself the new school's patron, and took responsibility for providing its first master and mistress. He chose Robert Barton, aged twenty-three, a baker from Cambridge, as Master and his wife Sarah (daughter of Edward Green, tenant farmer of Preston Farm) as Mistress, enlisting help of his friend Mr R.C. Hales of Magdalene College, Cambridge (who had recommended the Bartons), to arrange matters. Mr Mildmay interviewed them and thought that they would 'serve his purpose', emphasizing that the duties of the school would fall chiefly on the Mistress. He was somewhat taken aback by Robert Barton suggesting that they should have 'something in the shape of a "written agreement"', but Mr Hales in his letter to Barton asked him not to press the point, knowing that no 'written agreement' would be forthcoming. He nevertheless assured Barton of Mr Mildmay's wish to retain his services saying that, and 'nothing short of actual misconduct or something unbecoming would induce him to dismiss you'; besides, 'you might be sure Mr. Mildmay was anxious to keep you in your situation by the fact of his already having given orders that the tiled floor of your own room should be overlaid with wood'[8]

The letter makes clear the status of teachers at that period, as upper servants. The school was one of the first of twenty-four schools in Kent built between 1833 and 1840.[9] Clearly the Bartons proved satisfactory, because in 1846 Mr Mildmay presented a large leather-bound Bible to him with this letter:

Barton
We did not succeed last spring in finding a Book such as we wished to give you, but I hope the one Mr. Mildmay now requests you to accept will prove a useful addition to your library . . . we beg you to consider this as a testimony of our Entire Satisfaction with the zeal and fidelity with which you have discharged your duties at Shoreham.[10]

We do not know why ten years later in 1856 the Bartons left the school and Shoreham to go as free emigrants to Australia, a colony where convict transportation was not to end until January 1868. Perhaps it was the lure of gold and adventure that was attracting navvies and viscounts[11] or possibly the description of 'a fine country and a beautiful climate' (from a letter quoted by Dickens in *Household Words*[12]. But Robert Barton never forgot Shoreham. In 1877, a successful retired shopkeeper, he built himself a new house to the north of Melbourne in the colonial style. He named it Shoreham and it remained in the family until the 1950s.

There was no change to the fabric of the church during the nineteenth century until 1863, but W.P. Griffiths FSA, surveying 72 churches in Kent in the years 1838-56, has left a description of the interior of Shoreham church, which he visited in May 1843.[13] Until then no record of the gallery at the west end of the church was available, although it was common knowledge that it existed. Griffiths described the west end of the nave and south aisle as 'enclosed by modern wainscotting (panelling) above which was a gallery'. Behind the wainscotting was the stair to the gallery and space enough for a vestry room. The gallery might have been built in the Commonwealth period when it became necessary to seat as many parishioners as possible to enjoy the benefits of the sermons then much in vogue, or possibly later, to accommodate the steadily increasing population, for a notice on the wainscotting read

> This gallery was enlarged and Beautified at the sole expense of the parishioners in the year of our Lord 1841.
>
> James Clark Rout
> William Yates
> Churchwardens.

On the front of the gallery in the south aisle was painted

> John Borrett Esq., left by will an. 1736
> £3 a year to the poor of the parish for ever.

Griffith's comment on this gallery was short and blunt — 'The gallery is out of character with the church, painted oak color.' He also remarked that 'some of the pews are painted wainscot color and the font is painted in imitation veined marble'. It was placed at the west end of the nave, but stood in a pew (probably the box type) used by the baptism party, a practice common in the seventeenth and eighteenth centuries. The altar railing was of wood 'painted stone color and very plain'. 'Grafted' above the rood-screen was still the Eastern Gallery which Sir Walter Stirling may well have restored (see p. 126), for Griffiths calls it a modern gallery on the east wall of which were 'the Royal Arms of the time of Charles 2nd'. Griffiths much admired the screen (part of which was under repair leaning against the wainscotting at the west end of the nave), but was less complimentary about the altar window — it was 'unworthy of notice, a stable window'.

The pulpit and lectern were in the same positions as they are today. They would have been a familiar sight to the old eyes of Edward Medhurst (brother of George the inventor) who until he died at the age of ninety-six in 1840 had been parish clerk for sixty years. His prayer book was presented to the church by one of his successors, Samuel Cheeseman, in 1929. Edward Medhurst's son Thomas was appointed to take his place, and was given a salary of £12 a year to keep the church clean, attend to the fires, cleaning the stove and its pipes, to wash the surplices and toll the bell for all vestries.[14]

Griffiths reported on the church in the same year as Canon Edward Repton came to Shoreham as vicar (1843), replacing Robert Price, who had died the previous December. On 8 August 1845 an event took place which few parishioners can have noticed. Since 1018 Shoreham had been a peculiar of the Archbishop of Canterbury, but on that August day the special administrative relationship was ended for Shoreham and many other peculiars by an Order in Council as part of ecclesiastical reorganization. Shoreham then took its place in the diocese of Canterbury, but was transferred to the diocese of Rochester in 1905.[15]

When he came to Shoreham, Canon Repton decided to add the south wing to the vicarage in rag-stone. He had been prebendary of Westminster Abbey for five years, and was to fulfil the double duties of prebendary and vicar until his death in the village in 1860. This had advantages and disadvantages. In 1847 during a refurbishing of the Abbey this forceful and enthusiastic man was able to obtain the organ made by Christopher Schreider, the principal Abbey pulpit and part of the choir stalls which he gave as very valuable additions to Shoreham's church.

On the other hand, a certain amount of friction showed itself between the vicar and the vestry. In 1855 Canon Repton, it seems, had given permission to the Gregory family (now firmly established at Shoreham Cottage) to have alterations made to their pew. Such was the dissatisfaction of the parishioners with these alterations that it was unanimously resolved in vestry that

> the alterations already made are so unsatisfactorily finished and have been left in so unworkmanlike a manner that no further alteration shall be made in the church until the party or parties wishing to carry out and execute the same will give a sufficient guarantee to the parish that he or they will bear the whole expense of the said further contemplated alterations and that they all be done in a substantial and workmanlike manner and certified as such by some competent surveyor to be appointed by the parish authorities . . . .

A tail-piece to this minute was added as a tactful rejoinder to Canon Repton — 'It was also resolved that a copy of this resolution be sent to Mr. Repton'.[16] In the following year the vestry had to admonish Mr Repton once more for having the screen repaired without consulting the churchwardens. It may have been tiresome for a prebendary of Westminster Abbey to remember that although he had undisputed authority in the parish church over matters spiritual, it was the vestry who controlled expenditure on things material. The vestry resolution is evidence in mid-century of an increasing sensitivity of members to those items of expenditure upon the church for which a church rate could be levied by the vestry, who acted on behalf of all rate-payers living in the parish regardless of their religious denomination.

Since the Toleration Act of 1689, the number of dissenters had increased steadily in the parish. Certain of the Colgate family had been faithful supporters of the Baptists throughout the eighteenth century. Following the upheavals of John and Charles Wesley with the encouragement of the Rev. Vincent Perronet (see Chapter VIII) there had been a steady consolidation of the Methodists' position in Shoreham. On 25 February 1820 a certificate was presented to the Justices in Maidstone stating

> that the dwelling house of William Smith at Ramley [sic] Street, in the Parish of Shoreham . . . is intended and designed to be used as a place of public worship of God occasionally by a congregation of protestant dissenters from the Church of England

and William Smith, James Booker, John Wood and Robert Wigzell requested 'the same may be duly registered and recorded agreeable to an act of Parliament made on that behalf.[17]

In 1836 the Shoreham Methodists began to build their first chapel in the village. They leased for a peppercorn rent a piece of land belonging to William Groombridge and a smaller piece next to it which William Verrells, the saddler and collar-maker, and his wife had been unwilling to sell to Sir Walter Stirling for his aborted turnpike road. Of the twelve trustees named for the chapel, four came from Knockholt; two were farmers, Samuel Vaughan and Richard Groombridge; one was William Groombridge himself (described as a 'yeoman'); there were three labourers — Harry and Jessy Townsend and John Wood; the Shoreham carrier Robert Foreman; and two harness-makers, Thomas and Streatfield Verrells. The chapel was situated in an inconspicuous corner of the village behind the cottages to the east of the bridge, and next to those now called appropriately Chapel Alley Cottages. 'It was built for the use of the people called Methodists . . . in the connection established by the late Revd John Wesley'.[18] This modest chapel was to serve the Methodists for the next forty-two years until a new chapel was built in a more prominent position in the High Street.

For four years the Anglican curate, the Revd R.H. Auber, had owned and occupied Water House near the original chapel, but in 1842 he sold it (for £700) to the Revd John Briggs, the minister of the congregation of Old General Baptists at Bessels Green, so the challenge of the Non-conformists to the Established Church must have seemed to Canon Repton to be increasing when he came to Shoreham in 1843. When his successor, the Revd Lovett Cameron, took over in 1860 he expressed his certainty in a letter to the Dean of Westminster Abbey that 'dissent is rife — pervading indeed the great mass of the labouring population, but I do not despair of seeing many drawn into the fold of the church who now hold aloof from her communion'.[19] He had moved to Shoreham at the beginning of winter, but was evidently feeling more optimistic in February, as he and his family were 'beginning to feel a little settled and I am sure you will be glad to hear that the more I see of this place and its inhabitants the better I like it and them.'

Up to 1860 a barrel organ installed in the west gallery was being used instead of the organ transferred from the Abbey, which probably needed repairing (it was very completely restored in 1863). Samuel Booker, the sexton, was the last performer on this barrel organ: 'Its tunes were few and dirgeful.' Elizabeth, Lovett Cameron's daughter who played the Abbey organ from 1865 to 1888, showed a delightful sense of humour when she commented on the old barrel organ — 'we seem always to be "fainting in the sultry glebe"'.[20]

With John Gregory's death in 1860 Shoreham Cottage passed to his son George Burrow Gregory, who as Treasurer of the Coram Foundling Hospital was able to live in the Treasurers' House in London. He also had a country estate, Boarzell House in Sussex, and decided therefore not to occupy Shoreham

Cottage. In fact, the following year the vicar and his family moved into Shoreham Cottage for a while.[21] Other families were to rent it also, until Roger Gregory inherited the property and occupied it in the opening years of the twentieth century, first as a week-end house and later as his permanent home.

There was in mid-century a growing feeling of optimism among farmers and landowners. The riots of farm-labourers in the early 1830s were but a memory. The Government had taken drastic action in 1834 with the Poor Law Amendment Act to halt the increasing burden of the Poor Rates. These had previously been raised not only to meet the needs of the sick, the aged and unemployed but also to subsidize labourers' wages (a practice begun in the opening years of the Napoleonic wars) which hit farmers as rate-payers and pauperized and demoralized farm-labourers. The subsidizing of wages ceased, and although farmers had in future to pay the full market wage, demands on their pockets were reduced by the decrease in rates. The irritations of the medieval system of tithe payments to the Church were removed from farmers and landowners by the commutation of tithes to corn rents which began for Shoreham with a meeting at the George Inn of 24 May 1838[22] and was completed by 24 February 1843.[23] (The church living remained fairly constant at about £371 per annum until the end of the century.) Population pressures may also have decreased in the 1840s with the migration of farm-workers seeking work in London and farther afield in the growing industrial towns.

There was a more positive reason for optimism in the 1850s and 1860s — the Agricultural Revolution begun a century earlier was coming into its own. The countryside prospered as a result of the use of new machinery and the application of new scientific knowledge on farms. It was a time of high farming: high investment and high returns, matching the mid-Victorian economic boom. The farmers and landowners benefited, and even farm-workers' wages increased by 20 per cent to 13 or 14 shillings a week.[24] This prosperity showed itself in new building, as at Home Farm, but also in the church.

Although the parishioners assembled on 6 March 1863 were asked to consider plans for 'reseating the church',[25] in the event a great deal more was involved, and it was decided that the whole of the expense was to be paid by private subscriptions without calling upon the parish for any rate. Significantly, the vicar, Mr Lovett Cameron, agreed to guarantee the completion of the work according to the plans without any demand being made on the church rate. A committee was formed to supervise the work of Humphrey Francis Mildmay Esquire (who had inherited the estate on his father's death in 1853), the vicar and churchwardens. The reason for these special precautions was the high cost of the plans, the main element of which was the building of an entirely new vestry to the north of the chancel and east of the Buckland chapel with space enough in it for an organ chamber.

It seems reasonable to suppose that this considerable addition to the structure of the church resulted from dissatisfaction with the limited space available for a vestry beneath the gallery and the clear advantage of having the organ where it is today. In the absence of records it is also reasonable to suppose that both galleries were removed in 1863 along with the box pews, which were replaced by benches similar to those of today. In this year of renovation George Wood took over as parish clerk. He was a wonderful craftsman in wood. He had already added to the charm of the church by building the lych-gate. He then carved and built a screen — a worthy companion to the present Tudor screen. Until 1869 the large Tudor arch separating the main chancel from the south chancel, according to W.P. Griffiths had been 'filled up having only a small square headed doorway connecting the two chancels'[26] George Wood's beautiful screen opened up the arch and allowed light to stream into what must have been a dark corner of the chancel. It also provided a fine element in making what was to become the Mildmay chapel. George Wood's lych-gate may well have inspired Mrs Georgiana Mildmay, the wife of Henry Bingham Mildmay, who had inherited the Shoreham estate from his brother in 1866. Mrs Mildmay had the eye of an artist, and was a considerable painter in water-colours. She was also a pioneer photographer. The entry into the churchyard through the lych-gate needed enhancing, she thought, with a more stylish approach to the church, and so in 1867 she arranged for the building of the path in red bricks, flanked by an avenue of yew-trees leading to the south porch and continuing on to the gate in the eastern boundary of the churchyard.

Thus Shoreham, as one of the providers of food to the ever-growing capital city, shared in the prosperity of mid-Victorian England — a country whose wealth and prosperity grew with its industry and empire, and its parishioners expressed their gratitude by embellishing their church. Both Canon Repton and Mr Lovett Cameron were very much men of their time in that their sons were active in the expansion of the Empire and exploration overseas.

Canon Repton's three sons ended their days in India; Edward served in the Bengal Civil Service, Humphrey and William in the 47th and 56th Bengal Native Infantry. All three died young, and Canon Repton gave two stained-glass windows to their memory, depicting women weeping at the tomb of Lazarus. Mr Lovett Cameron gave a window in memory of his son Philip, who died in Canada aged twenty-seven.

His other son Verney had already been three years in the Royal Navy in 1860 when his family moved to Shoreham. He was then only sixteen. After serving in the Mediterranean, the East Indies and the Indian Ocean he was appointed senior lieutenant on HMS *Star* of the East African Slave Squadron, formed to frustrate Arab purchase of African slaves. There he saw at close hand the horrors of the slave trade, and this experience convinced him that its suppression could only succeed by action in the interior of Africa. His thoughts turned to the work of Dr Livingstone. In 1872 HMS *Star* was put out of commission, and Verney was appointed to the Steam Reserve in Sheerness. He was twenty-eight, and impatient for more active work. He offered his services to the Royal Geographical Society to go in search of Livingstone. He was not chosen, and bitterly disappointed he withdrew to his family home at the Vicarage in Shoreham and to prepare himself the better for Africa studied Steere's *Swahili Grammar*. The following year the Royal Geographical Society changed its mind and selected him for the second expedition to search for Livingstone.

He set out with W.E. Dillon, a naval surgeon, and Lieutenant Cecil Murphy, RA. Not long after the expedition had left Zanzibar they met Livingstone's servants bearing the dead body of their master. Verney's two companions turned back, but he continued his march and reached Ujiji on Lake Tanganyika in February 1874, where he found and sent back to England Livingstone's papers. He pressed on following the course of the Lualaba river, across the continent and reached the west coast at Benguella in November 1875.[27] In recognition of his achievement he was promoted to the rank of Commander, made a CB and received the Gold Medal of the Royal Geographical Society.[28]

These honours were no doubt enjoyed by Verney, but possibly not as much as the welcome home he received in April 1876. The train he arrived in was

The 'Spy' cartoon of Verney Lovett Cameron. (*Vanity Fair*, July 1876)

decorated with bay and laurel; at Shoreham station a band played *Hail the Conquering Hero* and George Wilmot presented him with a congratulatory address. The villagers took the horses out of the traces of the waiting carriage and themselves pulled it down the hill, preceded by the band to the church, where his father, mother and the rest of the village awaited him. The scene has been imaginatively captured in oils by Charles Cope RA on a large canvas now hanging in the church but originally commissioned by Mr Mildmay. The schoolchildren were given a two-day holiday, and after the welcome at the church athletic sports followed. In the evening the vicar was presented by his parishioners with an illuminated address on the safe return of his son.[29] In the painting Jacko, the young African who was Verney's companion on his expedition, can be seen standing by him in the carriage as they reach the church porch. Jacko had been freed by Said Ibn Salim, the Arab Governor of Unyanyembé in November 1873, and accompanied Verney on the rest of the long and difficult trek to the west coast. Jacko was so ill at one time that he had to be carried in a litter.[30] Jacko remained in Shoreham. When he was baptized on 17 March 1878 his name was given as Jack Francis, native of Ubis in Central Africa whose parents were supposed to have been killed by slave traders.[31] In 1881 he was living at the vicarage as an indoor domestic servant and according to the census return was thirty-five, unmarried and partly deaf and dumb.

Verney's restless spirit took him the following year to China for the China Inland Mission and then to the Euphrates. Finally in 1882 he accompanied Sir Richard Burton on his West African journey. The following year he married Amy, the daughter of William Morris, the poet and painter. When he was just short of his fiftieth birthday, in 1894, death came to him suddenly in this country. He was out riding to Lord Rothschild's staghounds near his home in Soulbury and was dismounting but had one foot in the stirrup when his mare was startled by a boy playing a mouth-organ. The mare returned home riderless, and Verney was discovered unconscious with a large and ugly bruise on his forehead. He did not recover. His coffin was brought by train to Shoreham for a service conducted by his father's successor, Mr Bullen. Hundreds were present at the graveside. The tattered flag (sewn from parts of the expedition's clothing as Lady Gregory reported in the 1930s) of his first African expedition rested for many years in the west end of the south aisle.

The Victorians at home were stirred by the heroic exploits of their sons in Africa, India and other corners of the Empire and they were fascinated by the writings of Sir Walter Scott, Malory's *Morte d'Arthur* and others who described in fiction and non-fiction the exploits of knights of old. This feeling found expression in 'Victorian Gothic' architecture and the display on houses of coats of arms and in churches of hatchments exhibiting family armorial bearings. It was probably in this period that one such hatchment was hung on the north wall of the nave in Shoreham church, remaining there until the early 1950s. The details of the hatchment in heraldic terms are 'Argent on a chevron azure three fishes hauriant argent. Crest: Gules and argent. Motto: Resurgam.'[32] The shield is gold-rimmed and painted silver with a blue chevron in the centre on which are three vertical silver fish, gasping for air. The crest is a right-handed mailed fist holding a scimitar.

The crest is very similar to that of Petley, but the arms are not. They belonged in fact to a family called Peniles living in Lupton, in Devon, in the reign of Henry VI (1422-1461): a family which expired with the death of an heiress in the sixteenth century. Between 1400 and 1428 there was a John Pemyll farming

THE NINETEENTH CENTURY (2)

some twenty acres in Goddeston and Timberden yokes in Shoreham (see p. 30), but from then until 1751 we have found no mention of the Pemylls. However, Peter Pemell was a member of the vestry in 1828, dying at the age of thirty-two in 1832, and his relations, the Pemell Ricketts, lived on at Colgates into the 1850s. It seems probable, therefore, that during the Victorian Gothic period the Penile arms may have been revised in favour of the Pemell family, and that it was they who placed the hatchment on the north wall of the nave.[33]

The church's tithe barn had stood for centuries in its yard just beyond a row of elms to the north-west of the church in what became the new graveyard consecrated in June 1878.[34] The function of the barn had ceased with the commutation of the tithes in 1840. There is an oblique reference to the Parsonage Barn Yard in the churchwarden's cash-book for 1861, but in the Ordnance Survey 25 in. map of 1869 there is no sign of the barn. It seems, therefore, that it disappeared between 1861 and 1869 without any record of its departure after centuries of service. Augustus Payne mentioned in 1930 two cottages standing near the tithe barn but now gone, and adds 'The incumbent still (1930) possesses right of way along Parson's Pound towards what is known as the hearse-house (now gone) and a solitary apple tree a relic of the farm adjoining the low boundary wall.'

The railway has already thrust itself into the story of Shoreham, but how and when did it get there? The 2nd of June 1862 was a special day for the village; people might have been seen walking up towards Copt Hall — not to visit the house or farm but to go to the new railway station. They were gathering on the platform to watch the special train pass through from Victoria Station in London carrying the directors of the Sevenoaks Railway Company on their way to celebrate the opening of their branch line from Swanley Junction (then called the Sevenoaks Junction) to the terminus at Bat and Ball. By a happy irony, in their haste to beat their competitors the South Eastern Railway (who were building the other line to Sevenoaks and Tonbridge through the tunnels of the North

The Kentish railway network. (R.R. Sellman, *op. cit.*)

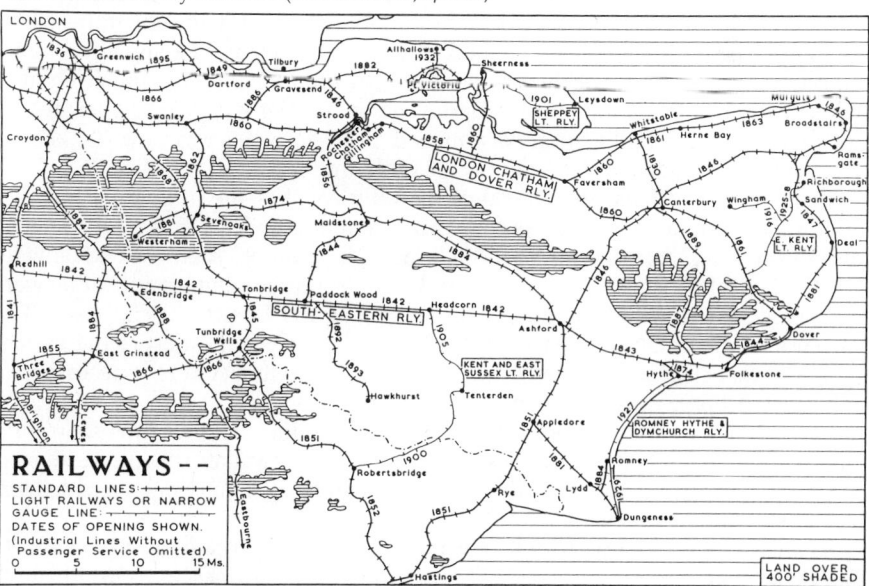

Downs), the directors of the Sevenoaks Railway Company decided to open their service with only one station ready to receive customers: the one at Shoreham, the birth-place of George Medhurst the inventor and pioneer of the atmospheric railway (see p. 119).

The building of the branch line was made possible by the completion in 1859 against all the financial odds of a line from Dover to London by the London, Chatham and Dover Railway Company. This meant that Sevenoaks was to be only eight miles down the Darent Valley from a main railway line. The nearest existing station for Sevenoaks at the time was Penshurst on the London to Folkestone Line via Croydon and Redhill. Local landowners, realizing that Sevenoaks had become somewhat isolated, were keen to see it regain its place in the world, especially as a dormitory town accessible to the city of London. The Sevenoaks Railway Company, was formed under the chairmanship of Lord Amherst following a meeting at the Crown Hotel, Sevenoaks, on 29 December 1858. Humphrey Francis Mildmay's name was not among those of the landowners attending the meeting. Since he was an invalid he was probably represented by an agent. The landowners were successful in having the track laid as close to the eastern edge of the downs as possible and parallel with the Dartford − Sevenoaks turnpike road, and running into a cutting at the point nearest to Shoreham Place. The Mildmays secured the right − of which they availed themselves from time to time − of stopping a train, even an express, on either the up or the down line. This privilege was limited to one train a day either way. The railway navigators (or 'navvies' as they were known) who were brought in to build the railway were lodged in Eynsford, where Navigators Row bears witness to their temporary presence.

After a period of uneasy co-operation with the London, Chatham and Dover Railway Co., the Sevenoaks company was absorbed by the LCDR in 1879. Their rivals, the South Eastern Railway Company were not far behind in building the more difficult extension of their line from St Johns to Tonbridge Junction. Greater difficulties were experienced than on the Swanley − Sevenoaks line, and the building of the Elmstead Woods tunnel was troublesome, as were the 80-ft Orpington embankment and the Polhill Tunnel with its 1 mile 851 yd length and five air-shafts between 122 ft and 258 ft deep. The appalling living and working conditions of the navvies building the tunnel and living at Dunton Green even brought comment by Karl Marx in his *Das Kapital*.[35] Nevertheless, by 1868 the Tubs Hill station was opened and Shoreham was now flanked by two turnpike roads, and a railway to both the east and the west.[36]

Benefits flowed from the arrival of the railways. For the individual traveller Victoria Station (as estate agents were quick to point out) was now only one hour away from Shoreham station, and the farming community soon took advantage. By 1867 oilcake, oats, hairwaste, dung, blood, manure, potatoes and stone were all being carried in bulk to and from Shoreham and Sevenoaks stations.[37] The Halstead station played its part a little later for farmers in the west of the parish.

There was clear advantage for the paper-mill. No longer was it necessary to rely on the horse-drawn wagons to bring from London the rags of which the paper was made, or to carry back the finished product. A track was soon built between the mill and the railway which is still used by walkers today. Moreover, after 1862 a faster delivery of drawing-paper and paper for books and ledgers could be offered to customers.

The George Wilmot who took over the mill in 1841 was only twenty years old but he remained in charge, taking it through its most prosperous period in 1879

THE NINETEENTH CENTURY (2)

George Wilmot, who took over the family paper-mill at the age of 20 in 1841, retiring in 1902. (R.H. de Burgh Wilmot)

when some 70 workers were employed. In 1851 he was employing 58 workers: 15 men, 29 women, 13 boys and 1 girl.[38] These workers were not only those born locally but some with special skills (such as Edward Berrey, an engineer) were attracted from East Anglia, South and South-West England.[39] According to the rules of their union, the Original Society of Paper Makers (OSPM), they were supposed to work from 6 a.m. to 3.30 p.m., Mondays to Fridays, and 6 a.m. to 12 noon on Saturday — a 53½-hour week. On the other hand, at a meeting of vat paper-makers at Maidstone in 1853 Wilmot (he seems to have dropped an 'L' and a 'T' in the course of the century) stated that the wages he paid for a ten-hour day were: a vatman 6s. 1d, a coucher 5s. 10d. and a dry worker 5d. He described the dry worker's job as an asylum for the old hands. The OSPM exacted 6s. a month of its members, but that subscription covered sick and unemployment benefit, an allowance for travel in search of work, superannuation and a funeral allowance, and even an allowance to emigrate.[40]

In the 1850s the Wilmots had a domestic staff resident at the Mill House of a cook, three housemaids and a groom. A further indication of the increasing prosperity of the paper-mill following the opening of the railway station was the fact that by 1869[41] George Wilmot had built his new house, The Mount, in a large garden above the water meadows between the mill and the churchyard, approached from Shoreham Street by a secluded drive. Yet another sign of growing local affluence was the building of Crown Road. In the 1870s and 1880s the increase in population was reaching a peak, overcrowding was considerable and new housing was needed. Although the 1869 OS map (25" to the mile) shows Crown Road only as a double pricked line without as yet any houses, already arrangements were far advanced for what was to be an uncompromising industrial housing development to accommodate the mill workers in the 1870s. By 1885 it was necessary to add a third vat at the mill to meet demand, and that at a time when English agriculture had entered a deep economic depression. Wheat in 1870-4 was selling at an average of £2.75 per quarter and in 1895-9 at £1.40 per quarter.[42] The *Sevenoaks Chronicle* of 1886 reported an unusually large number of farms becoming vacant at Michaelmas. Shoreham was fortunate in having a prosperous paper-mill.

It was fortunate also that during the prosperous times of the 1850s and 1860s the farmers had been grubbing up woodland and increasing their acreage of fruit and vegetables. The note-book of John Bowen of Timberden shows that during the spring of 1867 he carried from various coppices in the district some 36,000 poles, which from their size were most probably for use in hop gardens, and were sufficient for between 15 to 20 acres of hops.[43] Another entry for 2 March 1868 reads: 'Received from Mr. D. Foreham 1200 raspberry canes.' At Filston Farm hop-growing seems to have increased noticeably between 1869 (when the oast house had one drying kiln) and 1897 (when there were four kilns). Castle Farm also had well-established hop gardens, and other farms such as Sepham were also growing hops. Of the Blundell family, whose branches spread from West Wickham to Shoreham, two living in Chelsfield, James (born 1805) and Charles (born 1807) played their part in developing the north-west of the parish. They started fruit-growing in a small way on land rented from Sir Percyval Hart Dyke probably at Cockerhurst, and within a few years they settled in Well Hill and Halstead leasing land from the Polhills. They cleared it of rough woodland and planted thousands of strawberry plants. Eventually their successful introduction of the strawberry into the district and the growing of other fruit such as gooseberries, black and red currants and raspberries enabled them to invest in land of their own and to produce vegetables as well as fruit.

Charles's son George carried on the fruit and vegetable trade into the twentieth century. It was the enterprise of the Blundells and those like them who by diversifying their crops enabled Shoreham to ride the depression better than those in the corn-growing regions. With London always greedy for fruit and vegetables, and with the railway available to take fresh produce to the city, the orchards and market gardens flourished.[44] Charles Blundell died in 1899 in his ninety-third year. Although in 1845 two carriers of fruit and vegetables had made four journeys a week to the Queen's Head in Borough, by 1899 only one, George Blundell, continued to deliver goods once a week, on Thursdays.[45]

Two subsidiary advantages which the railway brought with it were first the telegraph which in 1878 was still at the station[46] although it had been made an integral part of the Post Office system in 1868, and secondly easier transport of coal. Isaac Loveland who ran the general stores at Lovelands (alias Record) until 1908 was also in business as 'a coal and hay merchant at the wharf on the Railway premises adjoining Shoreham station.[47]

The Post Office also improved its services during the century. In 1845, five years after the introduction of the penny post, London letters arrived by foot post from Dartford at 10.30 a.m. and were dispatched by the same route at 4 p.m. The postman had in the meantime travelled on to Sevenoaks with the mail, returning to Shoreham in the afternoon. By 1899 the Post Office was a money order and telegraph office and could provide express delivery and parcel post services, as well as being a Savings Bank, Annuity and Insurance Office.[48] Shoreham was being steadily linked into the nation's communication networks.

XII
THE NINETEENTH CENTURY (3)

AFTER Mr and Mrs Barton went to Australia in 1856 there is no record of Shoreham School's activities until 1862, and there is a further gap of thirteen years later in the century.[1] Nevertheless, a picture can be formed of its development and its place in the community, incomplete though it may be. It is known that Alfred T. White was headmaster in 1862, and his pupils numbered 87.[2]

The average age of entry in the National School seems to have been 5½ years, and about half of the children appear to have received some previous instruction at a dame school. Such a school was run almost certainly at the cottage now known as Friars and Pilgrims in the High Street. There is no evidence that it existed after 1870, when the infant school was opened in what is now (in 1989) the school dining-hall, with 75 children under Miss Booth. Entry into the infant school seems to have been at three years plus. Officially, the school-leaving age until 1893 was eleven, raised to twelve in 1899, but in Shoreham twelve had been quite a popular leaving age from about mid-century. For example, Frederick Britter, the gamekeeper's son, was admitted in February 1857 at 5 years 10 months after attending a dame school, and left in May 1864 to work at the Brickfields; Rosetta Saker, the bricklayer's daughter, was admitted in the same month after dame school and left in January 1864 to go into domestic service. Of course, some children left earlier, at eight or nine, to 'assist at harvesting' or as in the case of Jesse Harding 'to assist his father', a shepherd.

When Gilbert Yates entered the school in 1863 the fee his parents had to pay was threepence per week, and although the scale of charges was adapted to the circumstances of the parents there were always some who were reluctant to pay. In some cases children were even expelled for non-payment of fees. At the end of February 1883 the log book mentions 'school fees raised this week for all children who do not attend regularly', and a week later 'average attendance much improved'!

The Committee of the Privy Council for Education had already (1862) tightened their control of standards at State-aided schools by establishing Her

Majesty's Inspectorate. The Inspectors (HMIs) paid regular visits to Shoreham. The Government grant for 1865, which covered the headmaster's salary, pupil teachers and school materials, was £39 11s. The grant had been reduced to that sum by £10 because the HMI had refused to approve George Walker as an assistant teacher. Alfred White the headmaster appeared to satisfy the HMI in 1867, but, surprisingly, in the following year the HMI reported 'Mr White is about to leave the profession. I hope he has done his duty to the last, but appearances are against him.' The school was described as being in a very unsatisfactory state: discipline was bad, religious knowledge meagre, reading moderate, writing unsure, spelling moderate and arithmetic a total failure. The reason for Mr White's fall from grace is unknown and he lived on in the village as an overseer of the poor in 1870 and as constable in 1871.

The vicar, Mr Cameron, ran the school for the first few days of 1869 until the new headmaster, William Day, arrived. One of the first positive signs of improvement was that the most industrious pupils were encouraged by being allowed to take books home to read. During the spring Charles Potter the curate visited almost daily to teach Scripture and the catechism. William Day remained at the school for six years, and discipline gradually improved.

The Mildmays as patrons of the school always gave their support to the headmaster, as did the Gregorys at a later date. Mrs Bingham Mildmay on one occasion lent Mr Day a harmonium and provided him with a 'musical board' (possibly a blackboard lined for the writing of music) and cards and a box of chalks.

One of the problems facing the headmaster was the ratio of pupils to teachers. His wife as was customary became the needlework teacher, but in addition Mr Day had to rely on monitors to supervise classes. Monitors were selected from pupils of the first class, but few were able to maintain good discipline. Mr Day suggested that paid pupil teachers should be introduced, but Mr Cameron was against the idea, in spite of the fact that they had been employed as assistants in rural schools as early as 1849. Pupil teachers from the age of thirteen were required to serve a five-year apprenticeship, at the end of which they sat the Queen's Scholarship Examination, in order to obtain grants of £20-£25 at a teacher-training college.[3] Mr Day seems to have won over the vicar, because his son Herbert was appointed as pupil teacher to Shoreham school in 1873.

In 1872 the headmaster commented on another problem he was facing, absenteeism at the school. 'Denominational schools have no power to compel the attendance of children . . . . their fruit-picking has a demoralising effect on the children as a school [sic]. It tends to lessen the importance of education in their estimation.' On 5 October he noted 'only 5 children present this week'. Some children were absent for six months at a time. 'Surely if the government were aware of the readiness of the parents to keep their children from school for a trifle, they would extend compulsory attendance to rural districts.' The summer holiday was in some years seven weeks and in others ten depending on the seasons' harvests when the children were required by local farmers and their labourers to help 'fruiting and podding' in the mid-summer and 'hopping' in September and October. But in June 1872 a boy was kept at home to 'watch the bees', and in April 1873 three children were absent engaged in stone-picking (off the fields).

Yet attendance was important because it governed the size of the Government grant, together with the performance of pupils in examinations. A grant of 6s 6d per head was paid if a satisfactory report on children under six was furnished by the HMI. The older were grouped in six standards and tested in reading, writing and arithmetic and (for girls) plain needlework. Each child could earn a total grant of 4s for merit and attendance and 8s for a pass in the three R's; failure in the latter reduced the grant by 2s 8d.[4] On 17 January 1874 'Mr. Frank Mildmay distributed prizes to those children who had attended 250 times' (presumably during the past year).

The difficulty in budgeting for the school is made clear by comparing the HMI reports for the years 1875 and 1877. In December 1875 those presented for examination numbered 48, and of them:

Passed in Reading	47
Passed in Writing	35
Passed in Arithmetic	18
	grant £39 4s.

and the HMI report for December 1877:-

Presented for examination	72
Passed in Reading	67
Passed in Writing	56
Passed in Arithmetic	41
	grant £62 12s.

The increase in the number of children ready for examination in 1877 may in part have been due to legislation passed in 1876 which established the principle that all children up to the age of twelve should receive elementary education and Attendance Officers were appointed to whom children were reported for absenteeism. Their authority was limited, though, and the problem that deeply concerned William Day was to trouble his successor also.

The population of Shoreham had grown steadily over the past decades, and in 1871 stood at 1300. More space was needed in the school, and it was decided to build a new class-room. This gave pupils more elbow-room, but exacerbated the ever-present problem of bad lighting in the days before electricity, and when there was no gas in the village. In January 1874 the headmaster was constrained to write 'slate or paper work during the last hour is next to impossible in the middle of the room' and he found his own eyesight was also weakened. Mrs Day was now confined to her bed, and Dr Worship, the doctor for the Shoreham Amicable Benefit Society, had forbidden her to continue teaching. By March 1875 she was seriously ill and Mrs Griffiths had to take over the teaching of the needlework. Mrs Day had but a month to live, and at the end of the year Mr Day decided to resign.

His place was taken with hardly a gap by Edwin Pittman, a 'certificated teacher of the 2nd class' from Selby in Yorkshire. Mr Pittman was a teacher full of enthusiasm, and found to his surprise a great number of parents who objected to their children taking lessons home. One father, Mr Wicking, 'came to school on Tuesday in a great rage because his child was kept in to do her work'.

The performance of pupil teachers did not please him, and he noted in the log 'Matilda Webb female pupil teacher (from Crockham Hill) lacked energy, has no control over her class and no ability to teach ... higher than standard I (5 yrs.) and 'the monitors are not much use'. Matilda was replaced by William Wood (aged sixteen), a paid monitor, but he was no improvement — constantly away, very backward in teaching arithmetic and grammar and he continually struck his pupils. However, three years later in 1879 William Wood 'passed fairly' as a 5-year pupil teacher (presumably to attend training college) and was presented with 'a lever watch and chain' from the school. More reliable assistance for the headmaster arrived in 1881 in the person of Arthur Willis from Doncaster as an assistant master.

Mrs Ella Booker recalled for us the time in 1889 when at the age of three she went to the infant school. Her early teachers were Miss Santer and Ted Rickwood. After two years there Ella moved to the 'big' school (which had recently been renamed The Shoreham Parochial Mixed School) and was much scared by the headmaster John Vincent Steane, but having passed through all seven grades she left school at twelve fully appreciating his strictness and thinking him a very good teacher — a judgment given by others who had studied under him during his many years of service. Ella Booker also recalled the year 1891 because on one particular day she had been given the sixpenny piece set aside for her schooling. She had offered it as usual to the teacher, but was told that in future schooling would be free and she could keep the sixpence. The effects on the school's financial situation following the legislation making elementary education free is described later. A strong belief in discipline came naturally to John Vincent Steane, who had been a sergeant of volunteers. His appointments to be headmaster of the school and organist and choirmaster of the parish church probably came almost at the same time in 1891, and his gifts as a musician and as a teacher were to be at the service of the community for some thirty-five years, interrupted only by seven years of military service during and after the First World War.

By the end of the century there were 150 pupils on the school register with an average attendance between 95 and 120. Illness accounted for absences, and made necessary occasional closures of the school. The illnesses of the children reflected the general health and hygiene of the village population. Measles was the commonest disease (nine outbreaks from 1866 to 1911), followed by whooping cough (four outbreaks 1870 – 1911). Then came scarlet fever and chickenpox (three outbreaks); diphtheria, mumps and influenza (two outbreaks); and finally one outbreak each of typhus (1862), scarletina (1864), typhoid (1870) and smallpox (1871).

The long summer holiday and working absences in the spring and summer accounted for the Easter week not being given regularly as a holiday. The Easter break in 1882 was cancelled because a week's holiday was given for the coming of age on 26 March of Mr Francis Bingham Mildmay, the eldest son and heir of Mr Bingham Mildmay, who was generally known as Frank rather than Francis. The fair held regularly on 1 May for the sale of toys, with donkey races and other festivities earned a half-day holiday, as did the Club Festival or Feast of the Shoreham Amicable Benefit Society which also included a church service preceded by a parade with the band. A holiday was given for a ploughing match in November 1868, and from 1879 a half-day was allowed for the Annual Flower show. Those selected to sing in the church choir enjoyed the annual outing to Canterbury, Brighton or Ramsgate.

The nineteenth century had begun with the government of the parish very largely in the hands of the Church Vestry under the watchful eyes of the local gentry as justices. Shoreham ended the century with an elected parish council and a rural district council similar to those we have today, as well as branches of government departments of state. The shifting of authority away from the vestry followed a steady progression triggered by the Reform Act of 1832. It began in 1833 with the Government's modest financial grant in support to locally initiated schools (see p. 139). The Poor Law Amendment Act of 1834 followed, introducing a national system of Poor Relief organized locally by a district board of guardians consisting of JPs, members elected by rate-payers and landowners. In 1839 the County Police Act was passed, enabling counties to establish paid police forces, but Shoreham Vestry continued to nominate constables in the 1860s.

Ever since 1555 the vestry had been responsible by law for maintaining the parish roads, providing labour and materials under its surveyor of highways or 'way warden'. In 1835 the Highway Act abolished statutory labour and empowered the levy of a highway rate and the unification of parishes into highway districts with a district surveyor, and the 1862 Highways Act gave compulsory powers to justices to implement these changes. The vestry at Shoreham resented this change and expressed this resentment in December 1864 in a strongly worded representation sent to the Highway Board of Sevenoaks District, pointing out that the board's mode of reconstructing the highways in the parish was unnecessary and ruinously expensive, involving a cost from £10 to £20 per mile. The principle on which highways of 25 to 30 feet wide were built did not apply, they maintained, to highways of 12 to 15 feet in width

> especially on side hills or uneven ground, as the water in the upper table must soak away under the Road, or be conveyed across by Pipes (an unnecessary expense), whereas if the narrower Road is formed on an incline (as in this parish) as far as any amount of water is concerned, it is self-acting and clears the Road as it falls.

It appears that the district surveyor had been concentrating on the reconstruction of the highways, but neglecting ordinary maintainance such as removing accumulations of soil and leaves and rubbish from water tubes. The vicar, Mr Lovett Cameron, invited the members of the Board to come to inspect the altered and unaltered highways of the parish.[5] A working arrangement seems to have been reached, for in April 1867 the vestry decided to ask the Highway Board to enter into a contract with Mr Charles Crisp (a vestry member) 'to collect all necessary materials, to break the same and put them on where needs any [sic] to the satisfaction of the said Board and their surveyor.'[6]

The nonconformist churches increased their members as the century advanced. The Methodists thought themselves strong enough in 1877 to plan a new and more imposing chapel on a prominent site on Shoreham Street (now 12 and 12a High St.) on land kindly given by Mr T. Townsend of Knockholt. They considered the old chapel to be 'ill-ventilated, incommodious and no longer adequate to the wants of the place'. The Trustees who met on 25 April to launch the new chapel with the minister, the Revd Robert C. Barratt, in the chair, included Richard Ashenden, William Saker, Edward Osborne, Robert Bye, William Stacey, John Chapman, George Baker and W.B. Pattenden. Their plans included a chapel to seat 200 persons, a school room for 100 scholars and two vestries (later reduced to one). John Willis of Shoreham was chosen to build the chapel, which was completed in 1878 at a cost of £1,450.[7]

The indenture for the purchase of the site for a Baptist chapel in Crown Road was drawn up as early as 1870, although the Baptist Directory shows the chapel being formed only in 1896.[8] The trustees who signed the indenture in 1870 were the farmers William and Percival Bowen; George Agate, a gardener; and three woodmen, John Wills and William and Albert Brooks, all of Shoreham parish, plus three others from Chelsfield.[9] Supporters of the plan to build the chapel were the Mills family at Water House and the Carpenters at Oxbourne House, whose businesses were in London and who had been keen worshippers at the Metropolitan Tabernacle. With the site secured, the Baptists — presumably through lack of funds — had to wait for fulfilment of their hopes until 1896.

In 1895 the son of one of C.H. Spurgeon's deacons, Benjamin Isaac Greenwood, came to live in Shoreham and was called by one of his friends 'my ideal of a Christian business man'. He was a builder, and in 1882 (when he was only twenty-two years old) he helped to found Holliday and Greenwood, the well-known London contractors who built among many other buildings the London Hippodrome and the Shakespeare Memorial Theatre at Stratford. He had been brought up at the Metropolitan Tabernacle, and was totally committed to the Baptist persuasion. On arrival in the village he immediately took action to fulfil the wishes of the Baptists to have their own church in Shoreham. The congregation was a modest one, and was at its peak of 41 in 1905-8 during the ministry of Alfred Walker.[10]

Before the turn of the century Mr Greenwood had built himself Darentdale, but not fully content with the result he decided to build another similar house higher on the downs to the west. Coombe Hollow was completed in 1903 with a cottage at the eastern edge of the property on Cockerhurst Lane for the gardeners. Along this lane (on someone else's land!) he planted an avenue of beeches to enhance the approach to his property.[11]

The majority of village families were still regular worshippers at the parish church, but the vestry minutes make it clear that its members realized in the 1860s that the Established Church could not for much longer continue to levy compulsory rates for church upkeep. It must have come as no surprise when Mr Gladstone in 1868 by Act of Parliament deprived it of that power. In future the maintenance of the church was to depend on subscriptions and voluntary offerings. The Anglican church-goers of Shoreham rose to the challenge. The average revenue from the compulsory rate for such work over the previous five years had been £54 p.a., whereas the average voluntary offerings for the years 1868/9 - 1873/4 was £66 p.a., so the church seemed to have benefited. Although there is no documentary evidence of objections by Shoreham nonconformists, they must nevertheless have been relieved at the change. A further change in the life of the village came in 1875 with the Public Health Act.

There were twelve wells supplying water to houses along Shoreham Street from Mill Lane to the Almshouses, but only one east of the river behind Ivy Cottage.[12] We must presume from this that those living along the present High Street were able to rely on the wells, while those to the east of the bridge had to rely mainly on the river for their watersupply. The Dipping Place opposite Riverside House seems to testify to that. These supplies of water seem to have been considered sufficient at the time, but as already mentioned during the years 1871-91 the increase in population reached a peak (1300 in 1871, 1544 in 1891), with considerable overcrowding and the continued use of cesspools throughout the district causing an obvious health hazard. In addition, smallpox was an occupational hazard in the Timberden and Well Hill areas, brought out from the Borough Market by the fruit and vegetable growers.[13] The terrible living conditions of the navvies at Dunton Green during the building of the S.E. railway to Sevenoaks has been noted, and following the passing of the Public Health Act of 1875 the Rural Sanitary Authority took decisive action and the Darent Valley Main Sewerage Board set about laying the 24-inch pipe from Westerham to Dartford. In 1881 Henry Bingham Mildmay received an award of £5,500 for damage to his property during the construction of the sewer.[14]

The battle which raged between the Otford Vestry under the fiery leadership of the vicar, Dr John Hunt, and the Rural Sanitary Authority over the linking of Otford to the main sewer has been fully described in Chapter 10 of *Otford in Kent*. The acceptance in Shoreham of the link-up with the main sewer was less dramatic. This was due in part to the different characters of Dr Hunt and Mr Lovett Cameron (who was nearing the end of his life) and in part to Mr Mildmay, who as a resident landowner was personally concerned with the living conditions of those on his estate. He had in the 1860s and 1870s carried through a substantial building programme in Shoreham. He had built Home Farm and rebuilt the Post Office and its house. He bought in 1873 from William Waring Esq. of Chelsfield the four brick and timber cottages standing immediately upon the road next to the National School and opposite the former work-house.[15] These he demolished and replaced with four new terraced brick cottages set back from the road. Cottage No 4 had a 'very strongly built detached room formerly used as a lock-up'; this was the Cage of ancient times which was to remain standing into the second half of the twentieth century. Other groups of estate cottages on the west side of Shoreham Street leading towards Mill Lane had also been built. These new dwellings compared favourably with those at Dunton Green and impressed the Sanitary Authority, but even so the sanitation of the village generally was far from satisfactory.

Mr Harris Butterfield, Medical Officer of Health for West Kent, reported on 1 February 1887 that he had found one or two cases of measles and one of scarlet fever in the village, but more serious were the sanitary conditions:

> The cesspools were full to overflowing, the privies, especially at the schools where, if anywhere, they ought to be models of cleanliness, in a most offensive condition. I also noticed slop water in some of the public gutters and generally the odour of sewage was perceptible throughout the village. A large portion of the excreta and refuse of the inhabitants is kept about their dwellings while the remainder goes to pollute the Darenth.

No time could be lost in connecting Shoreham with the main sewer which passed through the village.[16] At a first meeting with the RSA officers Shoreham home-owners were unwilling to accept this idea, but offered to put their sanitary arrangements in order. The sanitary inspectors were not satisfied. As a compromise Mr Mildmay offered to lay a pipe to convey slops from Lovelands shop to the main sewer in Wilmot's meadow and from any cottage between the two. Having received this offer the RSA tried to persuade him to undertake a full sewage system, but this he refused to do. The RSA stood firm and a public inquiry was held on 20 September 1887 in the National School before the Local Government Board Inspector, Arnold Taylor Esquire. Those present included Mr W.M. Roberts (for Mr Lovett Cameron), Mr Spencer Chadwick, the architect who had recently built himself a mansion at Highfield on the downs east of the village, and Mr Isaac Loveland. In March 1888 the plans for 1,550 yards of sewer with 6' ventilation shafts were finally agreed, though Mr Hennell of Westminster who drew up the plans 'regretted that in consequence of Mr [George Burrow] Gregory, as owner of "Shoreham Cottage" not being able to see his way to give similar consent (as other owners) for a pipe on his ground there is no ventilator on his ground on the East side [of the river]'.[17] As there was no main water-supply, George Blundell, the carrier and fruiterer, was given the contract to flush the sewers periodically. This in practice may not have proved satisfactory, and once more Mr Mildmay came to the rescue with a gift of £500 to bring a supply of water from Halstead for the purpose of keeping the sewage on the move.[18]

Thus with the technological, political and religious changes of the nineteenth century Shoreham with some reluctance accepted the intrusion of the larger world into the running of its life, but continued to attract to itself as it had done over the centuries those interested in a varied agriculture or paper-making, and those seeking a place of special beauty in which to live close to the capital city. It is possible with the arrival of the railway and the ending of the period of high and prosperous farming in the 1870s to detect the beginnings of the change in the life of the village from being the centre of an agricultural community to being one whose professions and work were centred on London and the towns of north-west Kent. Their reasons for choosing Shoreham were not that it offered a valuable investment in farming land but rather the peace and beauty of the countryside to be enjoyed in the evenings and at week-ends. It is perhaps pertinent to mention here that in 1865 the Commons, Open Spaces and Footpaths Preservation Society was set up, and in 1895 the National Trust was founded. During almost exactly the same period (1861 – 1901) the number (nationally) of farm-workers fell from a peak of one million to 609,000.[19] In Shoreham the decrease followed the national trend. As the agricultural labourers deserted the land, so the city workers in their ever-growing slums and suburbs sought the fresh air and open spaces of the country.

Joseph Prestwich was professor of geology at Oxford University, and in the year that he was president of the International Geological Congress (1864) he decided to build a large house on the downs to the north-west of the village. He called it Darent Hulme, after his seventeenth-century ancestors' home on the banks of the Irwell, now part of Manchester. The story is told that during the building of Darent Hulme the labourers who were digging the well for the house had dug to unprecedented depths and were for abandoning the search for water. They had not realized that the man who had ordered the well to be dug had some thirteen years earlier published an authoritative book on the water-bearing strata round London and knew the exact depth at which they were to find water. There is no evidence that Joseph Prestwich — who was gazetted a knight on New Year's Day 1896 for his work for science — was interested in building up an agricultural estate, but we do know that the garden at Darent Hulme was his great pleasure for the next thirty-two years.[20] He had lived and worked half his life in London, but now he and Lady Prestwich grew to love Shoreham, a love that is reflected in his bequests. When he died in 1896 he left £618, the interest of which was to provide £3 for the village nurse fund, £1 10s for the brass band and £6 to provide labouring men receiving a daily wage with a 1d weekly newspaper: the residue to go to the church.[21]

There is also no indication that when Spencer Chadwick, the architect, bought Highfield and built his modern country residence on the small farm estate he was interested in anything other than a choice place to live. When he died in 1893 and Highfield was put up for sale emphasis in the advertisement was placed on Shoreham being only '50 minutes by train from London', and that the West Kent Foxhounds and Mid-Kent Staghounds hunted the district. Mention was made also of the principal inhabitants. It was as a country residence that Sir Benjamin Louis Cohen, the philanthropist, bought Highfield, and we are told that Edward Plunkett (Lord Dunsany) as a boy moved from London to Dunstall Priory and 'loved it immediately and for ever . . . .' 'Mystery and imagination were what Dunsany admired and Dunstall set the scene for both.'[22] For him Shoreham was where he wished to live and die in community with his neighbours. In the late 1890s two other families (already mentioned p. 158), the Mills at Water House and the Carpenters at Oxbourne House, chose Shoreham in which to live near London. Mr Mills was a butcher in the Old Kent Road, and his wife was Mrs Carpenter's sister. Her husband was a leather merchant in London.

Thus as Queen Victoria's Diamond Jubilee approached Shoreham found itself, more than at any other time in its history, the centre of attraction of these several substantial families, all of whom were providing employment within the parish for ground and domestic staff. It was a time when the station-master at Shoreham (being of managerial grade) wore a top-hat. When Mr A.F. Tucker, station-master, left in 1883 after only four years' service at the station it was thought right and proper that 'the principal inhabitants' of Shoreham should give him a gold watch. The watch was presented by John William Plunkett, seventeenth Baron Dunsany.[23]

This was at a time when the country was facing an agricultural depression, and even if farmers in Shoreham fared better than elsewhere there were those on the bottom rungs of the village ladder who in the 1880s needed the soup kitchen. The parish magazine of December 1890 under the heading 'Coal Club and Soup Kitchen' referred to the fact that 'these charities . . are too generally useful to let drop' and the writer mentions 'the present crisis in the life of a little community'. Two years later there is reference to agricultural labourers 'whose wages were not more than eighteen shillings a week'. Again, on 20 March 1900 the *Magazine* reports 'The soup kitchen has been greatly appreciated this winter and Mrs. MacLening's cooking has been excellent.' In December 1900 out-relief was increased by sixpence per head per week 'as the necessaries of life have much increased' in price.

In 1890-91 Bingham Mildmay faced a crisis quite unrelated to the agricultural depression. The Mildmay family had throughout the century been closely involved with Baring Brothers & Co., the merchant bankers. In 1890 a crisis occurred in the City of London and 'was marked, according to *The Times* of 22 December 1890 by the downfall of the famous house of Baring . . . . (although) other great firms must share with them the blame of having encouraged the government and people of Argentina to "run before their horse to market".' To meet his commitments as a partner Mr Mildmay had to take drastic action in two directions which affected Shoreham. He put up for sale some 673 acres in the north-west of the parish including 'some of the best fruit land in the country' as well as Colgates Farm and property within the village,[24] land which had been brought into the estate by Humphrey St J. Mildmay's second wife. He also let

SHOREHAM

Mr Bingham Mildmay with friends at Shoreham Place. (The Mildmay Collection)

Shoreham Place to the Rt Hon. Sir Henry James, QC.

Mr and Mrs Mildmay withdrew from Shoreham Place. They decided to leave only a month after the crisis at the bank. The shock of their departure was deeply felt in the village. Ever since Henry Bingham Mildmay had inherited the estate in 1866 from his brother Henry Francis, he had carried through a programme of building, renovations and additions which preserve to this day the memory of that period of prosperity in Victoria's reign. His fondness for cricket led him characteristically to give the Shoreham Cricket Club one of the most beautiful of grounds. His support and that of Mrs Mildmay for the church was generous and continuous, and in untold ways both showed their deep commitment to the village and those who lived in it. The vestry recorded on 13 December 1890 their very great sorrow at the Mildmays' departure. Members hoped that the separation would be only temporary, and so indeed it was to prove. In 1897 Mr Mildmay, having reached the age of sixty-nine, decided to surrender his life estate and interest in the Shoreham estate to his eldest son Francis (Frank) Bingham Mildmay, MP for Totnes in Devon,[25] but at the turn of the century he and Mrs Mildmay visited Shoreham from time to time before Frank Mildmay took possession of Shoreham Place.

In 1869 Sir Henry James became a QC and entered the House of Commons as Liberal Member for Taunton at the age of forty-one. He soon gained the respect of the House and Gladstone's admiration. He was made Attorney General, and had he supported Gladstone over Home Rule in 1886 he could have been chosen to be Home Secretary or Lord Chancellor, but he was unhesitatingly against a change of policy for Ireland. The newly elected Liberal MP for Totnes, Frank

Mildmay, at that time went through the same heart-searchings, and possibly influenced by Sir Henry decided to oppose the Home Rule Bill. Sir Henry had a large circle of friends and was a keen sportsman, especially with the gun: he must have been attracted to the woods on the downs to the west of Shoreham, well stocked with game by the Mildmays. Out of office from 1892 to 1895 he acted as attorney general of the Duchy of Cornwall to King Edward VII, then the Prince of Wales.[26] They became close friends, and the Prince was only too delighted to accept Sir Henry's invitations to join the James's house parties at Shoreham Place and enjoy the pheasant-shooting. There must for some have been a feeling on those occasions that *la belle époque* had come to this secluded Kentish village. The schoolchildren used to look forward to the Prince's visits because it meant an extra holiday and the possible scramble for pennies thrown to them when he walked through the village.[27]

The introduction of free education in 1891 — coming as it did hard on the heels of the Baring Bank crisis and the departure of the Mildmays from Shoreham — required immediate changes in the financial arrangements of the school. The fees being asked of parents then were:

Infant School —for the first child	2 pence per week
subsequent children, each	1 penny " "
Mixed School —for the first child	3 pence " "
" two children	5 pence " "
" 3 or more children	6 pence " "

The vestry evidently reflected the determination of all rate-payers that the school should continue under the voluntary system and agreed to it having a voluntary rate. Sir Henry James used his influence to obtain donations to the school funds from the directors of the South Eastern Railway, and also the London, Chatham and Dover Railway companies. The vicar, Mr Ashington Bullen, took the cost of the Infant School upon himself, and a management committee was set up consisting of the vicar and churchwardens, Lord Dunsany, Sir Henry James, Mr Chadwick, Mr George Redman (Cockerhurst), Mr I.J. Beale (Filston), Mr George Hemphrey and Mr C. Carpenter (Copt Hall). In 1894 the school was leased from Henry Bingham Mildmay at a rent of £25 p.a., to include the surrounding land, the school house and yard and the headmaster's house.[28] With the new financial arrangements settled in February 1894, the good news was announced in the parish magazine that under Mr Steane's guidance and as a result of a recent favourable HMI inspection the school was to receive the full grant from the Education Department, 'which places the school in the best position attainable by a Public Elementary School'.

Miss James, Sir Henry's sister, played an active part in the village, and it was possibly she who was responsible for setting up the Shoreham and Otford Nursing Association, of which Miss James was the first President and Secretary in 1893. The Hon. Treasurer was P.J. Rogers Esq., and other members of the committee were: Mrs Bullen, Mrs Carpenter, Mrs Chadwick, Mrs Cornwallis (Twitton, Otford) and Mrs Prestwich.[29] The Association offered a continuous service until 1948, when the National Health took over. It provided the services of a fully qualified midwife for day and night care. This was given free to the poor and sick in their homes, except that in maternity cases when the nurse was acting alone 10*s* was charged (5*s* for the nurse). There was no charge if the doctor was present. The first nurse to be appointed was Nurse Taylor.

Schoolchildren and teachers outside Shoreham school in the late 1800s. (The Mildmay Collection)

There is some evidence (which further research may confirm) that Shoreham was attracting not only those wanting a pleasant place in which to live but also those searching for work and living in the 1880s and 1890s. About 1880 Ella Booker (formerly Cassam) moved with her parents from Bedfordshire when her grandfather bought her father a farm at Romney Street.[30] In 1896 Thomas Drew, his wife Emma and son Thomas left Downe and with all their worldly goods on a hand cart came to Timberden (their cat walked behind). At sixteen their son Thomas started work as a stable boy for the Russell Scotts (who had bought Darent Hulme after Sir Joseph Prestwich's death) and at twenty-one he moved to work at the paper-mill. His future wife Emma Buckman had been born (1880) at Little Chart near Ashford, and in 1906 came to work at Copt Hall for Mr Broom, bailiff to the Mildmays.[31] George Cheeseman had been working for the Mildmays, but in 1895 went for a short time to Penge, but returned to Shoreham as shepherd at Castle Farm.[32] About 1880 James Feltham came to work as foreman of the building staff of the Mildmay estate. He had been a player in a military band, and is reported to have had the idea of forming a village band. Certainly by 1882 there was an impressive group of bandsmen photographed in the grounds of Shoreham Place.[33] Somewhat later in 1908 the Hicks family came to Shoreham from Chilham near Canterbury when Mr Hicks at about sixty years of age obtained a foreman post at Castle Farm. His daughter Anne (later to become Mrs De Decker) went to work at the paper-mill.[34]

Two arrivals in the district in the 1890s point significantly to the fact that the Darent Valley was a comparatively well-favoured farming area during the depression. In 1891 James Alexander, his wife, son William (then nine years old) and three daughters left their 65-acre dairy farm in Renfrewshire and settled in the 100-acre Home Farm, Eynsford. Their son William was to take over

Castle Farm, Shoreham, during the 1930 depression.[35] In 1897 Thomas George Dinnis came by train with all his household goods and all his farming equipment to Dunton Green and with his seven sons took over Great Dunton Farm. He had been farming in Cornwall, but with the depression had found there was no money to be made there. From Great Dunton Farm the Dinnis family 'spread all over Kent', and Thomas took possession of Filston Farm, which was to remain in the family for four generations[36] to this time (1989). These examples show Shoreham as a place where people could farm and find work at a difficult time.

It is appropriate to make first mention here of Fort Halstead as a place of work for those living in Shoreham, although it was not until the late 1930s that employment there for substantial numbers was established, except perhaps during the First World War. In 1888 a scheme for the defence of London was drawn up, but it is not very clear when the building began of the chain of military storehouses – or forts, as they were commonly called – of which Fort Halstead was one.[37] However, about that time a Mr Brooks farming Timberden had used Shepherds Barn for stabling eight horses. He used these for carrier work, and one of his contracts was with Fort Halstead to carry earth for the development of the site.[38]

In the last decade of the nineteenth century there was a feeling that in spite of the difficulties progress was being made towards a better world – at least in Shoreham. The vicar, Mr Ashington Bullen (an energetic man), was able to report progress to the Dean of Westminster in June 1896. Already a Mission Room at Twitton had been opened (1890). The opening service 'would have been perfect had not the room been so tightly packed' with 75 worshippers and even an orchestra. The following February a mission chapel was opened in Otford Lane to seat 120 worshippers. Here 186 crowded into the opening service and many were left outside. The decision to build a mission chapel at Well Hill was taken 1889, and the subscription list opened with £20 from Lord Dunsany, £100 from Mr Mildmay and 15 guineas from Spencer Chadwick, who was appointed honorary architect for the chapel. Sufficient funds were slow to come, and it was not until June 1893 that the 'pretty and much admired chapel' was opened.[39] Mr Bullen was able to add in his report that the Band of Hope had 120 members, the Adult Temperance Society had 49 members and there were 188 communicants on the roll. In material terms the reredos in the parish church had been erected, the organ renovated, the vicarage was in throughly good repair and decorated, all at a cost of £550.[40]

1897 arrived, and Queen Victoria's Diamond Jubilee was celebrated in traditional style. The Shoreham Village Band was now firmly established with about thirty members and had its own band-room presented by Mr Mildmay. According to Arthur G. Booker,[41] the band, in their uniforms similar to those of the 10th Hussars and including a pill-box hat, were first invited to play at Seal and returned in the afternoon to play in Shoreham Place paddock where the village were celebrating the Queen's Jubilee.[42]

Behind the rejoicing the village was becoming increasingly conscious that 'the soldiers of the Queen' were involved in colonial troubles that had been rumbling on in distant South Africa, and in 1899 (when war broke out) the general feeling was that it had to be brought to a speedy conclusion. Edward Plunkett, trained at Sandhurst, was already with the Coldstream Guards in South Africa when his father died and he found himself the eighteenth Baron Dunsany. In the spring of 1900 the vicar (then Mr Norman Radcliffe) noted that the list at the church door

Shoreham Village Band in the 1920s. (G.W. De Decker)

of those 'who are serving their country in South Africa slowly grows longer'.[43] Two of Isaac Loveland's sons were on the list. Joseph, the eldest, and a cousin who had been a cowboy in the Klondyke were serving with one of the Rough Rider Companies (the 72nd) of the 20th Battalion of The Imperial Yeomanry, renowned for their long, rough and continuous saddle work. Isaac's younger son Reuben in The Queen's Own Royal West Kents described the hardships and starvation of the campaign — 'we were 91 days on 11 lbs. of dry flour a day and some stewed mutton for dinner. Part of the time on half those rations . . . . sometimes we had scarcely any clothes to our backs.' Both sons had periods in hospital.[44]

In August 1900 Lord Dunsany returned from the war and was welcomed home in Shoreham with an enormous bonfire. There was sad news in 1901. In May Frank Foreman was dangerously ill with enteric fever, and in September it was reported that Captain Alexander Mildmay, serving with The Rifle Brigade, had been killed. A meeting of condolence was held in the Infant School Room, a muffled peal rung on the church bells and the Dead March was played on the organ at the end of the Sunday service. His brother Frank, the future Lord Mildmay, later served in South Africa with The West Kent Yeomanry. Although a modest man, he had 'a touch of the grand seigneur' and 'his not inconsiderable baggage accompanied him throughout his service in a neat waggon pulled by four Boer ponies'.[45] The war ended in May 1902, and in

September a public dinner was held in the George Inn to celebrate the return of four warriors from the front: Driver Hayman (ASC), Trooper Cheeseman (Damant's Horse), Private Edwards (2nd West Kents) and Trooper Sandford (13th Hussars).[46] So the nineteenth century had opened with war and ended with war.

Harold Copping's portrait of John Bowers, first chairman of the Parish Council, — popularly known as the 'Mayor of Shoreham'. (Shoreham Village Hall)

XIII
THE TWENTIETH CENTURY (1) 1894-1918

LOCAL democracy took a step towards the twentieth century when the Local Government Act was passed in 1894 whereby elected rural district councils and parish councils were established. A parish meeting was called for the election of nine parish councillors at the parochial schools in Shoreham on 4 December 1894. Sir Henry James took the chair, and called for nominations. There were thirteen nomination papers, and so the chairman asked for a show of hands of those present for each nominee, and then asked if anyone wanted a poll. After waiting the statutory time he declared the following persons elected:

John Bowers (70 votes) J.W. Davis (51)
George Hemphrey (53) F. Booker (50)
William Hancock (52) W. Gadsden (47)
M.A. Taylor (52) I. Loveland (47)
John Wells (45)

John Bowers, a leading member of the Methodist Chapel, had been working for the Wilmots as a paper-maker for sixteen years, and was much liked and respected in the village. As he had received the most votes he was the clear choice for chairman of the Council, a position he was to hold until 1919. Only occasionally over the next fifty-two years was a poll called for and only in 1946 after receipt of a letter from the local Labour Party did the Parish Council (PC) decide to ask Kent County Council to make an order that parish councillors should cease to be elected at the parish meeting but should be elected by means of nomination, and if necessary a poll.[1]

The Sevenoaks Rural District Council (RDC) met for the first time in the Board Room of the Union Workhouse, Sundridge, on Thursday 10 January 1895, and among the twenty-eight newly elected members were Cecil Leventhorpe, tenant farmer of Castle Farm, who was already a Guardian, and Michael Angelo Taylor of the Crown Hotel, who were the electors' choice for Shoreham.[2]

The RDC and the Shoreham PC soon settled into a pattern of collaboration not unfamiliar to those involved in local government in the 1980s. Early in 1895

John Bowers and the Shoreham PC clerk A. Webster wrote to the RDC complaining of the deplorable condition of the roads known as Shacklands, Polhill Road and Faggenden (sic) Lane . . . it was so bad 'that it was impossible for excursionists to travel to the village via Shacklands which is the most important road'. The RDC agreed, and repairs with 'hard stone' were carried out over a two-year period. Such humdrum yet necessary interactions of the two councils were occasionally varied with other matters. In 1900 the Westminster Cyclist Touring Club felt constrained to write to the RDC of danger to their members, one of whom had mistaken Mill Hill (now Mill Lane) for the main road into Shoreham when approaching from the north-west. He failed to make the sharp right turn at the bottom of the hill and ended up in the mill stream, there being no protecting railing or fence. A new sign was needed at the top of Mill Hill to direct cyclists to the right down Shoreham Street. The mill stream continued to be a worry, and eventually twenty-eight years later the Highway Surveyor with Frederick Boakes (dairyman) and Alfred Henshaw (the fruit-grower), the RDC members for Shoreham, reached an agreement with Mr Foster, the owner of Shoreham Mill, to fence 'a dangerous portion of the mill stream adjacent to the public footpath'. The RDC offered to pay half the cost of the fencing.[3]

An interesting early building development reached the RDC in 1901 when J.H. North asked permission to develop Badgers Mount Farm as a residential area with a rateable value not less than £12,000. Michael Angelo Taylor and George Spender — another Shoreham innkeeper who had replaced Leventhorpe on the RDC — accompanied by the Council engineer opened negotiations, and the Badgers Mount Estate became a reality in 1903. The main rush of the house-building in the district (though not in Shoreham) was to come in the 1920s and 1930s after the laying of the mains water and electricity. Shoreham was fortunate in its principal landowners (see Appendix to Chapter XIII) who were determined to conserve the wild life of the parish and the health of its agriculture, keeping the ribbon developers at arm's length.[4]

At a time when the nation seemed more interested in the preservation and development of its Dominions and Colonies and in the glory of its Empire on which the sun never set than in the welfare of its farmers at home, let us mention briefly the story of Kentish wild white clover and its link with Shoreham. Dr Hugh Nicol, the Scottish agriculturalist, considered it in 1951 as a fodder crop to be 'possibly the greatest practical feat of purely agricultural research in this country' because of its incalculable and great effect on the production of meat, milk and eggs — i.e. protein — which sustained this country in the Second World War. 'Its sum of virtues is unapproachable.'[5]

For some years William Boddy at Dunstall Farm had been studying the character of the pure wild white clover (not the Dutch variety), collecting the seed and experimenting with it. He showed the seed to one of the judges at a silage competition he had entered. This man became interested, and took some of it home to Cheshire, where further experiments were carried out by G.A. Gilchrist on Mr Gladstone's estate at Hawarden. William Boddy then had a visit from a friend who was a Scottish seed merchant. He was so interested in what Boddy told him he took some seed back to Kelso and distributed it to friends. By 1905 he was able to begin extensive trials on a large farm in the Lammermuirs. These trials and others at Cockle Park in Northumberland led directly to the commercial sale of the seed throughout the country, and by the end of the First World War to the rest of the world. William Boddy with his patient and persistent interest in wild white clover took his place in agricultural history. His son returned to Shoreham in 1910 to Preston Hill.[6]

On the first day of January each year members of Shoreham families took part in an ancient ceremony dating back three hundred years. It was Doling Day, and on that day a group of villagers set out along the valley to Lullingstone because in the sixteenth century Sir John Peche, Sheriff of Kent, left a sum of money for the performance of certain works of piety and mercy, of which this Dole was one. The villagers attended a service at Lullingstone church, and afterwards received two loaves and four pennies. For some families Doling Day was a memorable event and the chance to receive a little extra food and money in a harsh world.

Alice Gibson[7] (*née* Cheeseman) was four years old in 1900, but probably not one of those walking to Lullingstone. Her father George Cheeseman was shepherd and general labourer at Castle Farm — and later at Preston Farm — so Alice, his eldest child, walked daily to school in Shoreham in her hobnailed shoes. (These shoes had been bought for 2*s* 6*d* from Callcutt, the cobbler living

Mrs Alice Gibson, *née* Cheeseman. (Photo by Ian Harper)

in Darent Cottages, Shoreham Street.) She finished school at fourteen and went to work in the fields at Castle Farm from 7 a.m. to 5 p.m. for 9 shillings a week. Her father was earning 15 shillings a week, but had a tied cottage on the farm and also received faggots and two tons of coal a year. Alice recalls when working in the hop gardens training three vineshoots up the poles and removing all others. During the growing season the process had to be repeated three times. For this work she was able to earn 16 shillings an acre. Her whole family used to work at it when they were big enough (there were nine children in George and Laura Cheeseman's family). If they were working close enough to the cottage they came home at midday for a hot meal, otherwise when too far away — say potato-planting — they took food with them to heat over a fire. Alice did all light work on the farm except pruning. Cabbage-picking meant arms soaked if it was wet; brussels-sprout picking meant fingers cut with the ice if it was freezing. Turnips, apples, plums, pears, strawberries and raspberries all had to be picked in season, and for a change she worked the turnip-cutter to produce fodder for the sheep and the cattle.

Fred Crouch at twelve and a half (about 1906), having passed the 'Labour Exam' with one other boy out of 300, got work at a nursery garden near his home in Hailsham, Sussex, and there learnt the skills for growing many varieties of glasshouse fruit. At eighteen he came to Shoreham and worked first for Lady Dunsany at Dunstall Priory. Fred was not very happy there because it was difficult to get his wages on time. In most gardens pay usually came through the head gardener, but Ernle, Lady Dunsany insisted that each gardener send a bill to her once a month — which was sometimes returned if it had not been put in the envelope correctly. In addition, the Dunsanys at that time were only growing figs in their glasshouses (according to Fred Crouch). So after six months Fred moved to the Mildmays where he got to know Sam Yates, who was working in the kitchen gardens. He stayed until early in 1914, when he transferred again, this time to Mr 'Jim' Russell, a racehorse-owner at Halstead.

Under Mr Frederick Drake Humphris, the Mildmays' head gardener who lived in the cottage in the walled garden at Shoreham Place, there were some twenty-two gardeners; these included three foremen supervising the gardeners in the 'grounds', the walled garden and the 3½ acre vegetable garden which ran parallel to Filston Lane below the garden of Old Cottage. The four 'inside' gardeners — i.e. those in charge of the glasshouses and frames — lived in the bothy, where Frank Russell's mother looked after them.

On becoming an inside gardener Fred Crouch was given charge of three vineries, all the frames, the tomato and the melon house. He was paid twenty shillings a week. He rose at 6 a.m. and began the day by watering and spraying his charges. Breakfast was at 8 a.m. From 10 a.m. until tea at 5 p.m. he worked as one of a team following Mr Humphris's instructions — e.g. potting, tying peaches, pruning etc. His midday meal came at 11 a.m., when the inside and outside gardeners gathered together and ate their food in the wood-shed near the bothy. Before 5 p.m. he returned to spray and water once again. In the summer the thinning of grapes had to be done after tea until dark because when the sun was out it was too dazzling during the day. One week in four he had to be on Sunday duty for all four inside gardeners. This meant rising at 4 a.m. and carrying on until 9 p.m., and involved stoking the glasshouse boilers. One particular boiler was lower than the rest and regularly flooded when the river rose, so the gardener on duty had to bail out the boiler and keep the fire alight no matter what the hour, day or night. Although no overtime was paid, prize money from flower and vegetable shows in the district was shared out.

Fred Crouch recalls the occasion of an important dinner party for some forty to fifty guests. The inside gardeners had to decorate the table following Mrs Mildmay's instructions given earlier to Mr Humphris on a tour of the gardens and 'flowering' greenhouses. When the butler had completed the setting of the table with his staff the doors of the dining-room were unlocked and the gardeners let in. They were then locked in while they laid out the smilax and arranged the flowers. Such precautions were to safeguard the family plate brought down from London and taken back again after the event in a specially arranged railway van in charge of the first footman.

The inside gardeners were a tribe apart from the other gardeners. They were specialists dedicated to their work, and tended to move freely from one employer to another in the South of England. On their Sundays off they would visit colleagues in other large establishments to compare ideas and practices. The kitchen and 'ground' gardeners tended to be local people, not changing employers. One such was Walter Cheeseman at Shoreham Place, who lived in the Lodge. Later in life Fred Crouch became head gardener at Lullingstone Place.[8] One who knew him, though he was nine years his junior, was Frank Russell. Frank went to Dunstall Priory as a lively gardener's boy of fourteen in 1916, where he learned his gardening skills under Mr Wilson the head gardener. Frank arrived just at the time that Edward Plunkett, Lord Dunsany, inherited the Priory from his mother, and was to remain with the Dunsanys for ten years before moving to more responsible work with the Mildmays.

It was the period up to 1914 that stands out in the memories of Shoreham's oldest inhabitants now living as a period of special beauty and peace. Although the turnover of inhabitants had been continuous throughout the centuries — made inevitable by the village's closeness to London — the pace of change had quickened as the twentieth century was reached; yet Shoreham was still remarkably stable as a community. It was essentially an estate village.

Following the crisis of Baring Brothers & Co. in 1890, a new generation took over a reconstituted Baring Brothers & Co. Limited. Frank Mildmay's younger brother Alfred joined as a clerk in 1890 and became a managing director in 1897, remaining until 1940; the firm cautiously and steadily rebuilt its reputation. Their father Bingham never quite recovered from the shock of the crisis and took no further active part in the company.[9] It was, however, possible for the family to reoccupy Shoreham Place and participate in the life of the village. They had visited Shoreham in the autumn of 1905 but returned to Devon, where their father had an attack of bronchitis. This took a turn for the worse on 31 October and the same night he died, with his two sons and daughter by his side. Mrs Mildmay had died a few years earlier.

On Thursday 2 November the Vicar Canon T.K. Sopwith, the tenant farmers, tradesmen and others gathered in the Reading Room (the old Methodist Chapel), and a letter of condolence was sent to F.B. Mildmay Esq MP.

It was Henry Bingham Mildmay's wish to be buried in the quiet corner of Shoreham churchyard with his family, and his funeral gave the villagers the opportunity of expressing their grief at his going and their gratitude for all that he had given them. The church could hardly hold the members of the family and his friends from the City and all who worked on the estate and the farms. 'The cottagers vied with those in the mansions to show respect to the memory of the deceased . . . almost every blind was pulled down and shutters obscured shop windows and business was suspended until after the ceremony'.[10]

The following year Frank Mildmay married Alice, daughter of Seymour Grenfell of Taplow. Alice was vivacious and full of fun, and liked to fill her house with young people. On 17 August 1907 Mrs Mildmay gave birth to their daughter Helen, and to express his happiness and gratitude Frank Mildmay went down to the walled garden and picked a large bunch of the finest sweet peas he could find and presented them to Alice. It was only later that he learned of the consternation expressed by Mr Humphris when he discovered that the master of the house — not usually interested in the garden — had proved himself a keen judge of quality. He had picked the flowers that Mr Humphris was cosseting for the coming flower show. Alice Mildmay had a deep love of the Shoreham Place garden and took a lively and creative part in developing it with Mr Humphris and later with Helen. Her particular creation and joy was the rose garden. The 29th of September 1907 was a day for rejoicing in the village when the Mildmays brought their daughter Helen down from London to be baptized in Shoreham church. Anthony, her brother, was born two years later.

Until 1914 the Mildmay family's visits to Shoreham tended to be governed by the sittings of the House of Commons, where Frank Mildmay was much respected as the conscientious MP for Totnes. During the spring and summer Helen and Anthony spent more time than their parents in the fresh air of Shoreham away from the restricted London routine of morning walks in Hyde Park and afternoon drives in the open landau. Their mother and father came at weekends, which were frequently busy social occasions. It was always a sense of release that Helen and Anthony felt as they ran from the Shoreham station platform through the swing gate and across the paddock of Shoreham Place to play in the maze and garden behind the house. Their mother used to wake them early on summer mornings to enjoy the dawn chorus begun by nightingales and taken up by the other birds. In the summer parliamentary recess the Mildmays disappeared to Devon only to appear again in Shoreham in the New Year. Frank Mildmay was of medium height, slim with clear and somewhat aquiline features. He always had the deep sense of responsibility of one born to great possessions. He was to prove himself an affectionate father, but his moods depended largely on his state of health. When he was feeling off-colour he was inclined to depression, but when in form he could not have been more approachable or a better companion. His family observed these moods with caution. If he was seen to be smoking his pipe — all was well. His pipe was known through the family as 'the barometer'.[11]

What of other leading members of the village community?

Edward Plunkett, the eighteenth Baron Dunsany, the author, had grown up at Dunstall Priory when not at boarding-schools, and had loved every minute of his life there. His grandfather had died when he was ten, so his father went to live and look after his estate at Dunsany Castle near Dublin, leaving Ernle, Lady Dunsany, at the Priory with Edward and Reggie his younger brother. They were very different characters, Reggie shy and withdrawn, Edward affectionate and boisterous. In a way Edward remained a schoolboy all his life, enjoying jokes and games. After his father's death in 1899 he left the Army to look after the family estate in Ireland, spending as much time as he could in Shoreham. In

The Mildmay family in 1912. (The Mildmay Collection)

1904 he married Beatrice, the daughter of the Earl and Countess of Jersey, and in August 1906 they had a son, their only child, to whom they gave the family name Randal.

In the closing years of the nineteenth century Roger Gregory took possession of his inheritance with his wife Mary Bertine. Among her many interests Mrs Gregory probably gave first place to her garden at Shoreham Cottage. Through her love and labour, and possibly for the first time in its history, it became truly a 'pleasure garden' — a description used in Sir Walter Stirling's time. To begin with the Gregorys continued to live in London, and Shoreham Cottage was a holiday home, but Roger Gregory was an active churchman who was nominated sidesman in 1908. They were both interested in the school, and Mrs Gregory soon established what became a seasonal event — the Christmas-tree and the party at the school when she gave a present to each child. (The Mildmays gave a children's party each summer at Shoreham Place.)

In 1906 the headmaster, Mr Steane, introduced rifle shooting as part of the curriculum, and Roger Gregory supported him in this surprising innovation by presenting the school with a small Winchester rifle. However, the Board of Education were not amused. Their letter stated 'Rifle shooting is not a subject which can advantageously be taught to children in Public Elementary Schools'.[12] The rifle was probably not intended for the classroom, but it must have been very useful in the controlled conditions of the Miniature Rifle Club, of which more later. John Vincent Steane was now firmly confident in his achievements at school and in the church. In his teens and early twenties he had studied the organ under Dr W. Belcher at Birmingham and under Dr W.T. Simms at Coventry Cathedral. When he came to Shoreham he had already been organist at churches at Dover and Ramsgate. He was fond of the Shoreham organ, and had already enlarged its range by making certain changes.[13] After fifteen years as organist and choirmaster he felt justified in asking for an increase in his salary of £21, and the vestry approved an increase to £30 per annum. We do not know what salary he received as headmaster, but in 1912 the HMI considered that the 'children are under a wholesome and refined influence'.[14]

Largely due to the enthusiasm and energy of Mrs Gregory, in 1910 the inaugural meeting was held of the Shoreham and Otford Habitation of the Primrose League, the organization founded in memory of Benjamin Disraeli, 'to infuse new life into the Conservative party'.[15] Louisa Lady Cohen accepted the position of Dame President and Mrs Gregory the secretaryship.[16] About 1912 Roger Gregory's elder brother George died unmarried, and left to him his considerable library and other assets which enabled Roger to add the library and the third floor to the house, thus transforming Shoreham Cottage into Shoreham House. It must have been at that time that the bell (the 'dinner bell', as some villagers called it) was placed in its little turret on the roof ridge, where it was rung regularly at 1 p.m. each day. It was probably then also that Mrs Gregory began to organize the valuable library service for the village in the Church Room: free for those under sixteen and one penny a week for grown-ups.

Shoreham House now became the Gregorys' permanent home, and the inhabitants of the village began to realize that Roger Gregory was a great character as well as a great solicitor (he had joined the Council of the Law Society in 1911), with a sense of fun which showed itself when he gave a house party at Shoreham House for articled clerks and young solicitors in his firm and the firm's cricket XI played Shoreham Village XI.[17]

The village did not see much of Sir Benjamin Cohen, who lived on the downs at Highfield with Lady Louisa, their three sons and their daughter. His main interests were centred on London as Member of Parliament for East Islington and in performing other services for the community. He was an active President of the London Orphan Asylum, and in recognition of that he was created a baronet in 1905.[18] But he also cared for those in need in Shoreham, and to this end gave to the vicar a sum of money each year for him to distribute to those requiring help. After his death in 1909 it was discovered that he had bequeathed to the vicar and churchwardens debenture stock, the income from which was to be used for the same purpose.[19] Lady Louisa also played her part in village life, gave her support to the school and was a committee member of the Shoreham and Otford Nursing Association.

After fifty-nine years service to the church and vestry George Wilmot resigned

Mr and Mrs Gregory came to live permanently at Shoreham House in about 1912. (Miss R. Waring)

as vicar's warden. His son Albert took over the management of the paper-mill and was nominated vicar's warden in 1906.

Benjamin Isaac Greenwood, now at the peak of his career, was successfully concluding many years of negotiations over a form of contract between the Royal Institute of British Architects and the National Federation of Building Trades Employers.[20] In a leisure moment in 1905 he chaired the annual meeting of the Shoreham YMCA at the Association's rooms at Winslade supported by his fellow-Baptists Mills and Carpenter as secretaries, and Isaac Loveland as Treasurer.[21]

The name of Harold Copping first appears in Shoreham records when at the age of thirty-seven he was listed among those qualified to serve on juries in 1901. He had already trained as an artist at the Royal Academy Schools and in Paris, and had visited Palestine and Egypt to gather material for his biblical pictures which were to appear in such works as the *Copping Bible* and *Scenes in the Life of Our Lord*.[22] In 1904 he rented Darenth Villa, a small cottage on the river bank at the bottom of Crown Road. Four years later his reputation as an artist was growing, particularly as an illustrator of religious works; he bought the cottage, and decided to transform it into the house we know today as the Studio.

Copping found Shoreham rich in living and lively models for his illustrations. The Cassam family lived next door to the studio in Crown Road, and in 1904 The Religious Tract Society published John Bunyan's *Pilgrim's Progress* with Copping's illustrations. In it William Cassam is portrayed as Mr Despondency, Sarah his wife as Timorous and their daughter Emily as Mercy.[23] Another inhabitant of Crown Road, Lyn Pysden, also caught his eye and so did Amy Higgins (née MacLening) who appeared in *Dickens' Dream Children* by Mary Angela Dickens.[24] In 1911 Harold Copping was elected to the Parish Council.

About this time a friend of Mr Mildmay and a managing director of Baring Brothers, Gaspard Farrer, was concerned to provide a home in the country to which could come the children of the parish of St John's church, Hoxton — a very poor district of London. Mr Mildmay made available Riverside House, which for some ten years was to be known as the Farrer Cottage Home, managed by a matron. One girl of fourteen, Maude Bradbury, came to the Home in 1916 and repeated the visit for the next six years. She recalls them as the 'happiest hours' of her life, especially remembering the boat trips on the river.[25]

There was indeed a great feeling of community at that period. How many were there like A.L. Balme, the wool broker living at Water House after the Mills family left in 1908, who with Mr Madge the vicar used to go visiting in the village and returned home saying of the vicar 'he cleared m' pockets out'?[26]

The first decade of the twentieth century was still the age of the horse. Beside farm carts and wagons there was little traffic. The Russell Scotts' carriage and pair was a familiar sight trotting through the village from Darent Hulme to the station, and Lady Gregory used to ride her horse about the village. The Randalls, living at Chapel Alley Cottages with their horses stabled behind Flint Cottage, ran a 'taxi' service for those wanting to go to the station or on to Sevenoaks. But the transport revolution was on its way.

Thomas Karl Sopwith, the vicar of Shoreham from 1903 to 1908, had a brother Thomas Octave Sopwith who taught himself to fly and was making his name as an aircraft designer and builder. In 1909 Blériot made the first crossing of the Channel in his aeroplane and C.S. Rolls the following June flew across the Channel and returned in a single flight.[27] That same year, much to his astonishment, Frank Russell — a lad of eight years old — saw a monoplane

THE TWENTIETH CENTURY (1)

An etching of Church Street by Harold Copping. (Mrs J. Saynor)

flying low along the Darent Valley — 'under White Hill' was how he described it. The plane managed to reach Kingsdown where he and others were taken by his father to see it. It was an historic flight of a Blériot XII by Jean B. Moisant and his mechanic Félieux. Because of unexpected stops on the way the flight from Paris to Beckenham took six weeks.[28]

The internal combustion engine came to the streets of Shoreham about the same time in the form of a three-wheeled A.C. car driven by Ben Greenwood, son of B.I. Greenwood, who was to become an air pilot in time for the First World War. Going home one evening from the station, being a 'go-ahead driver'[29] he took the corner at Waterfall Cottages rather too fast and hit the parapet of the bridge.

Although there were those for whom the soup kitchen was a godsend, Mrs Lyn Pysden may have been right in claiming that for many in the village 'it was seldom that people had to buy' but grew their own vegetables.[30] The allotments in the Town Field had been provided by the Mildmays since at least 1875, and fruit in season must have been cheap from the fruit-growers such as the Blundells in the north and west of the parish. Because of its continued though diminished isolation (the train fare to Bat and Ball was 3*d*. and to Tubs Hill 4*d*.) the parish could sustain a full range of shops: two butchers, two bakers, three cobbler's shops, two forges, at least three sweet-shops (one with toys), two grocers and most surprisingly three general stores offering groceries and draperies, one of which (Lovelands') was also a coal merchant.

Two fish vans visited the village each week. On Saturday the oil man came to top up the house supply of paraffin and candles; Sunday was the day for the muffin man and men from Gravesend with shrimps and winkles. Given the low wages of the times, the tallyman had his place, selling new clothes on the instalment plan of one shilling a week. 'The man from the hills'[31] came regularly to the village with 'bavins' (bundles of brushwood for firing the coppers).

Sickness was a catastrophe, a dark cloud most people had at the back of their minds. From Elizabethan times the parish had responsibility for the health of its inhabitants, paying an annual fee to the parish doctor until the 1834 Poor Law Amendment Act put an end to that system, replacing it only with care in the Union Workhouse. Self-help was the answer found by those who started the Shoreham Amicable Benefit Society in 1848. It gave assurance against 'sickness and death according to payments'. The usual rate was sixpence a week, for which one received ten shillings a week during illness. J.L. Worship was doctor to the Society which in 1892 had 130 members in the district and £1,600 in hand. The AGM in June was held in the school and as usual this was followed by members marching to the church led by the village band. After the service 'the Dinner took place in the yard of the George Inn where host Spender very successfully catered for the wants of all present'.[32] In hard times the SABS had to compete with the Slate Clubs run by other organizations, including the George Inn, the Royal Oak and the Two Brewers: these attracted the younger men because of the share-out to members but did not provide for their old age. The Two Brewers 'in 1905 received £105 3*s* 4*d* paid out £31 19*s* 9*d* in sick pay and shared out to the members £69 14*s*.'[33] Shoreham also joined with eighteen other parishes in the Holmesdale Medical Provident Club giving a similar service to the SABS, and there was also the Nursing Association providing the village nurse. In 1893 Mr Mildmay was replaced as a trustee of the SABS by James Blundell of Halstead, and in 1895 John Wells of Shacklands took over from the vicar, Mr Bullen. By 1905 the SABS found the competition too much — membership had dropped to 45 and the society was dissolved, just three years before the Government introduced old-age pensions and six years before national insurance guaranteed benefits in sickness, disability and childbirth and the services of the panel doctor.

There was in addition a doctor resident in Shoreham, Dr H.S. Desprez, who from 1901 carried on a general practice from his house Birkdale (now Orchard House). His practice covered a vast area, and the story is related that at the end of his long daily round he refreshed himself at a public house in Eynsford before his horse brought him home.[34] There was also Dr Archer of Sevenoaks who followed Dr Desprez and who looked after both fee-paying and panel patients. Then in 1909 Dr Aubrey Ireland moved into Birkdale and continued the practice, finding time from the spring of 1914 to be an active councillor on the RDC.

In a world without radio or television the village folk entertained themselves. The woods and meadows and the Darent were their playgrounds, as Samuel Palmer and his friends had appreciated. Villagers young and old were members of the Rat and Sparrow Club, which provided hunters with rewards when at night with lamp and net they trapped the sparrows flying scared from the ivy on the cottage walls. Before a corn stack was threshed netting placed around the base trapped the rats before they could escape. Members took the sparrows' heads and rats' tails to the George Inn, where their catches were recorded and in April the winners received an annual prize.

In the eighteenth and nineteenth centuries there were brief references to a fair in Shoreham on 1 May each year 'for pedlary' (Hasted 1797) but more usually 'for toys'.[35] It was not listed among the early medieval fairs (of the twelfth to fifteenth centuries),[36] and by the twentieth its place was taken in the village calendar by the circus and fair which came annually to the meadow now filled with houses in Forge Way, Palmers Orchard and Boakes Meadow.

Mr Mildmay kept his pack of beagles at Kennel Cottage, and in winter the West Kent Fox Hounds met in the village. In January 1910 the meet took place at Shoreham Station.[37] In April the Royal Artillery (Woolwich) Drag Hunt held their point-to-point over three and a half miles and twenty stiff fences at Dunstall Farm, and in the same month the sixty-seven members of the Shoreham Miniature Rifle Club held its AGM chaired by the Revd H.A. Madge. The football club, Shoreham United, had had a good season ending at the top of the Second Division of the Sevenoaks and District Football League, having won all eight of their matches.[38] The Cricket Club was firmly established and Sir Herbert Cohen had provided the Club with a pavilion in 1900.[39]

The big event of the summer usually took place on the August Bank Holiday — The Flower Show and Sports. The site was the Gregorys' meadow (now the football field) where marquees and tents were erected and a track was carefully prepared for foot and bicycle races. The strong and fit competed in the steeplechase, the tug o'war and the greasy pole. The village band, uniformed and with sparkling instruments, drew the crowds in to the meadow by the 'Gregory Close' entrance. For the Flower Show weeks of painstaking cultivation, especially by the teams of gardeners from the big houses but also by the keen cottage gardeners, ended in the marquees. The ladies competed with needlework, cooking, preserves and flower-arranging.

For the great festivals of the church the head gardeners of the Mildmays and Gregorys tended to take it in turns to supervise the floral decorations.

Vincent Steane, in 1911 a newly elected parish councillor, had set the older children to write an essay on celebrating King George V's coronation and he

Lord Dunsany and members of the cricket club. (I. Harper)

passed on to the council the children's thoughts. They wanted to celebrate the coronation by having a village recreation ground. The council took up the idea and after considering various sites decided on the one we know today. Mr Mildmay readily agreed and rented the land to the PC for 1s. per annum. Was it then or later that the bandstand was built where the tennis courts were laid out in 1965?

Music-making was important in the life of the village, and a key figure was Vincent Steane, who gave to the church his considerable musical talent and to the choir a necessary discipline. If a choirboy misbehaved during the sermon Mr Steane gave him a sharp rebuke in school on Monday morning. He was for a time master of the village band, and his organ recitals are still remembered. Isaac Brown, the blacksmith living at Forge Cottage, his wife Emma and his family were music-lovers. On winter evenings the Browns and their friends used to get out four or five fiddles and play tunes from the Union Tune Book such as *Eglon*, *Cranbrook* and *Rock of Ages*.

The local talent was constantly in demand to fill out village concert programmes. Concerts were one of the most popular social activities. The church, the chapels, the school and other organizations called on their members to sing in chorus or solo, recite poems and perform comic sketches. Dorothy Brown's name appears several times in the pre-1914 programmes of the Baptist church, where she was later to be organist.[40] Violet Blundell, a new talent, was discovered in 1910 — 'a tiny maiden who cannot be more than seven or eight years old . . . possessed a quite extraordinary voice and style and a wonderful memory' at the concert given by the Church of England Temperance Society in the Church Room. The Otford Lane Choir provided the majority of items in the programme.[41] The Church Room had been opened on 10 January 1903 by the vicar, Mr Radcliffe, and paid for by a lady's bequest.

In 1910 there were ten public houses and inns in the parish, six in the village which were sustained in large part by the increasing numbers of visitors coming by train or driving out at weekends from south-east London to refresh themselves in the country air. The Rising Sun beer-house by the bridge appeared to be under threat of closure. William Plane, ex Regimental Sergeant-Major of the 1st Battalion The Dorset Regiment, had been licensee since 1894 and was also a popular master of the village band. To save the beer-house he had mobilized his forces, with well over fifty signatures on a petition to the Licensing Justices. The petitioners considered it would be a great inconvenience to those residing in the south of the village to have to go 'to the other extreme and for the purpose of obtaining the Westerham Ales which are popular' (from the Crown Hotel owned by the same Westerham brewers). In addition to the farmers, gardeners, coachmen, butchers, bakers, grocers, bricklayers and carpenters who signed, the petitioners included footballers from Eynsford and Harold Copping living in Crown Road, who had his Westerham Ale delivered to his house by the Rising Sun 'at the extreme end' of the village. The Licensing Justices were evidently much impressed, and the Rising Sun and RSM Plane continued to serve their petitioners.[42]

The thirsts and appetites engendered by the ride to Shoreham in train, horse-drawn brake, pony trap, dogcart and bicycle were satisfied not only by the inns and beer-houses but by the several cafés and tea-gardens. One of the most successful and long-lasting tea-gardens was to be found at The Ramblers (No 5 High Street), begun by Granny Edwards in 1907. It immediately became popular with family parties, but soon in high summer they were catering for 140 children and adults of the Bromley Baptists' Sunday School; 54 from the Woolwich Tabernacle Cycling Club 'partook of a meat tea' and on Easter Monday 1909 a 'splendid tea was enjoyed by 30 boys of the 1st Swanley Company of the Boys Life Brigade'; and so it continued for many years to come.[43]

The Inland Revenue in 1910 having produced the 'Domesday Books' of Duty on Land Value[44] for the whole country, provides an opportunity for noting changes in land-holdings in Shoreham parish since the Poor Rate survey of 1835. In spite of the need of Bingham Mildmay to sell land and property in the 1890s his son Frank still headed the list of principal owners with property, the rateable value of which was twice that of Sir William Hart Dyke of Lullingstone, the second on the list. In contrast to George Wilmot's comparatively humble position in 1835, Albert de Burgh Wilmot owned a much more successful paper-mill and The Mount. He was now fourth on the list. As a reward for hard work and enterprise (and especially that of his father in pioneering strawberry-growing), Charles Blundell appears as seventh on the list, between the Ecclesiastical Commissioners and Lady Cohen. He owned 117 acres of land, eight cottages and two houses in the Otford Lane area.

There were still some thirty smallholders, but of these half were owners living outside the parish, and must have considered their property in Shoreham just as an investment. Such was A.H. Palmer, son of Samuel Palmer, who owned nine cottages. About ten were members of old-established families of the parish such as H. and G. Booker at Romney Street, Isaac Brown at the Forge and Mrs A. Walker at the Post Office.

The farmers had since 1835 enjoyed twenty years of prosperity in the mid nineteenth century, and were now enduring a longer period of depression. Although during the intervening seventy-five years restructuring had taken place with reduction of acreages on some of the main farms, there appears to have been no marked reduction in the overall acreage being cultivated — 3,455 acres in 1835 and 3,347 in 1910; the 108 acres difference being almost certainly accounted for by Charles Blundell's fruit plantations. This seems to bear out the conclusion in Chapter XII that although times were hard Shoreham was better off than elsewhere.

However, there is evidence that the condition of the rented dwellings of the great majority of villagers was deteriorating. In 1912 the six 'Post Office' Cottages were closed as unfit for human habitation. Frederick Boakes, one of Shoreham's rural district councillors, bought these from the Crowhurst family and eventually they were to rise again as Marne Cottages. Four cottages in Mill Lane owned by de Burgh Wilmot were condemned[45] and another cottage next to the greengrocer near the Royal Oak was closed in 1913 because it was becoming a retreat for tramps. On the other hand, Shoreham was one of the first parishes in the district to ask the RDC to undertake refuse-collection for the village in 1911. The matter was raised in the council by Harold Copping on 29 March. After studying the costs of collection at Westerham, the only other parish in the district having such a service at the time, the Parish Council decided to accept the charges. The RDC received two tenders for the task (from John Dinnis of Filston of £52 and Robert Buchanan of Cockerhurst of £68) and Dinnis won the contract.

Far removed from dilapidated cottages near the Post Office and in Mill Lane, and far removed from the refuse-collection, there was an international crisis. On 28 June 1914 Franz Ferdinand and his wife were murdered at Sarajevo, and some five weeks later the First World War broke out. On 3 August Germany declared war on France and a British Expeditionary Force was mobilized. On 4 August German troops crossed the Belgian frontier and Britain sent the Kaiser an ultimatum which expired that night, unanswered. The inhabitants of Shoreham were swept into the war which all thought would be short, sharp and victorious. No one could foresee the horrors of the four years to come.

There were only two reservists living in the parish and very few regulars in the Army and Navy. A recruiting office was opened at Balsatts (Reedbeds) to which the fit young men went to sign on. More than half the total of those who enrolled in the armed services joined up in the enthusiasm of the first year of the war.

Frank Mildmay was fifty-three and had some difficulty in joining up but his distinguished service in South Africa and his fluency in French helped him to find a place in the Army and in December went overseas with the 27th Division.[46] Sir Herbert Cohen and Roger Gregory (also over fifty) joined up and so did 'Benny' Greenwood. At first he was ADC to General Seely, but keen to use his skills as a pilot he transferred to the Royal Flying Corps in 1915. Lord Dunsany was over in Ireland and because of the ever-deepening political crisis there he was fully involved in managing the family estate; he saw active service in France only during 1917. Dr Ireland abandoned his practice, resigned from the RDC and joined the Royal Army Medical Corps in December 1914. The council as in other cases did not take steps to fill the vacancy, hoping no doubt that Dr Ireland's would be a short absence, but in the election of May 1916 John Dinnis took his seat on the RDC with Frederick Boakes.[47] The councillors' belief that the war would be dragging on into an uncertain future seemed to be reflected in their decision taken that year to connect the military camp now established at Shoreham to the main sewer.[48]

The slaughter on the Western Front drew more and older men into the Army, and in 1915 Vincent Steane was commissioned at the age of fifty for service in this country, leaving the school in the experienced hands of Mrs Steane. The vicar, Mr Madge, well over military age, whose only brother was killed in action that same year, twice visited France to serve the troops, first in the YMCA and in 1918 to work with the Church Army.

The Voluntary Aid Detachments (VAD) which had been formed in 1913 set up a small hospital in Shoreham at Church House under Mrs Wilmot as its commandant. Their first patients, five Belgian soldiers, arrived still wearing their field dressings. The hospital moved more than once — to Myrtle Cottage and then to Shoreham Place, where on a rare visit to Shoreham during the war in 1916 Helen Mildmay-White recalls as a young girl playing draughts with the convalescent soldiers. Its final home was in the vicarage when Miss Madge was commandant. The village Scouts, forming a rota, took over the rough work at the hospital. A hospital supply depot opened in 1915 under Miss Greenwood's direction to prepare bandages and surgical dressings. It operated three days a week.

Workers including Alice Cheeseman went daily to labour in the munitions factory at Lullingstone to make shell-caps. The paper-mill closed for the duration, and Anne Hicks — who had employment there for six years — found new work in a factory in Wandsworth making shells. There she met her future husband Mr De Decker, a Belgian soldier who had been evacuated unconscious and badly wounded to England. He was pensioned off from the Army and got work at the Wandsworth factory.

Trench warfare had soon developed across the Channel. The Shoreham Sandbag Service by 1915 had dispatched 3,562 sandbags to the front and thereafter the volunteers knitted comforts in great quantities for the troops. Harold Copping recorded the spirit of the times in his painting of Rose MacLening as a Red Cross nurse entitled *On Service*.[49]

By 1917 German U-boats were devastating shipping supplies to Britain; food and war materials were getting scarce, and permission was given to set up National Kitchens. The Scouts added to their duties by collecting waste paper and metal.[50] The farmers were immediately affected by the enthusiasm with which their workers enlisted for war service, and by the Army requisitioning horses and large quantities of fodder. By mid-1915 the shortage of food was being felt by both people and animals, yet it was not until 1917 that the Government intervened with a policy of guaranteed prices for corn, with deficiency payments and a minimum wage for farm workers of £1 5s a week, to encourage the ploughing up of additional acres.[51] The shortage of labour was alleviated by the formation of the Women's Land Army. Among the Land Girls sent to Shoreham were Miss Berkeley and Miss Cobbold, of whom more will follow in the next chapter. Some switching of hopland to other much-needed crops took place in the district. At Filston hop-production remained at an average of 165 pockets (large sacks) during the war until 1918, when there was a sudden drop to 65 pockets.[52] This reduction came after the harvest in 1917, the year of the Corn Production Act, when there was a resulting switch from hops to corn. The Shoreham Gardening and Food Production Society were cultivating three acres of land given to them by Mr Blundell.

Members of The Loyal North Lancashire Regiment, The London Regiment, The Middlesex and West Kent Regiments were billeted at times in Shoreham, and in the absence of the village boys they helped to enliven the social life of the community. The clatter of small-arms fire echoed around the hills from the rifle range on Preston Hill, which had been built in 1897 on land owned by Bingham Mildmay and leased to Lt Col G. Henderson of The Queen's Own Royal West Kent Regiment.[53] Fort Halstead to the south-west was used throughout the war for the storage of ammunition.[54]

Beatrice, Lady Dunsany had come over in 1917 from Ireland to take possession of Dunstall Priory after the death of her mother-in-law. She had just said goodbye to Lord Dunsany (returning to France from leave) and as she walked up from the station she was struck by a moment of beauty thrown up by the war. In the search for Zeppelins, twenty-one searchlights stabbed the clear, frosty night sky. The conflict seemed very close at times, and as the war dragged on into 1918 many in the village must have felt that no matter how weary they were they must continue to give of their best in factory, field and hospital. One who certainly felt this was Beatrice Dunsany: haymaking at Dunstall in 1918 with her eleven-year-old son Randal, she rested for a moment and heard the distant thunder of guns.[55] Perhaps this was the guns of Ludendorff's army in the last German attack on the Somme.

Mrs Mildmay, writing in the parish magazine in September about one of her favourite delights — the dawn chorus in Shoreham Place gardens — added 'gradually comes an accompaniment — the never ceasing rumble from far across the seas of the guns in France, which like muffled drums seem to give a sinister tone to the wonderful symphony'. Few then knew that Haig's guns on the Somme were the beginning of the end of the war. In January Lord Dunsany had been withdrawn from the 'mud and slaughter' and given a job at the War Office writing articles for the world press. On the 8th of November Lady Dunsany's diary reads 'Eddie came home last night with War Office news that the war is over . . . . Bells are ringing in Shoreham and farther away . . . .' The Kaiser abdicated on the 9th and a republican Germany prepared to receive the armistice terms.[56]

In four long years a total of 218 from the village had served in the armed services. Thirty-one had been killed, thirty-seven wounded and seven taken prisoner.

XIV
THE TWENTIETH CENTURY (2) 1919-39

EXHAUSTED, bewildered, hardly believing that the war was over, the village began to think of the future. Some bracing and very practical hints were given in the parish magazine on how to prepare for the home-coming of the men from the war:

Inside the house —
    Clean the windows.
    Get rid of furniture, carpets and mats no longer used.
    Clean the water-cistern, lavatory, sink and bath.
    Get rid of window curtains and other things that harbour dust.
    Get a polish on fire-irons, kettles and tea-pots.

Outside the house —
    Clean the dust bin and place it where no smell can enter the windows.
    Clean out the gullies and rainwater gutters.
    Scour out the yard and get rid of all cases, barrels, bottles, tins, etc. lying about in the garden.
    Try, both back and front, to grow either flowers or vegetables.

As he walked down from the station the returning veteran saw that the church and the George Inn were still there. The gentle sound of the water flowing beneath the bridge was unchanged, and as he paused on the bridge he caught the appetizing smell of new-baked bread drifting over from Sid Wood's bakery behind the post-office. Tom Drew, who had worked in the stables at Darent Hulme before the war, found work at 25 shillings a week as a team man with the horses at the Mildmays' Park Farm in Otford, and one can imagine him in the evening taking out his cornet and starting to practise in readiness for the first meeting of the band.[1] Anne Hicks had returned from Wandsworth in 1916 to care for her father after her mother died, and in 1919 married Mr De Decker. They both got work in the paper-mill when it reopened in 1921. Mr Madge the vicar returned from France and resumed his work at the heart of the community

Amy Higgins (*née* MacLening) with the manager at the door of the Co-op shortly after the war. (Ian Harper)

in church and as an elected member of the Parish Council. Nelson MacLening, having followed his father into the Royal Horse Artillery, finished the war as a lance-bombardier and entered the building trade. Enos MacLening had been a sniper in The Royal West Kents, but was a prisoner of war in Germany for two years before coming home to bricklaying and plastering.[2] At the Armistice Captain Vincent Steane was appointed Army Education Officer of the South Eastern Area, serving for 2½ years at the Royal Herbert Hospital.

Lieutenant Colonel the Rt Hon. Francis B. Mildmay returned without delay to political activity at Westminster, concerned with one of his main interests — public health. In the middle of the war he had been appointed to the Privy Council, and on his return the Privy Council made him a member and Treasurer of the Medical Research Council. However, in 1922 after thirty-seven years as MP for Totnes he decided not to stand again, and was warmly congratulated by the village when he was raised to the peerage as Baron Mildmay of Flete.

Major Roger Gregory was in 1919 able to return to peaceful pursuits, and accepted the wish of the electors in Shoreham to become the chairman of the Parish Council. John Bowers had been chairman for twenty-five years and during that time had been affectionately dubbed 'The Mayor of Shoreham' but at seventy-two he decided to retire. Roger Gregory became a justice of the peace for Kent in 1920, and in 1921 was made a knight. This honour came in recognition of the considerable service to the legal profession that he had given before and after the war, particularly on a number of important legal reform committees.[3] In June 1922 he added the duties of the vicar's warden to his other local activities.

One who perhaps had most difficulty in adjusting to the post-war world was Edward, Lord Dunsany. Something of the sorrow and bitterness he had experienced on the Western Front he expressed in writing *Unhappy Far-Off*

Things, published in 1919. Before the war he had made a reputation as a writer of short stories and short one-act plays. Now he found there was little demand for what was 'small and exquisite'.[4] Frustrated and over forty, he had to exert himself to draw out his tales to book-length; so when demobilized in 1919 he went to Dunstall Priory and started to write novels. In fact he completed nine of them between 1919 and 1939.[5] One of his relaxations was to shoot black vipers on the Downs above the house, which George Walkling (living at Chapel Alley Cottages) skinned so that he could wrap their skins round his head to cure headaches.[6] He had to contend with all the anxieties and dangers of the situation at Dunsany during the Troubles of the next three years, which at times were nothing short of civil war.

As the village inhabitants returned, so the broken threads of pre-war life were picked up and woven into a new pattern. The Rifle Club opened in the Church Room in February 1920, the Mothers' Union organized an entertainment at which John Humphreys (son of the landlord at the George Inn) gave impersonations and during the winter cinematograph shows were given in the Church Room. Even before the end of the war a new organization was started, anticipating the coming of peace. The parish magazine of July 1918 announced that the Women's Institute 'has been formed in the village . . . Open to all women over 18 . . . non-political, non-sectarian'. The WI President was Miss D. Scott, the Vice-President Miss Madge, the Treasurer Mrs Moore and the Secretary Mrs Walkey. At their first meeting 'Miss Clouting packed a hay box and cooked rice and potatoes by the hay box method'.

Those who had not returned from the war were ever present in people's hearts and minds. Their nearest and dearest since the Armistice had been wondering how best to remember them. It seems that it was Mr Madge, the vicar — who had lost his brother in the fighting — who first put forward the idea of cutting a cross in the chalk of the hill below Meenfield Wood. The idea immediately found favour. Roger Gregory also suggested the building of a village hall for entertainments and a working men's club as a memorial, and a further element was added — the stone memorial on the banks of the Darent by the bridge. Benjamin Greenwood offered to plan and help with the construction of the cross on the hill.

On Empire Day, Monday 24 May 1920, in brilliant sunshine the people of Shoreham paid their respects to those who had died in the war. In the village before the ceremony the Shoreham United Brass Band under Bandmaster Joseph Booker played *Lest We Forget* and then climbed the hill beneath Meenfield Wood with the rest of the village. The vicar Mr Madge conducted the memorial service and explained that people had wanted their memorial to be something very simple, something as close to nature as possible. It was fitting, therefore, that the chosen ground for the cross overlooked the village from which most of them had gone, and where they had earned the right always to be remembered. Colonel Mildmay in cutting the first sod said that his words would be few, but he thought that they would all agree that they were deeply indebted to Mr Madge for his conception of the cross on the hill as the best way of perpetuating the memory of those who had passed away. This was an occasion which lent itself not so much to public speaking as to silent thought. He said that there had been times in the war when things looked black, and a few had asked whether we should try to compromise. Thank God, England did not shrink. England had been determined to do its duty.

The band then played a funeral march, and after the music died away over the

Edward, Lord Dunsany. (Mrs P. Rye)

valley and there was silence, save for the stirring of the leaves in the wood, Lord Dunsany spoke as follows:

> It is the duty of the youngest to remember this ceremony, and in years to come to tell the children of it and to impress on them that the cross must be carefully tended. Thus it will become a custom that will not pass away, but the cross will remain white upon the hill like the oldest white horses in England. It may be in the future that the place we know as London will come over the hills, and if that happens this spot will still be kept sacred amid its streets and traffic . . . centuries hence it may be that nothing will remain but a few shepherds, but even among them the memory will

remain that there was once a great sacrifice by the men of the valley for the safety of the hills . . .

Joseph Booker sounded *The Last Post*, 'but even after its clear silvery notes had died away in the distance the people stood silently and reverently in homage to the memory of the glorious dead'.[7]

Men, women and children, the rich and the poor, set to and dug the trenches in the hard chalk and in the end the cross was cut: 100 feet in length, with the spread arms 58 feet. The upright of the cross is 13 feet wide and the depth of the arms 16 feet, to allow for perspective.[8] The construction of the cross and the riverside memorial was completed in September 1921. The inscription on the memorial reads:

> Remember as you look at the Cross on the Hill those who gave their lives for their country 1914-1918;

and the plaque at the head of the cross originally read:

> In gratitude to the Great Creator and in respectful memory of those men of Shoreham who gave their lives for their country 1914-1918.

The proposal to build a village hall was not dropped, but 'the appalling cost' of the first plans decided the committee to begin modestly with a 'memorial porch and a portion of the hall to seat about 100 persons together with the platform or stage and two small retiring rooms at an approximate cost of £3,000 to £3,500'.[9] All the voluntary societies set about raising funds. In January 1921 Harold Copping put on a dramatic show in the Memorial Hall, Otford, in aid of the fund. Harold appeared with Mrs Dorothea Wilmot in *The Boatswain's Mate*, and the two Land Girls who had remained in Shoreham after the war — Miss Berkeley and Miss Cobbold — joined him in the grave-diggers scene from *Hamlet*. Copping and Heath-Stubbs were the grave-diggers, Miss Berkeley the Prince of Denmark and Miss Cobbold Horatio.[10] Miss Cobbold, a 'bright and lively' person, was also the first captain of the Girl Guide Company (the 1st Shoreham) which she and Miss Berkeley started in 1920. They lived with Miss Berkeley's father, a much-respected South London surgeon, at Little Timberden.[11]

When Lloyd George called for a general election eleven days after the Armistice was signed it was soon realized that better housing was going to be a key issue. There had been ample evidence of Shoreham cottages that were unfit to live in before 1914, and no doubt the situation had worsened in four years of war. The RDC and PC were both keen for action. In October 1919 the RDC had approved with the parish a three-acre site, and on 1 June 1920 the land was purchased from Mr Mildmay and the Commissioner for Housing approved plans for twenty-four houses in Shoreham.[12] There was some delay in completing the plans because of uncertainty over the number of hands likely to be employed at the paper-mill which reopened in the spring of 1921, and delay also in the supply of materials, so that it was not until August 1926 that the houses were completed and tenants selected.[12] The first tenants were C.J. Cheeseman, H. Collins, F. Emery and T.W. Farmer. The following month the Parish Council recommended the names of the roads along with the houses were built. The first was Bowers Road after John Bowers, the much-loved 'Mayor of

Shoreham' whose portrait (painted by Harold Copping) was to hang in the Walnut Tree Club. The second was Mesne Way; this was an academic choice of name, the alternative spelling of Mesne being Meen as in Meenfield Wood. It implied land that in medieval times belonging to the Manor, rather than glebe land belonging to the Church.

The Parish Council under Sir Roger Gregory's chairmanship raised with the RDC various pieces of unfinished pre-war business, such as clearing the river Darent of weed and rubbish, but a more long-standing matter was the wish for a bridge to be built across the Darent at the bottom of the Crown Road. This had been first expressed in a petition presented at a parish meeting in 1909, when Frederick Boakes claimed that the path between the paper-mill and Water House was a public path. Albert Wilmot denied this, and asked Boakes for his authority. Boakes claimed it was in print in an old book at Westerham. The meeting was not impressed, and the matter was dropped. In 1919 the District Surveyor, Frederick Boakes and Sir Roger all agreed that the bridge would indeed be a great advantage to those in Crown Road and the north-west of the village going to the station, and as the only objector was Mr Wilmot, the chairman promised to talk to him.

Meanwhile the PC had agreed with the inhabitants that Crown Road needed making up. It was in such a bad condition that the RDC agreed to take responsibility for it, but only if the 'Frontagers' would pay for certain basic improvements first. After some objections and bargaining over the estimate for the preparatory work, all was agreed. The Parish Council were particularly pleased, as they had been pressing for such projects to alleviate the serious unemployment situation. By May 1923 the majority of Frontagers had paid their contributions, and work began in June. To the consternation of all in Crown Road, it was discovered that included in the plan for the road was a concrete wall and an unclimbable iron fence to be erected 'across the road adjacent to the River'. What had happened to their request for a bridge? A petition was hastily put together and sent to the RDC, whose Highways Committee considered it but recommended that no action be taken. The concrete wall and the iron fence were completed by 9 August 1923.[13]

The prospects of employment in the early 1920s were not good. Those seeking work at Fort Halstead were disappointed, as in 1922 the Fort was sold to a private buyer. Two enterprising ex-soldiers started a bus service to Sevenoaks, and fortunately about seventy hands were eventually taken on at the paper-mill. The *Paper-Mills Directory* for 1923 noted that George Wilmot Limited was making 'hand-made papers for ledger, writing and drawing. All papers entirely from rags. No machine or mould-made papers made.' Some may have realized even then that the hand-made paper industry was threatened when in 1922 Reed's Paper Mill at Aylesford was founded.

On his return to Shoreham Vincent Steane started the Boy Scout troop. However, Scouting really became a force in the village with the arrival in 1923 of Stanley and Barbara Brown. They had been active with the Scout movement in Bromley. Stanley — or Skipper as he soon was called — was in banking, and Barbara a teacher in Otford. The well-being of the 5th Sevenoaks (Shoreham) Group and its members became their life interest. The Scout camp for many youngsters was the only holiday they could hope for; it was the event of the year, usually taking place at Bexhill or Deal. The group was supported by a strong management committee chaired in the late 1920s by Captain Anthony Brown, with Major Miller as vice-chairman and including the vicar, the headmaster, Lady Gregory and Benny Greenwood.[16]

In 1923 there seemed to be a slightly more relaxed mood in the parish. Mr Madge suggested in August: 'Now that the band plays in the Recreation Ground more of us may be tempted to spend the last hour or two of the day there listening to them.' 1924 seemed even fuller of promise. With the fund-raising efforts of the various clubs and societies, the Village Hall was near completion in January, and on the 2nd of May the Village Hall trustees — A.H. Balme, B.I. Greenwood, Harold Copping, George May (the draper and Rural District Councillor) and Herbert Street (land agent to Lord Mildmay) — signed an indenture with Lord Mildmay and received the land on which the hall had been built. Almost at the same time the Walnut Tree Club was opened with its billiard table, library and beer licence. Mr Madge was full of enthusiasm for the opening of the hall; 'it is an event', he said, 'which we may well hope will be the start of an upward movement in our village. There are possibilities in the new Hall such as have not been presented by anything that we have had before'.[17] Spirits were rising. Even Lord Dunsany was finding some peace in Shoreham. After a rainy day he and Lady Dunsany walked along the Terrace beside Meenfield Wood, and up over the hill towards Shepherds' Barn, and from 10.30 to 11.00 p.m. they 'were surrounded by nightingales'. Isaac Brown the blacksmith and Edward, Lord Dunsany, had often met on the cricket field, and now they found another mutual interest in chess. Though Edward usually won, Isaac gave him a good game.[18]

As already mentioned, village concerts had for many years been a popular activity. A star performer who is still remembered from those years with pleasure and a smile was Lady Hart Dyke, playing a vigorous beat on her drum to a piano accompaniment. With the Village Hall available new possibilities opened up, and as if fate were taking a hand the right people seemed to have come together at that moment. Harold Copping was a trustee of the hall. A friend of his, Herbert Reginald Barbor, had been watching it being built with keen interest from his cottage 'Friars' in the High Street. Barbor had the love of the theatre in his veins. He had already made his name as a dramatic critic, contributing to the *Daily Telegraph*, the New York stage paper *Billboard* and others. Since coming to live in Shoreham he had been studying the inhabitants of the village, those labouring in the fields, in the shops, carpenters, butchers, bakers and teachers and decided that he could cast Shakespeare's play *A Midsummer Night's Dream*. Harold Copping spurred him on, as did Lord Dunsany. Franklin White was only too keen to design and paint the scenery with the help of his students and villagers. Olga his wife, a gifted violinist and a student of Kreisler, was also keen to help. Ernest Edwards the carpenter with the help of the schoolboys built the apron stage in his workshop next to Holly Place. His son Len took the part of Flute and his daughter Winifred — who normally looked after the Barbors' son 'Bim' — played a fairy. Vincent Steane was ready to produce the music with Joseph Booker and James and Frederick Drew from the band.

There were so many wanting to act that Barbor had to form two casts. Henry Geering from the butcher's shop at Walnut Tree Cottages shared the part of Theseus with Haydn George, while Percy Taylor at the Royal Oak and Malcolm James learned the part of Demetrius. Titania was played by Vera Draffin and Betty Coddrington, Harold Copping's daughter. Vera Draffin's father took

Egeus. Harold Copping not only designed the costumes but also played Bottom. Olga Harte (Mrs Franklin White) and Mable George shared Hermia, and Ernest Dowdy learned Quince's words as he went on his rounds as the village carrier. Greta Collins the saddler's daughter at fourteen made a lively Puck.

Naturally Lord Dunsany became President of the Shoreham Village Players, while Louisa, Lady Cohen and Lady Gregory were vice-presidents with Henry Ainley, the West End actor who added professional weight to the fledgling society. An actress of growing eminence, Edith Evans, was a close friend of Barbor's and was already committed to encourage rural drama groups. She often visited the Barbors in Shoreham to watch the progress of the Players, and donated £5 to the production.

Careful training and preparation was the order of the day, but at last in January 1925 Franklin White's scenery was built and painted and Malcolm James had installed the special acetylene lighting — Shoreham had no electricity at the time. The first night was on Monday 2 February, and Lord Dunsany took his special seat in the front row. The Players were astonished with the success of their hard work and the stir that they had caused. The national press had been alerted and the Tuesday editions of the *Daily Mail* and *Daily News* carried full and congratulatory notices. It was not the 1980s, when most villages have amateur drama groups; in 1924 the Shoreham Village Players — thanks to H.R. Barbor's imagination and patient work, and to the enthusiasm of the whole community — were among the first of the pioneers.

Six performances were given in the new village hall, and the demand was such that Lord Dunsany invited them to perform in the grounds of the Priory on 25 July. Reports in the *Evening News*, *Daily Graphic* and *Manchester Guardian* claimed that there were three to four hundred in the audience. A further performance was given in August at Somerhill Park, Tonbridge, at the invitation of its owner, Lieutenant Colonel d'Avigdor-Goldsmid. With this explosion of interest and achievement the Players attracted other professionals from London to see performances. Len Edwards recalled[19] a billiards match between Barbor and C.B. Cochran, the great impresario, in the working men's club next to the Village Hall. Len was acting as marker.

Cochran on that occasion said he was delighted with the production and would have taken it to the West End, but it would have clashed badly with a spectacular production of the *Dream* being put on by Basil Dean. The excitement aroused by Shoreham's *Midsummer Night's Dream*, followed by *The Shoemakers' Holiday*, drew into the village two interested composers who offered to help with a future production. Peter Warlock and E.J. Moeran were living in rooms opposite the Castle Hotel in Eynsford. The production in which they took part turned out to be a rustic review called most appropriately *Hops*. The Players over the next four years firmly established themselves and became a valuable cohesive force in the community, bringing together in a common purpose many from all sides of the village.[20]

Shortly before the war, at the end of his school-days at Prince Alfred College in South Australia,[15] Franklin White came with his art master on a tour of the 'old country' and Europe. He was completely captivated by the wealth of paintings that he found in the galleries: not only in London but with his 'rover' ticket on the railway, in Scotland, Burnham Beeches and St Ives in Cornwall. He soon realized that there was only one thing to do — paint and draw — and as he moved about the country he searched for the right school to meet his need to discipline his own unruly creative urges. He found such discipline at the Slade School of Fine Art at University College, London, but could only spend two terms there before war broke out.

During the war he worked as a draughtsman at the Admiralty, and benefited from the detailed drawing that he had to do there. He returned to the Slade in 1918, and after only five terms Professor Tonks invited him to join the staff. He became a tutor in drawing for three days a week, and was given a salary of £5 per week. It was the policy of the Slade to employ active and inventive artists. By paying them only modest salaries it forced them to do supplementary outside work, and certainly Franklin White had to work hard to augment his income to keep his wife and four children in the 1920s and 1930s. He was attracted to Shoreham but not as far as it is known by the work of Samuel Palmer, and lived first at Hope Cottage in Crown Road, but in 1920 acquired Reedbeds. It is one of the great ironies of Shoreham's history that Franklin White — who was to found the Samuel Palmer School of Fine Art at Reedbeds in 1958 — never discovered that it had been the home of William Belsote in the fourteenth century (see p. 60), and that it had been owned by Samuel Palmer in the 1830s. He only discovered the work of Palmer in 1926. In 1920 there were six dwellings in the house and six front doors, and those living there included the Russells and the Walklings. Franklin White began to teach drawing and painting at Reedbeds on a small scale, and held the first residential course about 1922. He was on the staff of the Slade School for thirty-eight years.

After the belated lift to farm fortunes in the last year of the war, prices began to fall sharply in 1920-1 and the Government was able to push through the Corn Production Acts (Repeal) Act which abolished price guarantees and minimum-wage control. Inevitably farmers started shedding labour, and the Union was powerless to prevent it. Wages by the end of 1922 had been reduced by 25 per cent on levels existing only two years earlier.[21] Shoreham parish council as already noted was deeply concerned to alleviate unemployment, though it was not as acute in the parish as elsewhere. Hops and fruit-growing were picking up since 1918. Between 1919 and 1923 the average annual number of pockets of hops produced at Filston was 144, and in the next five years 193. (In 1914-17 the figure was 165).[22]

The annual arrival in the autumn of the 'hoppers' to occupy their huts at Castle Farm and Filston Farm was an exciting disturbance of the daily round in the village. Whole families came. In the 1930s at Filston three hundred pickers were required. This was welcomed by young and old in the village as a seasonal increase in income, because with the hoppers required by Castle Farm there was ample work for the village and for the families coming from Dartford and elsewhere who needed their earnings from hopping to pay for their winter clothing. For the hoppers it was a five-week family holiday, hard-working, but an escape from the grime-filled air of the city streets to the fresh breezes of the country. Children as well as grown-ups picked: if necessary into upturned umbrellas. Each picker had a book to keep the record of bushels picked, and the measurer (earlier called the tallyman) kept the master book.[23] In the evenings after the strenuous work of the day, they seemed to have energy enough for practical joking, dancing round camp fires. On Saturdays they raced their horses and carts, 'Ben Hur fashion' (according to Nancy Teague) up and down the

The Geerings' butcher's shop at Walnut Tree Cottages, painted by Franklin White. (Mrs G. Franklin White)

High Street, and the villagers ran for cover. The fruit-growers seemed to be finding a growing market. *Kelly's Diréctory* for Shoreham listed six fruit-growers in 1924 and twenty-one in 1938. They too were in season a ready source of extra employment for the parish. There were others, mainly in the Badgers Mount and Well Hill area, who tried to make a living with poultry farming.

The harsh economic realities broke in on the heartening theatrical events centred on the Players in the village hall when in 1926 came the coal and the general strikes and for Shoreham the closing of the paper-mill. After more than 230 years the makers of hand-made paper could no longer compete with modern production methods, no longer compete against such large installations as Reed's paper mill at Aylesford. So the gates were closed at the bottom of Mill Lane, and the hooter no longer sounded at noon, 1 p.m. and 5 p.m. Those working for the Mildmay Estate, on the land, on the buildings and in the workshops considered themselves fortunate indeed. The search for work went on. Alice Cheeseman had been rag-cutting and cleaning at the paper-mill for thirty shillings a week; now aged thirty, she went up to London and stood outside factories in Silvertown and Millwall in the hope of being taken on. At this moment of crisis George and Mrs Summerfield moved into the George Inn with their two sons. After many years Mrs Walker had handed over the running of the Post Office to her niece Ann Spring and her nephew Fred Spring, who took the letters from Shoreham to Sevenoaks at 7 p.m. each evening (including Sundays) and brought the mail from Sevenoaks in the morning which Sam Yates delivered in the village.[24]

Since 1923 house-building had been slowly increasing. Bungalows had been appearing on small plots on the East Hill estate, and as a result the provision of passing places and widening along Fackenden Lane was carried out to accommodate increased traffic; owners of hedges were ordered to cut them back.[25] Such was the concern expressed in the parish council over the increase in heavy motor traffic that councillors suggested the closing of Shacklands and Filston Lanes to heavy vehicles. The RDC surveyor agreed that Shacklands Lane was totally unsuitable for heavy vehicles, but considered Filston Lane could be made suitable by widening it to 18 ft throughout (an application for a grant to the Ministry of Transport would probably be successful). Meanwhile the Post Office engineers had been improving communications by erecting overhead telephone lines to Coombe Hollow and Highfield, and a year later Messrs John Mowlem laid underground cable conduits throughout the village.

In relations between the rural district and the parish councils there had been, perhaps from their inception, an ambiguity over responsibility for the maintenance of footpaths: the RDC firmly refusing to accept what the Shoreham council saw as RDC responsibility. Sir Roger Gregory, one of the leading lawyers in the country (he became President of the Law Society in 1930), and chairman of the PC, decided in March 1924 to submit the whole correspondence between the parish and the RDC to the Ministry of Health — responsible then for local government. The immediate result of this move we have been unable to trace, but the impression is left that the ambiguity was resolved in the Parish Council's favour.

1927 began and ended with the loss to Shoreham of two of its prominent parishioners. Vincent Steane's health had broken first during his post-war appointment as Army Education Officer, and although he returned to his busy life as schoolmaster, organist and choirmaster and parish councillor, he suffered further breakdowns. He at last decided to ease off and gave up teaching at Easter 1926. He finally retired after thirty-five years as headmaster in the September. Easter Sunday was the last time he was able to play the organ he loved so much and which he had enlarged three times since 1891, the last time being just before Easter. He had only a few months of retirement and died in January 1927.[26] As if to emphasize the continuity of life, in that same month Miss Cohen planted a new replacement walnut-tree on the grass in front of the Walnut Tree Club.

John Bowers died at the age of eighty, having served the Methodist Society over fifty years in every office open to a layman, and having been in character if not in name the Mayor of Shoreham, as chairman of the parish council for twenty-five years. His last public appearance was to read the lessons in the parish church at the united service on Armistice Sunday, 6 November 1927, and to address the open-air gathering on the bridge near the memorial stone. Two weeks later he died, and Mr Madge assisted the Superintendent Minister Mr E. Pratt at his funeral service in the Methodist Chapel.[27]

The following year the Methodists celebrated the fiftieth anniversary of the founding of the chapel in the High Street. To mark the occasion they installed electric lighting in the chapel for £28, and presented the old oil-lamps to the Weald and Romney Street Chapels and gave one to the Shoreham Baptist chapel. It was, however, decided that no mains water would be laid on because water for tea meetings could continue to be drawn from a neighbouring well.[28]

If heavy vehicles were a worry to the councillors in 1927, of far greater concern was the plan to build an arterial road through the valley and through the village. Such a road was seen by higher authority as a valuable link between the

Dartford–Purfleet tunnel and a by-pass round Sevenoaks on the London to Hastings road (both at that time in the planning stage). The proposal aroused indignation and protest in the Sevenoaks area, and especially in Shoreham. A petition was sent to the Minister of Health, who having considered the objections informed the RDC that 'it is unnecessary and undesirable to make provision in the scheme for a new arterial road along the Darenth Valley'[29] and the plan was withdrawn. The good news was given in the parish magazine of September 1927: 'Our readers will be glad to know that there is no longer any probability of a new road through our valley. The scheme is now definitely abandoned . . .' This was somewhat premature, as the planners had returned to their drawing-boards and on 14 June 1928 the question of the line of the road was again raised in the RDC Planning Committee. 'After careful consideration it was resolved to recommend the Council to reserve in the scheme a line from the main London–Hastings road immediately north of the Sevenoaks By-Pass and swinging off in a north-easterly direction joining the main Farningham Road near Fackenden Lane, Shoreham.' Frederick Boakes and George May, Shoreham's RDC councillors, must have hurried back to Shoreham with this bad news. Once more the inhabitants of Shoreham went into action and a second and very eloquent petition was drawn up and sent to the Minister of Health. Extracts from this petition are given in The Appendix on p. 255. Again, the battle was won and no road was built. To celebrate the victory Lord Dunsany wrote a light-hearted play called *The Road* which the Shoreham Village Players included as part of *An Evening with Lord Dunsany* in 1956.

If the inhabitants of Shoreham beat off attacks from the transport lobby, they welcomed the coming of mains water and electricity into the village. Councillor George May in April 1928 asked the RDC to sanction electric light in the Shoreham council houses and the matter was referred to the Housing Committee 'to await a formal request from the tenants' who would have to pay for the electricity once the installation was complete. In that same year Lord Dunsany published his novel *The Blessing of Pan*. According to his biographer Mark Amory, 'His passion for the countryside round Dunstall floods through the book'.[30]

The continuity of the parish church and the community of which it was still a centre was brought home to parishioners in 1929 when certain gifts were made to the church of St Peter and St Paul. Samuel Cheeseman had been parish clerk and sexton from 1900 until he handed over his duties to Percy Stevens in 1927. He gave the church the prayer-book used by one of his predecessors, Edward Medhurst, who had begun his sixty years as clerk and sexton in 1780. Joseph Booker, the bandmaster, gave back to the church five early music books (rebound through the kindness of Lady Gregory) which had been in the care of his family but had been used originally by the church instrumentalists. Joseph's ancestor, William Booker the sawyer, had been an enthusiastic member of the church orchestra about 1841, and the books bore the following inscriptions: 'Shoreham Choir 1818-1820, 1829'; 'Richard Squib February 19th 1830'; 'David Baker April 16th 1833' with a pen and ink sketch added of a rustic player with his 'violinsello' (sic). Beneath are the words 'John Smith's book March ye 10 1830. This day aged 64 years.' Mrs Steane presented an ancient music book: *The Psalmist's New Companion*, 'set forth and corrected by Abraham Adams at Shoreham in Kent'. Abraham Adams, the eighteenth-century organist and musical editor, lived at Shoreham about 1760.[48] On their silver wedding day, 8 September 1929, and to commemorate their marriage there in 1904, William Draffin and his wife presented a Breeches Bible (1616).[31]

More than ten years had passed since the ending of the war, and although many traditional habits of mind remained inevitable changes were taking place. Meticulous care was observed in the rearing of the pheasants in the woods west of the village. The keepers, always in uniform with shot-guns and black (always black) retrievers at heel, patrolled the woods. To deter predators they hung rows of dead crows, weasels etc. on the five-barred gates. The nesting boxes lined the path at the top of the open field above Timberden Farm — just before the path goes into the wood. Small heaps of grit for the birds were placed at intervals along the lesser paths (not the Terrace) and village children were told not to walk near them at about 3 p.m., which was considered to be feeding-time. The men of the village acted as beaters and the shot pheasants were loaded into a cart at the end of the Terrace in the open field crossed by the track from Shepherds Barn to Filston. However, the Mildmays now let out the pheasant shoot to a syndicate.

Church-going was still an important and regular part of life for many. On Sundays during the midsummer months the Mildmays sat in their private chapel, while the Gregorys sat in the Buckland chapel (now known as the Gregory chapel). Lord Mildmay read the lessons very well, and so did Sir Roger Gregory, but Lord Dunsany was less successful, because, as a village wit remarked, he had not written the Bible himself. The new vicar, Mr Augustus Payne, shook hands with members of the congregation at the south porch after the service, and because there were no letters to deliver on Sunday Sammy Yates greeted friends at the lych-gate instead of at their front doors. Sam always sang very loudly and out of tune, making difficulties for the congregation. Newcomers to the village Mr and Mrs Kenneth Ritchie were surprised to discover that inhabitants of long standing called upon them, leaving their cards, and expected a courtesy call in return. Sir Herbert Cohen was now Lord of the Manor.[32] The pre-war social order had been shaken but still stood.

The village band was playing its valuable part in keeping up people's spirits. There had been some difficulty in regrouping it after the war, but eventually Joseph Booker succeeded in making it one of the best in the country. Certainly the quality of its playing attracted the two composers Peter Warlock and E.J. Moeran, who persuaded the band to try out some of their own compositions. On another occasion Sir Dan Godfrey, the conductor of the Bournemouth Municipal Orchestra from 1893 to 1935, composed a special piece of music for the band to play in the Crystal Palace Brass Band Competition. The band wondered what had hit them when he conducted them through it. They were much in demand to play at functions in the district, but the centre of their music-making was the band stand on the Recreation Ground. On alternate Saturday nights they used to play on a beat from the Royal Oak to the Two Brewers and on one from the bridge to the George Inn. There was also a time when on Christmas mornings they started playing at 5 a.m. — *Christians Awake* took on a new meaning. One bright spark given the task of taking the collection fixed the bag to a long pole so that those still abed could make their contribution through the bedroom window.[33]

The band played their hearts out on 14 April 1930 when an all-day party was given at Shoreham Place for the village to celebrate Anthony Mildmay's twenty-first birthday. Some claim the party lasted for three days. During the war years Mrs Mildmay had taken Helen and Anthony to Flete in Devon, where both had been able to enjoy the freedom of the countryside. It was there that Anthony's love of horses began. He got to know the sons of Lomas the groom and other boys at Holbeton. He was a very even-tempered boy, quite retiring, yet always interested in what those around him were thinking and feeling.[27] After the war on their visits to Shoreham he found his village friends growing in numbers, so that by 1930 the celebration of his twenty-first birthday was a really happy occasion.

He joined Baring Brothers, but rather naturally he found it difficult to adjust to City life at a time when even a clear Saturday away from the City was a rare event. He longed for life in the open air, preferably on horseback. As a compromise, he worked out a plan with a friend Peter Cazalet, who lived at Fairlawne near Tonbridge and who had started a training stable there. Peter Cazalet happily agreed that Anthony should keep a horse at his stables, and soon his weekday routine was to leave Shoreham at 6.15 a.m., have a ride at Fairlawne followed by a quick breakfast and catch the 8.15 train from Tonbridge for London Bridge in order to be at Barings by nine. From this beginning there grew what the horse-racing public came to know as the Mildmay–Cazalet Combination, and Anthony Mildmay found he had the entrée into the world of the amateur jockey.

By 1932 Anthony realized the compromise with the city was intolerable and an alternative had to be found. Plans were made for him to develop a market garden on the estate, and later to run Park Farm in Otford. Market gardening was entirely new to him, and he set to learning about it in a most businesslike way and with enthusiasm. For a year he studied it at the Golden Green Nurseries near Tonbridge and then returned to Shoreham. The site he chose for his Kent Fields Nurseries was that where now a garden centre operates, close to the London–Hastings road and opposite what at one time was the Black Eagle public house. An acre of glasshouses was built and a start made but not without many difficulties. These were only resolved when Anthony persuaded a Mr Coutts to help him. Mr Coutts, a stern Scot, had till then been head gardener at Fairlawne, but he took well to market gardening and soon the roadside stall was taking over £100 a week in summer. There was a permanent staff of eight. Anthony himself did a good deal of hard labour, and would often be seen hoeing away at eight in the morning.[34] Frank Russell, towards the end of twenty-three years of service with the Mildmays in the Walled Garden and the Top Garden, took over as foreman at the Kent Field Nurseries when Mr Coutts had to retire through illness about 1945.

After taking over the management of Park Farm, Otford, and being intensely interested in clean-milk production Anthony acquired from William Alexander senior in 1938 twelve heifers from his noted herd of Friesian cattle at Eynsford. To these were added some carefully selected females to found the Bingham Herd. His activities in market gardening and farming in no way impeded his growing reputation as an amateur steeplechase rider, in spite of the extremely serious injuries he suffered when riding Irish Flight in the Foxhunter's Chase over the full Grand National course in 1934. He made a remarkable recovery, and had fourteen wins the following season, with his eye on the Grand National in 1936. That year Grand National Day was bright and sunny, but the betting odds of 100–1 were heavily against Anthony winning on Davy Jones. Many in Shoreham, however, put their money on them and even more had their ears to the radio at the 'off'. The excitement was almost unbearable as the race developed and it seemed a possibility that the amateur outsider might win.

Anthony was leading at the second to last fence. It looked a certainty, and to give Davy Jones every chance over the last, Anthony 'let slip his reins to the very buckle, and then in one nightmare moment, disaster descended. The prong of the buckle in some way managed to slip through the hasp, and in a trice, there were the reins flapping loose round Davy Jones's neck.'[49] In spite of Anthony's efforts, Davy Jones ran out to the left, leaving Reynoldstown to win.

By 1939 Anthony had found his experience at Baring Brothers had been of value. He proved himself an efficient business manager as well as an increasingly successful jockey, and Lord Mildmay — now seventy-eight — decided that the time had come to make over both Flete and the Shoreham estates to his son and heir.

One of the results of the war and the following years of depression was the 'ubiquitous, despised and unwanted minority'[35] — the tramps. They were much in evidence in Shoreham, sometimes sleeping in the shelter on the Recreation Ground. They were indeed attracted to the village because of the action of two people who felt compelled to help them. Miss Berkeley and Miss Cobbold as part of their work for the Southwark Catholic Travelling Mission to sequestered villages in the South-East decided to convert one of the barns at Little Timberden into a refuge where tramps could spend a night. On leaving each man was given 2s. 6d. and a mended pair of boots. Part of the barn nearest to the road was used for the same purpose, while part they converted into a small chapel to which Catholics in the district came for their devotions. When her father died and was buried in Shoreham churchyard Miss Berkeley erected a crucifix in his memory. The cross was 15 feet high with a life-size figure of Christ carved in teak by a well-known Austrian wood-carver, Mr Dapre. The crucifix stood on the upper bank above the junction of Cockerhurst Lane and the Shoreham–Eynsford road. The ground there at the chapel was consecrated so that on occasion Canon Donnelly would say Mass. In 1938 after Miss Berkeley had left Little Timberden a community of American Franciscans, the Friars of Atonement, was established to maintain the work on a full-time basis. However, this ceased in 1940 and only travelling missioners used it subsequently.[36]

On 29 September 1934 an Airspeed Courier aircraft belonging to London, Scottish and Provincial Airways piloted by Ronald Maxwell Smith took off from Heston for Paris. Maxwell Smith was an experienced pilot who had flown with the RAF and was shortly to be married. There were three passengers on board. At 5.20 p.m. on that day the Courier crashed in the valley between Little Timberden and Coombe Hollow. All on board were killed. Miss Berkeley placed a memorial stone to the dead close to the site of the crash.[37]

The full life of Benjamin Isaac Greenwood came to its end in February 1936. He had lived in Shoreham for more than forty years, and had enjoyed sharing not only the life of the Baptist Church but many of the village's activities: the construction of the Cross on the Hill, the building of the Village Hall, the YMCA — everything that promoted the well-being of the village. His funeral service at the Baptist church was taken by three student pastors, and Dorothy Brown was at the organ. The congregation then walked on foot through the village to the churchyard where a committal service was conducted by the vicar, Mr Augustus Payne.[38] His son Benny and his family were to live on, playing their full parts in Shoreham life.

The crucifix erected by Miss Berkeley in memory of her father. (The late Miss Dibley)

During 1932 a general survey had been made to decide the number of new dwellings required to rehouse those with dilapidated dwellings, but although Bowers Road and Mesne Way were established it was not until 1935 that the RDC applied for a loan to purchase a two-acre site for additional council houses. Fifteen years were to pass before the houses were built.

One consequence of the arrival of mains water and electricity in the valley was a marked increase in private-house building. The principal landowners had always agreed to keep speculative building away from the valley surrounding the village. Ribbon development had come close in 1925 along the Shoreham Road in Otford.[39] In 1928 the RDC had approved the layout for 103 houses in the Badgers Mount area but it seems that only 17 of these were built, and it was not until 1937 that further building took place along the Orpington By-Pass,[40] the year in which work began on the Dartford–Purfleet Tunnel. By 1938 as Badgers Mount grew so services developed there: William Honess was running a grocer's shop, Arthur Lemon the Post Office and stationers, and Alfred Jeffrey a joinery business, while Frederick Beckett and E.H. Elderfield were builders. A garage which covered both the London–Hastings Road and the Orpington By-Pass was run by Bernard Blundell and F. Fox ran Badgers Mount Garage.[41]

The motor-car was making an increasing impact on people's minds, although the impression left on Mrs Phillis Ritchie was that in 1935 when she and her

THE TWENTIETH CENTURY (2)

husband Kenneth Ritchie came to live at Church House there were only about ten cars owned by inhabitants; but then as in the 1980s a week-end invasion by cars as well as train and bicycle was beginning, providing customers for the still flourishing Ramblers and eight other refreshment rooms in the parish, not to mention the public houses. Even the comparatively few cars seem to have caused fierce exchanges between Franklin White at Reedbeds and the headmaster, H.J.A. Shoolbridge. The story is related that Franklin White hung a notice on a tree facing Church Street and the school-house which read 'Keep your cars off here — murderers' and Shoolbridge replied with 'Mind your own business.'

Although Sir Roger Gregory was still a parish councillor, he was feeling his seventy-four years and decided that he could no longer carry the responsibilities of chairman of the PC, so H.J.A. Shoolbridge, the headmaster who had topped the poll in 1928[42] and who had been re-elected since, took Sir Roger's place in 1935.[43] Ernest Dowdy became clerk to the parish council. Ernest, who had come to Shoreham on discharge from the Army in 1915, had a milk round and was in the haulage business. He had taken the part of Quince in the Players' original *Midsummer Night's Dream* and was still taking prominent parts in productions which at this time were mainly farces or thrillers. Vera Draffin (whose family were now living at Colgates) and Robert Pattenden at The Mount were the producers.

As if the play was recognized as an antidote to depression, the village leaders gave their full support. Lady Gregory was the Players' President, the vicar Mr Payne was the chairman and the vice-presidents were Lord and Lady Mildmay, Lord and Lady Dunsany, Sir Herbert Cohen, A.H. Balme Esq and G. Robertson Esq (living at Darentdale). For their part in celebrating King George V's Silver Jubilee the Players gave a free performance of *Ambrose Applejohn's Adventure* to the schoolchildren and old-age pensioners, as well as two other performances for paying audiences. In preparing for the Jubilee celebrations the PC suddenly realized that there was one important element which had been an essential feature of all Royal celebrations over the past sixty years, but which might be missing in 1935 — the village band. Joseph Booker was approached, but after much thought and heart-searching, he saw that it would need months of hard work to revive the band, and he did not feel capable of doing it. The village band had quietly died. Without the band, the plans for celebrating King George V's Silver Jubilee went ahead under the efficient direction of Mr Shoolbridge. There would be no bonfire or fireworks, but souvenir mugs would be given to the children and tea for six hundred. Houses were decorated, and there was dancing round the maypole, a fancy dress dance, a whist drive and sports. On Sunday 7 April one pink and one red chestnut tree were planted on the Recreation Ground, and Isaac Brown made the iron guards to protect them. All too soon (February 1937) a public meeting was called to discuss the celebration of George VI's coronation. A penny rate was agreed so that £45 could be spent on a programme very similar to that of 1935.

'In January 1938 with much regret Lady Gregory decided that because of other demands upon her time she would have to stand down as President[44] of the Shoreham Village Players.' Beneath those bland words lay the harsh fact that Sir Roger had for some time been ill, and he died on Sunday 27 February 1938. In a letter to *The Times* on the following Tuesday Sir Reginald Poole wrote 'Roger Gregory was first and foremost a great solicitor', and this was clear from the honours he had attracted not only in this country but also in Canada and the USA. He was a great solicitor because of his qualities as a human being, as the

SHOREHAM

The last picture of the Village Band, c.1930.

people of Shoreham could testify. He was approachable by everybody, and sympathetic to those who needed his advice. He was very largely responsible for the introduction of the Poor Persons procedure when this was taken over by the Law Society, and as the Treasurer he took a keen interest in the Foundling Hospital (see Chap. X, p. 136). Sir Roger and Lady Gregory had become part of the heart and soul of the community, and his many village friends were joined in the parish church by those from London and Kent who wished to pay their last respects when on the Wednesday David Madge returned to Shoreham to assist Augustus Payne at his funeral service. Because of his deep attachment to the church and the importance to the whole community over the centuries of the tidings of joy and sorrow which they had sent winging across the meadows and over the woods, Lady Gregory arranged for the church bells to be refurbished in his memory.

On 18 February 1938 the *Sevenoaks Chronicle and Courier* carried the headline 'Darenth Valley Threatened'. The planners were active once more, and the South Orbital Road was the subject of their attention. Otford Council had sought information from Shoreham (who seem to have been first with the news), and by mid-February Sevenoaks RDC had 'carefully considered the possible threat to the amenities of the Darenth Valley' if the road were constructed, and objections had been forwarded to the County Council on the following grounds:

Building development would follow.
The valley provided excellent farming close to London.
The valley formed part of the Green Belt and 'it may be possible to secure the preservation of the valley for all time if the road is abandoned'.
The cost of making and maintaining the 15 miles of the road would be an unnecessary burden.

John Dinnis as chairman of the annual parish meeting reported that Shoreham with other councils had taken every step to protest against this plan for a South Orbital Road, and he thought their efforts would be successful.[46]

Agricultural prices nationally had fallen by 36 per cent between 1929 and 1933. Many farmers had major financial difficulties, including D. McN. Templeton, from whom William Alexander took over the tenancy of Castle Farm in 1932. Government assistance to farmers in the next five years had been tentative (price guarantees for wheat were introduced in 1932), and it was not until the Munich crisis (1938) and the German invasion of Czechoslovakia that decisive action was taken and agriculture was once more put on a war footing. In support of a thesis running through the Shoreham story — that the valley of the Darent was a favoured place in which to farm — one can give Cockerhurst as an example of a potentially healthy mixed farm when in 1939 it was sold following the death of William Milvain.[47] Of its 283 acres the fruit plantation covered 48 acres, producing Cox's Orange, Miller Seedling, Worcester Pearmain and Bramley Seedling apples; Conference and Comice pears; Giant Prune, Victoria, Monarch and Yellow Gage plums. The 216 acres of arable land was considered suitable for growing potatoes, soft fruits and other market produce in addition to the usual corn crops. There were also 15 acres of pasture, and among the farm buildings stalls for 98 cows.

XV
THE TWENTIETH CENTURY (3) 1939-50

EVEN in 1937 there were signs locally that the Government was facing the possibility of war against Hitler and Mussolini — the War Office bought back Fort Halstead from its private owner for use on experimental work. In 1938 the Shoreham fire brigade which had been set up on a voluntary basis in 1915 was taken over by the RDC, and became part of the Seal Fire Brigade.[1] In February 1938 Colonel G.D. Bruce, the Chief Air Raid Warden for Sevenoaks district, explained in the *Chronicle and Courier* his plans for building a network of wardens,[2] and during the year an official visited parish council meetings to discuss air-raid precautions and proposals for public trenches, although the RDC in this was running ahead of Home Office instructions.

Individuals made their moves also. Kenneth Ritchie, the London solicitor now living with his wife and two young daughters at Church House, thought war was inevitable and learnt to fly, but was deeply disappointed when he was turned down as a pilot or an air gunner because of his age. Anthony Mildmay decided to join the local Territorial regiment (an anti-aircraft unit) to prepare himself for active service. He transferred to the Commandos and later to the Welsh Guards in 1941, and in the 1944-5 European campaign proved himself an excellent and courageous officer in the Guards Armoured Division.

In August 1939 the parish magazine gave no indication of concern that war was imminent. It reported that the weather had caused some anxiety on the day of the annual Garden Fête: ices did not sell very readily. The Women's Institute had held a delightful meeting at Shoreham Place, invited by their President the Hon Helen Mildmay.

On the morning of Sunday 3rd of September 1939 Neville Chamberlain, the Prime Minister, announced that Germany had invaded Poland, and that as a result Britain was at war with Germany. The air-raid siren sounded almost immediately after this broadcast. The Shoreham Village Players could not have produced a more dramatic opening to what was to be for Shoreham the most testing drama in its 1,100 years of history. The sky above its fields and woods was to be a crucial battleground of the Second World War. The village was fortunate in having the men and women to meet the challenge. Gas-masks and ration books were distributed with remarkable speed, and for the first year gas-masks were carried at all times; children were sent home from school if they had forgotten them. Even as late as May 1941 the parish magazine instructed:

> You will note and please pass on the information that there will be a hose and nozzle with running water hanging from the bathroom window of the School House, so that anyone who has come into contact with gas-vapour can rinse their eyes and hands if it is quicker than going home.

It was the coming of the evacuees to the village, from what were thought to be high-risk areas — Bellingham and Catford — that showed that the war had begun in earnest. The two billeting officers, members of the Women's Voluntary Service (WVS), were Mrs Ritchie of Church House and Mrs Lockett of Oxbourne House. There was no compulsion to take children but those with spare rooms were expected to take at least one. Every Saturday from 2 – 5 p.m. the Church Room was open so that children evacuated to the parish could meet for recreation and games, and every Sunday from 12.30 to 6 p.m. parents could meet their children there. The room was comfortably heated, and facilities provided for making tea. One father delighted his small son by always wearing his full Fire Service uniform, including his axe.

The few months of the 'phoney war' gave the various services time to organize themselves. The feeling of optimism at that time was perhaps expressed by one of the last entries in the visitors book of the Ramblers tea-room:

> A chap came down here for a spin
> Shoreham and Eynsford for to see.
> Britain was at war, but he knew they'd win
> And so he enjoyed his tea.

There was no Government hesitation this time, with the experience of the First World War in many minds. The plan was to make the country as self-sufficient as possible. The Kent War Agricultural Committee (KWAC) under Lord Cornwallis was set up, and John Dinnis of Filston — although becoming infirm — joined the local committee. He had been on the RDC during the First World War, and had been re-elected in 1937 and elected chairman of the parish council in 1938. His younger son Harold after only a year at Wye Agricultural College returned to help on the farm and assist his father with his wartime duties. Mr Dinnis carried out a survey of fields in the parish to decide how to increase production, and Harold when not working the land drove his father round the ten square miles of the parish to help him prepare his reports.

For the first time in its history the three Dinnis brothers began to bring into cultivation the fallow land of the eastern slopes of the Downs from the Rifle Range in the north, past Dunstall Priory to the Otford boundary in the south: 'My sons will do it in their spare time,' their father told the KWAC. The richness of the soil coupled with two exceptionally fine summers in 1940 and 1941 resulted in record harvests, and double summertime enabled work to continue until 11 or 12 o'clock at night. On the western slopes of the Downs above the High Street the Cross on the Hill, an obvious landmark for enemy aircraft, was covered with earth. From Sepham Bank to Timberden a great deal of unproductive scrub and grassland — the habitat of wild flowers, herbs and insects — had to remain, but all land above the plough-bank (dating from before

THE TWENTIETH CENTURY (3)

Domesday Book, which marked the limit of modern cultivation) that was not woodland or too steep was ploughed up to produce barley, wheat and oats. On the old Blackberry Common the ancient trackway (see Chap. I) leading from Shepherds Barn down to the river crossing disappeared under the plough. During the war the country's self-sufficiency was increased from 40 per cent to 75 per cent and no one went hungry. Individuals played their part, and the slogan 'Dig for Victory' was translated into practical terms in the cottage gardens and allotments. Where there was more space, as at The Mount, chickens, ducks, geese and rabbits were raised.

An exotic-looking crop, unknown locally since the great days of the Kentish weavers, was flax. Before the United States introduced nylon for parachute cords these were made from flax, and Shoreham's crop went to a factory in Ashford. The sight of Magpie Bottom blue with flax flowers was not easily forgotten. The hoppers from London could no longer come to Shoreham to gather the large wartime harvests of hops, so everyone in the village was called on to pick, at 6*d.* a day. As well as the staple vegetables, the luxury crop of strawberries was still farmed and sent to the large London hotels. The land now Palmers Orchard and Forge Way was used for pigs and hens, and of course the Townfield allotments were fully cultivated. The farmers and their labourers worked a sixteen-hour day, in spite of constant aerial attack from 1940 onward. Many farm workers were called up for the Services, and the contribution of the land girls cannot be overestimated.

Several centuries had passed since the legal duty of every able-bodied man between sixteen and sixty to serve in his country's Militia had been implemented. In 1939 the probability of air attack and the possibility of invasion led to the formation of distinct services to protect the inhabitants and defend the land: the Home Guard (originally called the Local Defence Volunteers), Air Raid Wardens, Special Constabulary, the National Fire Service and Fire Watcher patrols. Of these the Home Guard most nearly approximated to the militia of past centuries.

Recruitment to the Home Guard in May 1940 was by the civil police, and Shoreham, together with Otford, Kemsing and Seal, formed 'B' Company of the 20th Kent (Sevenoaks) Battalion. The members of the Shoreham contingent were mostly ex-WWI soldiers, but boys of sixteen could join — as in the Elizabethan militia. The company headquarters was at Coombe Hollow, the house of their commanding officer, Major Ben Greenwood. The second-in-command was Kenneth Ritchie of Church House, and after he left to join the RAF, Ted Dinnis; the platoon commander was Mr Cresswell of Cockerhurst; Ronald Hillier — Lord Mildmay's land steward living at Copt Hall, who had been an active rural district councillor since 1934 — became the platoon sergeant. Other members were Jack Cheeseman, Ray Cornwell, the other Dinnis brothers, Jack Marriott, Horace and Alec Martin and Jack Wood.

Lord and Lady Dunsany were over in Ireland in the summer of 1939, with Randal their son home on leave from India. Vera his wife had just given birth to Edward John Carlos. His grandparents were enjoying their family reunion when news of recruitment to the Home Guard reached them from Shoreham. Lord Dunsany immediately prepared for his return to Dunstall Priory, but was delayed because of complications over his determination to take various weapons (but no ammunition) over with him.[4] The only other weapons available then were those used by landowners, farmers and game-keepers and it was several months before weapons were actually issued. Meanwhile training took place at

209

Members of the Shoreham contingent of 'B' Company of the 20th Kent (Sevenoaks) Battalion, Home Guard. (The Shoreham Aircraft Preservation Society)

least twice during the week and on Sundays: tactical exercises on the hills and weapon training in the Village Hall, and later the rifle range once more was in constant use. Every man was given duties suited to his age and abilities, such as manning observation posts, defending road blocks, despatch riding, administration and cooking. Once the Blitz began the Home Guard was on duty every night, usually after finishing their daytime work. One meeting-point for duty turn was up on East Hill at the crossing of five roads near Romney Street. Here Dan Ashby, Jim Morse and others would meet.

Even those air raid wardens who remembered the Zeppelin raids could not have any idea of what to expect, and during the phoney war their main task was to train the inhabitants in the disciplines of the black-out. 'Put out that light' became the catch-word of the moment. Visits to seek suitable black material revealed that it could only be found at the local undertakers. The chief air raid warden was Major Joseph Charles Miller, veteran of the Boer War and the First World War, and his headquarters was in his home, Wayside, opposite the Co-operative Stores. The windows of the control room on the ground floor were protected by sandbags. It was bare of furniture except for two camp beds, chairs, tables and a telephone with maps on the walls. Props and wooden beams reinforced the ceiling, and there was no fire.[5] There were eight wardens, who included Will Cheeseman, Charles Hodges, the vicar Mr Guy Ford and Harold Goodban when he became headmaster of the village school in 1944. Theirs was a vital task in ensuring that no chink of light escaped from windows, as well as knowing the occupants of all the dwellings. They patrolled the streets with large gas-rattles to give warning of a gas attack, but mercifully did not have to use them.

The village fire-fighting service had to be extended. Before 1939 the Fire Station was the small brick building beside Walnut Tree Cottage. On 3 September 1939 one of Mr Ashby's coal lorries was commandeered and taken from the station coal-yard as an extra vehicle. It remained in use throughout the war. In December 1940 a much larger station was built on the site of Townfield Cottages, opposite Orchard House, after their destruction. In addition a fire pump and buckets were stored in the stable between Flint Cottage and Chapel Alley Cottages manned permanently by firemen Roger Cheeseman, Mick Smith, Mr Tooth, George Walkling and others. Dan Ashby at that time left the Home Guard and became leading fireman for Shoreham with a team of three including Reg Lawrence. Their motive power was an old Buick car behind which they towed the pump. As well as the Fire Brigade proper, fire-watching patrols were on duty every night consisting of girls working in pairs. One patrol route was from Shoreham Place to the High Street, the second along the High Street. In the depths of the black-out this was not a popular duty. Most homes kept a stirrup pump, bucket and sandbags ready to put out incendiary bombs.

At the permanent centre of civil authority was Police Constable Reuben Mannering, responsible for keeping law and order on his large and hilly patch. His headquarters were in his house on Church Street, which had a small notice outside the door that stated 'Constabulary'. His wife manned the telephone. To cover the 5,500 acres of the parish he used his bicycle, and he wore the uniform of a police cyclist — navy blue breeches and puttees. As in the First World War, the special constabulary was set up to work with PC Mannering. The 'Specials' had their headquarters at Orchard House, where they were directed by Capt W.A. Brown. They included Bill Gillham, who had been the Gregorys' groom; Arthur Offen, the butcher; Bernard Herrington of Home Farm; Henry Hitchcock of Oxbourne Farm, two Cheesemans and two Santers.

There were no doctors resident in Shoreham during the war, but Dr J.F. Alexander and Dr P.A. Mansfield in Sevenoaks both covered Shoreham, as did Dr Archer and Dr Peyton in Otford. The district nurse, Nurse Harlow, living in Bowers Road, turned her attention from delivering babies to caring for the injured. Shoreham's first-aid post was at Orchard House, and if an ambulance was required one was sent from the first-aid post in Otford, driven on occasion by Mrs P.L. Whyte of Darent Hulme. There were also fully trained first-aid groups in the Home Guard, and in a St John Ambulance section. PC Mannering (also trained in first-aid) found that there were fewer casualties for him to deal with during the war than there were cycling casualties in peacetime.

When the air raids began in 1940 many villagers stayed in their corrugated iron Anderson shelters in their own gardens, or in shelters dug into the hillside to the west of the High Street. The Specials had one such dug in the garden of Orchard House. Only after many months was a public shelter dug at the top of the steps in the recreation ground next to the village hall. Some living in the older cottages put their trust in the chimneys which had stood for centuries and sheltered beside them. Later in the war Morrison table shelters erected in downstairs rooms were issued by the Government, under which two or three people could sleep.

Shoreham Place and Shoreham House were requisitioned by the Army. Lord Mildmay, already living in Devon, kept a room or two to live in and the remainder of Flete became a wing of the General Hospital of Plymouth where Helen Mildmay was nursing at the Naval Hospital. Three troops of 150 were in Shoreham Place at any one time, largely from the Royal Artillery, Royal

Engineers and Royal Armoured Corps. Nissen huts were erected in the grounds for ATS girls, and the outbuildings were used for the regional NAAFI stores. Margaret Butler (née Osborne) worked there, and recalled the hard manual work involved as well as endless checking and book-keeping. Her most vivid memory was of boxes and boxes of Swiss rolls. The Quartermaster would occasionally give the girls some extra food to take home (rationing was strictly observed), and Margaret would creep home round the back of the church, instead of walking down the road, to avoid an encounter with PC Mannering.

By February 1941 Shoreham House was also requisitioned. Lady Gregory wrote in the parish magazine 'I was deeply shocked when I found it was required for other purposes, as other people's homes have been'. It was probably at that time that she disposed of her collection of village library books at threepence a copy to anyone who wanted them. Shoreham House was used primarily as the officers' quarters — twelve living there with their batmen. It was also the clerical and administrative centre where the ATS worked. The officers' mess was in the former library, the guard house in the old kennels. Darentdale was also an officers' mess.[6]

The war began in earnest in the summer of 1940. With France and the Low Countries occupied, Hermann Goering, Commander-in-Chief of the German Air Force, assembled some 3,000 bombers and fighters to carry out the destruction of England's southern ports, the annihilation of Fighter Command, the destruction of London and the morale of its inhabitants — all in preparation for the invasion of Britain on the 21st of September. In August Shoreham realized that it lay directly beneath one of the principal routes taken by the German air force in their attacks on London. The evacuees were hurriedly moved to safer areas. The wail of the air-raid sirens at first scared the villagers as much as it did the pheasants in the woods, but soon the sirens, the throbbing drone of approaching bombers, the ear-splitting crash of the Ack Ack batteries opening-up were received calmly and men, women and children knew what action to take. They soon realized another truth of their situation: their Army neighbours on the Downs were providing a very efficient anti-aircraft barrage against the invading planes, so strong and so efficient indeed that 'many of the raiders preferred to drop their bombs in N.W. Kent rather than face the terrific barrage' according to H.R.P. Boorman.[7]

So the day and night raids began, and rolled on until the climax came on Sunday, 15 September, when a thousand aircraft were sent against London. Understandably, the memories of that day are mixed. One hundred bombers attacked shortly before noon on a ten-mile front, and were met by no fewer than nine RAF squadrons. The battle developed into a series of individual dog-fights. Jack Marriott, on duty at the Otford First Aid Post, received a message that hop-pickers at Castle Farm had been machine-gunned from the air. One had in fact been shot in the leg by a bullet from one of two Spitfires of 609 Squadron, attacking a twin-engined Dornier bomber. David, a boy of fourteen, one of the Hewitt family at Castle Farm, saw one of the Spitfires circling the Dornier after it had crash landed, with the cockpit canopy pulled back and the pilot signalling to the growing crowd to keep back. The wounded German wireless operator was attended by one of Kenneth Ritchie's First Aid Party and taken to Sevenoaks Hospital, but was dead on arrival. The rest of the crew were arrested by the police and the Home Guard, and Jack Summerfield, at that time a Special Constable (he was called up the following month) recalled that Major Greenwood bought the German crew a drink at the George before taking them to

Townfield Cottages, seen from across the river and allotments.

Sevenoaks police station. Coming back, the Home Guard members asked each other 'Did you have any ammunition?' None had a single round.

Sixty enemy planes were destroyed on 15 September at a cost of twenty-six to the RAF. It proved an historic British victory. Two days later the invasion of Britain was indefinitely postponed. It is no wonder that the Battle of Britain has been celebrated ever since on 15 September each year. The village was reminded of what might have occured had Hitler invaded when part of Holly Place was rented by a refugee Hungarian historian Dr Karl Polanyi. His wife, broken in health, was able to join him in Shoreham later: influential British friends had obtained her release from a concentration camp.

Day and night raids continued until November and there was only one night when there was no raid on London. It was perhaps on that unusually quiet night that the Dunsanys arrived back at the Priory from Ireland but the following night two planes were shot down, one German and one English. Lord Dunsany for a day or two sat on the verandah at Dunstall Priory with a rifle, but feeling rather foolish he found a niche for himself with his neighbour Sir Herbert Cohen and the Home Guard spotting falling aircraft from a high point on the Downs above the house.

On 8 December 1940 Dan Ashby, a leading fireman with Jim Morse, was driving past the Crown during a raid when a bomb fell on the road directly in front of them. They were both unhurt but the car was damaged. They saw that a second bomb had fallen but not exploded on Townfield Cottages, an old group of cottages built at right angles to the High Street opposite Orchard House. They found it had lodged under the front wall, and Mrs Maxfield and her daughter (Mrs Pam Ayling) had been sitting beside it. The air raid warden took them quickly to the shelter on the recreation ground. Another elderly couple from Townfield Cottages were given tea and comfort by Mrs D'Eye at Friars and they could not help laughing through their tears when she showed them their blackened faces in a mirror — 'we look like city minstrels!' Hours later the bomb exploded and some of the oldest cottages in the village were totally destroyed, and with them all the precious possessions of their occupants. That same bomb made No. 77 High Street uninhabitable, and Frank Russell and his family were moved to the head gardener's cottage in the Walled Garden at Shoreham Place, and they were able to use as an air raid shelter the 'vegetable cellar' built into the ground in a time of peace for storing vegetables.

There was always a risk during daylight raids of casualties in the fields and roads from German planes flying low and machine-gunning anyone in sight. Mrs Hitchcock senior was on one such occasion delivering the afternoon milk when she was forced to shelter under the milk-float at the corner of Filston Lane and Bowers Road. On another occasion, Home Guard members infuriated by such an attack were seen running along the High Street, shooting at the dive-bomber. The intense attacks of the 'Blitz', as it was called, ended about May 1941 with a total loss of 1,733 German planes against 915 of the RAF.

The ladies of the village breathed a sigh of relief and set about knitting comforts for the Services: almost 800 socks, body-belts, pullovers and balaclava helmets by 1942. At a garden social in the vicarage grounds organized by Marjorie Ford, the vicar's wife, Barbara Brown, ran a stall entitled 'Nails in Hitler's Coffin' and Phillis Ritchie ran the toy stall. She found people like Mr Bowler, who were most ingenious in making toys, while others who were clever in searching out toys for resale. The parish council in April 1942 instructed the Clerk to inform the Demolition and Recovery Officer of the Ministry of Works and Buildings that there was still scrap metal waiting to be collected at Oxbourne, Timberden and Romney Street Farms. There was also the 'large iron wheel' still on the site of the old paper-mill. The vicar, Guy Ford, a man of a retiring nature, reflecting on his experience as an air-raid warden saw that air raids could:

> knit far more closely together than ever before the community that experiences them, and the total failure of a bomb to distinguish between the social grades or to respect the bank balances of its victims does tend to turn a population into a community. That is to say, an air raid can have, among its effects, one that is of religious value.[8]

Kenneth Ritchie was now transferred from the Home Guard to the RAF, and was able to put his skills as a pilot to good effect as a flying instructor. Lord Dunsany was invited by the British Council to take up an appointment in Athens, and after an 83-day journey round the Cape he arrived to replace Laurence Binyon as Byron Professor of English at Athens University. For a short period the Priory was used again for housing evacuees, but was then occupied by Anthony Powell the writer, his wife Violet and their young son. Anthony Powell was then working in Military Intelligence. He found that:

> Shoreham was still the scene of Palmer-like cloud effects in the Northern sky at evening. At the end of a summer day the black smoke of London would drift south and then, as it were, stop dead in the heavens at a given point towards the setting sun . . . There was in any case something strange about the Shoreham landscape, which caused foreign visitors to Dunstall in war time — Polish, Belgian, French — all, to insist that the wooded hills

and water meadows that surrounded the house, strikingly recalled their own country . . . [and Anthony Powell continued] The only occasion during the war when I descended to a cellar during a raid was at a Dunstall week-end . . . a fierce raid began which went on just above the house and it seemed wise to move Tristram from the room upstairs . . . . for a moment abandoning the curry.[9]

On 31 January 1944 as if pagan gods were taking part in the war a gale blew down Miss Berkeley's crucifix and Major Greenwood found time from his Home Guard duties to repair and restore it to its consecrated ground. By this time the anti-aircraft response to air attacks was considerably increased — 'out of all proportion' compared with the earlier attacks — 'in fact the stuff (shrapnel) comes down like hail' was Major Greenwood's description.[10]

One night that same month German pathfinder planes dropped flares which flooded the valley with light, and bombers followed these with incendiary bombs (some reports claimed 16,000) and finally forty-five HEs. The brunt of the attack was taken by Filston Farm. The three Dinnis brothers and their farm-workers rushed to release their trapped animals from the burning buildings while Mrs Dinnis on the watch indoors saved Filston Hall itself by throwing the fire bombs out of the attic windows as soon as they landed. Five bullocks were lost. Dan Ashby was mightily relieved when the Sevenoaks Fire Brigade arrived and took charge of the fire. It was too large for the village team to contain. A string of high explosives fell across the churchyard, destroyed the parish hearse in its shed in the north-west corner of the yard, blew out the church windows and killed a sentry on duty at the lodge of Shoreham Place. A direct hit caused an even greater tragedy at Preston Hill Farm. The farm-house and outbuildings were completely destroyed, and Major Miller, the head ARP Warden, knew that there were ten people living up in that inaccessible place. The rough cart-track up the side of the steep hill was slippery with rain, yet the women drivers got their ambulances up. So did Major Miller with PC Mannering and the rescue party. First aid was given to six walking injured and they were sent to hospital. The rest were buried under debris and it took some time to get out the first one, a young girl still alive, but five of the McCaughen family were killed.

Anthony Powell recounts:

> When the Belgian Military Attaché . . . spent a Sunday with us, we went for a walk in the afternoon through fields which seemed to have been sown with dragon's teeth, incendiary bombs exploded and unexploded lying every few yards, including a whole basketful which had failed to ignite.[11]

On that particular night in January were the Germans with their flares trying to light up a particular target on which to rain down such massive destruction? Ken Smart, who lived in the village, thought about the attack and years later wrote 'I remember clearly seeing . . . a green marker flare being dropped over the Shoreham valley by one of the German path-finder aircraft.' He wondered whether the bombs that night were aimed at Fort Halstead.[12]

At the annual parish meeting in March Miss Brown was able to report that the year's total for the War Savings Group was £1,906 10s. 6d. and £283 13s. 3d. saved by the schoolchildren. This was the highest figure reached in the war years, but never reached again.

There was a desperate need for more Morrison table shelters, and that same month Mrs Hillier's petition to the RDC was successful in obtaining a further supply for the village. In the parish council Mr F.C. Jewell pressed for a static water tank for Badgers Mount. Amid the scenes of battle the needs of the children were not forgotten by the PC, and Mr Boakes was asked to provide a new seat and chain for the baby swing and new bolts, eyes and a new wooden seat for the large swing on the recreation ground.[13] About this time it was noticed that the field between the church and the station was full of fine mature cabbages, but with the stresses and strains of war farm-hands were not available to do the picking. Rather than see good crops wasted, at night in the black-out shadowy figures could be seen helping themselves.

In June 1944 Hitler's V1 flying bombs were launched against the south-east of England and it was decided to evacuate the village children to Beer in Devon. To prevent the flying bombs reaching the built-up areas the balloon barrage was moved farther out from London and the grey monsters hung over the village and along the valley in a zig-zag line every half-mile. Twenty-one flying bombs were brought down in Shoreham parish, the great majority on the hills and in the fields, though two caused tragedies. Three members of the Puxty family died when one fell at Badgers Mount and another destroyed one of the most beautiful village homes in the meadow close to Water House. At Meadow Cottage (formerly a malt house where Richard Squib the maltster had worked a century earlier) miraculously Mr and Mrs Barker were saved by the ancient beams which prevented the debris from crushing them. The flying bombs were perhaps the most trying to the nerves of all forms of air attack, and certainly one V1 severely tested the devotion of the congregation in the war-battered church of St Peter and St Paul when it flew over the church in the middle of Mr Ford's sermon. At least one member of the congregation wished the vicar had ended his sermon so that all could take shelter![14] The tiny Catholic chapel at Little Timberden suffered bomb damage at this time, and the travelling missioners ceased to use it. Instead the Catholic centre for the rural area moved from Shoreham to Otford, where the old Methodist chapel was purchased as a chapel of ease of St Thomas's in Sevenoaks.[15]

The advance of the Allied armies in France had removed the risk of invasion, and by the autumn of 1944 the Home Guard was no longer required. Representatives of the 20th (Sevenoaks) Bn. of The Queen's Own Royal West Kent Regiment were among the 3,000 men of the Kent Home Guard who attended a Stand Down Service in Canterbury Cathedral on 5 October.[16]

Fortunately, Shoreham was spared the devastation caused by the V2 rockets, but the tally of bombs for the war was enough:

High explosive bombs	474
Oil bombs	10
Incendiary bombs	22,000
Flying bombs	21[17]

This time the inhabitants of Shoreham had not only heard the distant thunder of guns over the Channel in France, but had waited courageously and stoically for the enemy to attack them in their homes. Nine lives were lost in those raids, and eleven more were lost in action. Nine lives were lost in those raids, and eleven more were lost in action or on active service elsewhere. Their names were inscribed upon the memorial by the bridge and in the parish church, after the war in Europe ended on 8 May 1945.

The 8th of May was a sparkling, beautiful spring morning and everywhere in the village there was an atmosphere of relief and rejoicing, and much light-hearted chatter in Mrs Bell's shop at No 1 High Street. Everyone was on the move preparing for the parade of all the organizations that had played a part in the war. Reuben Mannering headed the parade, which began in the High Street and ended at the War Memorial on the bank of the river. After a pause 'everyone it seemed — young and old — was climbing up to the Cross on the Hill', now cleared of earthen camouflage and gleaming white once more. There Paul Gliddon, the vicar, led the village in a thanksgiving service:

> As we looked down on the valley of vision from the cross everyone was united in a spirit of thankfulness that this beautiful valley had not been desecrated by invaders and of gratitude to those who had made it possible now to hope for our children's future . . . . That night all the lights shone out in Shoreham — no more blackout and Shoreham church was floodlit. We knew we could sleep in peace that night for the first time for nearly five years.[18]

The war against Japan ended on 15 August, and on 8 June of the following year Shoreham joined the rest of the country in victory celebrations. In spite of food shortages sports were organized for the children (savings stamps for prizes) and a tea-party for all under sixteen. For the adults a dance and a whist drive were held. A credit balance of £8 19s. 4d. from the celebrations was spent on repairing the swings on the recreation ground.

The village already had built its memorials to those who had died in the First World War, and the names of those who had died in the Second World War were inscribed on the memorial stone. As a positive act of remembrance, on 15

The parade to celebrate Victory in Europe, 8 May 1945. (Mrs M. Lewis)

The service of thanksgiving at the Cross, 8 May 1945. (Mrs M. Lewis)

March 1948 the Shoreham (Kent) Branch of the British Legion was founded.

There had been twelve marriages between soldiers stationed at Shoreham Place and village girls, and four of the couples lived on in Shoreham. Nancy De Decker met George Pallant at a village 'hop' and they married in December 1941. He ended the war as a sergeant-major and had been twice mentioned in despatches. Mr and Mrs Flower had met in 1942, and were married in the parish church on 10 April 1943. Several young evacuees who had stayed in Shoreham during quiet periods of the war kept their links with the village as they grew up. Victor Dean had come to live with Mr and Mrs Farmer when he was eight, and remained in the village ever after. He married here and became a leading member of the community, particularly of the Horticultural and Cottage Gardeners' Society.

The next few years were frustrating for many. Unlike the First World War, during the Second a great deal of hard thought had gone into plans for a new and better world after the terrible destruction. The Butler Education Act for reforming our education system became law in 1944; the Town and Country Planning Act followed in 1947; the National Health Service and National Insurance in 1948 and the Access to the Countryside Act (1949) were other legal expressions of reform. But the country had spent all its material and financial resources on winning the war. Parish and Rural District Councillors wanting to get on with post-war reconstruction found progress hard to achieve.

No matter with what persistence Mr F.C. Jewell pressed for a bus shelter at the Badgers Mount roundabout, or a public telephone and post-box at Cockerhurst they were considered luxuries for the future.[19] The RDC hopefully approved the building of the bridge at the bottom of Crown Road, but for the third time this century it was not built.[20] On the credit side, new council houses that had been planned but delayed by the war were available comparatively soon after it and the sixteen houses in Bowers Place (to be renamed Mildmay Place in 1960) were occupied in 1946.[21] It was four years, though, before the four Hopgarden Cottages were ready for use.[22] On 19 February 1948 Councillors

THE TWENTIETH CENTURY (3)

Page and Skinner expressed the frustration of many in proposing to the RDC that 'This Council requests the Minister of Health to reconsider his decision to allow only twelve permanent houses to be commenced in this Rural District during the next six months. This Council asks to be allowed to build to the capacity of the local building industry.' At the same session Mr Hillier, Chairman of the Housing Committee, asked for £150 to be spent to make No. 3 Chapel Alley Cottages, Shoreham, habitable.[23] Rationing of food, clothing and domestic materials continued, and ironically bread-rationing — avoided during the war — had to be introduced. Major Miller, having dismantled the Air Raid Wardens' Headquarters at his home Wayside, was asked by the RDC to be the Voluntary Food Organizer for Shoreham.

In 1948 the National Health Service was set up and Dr Donald Campbell arrived in Shoreham, while Dr William Lothian came the following year. With the NHS established, the work of the Shoreham and Otford Nursing Association in providing a nursing service for the parish was no longer required. When the Association wound up it was able to hand over to the Terry Charity a donation of £102.[24]

When the flying-bomb attacks were easing off in 1944 the Rev. Paul Gliddon took over from Guy Ford as vicar. He found the church standing, firm but battle-torn, its windows blasted by bombs and their empty frames covered with tarred felting. All except one of the nine stained-glass windows had been blown out. The one that remained was the Burne-Jones window 'Joy, Creation and Love', dedicated in 1903 to the memory of Sir Joseph Prestwich, his wife and sister. Miraculously, the small picture of a pelican in the crest of the most westerly window of the north wall of the nave (see p. 46 in Chap III) survived. Sir Herbert and Lady Cohen were to bring colour and light back to the south wall when they presented the window depicting St George with the village and the Cross on the Hill in the background, in memory of their sons Nigel Benjamin and Captain Stephen Behrens.

Paul Gliddon was interested in drama, and introduced nativity plays into the church (the Ashby girls are remembered as angels appearing on the Rood-screen). In January 1946 he was delighted to discover an enthusiastic group of members gathered in the Church Room to revive the Shoreham Village Players. Clyde Fitzgerald, a founder member, was in the chair and with him was a strong nucleus of experienced actors: Ernest Dowdy, Lilian Wood, Roy Cornwell, Jack Marriott, Mary Brashaw and Nancy Drew. Vera Draffin was there to produce. From the real-life drama of war Reuben Mannering turned his untiring optimism and energy to managing the business side of the Players for fifteen years, fourteen as chairman. Paul Gliddon joined the Players' committee in 1948 and helped with the production of Ronald Pertwee's *Pink String and Sealing Wax*.[25] In the same year he produced the fifteenth-century morality play *Everyman* in the church with Kenneth Ritchie, an active supporter of the Players, taking the part of Everyman. Some of those attending objected to the use of the church in this way, but the majority were in favour.[26]

Kenneth Ritchie — who had been awarded the AFC — after release from his wartime duties had returned happily to life in Shoreham. He was elected with Ronald Hillier to the RDC in April 1946. He also discovered an absorbing interest in bell ringing and organizing the ringers, as well as being chairman of the Cricket and Football Clubs. Later he became a justice of the peace and was chairman of the combined village charities that came to be known as the Walnut Tree Trust. It fell to Kenneth Ritchie to speak in appreciation of the twenty-five

219

years which Ernest Dowdy had spent as clerk to the Parish Council.[27] Ernest in 1946 felt the need to retire, but continued to give advice to those who wanted it from behind the bar at the Two Brewers.

One who had played a full part during the war in spite of ill health was John Dinnis but with the battle for food production over he had to let go the reins. He resigned as a Rural District Councillor in November 1945 and in the following March as chairman of the Parish Council. Harold his son was to carry on his good husbandry at Filston and was soon working with William Alexander of Castle Farm on the development of seedless hops, an important experiment for the country as a whole.

Even before the war in Europe was over Anthony Mildmay and Peter Cazalet were looking forward to a future in steeplechasing, buying horses of the highest calibre which Peter would train and Anthony would ride to victory in the Grand National. During the 1946-7 steeplechasing season Anthony found himself the leading amateur jockey, a position he was to hold for the next four years. He achieved this success while at the same time taking over the Mildmay estate in Devon, and while attending to all that needed to be done in Shoreham. He found Shoreham Place devastated by six years of military occupation and the direct hit of a bomb dropped in January 1944. He decided to abandon the house and concentrate on restoring the estate cottages and attending to the needs of their occupants, making renovations at Park Farm and the market garden and assisting tenant farmers in the parish. From time to time he would drop in on Harold Dinnis at Filston with the simple inquiry 'What's to be done?' and would help with whatever needed doing.

Lord Mildmay died in 1947 in his eighty-sixth year. His funeral at Holbeton, Devon, and memorial services at St Mark's church, North Audley Street, London, and at Shoreham were held simultaneously at 3 p.m. on 12 February. Although Lord Mildmay was not as easy a person to know as his son, his death led Arthur Wood to express the sorrow of the Shoreham Village Players at his going. Arthur Wood had been secretary of the Players for twenty-two years, and remembered him as a man of gentle charm and kindly manner, who had cared for those living and working in Shoreham during a hard and depressing period of the twentieth century.[29] On the day Lord Mildmay's memorial services were held Thomas Drew, employed on the Mildmay estate for twenty-five years, died at Laburnum Cottage in the High Street. He had never really recovered from the loss of his son Tom in the RAF in 1944. Like his daughter Nancy (Teague), Thomas had been an active member of the choir and at the funeral service the choir was present to lead a large congregation to honour his going. As if to emphasize the continuity of life, a happier event took place in April when Helen (née Mildmay) with her husband John White brought their daughter Elizabeth to be christened in Shoreham church, where she herself had been christened in 1907.

As the successes of the Mildmay–Cazalet combination in steeplechasing continued, it became clear from 1948 onward that the interests of Anthony, the second Lord Mildmay, lay in Devon and in the Tonbridge area. He had inherited from his family a very real sense of responsibility towards those dependent upon him, and it was this quality that coloured his actions as he made only a gradual withdrawal from Shoreham to concentrate on his interests at Fairlawne and Tonbridge. He decided that tenants of the Shoreham estate should be given the opportunity to buy their farms or their cottages at prices which were within their means. Thus over the next few years the Mildmay estate

In the 1946 steeplechase season Anthony Mildmay became the leading amateur jockey. (The Mildmay Collection)

at Shoreham — first established in the 1830s — was transferred for the most part to the occupants of the properties.

Ronald Hillier, who had taken over as chairman of the Parish Council from John Dinnis in 1946, had for some years been land steward to the Mildmays, and was therefore in a good position to guide this quite complex transfer of properties to a successful conclusion. As chairman, Mr Hillier called a parish meeting for 14 April 1950 to obtain the villagers' wishes on acquisitions by the parish. It was proposed that the parish purchase the 4½ acres of allotment land known as Townfield at £100 per acre; the existing recreation ground and the cricket ground were offered as a gift to the parish. These proposals were readily agreed.

Exactly a month after this meeting the Plymouth daily paper *The Western Morning News* of Saturday, 13 May 1950 carried the following headline:

NO TRACE OF LORD MILDMAY FOUND

On the previous morning at Mothecombe Anthony had gone down to swim before breakfast, as was his invariable custom. He never returned to the house. An all-day search by RAF planes and naval launches, the Plymouth lifeboat, marine commandos, coastguards, police and estate staff failed to find any trace of him. It is thought that the cold morning water had almost certainly brought on an attack of cramp; injuries to his neck in a riding accident made him more liable to such attacks. The search continued for days, and a voluntary watch by employees and tenants went on for three weeks.[30] Memorial services were held simultaneously at his home, in London and at Shoreham, where the church windows were decorated with blue forget-me-nots and white lilac, Anthony's racing colours. The whole village mourned for him, and the church was packed to capacity — so much so that the vicar, Mr Victor Edwards, held up the service to have chairs brought in for those standing in the aisles. During the service it was the wish of the nearest relations that there be no sermon or oration, but Mr Edwards said: 'I am speaking on behalf of all here and in many places elsewhere in expressing the real sense of loss that we all feel and yet we feel a deep sense of gratitude for the character of him whom we are now remembering.'[31]

> He was buried at Mothecombe at eight o'clock on a bright summer morning. Besides the men who carried him to his grave there were present only his brother-in-law John White, his sister Helen, to whose unselfish love so much of his happiness had been due and his devoted friend Peter Cazalet, with whom he had been so closely bound in every aspect of his life for the past eighteen years.[32]

With Anthony's death the long and close relationship between the Mildmay family and Shoreham came to an end. With it ended that almost continuous presence of a father-figure in the village that had endured since Archbishop Wulfred accepted the gift of a place called Milton from Cedwulf, King of Kent, in AD 822.

EPILOGUE

THE tragic death of Anthony, Lord Mildmay, caused some delay, but eventually his wishes for the Shoreham estate were fulfilled. His death was a traumatic experience for those in Shoreham, coming as it did at a time when other deep-seated changes were taking place in the parish and the country. In the wartime struggle for survival one had scarcely noticed that the horse as a working animal was being put out to grass. The rapid advance of technology made possible by the war brought not only the tractor but also the combine harvester into the fields, and the grain-drier and the milking machine into the farm. In the 1950s the slow-improving standards of living made hop-picking less attractive for Londoners. Technology provided a more reliable alternative for the farmer: a hop-picking machine. Mixed farming continued in the valley, though now cattle can only be seen at Castle Farm. Timberden and Warren Farm still have their flocks of sheep. The brilliant yellow flower of the oil-bearing rape has added its colour at Preston and Filston to the fields of winter wheat, barley, linseed, maize, peas and beans.[1] The private car in ever-increasing numbers has brought town folk to the parish to 'Pick Your Own' fruit and thereby cut the producers' labour costs.

Quite suddenly and fundamentally, mechanization of farming had changed the character of Shoreham, which had been the home of 645 agricultural labourers in 1841, and in 1988 the farms in the valley have an average of three working in the fields. Yet the population has grown steadily from 1,589 in 1931 to 2,007 in 1981. Shoreham is no longer an agricultural community but a residential and recreational community of those who work or have worked elsewhere.

The fact that the nation's wealth had drained away in the defence of its freedom also meant change for Shoreham. The gaping wound of the derelict Shoreham Place had even in the 1950s become a 'haunted ruined mansion' for one young girl, 'with its sagging floors and staircases, owl pellets and mildewed leather binding peeling from the false wooden books in its walls'[2] and it had to wait some ten years before developers decided that it was best to set fire to it and burn away the dry rot before clearing the rubble to make room for twenty-four new dwellings in 1964. The disappearance of the 'big houses' from Shoreham had begun earlier when Lady Gregory — who during the war had retired to the Garden Cottage — rented out Shoreham House in 1947. After quite a brief period the home of one family became that of several. It only remained for

Harold Seager to buy the property in 1949 and to divide it into six flats. Later Darent Hulme was to become the home of three families, and Coombe Hollow the home of two families instead of one.

One of the pleasant winter season's events in the early 1950s was the Boxing Day meet of the West Kent Hunt which took place at Highfield, where Constable Mannering stood at the door to keep out undesirables. By 1969 Highfield had been transformed by Sir Bernard Waley-Cohen (Sir Herbert's cousin) into six apartments. The small flat or house was the requirement of the times. In 1954 the twelve houses of Forge Way had replaced the timber-yard and saw-mill which had caused such aggravation to those living nearby. It was not until 1971 that the twelve houses of Palmers Orchard filled the space between Forge Way and Boakes Meadow. The Old Peoples' Bungalows on part of Townfield in 1975 completed the District Council's effort.

Dunstall Priory was the only large house that did not become fragmented. Lord Dunsany lived on there after his return from Athens, but during a visit to his son Randal at Dunsany he died of an appendectomy in 1957. Before the operation he asked for paper and wrote 'I want to be buried in Kent in the churchyard of Shoreham so as to share with every one of my neighbours whatever may be coming, when dead, as I shared it through the summer of 1940 when alive,'[3] and so he returned to Shoreham for the last time. Dunstall Priory was bought by Lord Gowrie, although some land was retained by the Plunkett family.

Mills on their present sites had served the community almost certainly for nine hundred years: the one to the north producing flour and then paper has left the Mill House as a reminder of its existence; the one to the south in medieval times was a corn-mill, and in Tudor and Stuart times a fulling-mill. In the eighteenth and nineteenth centuries it returned to flour-milling, and in about 1890 it became a saw-mill with a timber yard nearby. By 1910 its power was also pumping water and generating electricity for Shoreham Place. It is now a family home.

There was the merest ripple of cold war that touched Shoreham in the 1950s when it was thought that a Communist cell was plotting to take over the village. There was a small branch of the Party run by the redoubtable and generous Jean and Lewis Feldmar. They were so successful in selling the *Daily Worker* that they won a prize of a fortnight's holiday in Russia for achieving the highest per capita sale of the paper in any village in England. The forces of the Right mobilized, and in the RDC by-election of 1950 Harold Dinnis gained 585 votes to Jean Feldmar's 90. At a later date Jean Feldmar was to become a popular chairman of the Parish Council.

The personal control of the parish environment of the principal landowners had disappeared, and power was dispersed to elected bodies, individual farmers and householders. It was of significance, therefore, that Kent County Council in August 1950 made a Preservation Order covering a wide range of woodland between the Darent Valley and Polhill, including Pilots, Meenfield and Andrews woods to ensure that felling would be controlled and replanting take place.[4] At the end of 1988 the Forestry Commission (which had taken care of the woods from the 1950s to the present day) declared their intention to relinquish them, and in April 1989 the Parish Council reported that Sevenoaks District Council might wish to purchase them. The Woodland Trust could also be interested.

EPILOGUE

Also during the 1950s other statutory measures were being introduced for the protection of the environment, but the menace of the internal combustion engine was increasing. The Dartford Tunnel was under construction, permission was given for building four factories in the Vestry Estate area despite the protests of the Otford council.[4] The parish councils felt impotent standing alone, and as a result the Darent Valley Consultative Association was formed by 1958, comprising council representatives of Otford, Shoreham, Eynsford, Farningham, Sutton-at-Hone, Darenth and Horton Kirby, to ward off the traffic menace.[5] Another threat to the agricultural heritage and beauty of the valley was the exploitation of the valuable gravel layers beneath its top-soil. Gravel had for some years been extracted south of Otford, and an application submitted in 1960-1 to extract it between Otford and Shoreham was successfully thwarted by the Rt Hon S.C. Silkin QC MP, a lover of the valley, briefed by an unofficial group from Shoreham. Above all there was the threat of the South Orbital Road round London.

Influence and power now rested with Members of Parliament, the County Council and the District Council (which after 1974 was to lose its rural connotation and had to embrace both the rural and the urban areas between Sevenoaks and Swanley). This left the Parish Council with little power with which to stir those to action higher up the ladder. In this situation Shoreham inhabitants felt the need to form an organization to give strength to their voices in supporting the council in the corridors of power. At the end of 1961 the Shoreham Society was founded with the mild-sounding aim of enhancing 'the amenities of Shoreham village and to maintain the agreeable rural character of its surroundings'.[6] The battles to come which the Society had to face were to require courage and determination, hours of devoted work and thousands of pounds raised to engage expert advisers and lawyers. In the final attack on the Ministry of Transport's plans for the South Orbital (M25) route, the Shoreham Society fought alongside the Darent and North Downs Action Group. The attacks of the internal combustion engine had been beaten off in 1927, 1929 and 1938, but the battle in the 1980s was lost after a long, hard fight which necessitated taking the struggle to the High Court and the Court of Appeal. It is certain that there will be future battles to be fought (the Channel Tunnel?). Lord Dunsany in 1920 said 'It may be in the future that the place we know as London will come over the hills.' Will his words come true? Meenfield and Pilots Woods are now protected only by the unwelcome and uncertain barrier of the six lanes of the M25 motorway.

After the war Pastor O'Connor hoped that numbers of those worshipping at the Methodist chapel in the High Street would increase. They had been falling since 1937, and in 1962 the trustees recommended that Shoreham Methodists should cease to hold services there as from 2 December. The following year the trustees decided that the site and the building should be sold, and that outline planning permission be obtained.[7] (Since 1965 Nos 12 and 12A High Street have in fact stood upon the site.) A similar fate was awaiting the small group of Baptists in Shoreham. In 1962 the membership of the Baptist chapel in Crown Road was thirteen, and in the next twenty years it did not rise above fifteen and for the last ten years above ten, so in 1982 it was decided that it should be closed. In 1986 it became a private house.

One night at the end of October 1960, when the flowers had faded on the tangle of wild roses in which it stood at the corner of Cockerhurst and Castle Farm Lanes, the crucifix was torn down by vandals.

> The Figure's feet and the foot of the cross were sawn through. The cross fell and the Figure's arms were broken off . . . . Mr. Viner rescued all he could and eventually the pieces were taken to the workshops of Burns Oates Ltd. . . . . where a son of the original carver (Mr. Dapre) repaired them with teak of the same age and stock.[8]

Miss Berkeley, who had erected the crucifix in memory of her father (Chap XIV, p. 201) then presented the Figure to Sister Mary (formerly Margaret Cobbold) at the Carmelite monastery of Quidenham in Norfolk, where it now stands in the garden. At its former site the seat and stone pillar which had long been covered in undergrowth had been cleared and the view restored according to *The Shoreham Gazette* in April 1989.

The bells of Shoreham church still send out their powerful and enduring message, and continue to attract devotees such as Ron Booker, Kenneth Ritchie and Michael McDonnell to care for them and attract others to their service. The strength of their place in the community made it possible in 1981 and 1982 for a complete rebuilding within the tower of the bellframe, the recasting of two and the retuning of others of the eight bells by the Whitechapel Bell Foundry. The £20,000 needed was raised within the twelve months from the parish and elsewhere, including a bellringers' race at the Brands Hatch motor racing circuit. It was largely a team of local volunteers who dismantled the bellframe and carried out the renovations, while one of them with his lorry provided the transport required for the operation. At the dedication of the bells by the Bishop of Rochester on 12 September 1982 Michael McDonnell, the Tower Captain, read the first lesson and Lionel Mathias the second. The bells have been rung ever since by an enthusiastic team of ringers.[9] The church, shorn of its civic duties, is at the centre of Shoreham life. It provides for the spiritual needs of the community, and through the exceptionally valuable parish magazine, *The Shoreham Gazette*, it helps in a very practical way to solve the problem recognized by Paul Gliddon in the 1940s. He found Shoreham so full of different personalities he could not 'weld them together'.[10]

Certainly Shoreham in the 1980s is wonderfully rich in the variety of its people, coming as they do from all walks of life — electricians, civil servants, teachers, publicans, artists, authors, journalists, photographers, engineers, lawyers and those who still work on the land. Inhabitants whose families have lived in Shoreham for three or four generations have received the newcomers with friendship and with surprisingly little resentment; but of course newcomers have been arriving in the village for centuries, though never in such numbers as now. The twenty-odd organizations and clubs active in the village testify to its vitality. Many of them, such as the Shoreham Village Players (with the production of seven of Shakespeare's plays and many others to its credit), help to integrate a wide range of people in a common purpose. The Shoreham Countryside Centre set up by the Shoreham Society and the Parish Council at the railway station in April 1988 seems to show the confidence of the community in its past and in its future.

The school survived the war with fluctuating attendance, depending on the intensity of air attacks and the requests of farmers for help in gathering their vital harvests. Its buildings suffered only superficial damage, and in the 1980s

Shoreham Primary School is a lively and flourishing establishment at the very centre of the community and a guardian of the village's existence.

In the period of 1900–14 there were some twenty shops, providing all the necessities of the village from coal to spinning tops. In the 1930s for those wishing to shop in Sevenoaks and elsewhere the railways — electrified in 1934 — provided a service unequalled in frequency of trains and cheapness of fare since WW1, and the same can be said of the bus services. The result was a reduction of shops in Shoreham to about eleven. In 1988 there are three, and the Post Office operates from within the Shoreham village store. Rising standards of living resulting in the rapid increase in ownership of private cars have led to the growth of the supermarket as a challenge to the village shops everywhere. The inhabitants of Shoreham itself face the challenge of plans for a mega-market on the land of the ancient manor of Hewitts. Elsewhere in Britain the first signs of the break-up and disappearance of a village community is when the school and shops have to close. There seems little danger of Shoreham's school closing but one would like to see the decline in the number of village shops halted, and indeed reversed.

Nature and man over the centuries working together had composed a unique harmony in the Shoreham valley of river, field and hill, but in 1973 the accustomed pattern of the landscape was upset when disease struck the ancient elms and deprived the valley of hundreds of its most beautiful trees. Worse was to come. In the small hours of Friday, 16 October 1987 — the same year that had experienced the most severe snow-fall in living memory — with a growl and then a roar Nature hurled a hurricane at the Darent Valley, terrifying in its suddenness and power. For four hours winds of 100 mph tore into the valley from the south and left a tangled mass of trees, great and small, on the hills and across the roads and lanes. The people of Shoreham, with electricity and telephone lines cut, waited in their homes for daylight. When it came they saw then the devastation in their village and the valley — a scene never to be forgotten by those who lived through it.[11]

Now in 1989 the wounds are healing, houses and buildings have been repaired, the clearing of fallen trees continues on the hills, and the planting of saplings is well under way.

NOTES

CHAPTER I

1. S. Pittman, *Lullingstone Park: The Evolution of a Medieval Deer Park*, Meresborough Books, 1983.
2. AC XCVII 1931. p. 32. 'Remains of mammals from the Darent river gravels at Sevenoaks Reserve, Kent' by D.L. Harrison, J. Clutton-Brock and R. Burleigh.
3. Op. cit. p. 42.
4. AC XCIV 1978 p 233 'Danes Trench and Pre-historic Land Division in the Upper Darent Valley – J.A. Pyke.
5. 'The Cantiaci' by A. Detsicas, Alan Sutton 1983 p.1.
6. E. Ekwall, *Concise Oxford Dictionary of English Place Names*, 4th ed. p. 419. Clarendon Press, 1980.
7. Detsicas, op. cit. p.2.
8. *Conquest of Gaul* trans. by S. Handford (Penguin Classics 1960).
9. AC vol. C 1984 p.61: G.W. Meates, 'Christianity in the Darent Valley.'
10. G.W. Meates p.8. unpub. 1981, *Pre-history and the Influence of Rome*.
11. AC vol. LXIV (1951), p. 161.
12. Detsicas, op. cit. p.180.
13. Ibid pp. 183 & 184.
14. E. Ekwall op. cit. pp. 408 & 419.
15. AC XCII 1976 p. 22, A Everitt, 'The Making of the Agrarian Landscape of Kent.'

CHAPTER II

1. Venerable Bede, *The Ecclesiastical History of the English Nation* p. 22 (Dent, 1930).
2. Ibid, p. 22,
3. AC XCIX 1938 p.1 'Joint Kingship in Kent', B. Yorke,
4. Dr M. Metcalf MA, Ashmolean, Oxford on 28 March 1982 at Wye College. The title of his lecture was 'Anglo-Saxon Coinage in Kent'.
5. E. Jacob, 1774.

SHOREHAM

6 F.R.H. Du Boulay, *The Lordship of Canterbury* p. 28 (Nelson, 1966).

7 AC XCVI 1980, p. 312. 'Recent Investigations at the Anglo-Saxon Cemetery, Darenth Park Hospital, Dartford', R.M. Walsh.

8 D.J. Philp, *Excavations in West Kent, 1960-1970* (1973) p. 201.

9 AC LXXIII, p. 216.

10 F.C. Elliston – Erwood AC LXV, p 144.

11 Clarke and Stoyel, OIK, p.38.

12 AC LXXVII 1962, p 135. 'Filston in Shoreham' N.H. MacMichael.

CHAPTER III

1 V.H.Galbraith, Studies in Public Records London, 1948.

2 W.S. Churchill, *A History of the English Speaking Peoples*, Vol 1, p. 131 (Cassell, 1958).

3 H.F. Baring's study in 1906 is mentioned in OIK p. 40.

4 OIK p. 40.

5 F.R.H. Du Boulay, *The Lordship of Canterbury* p. 145.

6 Sir Frank Stenton 'Anglo Saxon England', *The Oxford History of England*, 3rd Edition, p. 299.

7 Du Boulay, op. cit. p.52.

8 Joy Saynor, 'Aspects of the History of Shoreham (Kent) in the Eighteenth and Nineteenth Centuries'.

9 AC vol. LXXIII p. 216: 'Recent Discoveries at Shoreham Church' by A.D. Stoyel.

10 R. Welldon Finn, *An Introduction to Domesday Book* (Longman, 1963).

11 Canterbury Cathedral MS E. 24 ff bqv to 74 v, translated by Dennis Clarke.

12 Sir John Clapham, *A Concise Economic History of Britain* p. 95 (C.U.P., 1951).

13 Owned by Wm. Alexander.

14 *Concise Oxford Dictionary of English Place Names* p. 462.

15 G. Ward 'Polhill' 10/121 (SL).

16 Diedrich Saalfeld in *Our Forgotten Past* (Thames & Hudson, 1982).

17 Du Boulay, op. cit. p. 186.

18 SL C.T.Phillips MSS Vol 5.

19 OIK p. 86.

20 We are grateful to H.G.F. Lambe for drawing our attention to William of Shoreham and to Helen Wheeler MA for her study of his poems and her translations. We hope that her study (1985) may one day be published.

21 OIK p. 81.

22 Du Boulay op. cit. p. 218.

23 Lambeth Court Roll 804, 805, 808, 809, 813, 814, 820, 821, 825 (Hesketh trans.).

24 Du Boulay, op. cit. p. 306.

25 Lambeth Roll 875.

26 Clapham, *Concise Economic History of Britain*, p. 110.

27 Du Boulay, AC vol. LXXIII, 1959.

NOTES

28 John Stowe, *Annals of England* quoted by Sir John Dunlop in *The Pleasant Town of Sevenoaks*.
29 Sevenoaks Preservation Society – History Notes No. 5.
30 We are indebted to Anthony Stoyel, Director of Studies of the SDAH, for the details of Chapel Alley Cottages and Holly Place.
31 PRO C/47/9/59 Lambeth MS 1212 L. 148-57; references kindly provided by Jennifer C. Ward.
32 Edward Hasted, *History and Topography of the County of Kent*, vol. III (1797).
33 Joy Saynor, op. cit. p. 64.
34 Hasted, op. cit., vol III.
35 Lambeth Roll 837.
36 R.G. Bennett, (1958, unpublished) *The Kentish Polhills*, p. 11.
37 Hasted, op. cit., vol III.
38 Lambeth Roll 836.
39 W.H. Ireland, *History of the County of Kent* (1830).
40 KAO U 1007 T 211.
41 KAO U 1007 T 234.
42 Du Boulay, op. cit. p. 71.
43 Kent Records 'Calendar of Kent Feet of Fines', vol XV 1956.
44 Hasted, vol II.
45 Kent Records 'Calendar of Kent Feet of Fines', vol XV 1956.
46 S. Pittman, *Lullingstone Park* (Meresborough Books) p. 30.
47 Hasted, op. cit.
48 Clapham, *Concise Economic History of Britain*.
49 OIK p. 129.
50 A. Payne, *History of Shoreham Church*, chap IX.
51 C. Hesketh, transcription of Reynolds f 24 b, Lambeth.
52 SL C.J. Phillips MSS vol. 5.
53 C. Hesketh, transcription Islip f 69 a, Lambeth.
54 OIK, p. 78.
55 Leland L. Duncan FSA, AC XXIII 134.
56 *Testamenta Cantiana* 1907.
57 *Invicta Magazine* vol I No. 5 March 1910, p. 221.

CHAPTER IV

1 Asa Briggs, *Social History of England* p. 94 (Weidenfeld & Nicolson, 1983).
2 OIK, p. 100.
3 AC LXXIII, p. 219.
4 1540 Survey of the Manor of Otford, SL GW Box 4.
5 *Testamenta Cantiana* 1907.
6 L.L. Duncan, AC Vol. XXIII, p. 134.
7 PRO, L & P 1534 item 1035.

SHOREHAM

8 PRO, L & P 1305.
9 OIK, p. 128.
10 Youings; 186.
11 R.A.C. Cockett, Fawkham & Ash Archaeological Group, 24.7.1985.
12 G.W. Petley Notebook I, SL.
13 A.Fraser, *Cromwell Our Chief of Men*, p. 7.
14 F.R.H. Du Boulay, 'Late-Continued Demesne Farming at Otford' AC LXXIII 1959.
15 For a fuller discussion of this matter readers should see the correspondence between Major Hesketh and H.W. Knocker in the Kent Archives Office, U55 219.
16 SL, G.W. Polhill 6.
17 SL, GW Box 22, Patent Roll I Edward VI part 9.
18 SL, GW Box 4, Patent Roll, 2 & 3 Philip and Mary pt. 3, Hesketh transcription.
19 DNB.
20 WCM, 14372.
21 Asa Briggs, op. cit. p. 123: figures taken from the Phelps Brown/Hopkins selective price index quoted by Professor Briggs.
22 OIK, p. 121.
23 WCM.
24 Archbishop Parker's Register Canterbury and York Society Vol. 36 pt. IV, dated Sept. 1914.
25 WCM 14387.
26 AP, p.49.
27 WCM, 39900-39902.
28 OIK, p.131.

CHAPTER V

1 Prof Joyce Youings, 'Sixteenth Century England', in *The Pelican Social History of Britain* (1984) p. 157.
2 SL G.W. Polhill II.
3 Owned by L.A. Mathias.
4 K.A.S. Library Maidstone.
5 R.G. Bennett TKP App B 1.
6 W.I. Curnow, *Eynsford* 1953.
7 OIK, Chap. VI.
8 SL G.W. Pol. V.
9 AP, Chap. VI.
10 KAO, VI 007 M 23.
11 SL G.W. Pol. Box 22 (Shoreham).
12 IPM Thomas Polhill 1589 PRO C. 142/220 No. 20.
13 Youings, op. cit., p. 151.
14 LHE, 204.

NOTES

15 Youings, op. cit., p.250.
16 T.A. Bushell, *Barracuda Guide to County History*: Vol. I, 'Kent'.
17 Lena Bamping, 'West Kingsdown' 1983.
18 From *Vox Populi, Vox Dei*, pp. 9-10, quoted by Christopher Hampton in *A Radical Reader*, p. 101 (Penguin, 1984).
19 W.G. Hoskins, *Old Devon*, p. 150 (Pan Books, 1971).
20 PRO SP 12 LXXXIX 19.
21 Dunlop, p. 102.
22 PRO SP 12 139 (45).
23 G.M. Trevelyan, *History of England* 3rd Edition, p. 199 (Longman, 1945).
24 Trevelyan, op. cit. p. 278.
25 KAO, QM/SI and QM/SRC.
26 Youings, op. cit., p. 275.
27 KAO, QM/SI.
28 KAO, QM/51, 1610/21.
29 KAO, QM/SRC.
30 KAO, QM/SRC.
31 KAO, Kent Sources Vol. VI.
32 AC Vol. Cl, Pl 57, W.R. Briscall.

CHAPTER VI

1 KAO, Q/SO W1 ff 152 r and 162 v.
2 Dating assessment by Anthony Stoyel.
3 Ibid.
4 Survey by FAAG 24.7.85.
5 The descriptions of crafts and trades in this chapter are taken from wills and probate inventories in Lambeth Palace Library, VH 96.
6 C. Wilson, *England's Apprenticeship 1603-1763* (Longman, 1965) p. 23.
7 Ibid p. 25.
8 See SDAH Shoreham Study No. 1.
9 OIK, p. 165.
10 BL 26 785 ff 95 add.
11 OIK, p. 152.
12 AP, p. 55.
13 Wilson, op. cit., pp. 13 & 21.
14 AC vol LXXV, p. 26.

CHAPTER VII

1. TKP Supplement No. 6, Sevenoaks Local History Library, Otford.
2. KAO QM/RL.
3. SL GW. Pol 4.
4. PRO E 179 128/616 4 Chas I.
5. William Berry, *Kentish Genealogies* 1830.
6. B.D. Clarke, 'Quarter Sessions Orders for West Kent 1625-1648', 27.12.1964, KAO.
7. Shoreham tithe list, WCM No. 14333.
8. KTGR, p. 189.
9. KTGR, p. 241.
10. P. Bloomfield, 'Studies in Modern Kentish History', KAS 1983 p.11.
11. Ibid p.23.
12. OIK, p. 158.
13. W.H. Ireland, *History of the County of Kent* vol III, p. 350.
14. W Berry op cit.
15. PRO Cal. Committee of Compounding.
16. WCM 14236 and 14454.
17. WCM 14452/3.
18. AC vol. 94, p. 61 'Original Compton Census Returns', Mary J. Dobson.
19. KAO Q/SB9.
20. BL EG 2958 f 254 Add.
21. LPL Canterbury Peculiars VP 11/4 Shoreham, vol. 1 p. 128.
22. Smiles, *Huguenots in England and Ireland* (1876 edn).
23. *Miscellanea Genealogica et Heraldica*, New Series 1874. KAS Library.
24. PRO E 179/129/702/24.
25. Dard Hunter,'Papermaking' p 119, 2nd Ed. (The Cresset Press, 1957).

CHAPTER VIII

1. OIK, p 163.
2. SL GW, Pol 5.
3. D'A NB, KAO U 442/045.
4. WD Diary, Sl.
5. Information provided by Mrs Gertrude Franklin-White.
6. KAO, Shoreham Church Register.
7. KAO U 442/045.
8. KAO U 442/045 Op. cit 30 Sept. 1708.
9. AC vol. 26 p. 32a *The Palatines*, Richard Cook.
10. G.W., Sevenoaks Essays, p. 232.

NOTES

11 F.F. Nicholls, *Honest Thieves: The Violent Heyday of English Smuggling* (Heinemann, 1973).
12 J.H. Plumb, *England in the Eighteenth Century* (Penguin, 1963).
13 Copy available in Sevenoaks Library.
14 DNB.
15 DNB XLV, p. 16.
16 Dr John Hunt 'A Kentish Parish' (unpublished).
17 Price, *On Civil Liberty* 1776 – quoted by J.H.Plumb op. cit. p. 135.
18 F.L. Clark, *The Perronets of Shoreham* (London and Home Counties Branch Bulletin Wesley Hist. Soc, 1984).
19 LPL MSS MS 1134/6.
20 Plumb, op. cit, p. 93.
21 J. Wesley, *Journal* Vol I, p. 35.
22 Ibid, *Journal* Vol 3, p. 159.
23 C. Wesley, *Journal* P. Vol 4, p. 271.
24 LPL, VH 55/1, pp. 221-8.
25 LPL MSS V.P. II 2/4 221.
26 SL. GW. Baptist Notes.
27 KAO Shoreham Land Tax list, 1792.
28 GW Baptist Notebook.

CHAPTER IX

1 Hasted, Vol I p. 317.
2 SL. GW. Court Baron and Court of Election 13 Nov. 1781.
3 PRO.
4 SL. GW. Pol. 6 Indenture 28 July 1741.
5 Hasted, Vol III 1797.
6 SL. GW. Pol. 5.
7 LPL MS 1134/677.
8 Maidstone Library K 362.
9 KAO U. 36 T 446.
10 Plumb op. cit., p. 82
11 WCMR RCO 64.
12 WCMR 57372.
13 (a) WCMR RCO 64, (b) Hartley Survey WCMR 55506, (c) Petman Survey WCMR RCO 64.
14 In the possession of William Alexander.
15 See *Shorter Oxford English Dictionary*.
16 LPL VH 96 5732.
17 See Indenture May 3, 1777 in possession of Lt Col T.E. Morgan.

235

18 AC Vol. 94 p. 61 Mary J. Dobson and 1801 National Census.
19 OIK, p. 174.
20 J.S., p. 50.
21 SL. GW. Shoreham notebook.
22 Vestry Book (VB) 4. Jan. 1793.
23 VB Jan 4. 1783
24 VB 30. Oct., 1785
25 VB 4. Jan., 1787.
26 VB 17. Oct., 1802.
27 County Library Maidstone K 362, p. 144.
28 C. Seymour, *A New Topographical Survey* 1776, p. 727.
29 LPL VH 55/1, pp. 221-8.
30 KAO Q/AB 51.
31 VB Jan. 1804.
32 DNB.
33 DAO Land Tax list 1809. SL holds William Danks Diary (D/876,F680).
34 VB 5 April 1805.
35 DNB Vol. III pp. 296-9.
36 An estimate received from Anthony Stoyel.
37 SDAH Group Shoreham Study No 2.
38 Information from Mrs Katharine Moore.
39 Anthony Stoyel letter of 13.12.1986 to C.A.M. White.
40 Information supplied by Peter Schabacker.
41 F.C. Elliston Erwood FSA, AC Vol. LXV p 144.

CHAPTER X

1 Indenture 17 Sept. 1831 between John Bonham-Carter, Sir W. Stirling, N.W. Bowers and George Phillips, Foster Gregory in possession of Messrs Buss Murton, Solicitors, Tunbridge Wells.
2 R.G. Thorne *The History of Parliament: The House of Commons 1790-1820* p. 298 (Secker and Warburg, 1986).
3 SL 1000/9 M 34.
4 Letter to C.A.M.N 19.12.86 from M. Carter, W. Kent Archivist SL.
5 KAO Q/AB51 letter dated 24.7.1808.
6 WCMR RCO 64.
7 AC vol CIII p. 119 – *Kentish Churches before Restoration*, Nigel Yates.
8 AP, p. 15.
9 SL F1014 House of Commons minutes of Evidence 30.5.1811, Shoreham turnpike.
10 Ibid.

NOTES

11 The Nash family had farmed in Shoreham as yeomen in the seventeenth and eighteenth centuries (see Appendix, Shoreham Farms 1835).

12 This account is taken from the House of Commons minutes of Evidence, to be found in Sevenoaks Library: ref F1014.

13 KAO, Q/RU m 110 Quarter Session Records.

14 KAO, Land Tax 1824.

15 SL 1835 Parish property valuation.

16 R. Lister, *Samuel Palmer: a Biography* p. 57 (Faber, 1974).

17 Based on Shoreham Parish valuation 1835, SL.

18 A.M.W. Stirling, *Richmond Papers* (Heinemann, 1926).

19 Ibid.

20 Ibid.

21 *Letters of S. Palmer* (vol I) ed. by R. Lister (Clarendon Press, 1974).

22 The solicitors Buss Murton of Tunbridge Wells hold the leases dated 22 & 23 March 1830 between J. Bonham-Carter & Samuel Palmer, a lease of 28.4.1867 between S.Palmer and William Yates and indentures of 25.3.1887 and 25.1.1888 and generously allowed us to examine them.

23 We are much indebted to the authors of OIK for the contents of this passage: see OIK, Chap. 9.

24 KAO Gaol Calendar, Maidstone 1833-1851 C/10 (12-15 BM).

25 SL.

26 SL.

27 The vicar in 1807 reported that the parish contained 4,708 acres and 150 dwellings. LPL VH55/2b ff 119-21.

28 The 5 public houses identified in the 1841 census were: The George Inn, Crown Inn, Pig & Whistle, Polhill Arms, Wheatsheaf.

29 OIK, p. 191.

30 KAO U442/081/3 Cert. of Tax Assessment Shoreham 1842/1843: Burton taxed on 27 windows.

31 *Buildings of England*: John Newman, 'West Kent and the Weald'.

32 AP, p. 62.

33 Indenture in possession of the Buss Murton Partnership, Tunbridge Wells 26.3.1987.

34 Information from notes kindly provided by Mrs Hazel Pollock based on *Number One, A History of the firm of Gregory Rowcliffe & Co. 1784-1984* by Patrick Davis (London 1984).

35 *An Epitome of County History*, Vol 1 'County of Kent' (C. Greenwood, 1838), p. 86.

CHAPTER XI

1 DNB; PRO Calendar of State Papers Commonwealth 7 Vol. LXXIV and Cal. S.P. (DOM) Charles II, Vol. XLVI, LII and LIX.

2 Mildmay papers: No.M(S) 1. The list of Mildmay Papers is held by J. Saynor.

3 KAO U442/081/3 Certificate of Assessed taxes 1842/43.

4 Mildmay Paper: M(S)2.

5 H.J. Habakkuk, 'Marriage Settlements in the Eighteenth Century'. *Royal Hist. Soc. Transactions* Vol. XXXII.

237

6 E.L. Woodward, *The Age of Reform* (Oxford Hist. of England), p. 455. (OUP 1949).
7 S. Curtis and M. Boultwood, *An Introductory Hist. of English Education since 1800*, p. 56. (University Tutorial Press, 1966).
8 Quotations from Mr Hales's letter to Barton, in Mrs Meg Chapman's family papers, Melbourne, Australia.
9 F.W.Jessup, *Kent. Hist. Illustrated.* p. 64 (KCC, 1973).
10 Meg Chapman family papers.
11 R. Hughes, *The Fatal Shore* p. 571 (Pan, 1988).
12 Letter quoted by Dickens in *Household Words*, p.557.
13 KAO U2189 Z 3/5.
14 VM 17 April 1841.
15 *Barracuda Guide to County History* (Vol. 1).
16 VM 29 March 1855.
17 KAO, Q/SBW 81 Easter 1820.
18 Mildmay Papers No 13.
19 WCMR RCO 64 Letter dated 5 Feb. 1861.
20 AP p. 20.
21 1861 Census Returns.
22 SL D750: Letter 9 May 1838 Calverley Cole to Chas. Willmott.
23 KAO CTR 335A & B, Tithe Commutation.
24 Howard Newby, *Country Life* p. 134 (Weidenfeld & Nicolson, 1987).
25 VM 6 Mar. 1863.
26 KAO U2189 Z3/5.
27 Certain information kindly supplied by the late Robert Bell; *Encyclopaedia Britannica*; Annual Register 1876 Pt. 2 p. 35.
28 DNB.
29 SL, Kent and Sussex Courier 17 April 1876.
30 *Across Africa* by V.L. Cameron (1877), Vol. I p.171; Vol. II p. 229.
31 Baptismal Register.
32 Letter from Peter Summers, Oxford OX9 6BL to A.E. Whitworth of 11 Sept 1984.
33 Letter to Joy Saynor from C.R. Councer FSA 5.2.1985.
34 Shoreham Vicarage, Church Wardens' Cash Book 19.6.1878.
35 *Sevenoaks Chronicle*, 27 May 1978.
36 We are indebted for much of the information for this section to *Railways to Sevenoaks*, By Charles Devereux. (Locomotion Papers No. 102, 1976). The Oakwood Press.
37 The evidence is found in notebook and accounts (1867-9) of John Bowen, running a carrier business from Timberden. The notebook and accounts were kindly lent by Frank Hitchcock.
38 Geoffrey Wakeham, *20th Century English Vat Papermills* (The Plough Press, 1980).
39 PRO. HO. 107. 485/6.
40 A.H. Shorter, *Paper Mills and Paper Makers in England 1495-1800* The History of paper, Gen. Ed. E.J. Labarre 1957
41 See O.S. map 25" to the mile 1869.

NOTES

42 Howard Newby op cit, p. 100.
43 Harold Dinnis gave this estimate, bearing in mind the method of growing hops at that time.
44 We are indebted to Dorothea Teague for allowing us to use material from her book *Shadrach Blundell, His Family and Property 1580-1880*. (Synjon, 1985).
45 Kelly 1845 and 1899.
46 Kelly 1878.
47 Memorandum of agreement: J.G. Moore 14.11.1908 in possession of Lt Col T.E. Morgan.
48 Kelly 1899 Directory.

CHAPTER XII

1 Log Books are available covering the following periods: Dec. 1862 – Nov. 1883, Dec. 1895 – June 1912.
2 LPL MSS V.C. 2/7b 317.
3 S.J. Curtis and M.E. Boultwood, *History of English Education Since 1800* p.62 (University Tutorial Press, 1966).
4 Op. cit. pp, 70-1.
5 VM 9.12.1864.
6 VM 3.4.1867.
7 SL M2/2L/3/1 Minute Book of New Chapel, Shoreham.
8 Letter from J. Barfield 28.8.1987, The Baptist Union Corporation Ltd.
9 The 1870 Indenture, examined by kind permission of Mr and Mrs S.G. Gulliver.
10 Letter from Revd G.R. Breed 30.1.1988 to C.A.M.W.
11 Information on her father kindly provided by Mrs Gillian Webb, 6.3.1988.
12 O.S. 25" map 1869.
13 SL Minutes of the Rural Sanitary Authority RD/SE AM1/1, AM1/2 and AM1/3.
14 Mildmay Papers No. 17.
15 Mildmay Doc. No. 12. Particulars and contract of sale Sept. 1873.
16 SL. Minutes of the Rural Sanitary Authority AM 1/4 1886-89.
17 Op. cit. p. 341.
18 OIK p. 219.
19 Howard Newby, *Country Life* p. 133. (Weidenfeld and Nicolson, 1987).
20 DNB.
21 Vestry minute 15.4.1900 shows it was Sir Joseph's will to bequeath £800, but other demands on his estate reduced this sum to £618.
22 Mark Amory, *Lord Dunsany: A Biography* (Collins, 1972).
23 *Sevenoaks Chronicle* 18 May 1883.
24 Mildmay Paper No. 22.
25 Ibid, No. 25.
26 DNB.
27 Mrs Ella Booker interview 29.3.77.

28 Mildmay Paper No. 21.
29 Annual Reports of the SONA are available at the Vicarage.
30 Mrs Ella Booker interview 29.3.77.
31 Mrs Nancy Teague interview March 1976.
32 Mrs Alice Gibson interview *c.* 1980.
33 Published in W.I. Booklet.
34 Mrs De Decker interview c 1980.
35 Letter from W.G.G. Alexander to C.A.M.W., 25.5.1988.
36 Harold Dinnis interview 28.1.1988.
37 'A Short History of The Establishment' kindly provided by Lt Col T.E. Morgan.
38 Interview with Bill Rushen, 3 Crown Cottages, Halstead 6.5.1983.
39 *Shoreham Gazette*, July and August 1983.
40 WCMR RCO 64.
41 *Sevenoaks Chronicle*, 26 January 1951.
42 Op. cit.
43 SPM 20 March 1900.
44 *Sevenoaks Chronicle*, Feb 1901 & SPM 20.2.1901.
45 Roger Mortimer, *Anthony Mildmay*, p. 11.
46 SPM 17 Sept. 1902.

CHAPTER XIII

1 The activities of the Shoreham Parish Council are taken from the records of the annual parish meetings and parish council minutes held by the Clerk to the PC.
2 SL, RDC minutes RD/SE AM1/6 etc.
3 SL, RDC AM1/9 and AM1/32.
4 An opinion forcefully expressed by the Hon Helen Mildmay-White to C.A.M.W.
5 Professor Hugh Nicol, *Fertilizer and Feeding Stuffs Journal* Vol. 37, 1951.
6 We are indebted to A.E. Whitworth for this account of Wild White Clover.
7 Taken from an interview of Mrs Gibson by C.A.M.W. 21.1.1980.
8 This description of the inside gardener's life was given to C.A.M.W. by Frederick Crouch, 1.10.1980.
9 *The Sixth Great Power, Barings 1762-1929*, Chap. 14 & 15, by Philip Ziegler (Collins, 1988).
10 SL, *Sevenoaks Chronicle*, 10.11.1905.
11 Extracts with slight amendments from *Anthony Mildmay* by Roger Mortimer (MacGibbon & Kee, 1956).
12 School log-book 1895-1912.
13 SL, *Sevenoaks Chronicle*, 28.1.1927.
14 Op. cit.
15 *Chambers' Encyclopaedia*, Vol 11.

NOTES

16 SL, *Sevenoaks Chronicle*, 13.5.1910.
17 Information kindly supplied by Mrs Hazel Pollock and Miss Rosemary Waring.
18 *Who Was Who* 1897-1916, p. 146.
19 Letter from Sec. Charity Commission RCB/62467 Clerk PC Shoreham 25.11.50 to H.E. Saker.
20 Information from *The South African Builder* (Johannesburg, 1909), cutting supplied Mrs Gillian Webb.
21 SL, *Sevenoaks Chronicle*, 22.12.1905.
22 See *A Dictionary of Contemporary British Artists* Ed. Bernard Dolman (Antique Collectors Club 1929, Reprinted 1981), & *Who Was Who* Vol. VI.
23 Mrs Ella Booker, interviewed 29.3.1977.
24 Mrs Amy Higgins, interviewed 28.2.1978.
25 Letter in possession of Mrs Katharine Moore, dated 4.5.1983.
26 Mrs Ella Booker, interviewed 29.3.1977.
27 *Barracuda Guide*, Vol. 1. p. 104.
28 The details kindly supplied by David G. Collyer, Archivist, Kent Aviation Historical Research Society.
29 A description used by his daughter, Mrs Gillian Webb.
30 Mrs Lyn Pysden, *Shoreham Memories* 1976.
31 Description used by Mrs Lyn Pysden.
32 *Shoreham Gazette* October 1983.
33 SL, *Sevenoaks Chronicle*.
34 We are indebted to Dr William Lothian for information on the medical services.
35 *The New British Traveller* (1784); *The Post Office Directory* (1845).
36 PRO, *Palmer's Index* No. 93.
37 SL, *Sevenoaks Chronicle* 14.1.1910.
38 SL, *Sevenoaks Chronicle* various.
39 SPM 20.3.1900.
40 Dorothy Brown interviewed in 1978.
41 SL, *Sevenoaks Chronicle* 11.2.1910.
42 Petition lodged in the Sevenoaks Library.
43 Details from *The Ramblers Visitors Book* kindly lent by Peter and Viezonie Hodges.
44 KAO IR4/135.
45 RD/SE AM1/20 and 22.
46 *The Times* obituary 1947.
47 SL, RD/SE AM1/23.
48 SL, RD/SC AM1/24.
49 A copy is in the possession of Mrs Amy Higgins.
50 SL, RD/SE AM1/24.
51 Howard Newby, *Country Life* p. 159.
52 The averages are derived from the numbers of the pockets harvested for the years 1886 to 1979, found recorded on joists and walls of the oast stowage at Filston during an examination in February 1981 by the SDAH Group.

53 Letter from the Secretary, South East TAVR Association to C.A.M.W. 9.2.1988.
54 A Short History of the Establishment supplied to Lt Col T.E. Morgan.
55 Mark Amory, *Lord Dunsany: A Biography*, pp. 151 & 153 (Collins, 1972).
56 Keith Feiling, *A History of England*, p. 1073 (Macmillan, 1950).

CHAPTER XIV

1 Mrs Nancy Teague interview March 1976.
2 Information from Mrs Amy Higgins, June 1988.
3 Patrick Davis, *Number One: A history of the firm Gregory, Rowcliffe & Co. 1784-1984* (London, 1984).
4 Mark Amory, *Lord Dunsany: A Biography* (Collins, 1972).
5 Op. cit.
6 Frank Russell interview, 10.12.1981.
7 SL. *The Sevenoaks Chronicle and Courier*, 28.5.1920.
8 *Shoreham, Kent: A Village Booklet*. (WI Shoreham 1988).
9 SPM June 1920.
10 SL. *Sevenoaks Chronicle*, 7.1.1921.
11 Letter from Miss Dorothy Durrant to C.A.M.W., 13.6.1988.
12 SL. RD/SE AM1/25 and 26.
13 SL. RD/SE AM1/26 & 28.
14 Mrs De Decker, interviewed c 1980.
15 *A Dictionary of Contemporary British Artists*, Ed. Bernard Dolman 1929. Antique Collectors Club (reprinted 1981).
16 Information kindly supplied by Ray Cornwell.
17 SPM June 1924.
18 Mark Amory, *Lord Dunsany: A Biography* (Collins, 1972).
19 Interview 6.10.1984.
20 A fuller description of the Shoreham Village Players can be found in *The Shoreham Village Players 1924-1984* by Malcolm White (The SVP, Shoreham, 1984).
21 Howard Newby, *Country Life*.
22 Figures recorded by the Sevenoaks District Architectural History Group, in the Filston Oast before its conversion.
23 Information supplied by Harold Dinnis 1988.
24 Interview Frank Russell, 10.12.81.
25 SL. RD/SE AM1/28.
26 SL. *Sevenoaks Chronicle* 28.1.1927.
27 SL. Shoreham Methodist Society M2/2L/1/1.
28 Op. cit.
29 This passage is quoted from *Town Planning, Shoreham Kent April 1929* — petition to the Minister of Health, Road across the Darenth Valley.

NOTES

30 Mark Amory, *Lord Dunsany: A Biography* (Collins, 1972).
31 AP.
32 SL. Box D 889 Herbert Knocker, Misc. Papers.
33 Information given by Mrs Nancy Teague.
34 Roger Mortimer, *Anthony Mildmay* (MacGibbon & Kee, 1956).
35 OIK, p. 252.
36 OIK and A.E. Whitworth, *Shoreham Gazette* (March 1980).
37 Taken from description by J. Saynor and A.E. Whitworth, *Shoreham Gazette* Vols. 17 & 18 1985/6.
38 Obituary provided by Mrs Gillian Webb.
39 SL. RD/SE AM1/30.
40 SL. RD/SE AM1/36.
41 *Kelly's Directory* 1938.
42 PMM, 17.3.1928.
43 PMM, 22.2.1935.
44 Malcolm White, *The Shoreham Village Players 1924-1984*.
45 SL. *Sevenoaks Chronicle and Courier*, 18.2.38.
46 Minutes of Shoreham annual parish meeting 25.3.1938.
47 Sales prospectus kindly lent by Mrs Ann Ball.
48 *Grove's Dictionary of Music and Musicians* Vol. I., 1954.
49 Roger Mortimer, *Anthony Mildmay* (MacGibbon & Kee, 1956).

CHAPTER XV

1 Minute of Annual Parish meeting 17.3.1939.
2 SL, *Sevenoaks Chronicle & Courier* 11.2.1938.
3 *The Ramblers Visitors Book* kindly lent by Vizonie and Peter Hodges.
4 Mark Amory, *Lord Dunsany: A Biography* (Collins, 1972).
5 Details from *London Calling* No. 237 April 1944.
6 Much of the information in this account of Shoreham at war is adapted from *Shoreham Remembers 1939-1945*, compiled by Joy Saynor and Daphne Wildbore in 1985.
7 H.R.P. Boorman, *Hell's Corner*, 1940.
8 SPM October 1940.
9 Anthony Powell, *To Keep the Ball Rolling*, Vol. 3, *Faces In My Time* (Heinemann, 1980), p. 146.
10 *London Calling* No. 237.
11 Anthony Powell, op. cit. p. 146.
12 SL, D400 *Sevenoaks Chronicle* 3.5.1985.
13 Minutes of Parish Council meetings 17.3.1944 and 21.4.1944.
14 A recollection by Mrs Phillis Ritchie.

15 OIK, p. 252.
16 *Barracuda Guide to County History* Vol. 1 T.A. Bushell, p. 116.
17 SL, *Sevenoaks Chronicle* 11.5.1945.
18 Quotations from recollections of the day by Mrs Mollie Lewis.
19 APM 1946.
20 APM 1949.
21 ER 1947.
22 ER 1951.
23 SL, RD/SE AM/1.
24 APM 30.3.1949.
25 Malcolm White, *The Shoreham Village Players* (1984).
26 VM 13.1.1948.
27 APM 13.3.1946.
28 Roger Mortimer, *Anthony Mildmay* (MacGibbon & Kee, 1956).
29 *Sevenoaks Chronicle* 17.2.1947.
30 Roger Mortimer, op. cit.
31 *Sevenoaks Chronicle* 19.5.1950.
32 The closing words of Roger Mortimer's biography.

EPILOGUE

1 *Shoreham, Kent: A Village Booklet* (Shoreham WI, 1988).
2 Shena Mackay, 'My Country Childhood' in *Country Living*, 1987.
3 Mark Amory, *Lord Dunsany: A Biography*, (Collins, 1972).
4 *Sevenoaks Chronicle*, 18.8.1950.
5 OIK, p. 256.
6 A circular dated October 1961 to Shoreham residents concerning the formation of the Shoreham Society.
7 SL M2/2L/1/1 and M2/2L/2/1.
8 Written by A. E. Whitworth, *Shoreham Gazette*, March 1980.
9 *Shoreham, Kent: A Village Booklet* (Shoreham WI, 1988).
10 Mrs Phillis Ritchie mentioned this in a letter to C.A.M.W. in 1988.
11 See Bob Ogley's *In the Wake of the Hurricane* (Froglets Publications Ltd, 1987).

APPENDIXES

CHAPTER III

THE YOKE OF TEFLYNGE

Alan of Godyngestone,
John of Teflynge,
Simon, son of Roger Porter,
John le Steer,
Cecilia, widow of Hamon le Pendere

Guinild,
Alicia   daughters of Robert Fyke, and
Edith

William of Chelsfeld hold one yoke in Tefflyng, for which they will plough, sow and harrow 2 acres in winter for wheat and 2 acres for oats at Quadragesima. And they shall seek the seed at the lord's granary. They will mow half an acre of meadow. They will ted, gather, cock and bring in to Shorham. They will reap in autumn 3 acres 1 rood of corn. They will bind and bring to the same place.

Item they will reap 2 acres of barley or oats. They will bind, stook and leave in the field and they shall have 8 loaves. They will perform 4 carrying services a year when the lord is present from Otford to Lambeth, Croydon, Bixle, Northflete, Wrotham, Pencestr' and they shall have four loaves. They will enclose 3½ perches of the Burghyard around the lord's court with the lord's wood which they shall ask for. They will carry from the lord's wood five loads [*carratas*] or ten half loads [*carrectatas*] of fire wood to the court of Otford of Gavelwode between Hokeday and the feast of the blessed St Peter ad Vincula.

They were accustomed formerly to find forage of corn [*stramine frumenti*] for five horses in their own homes. And they used to have allowance of food from the court of the lord Archbishop and provender for their horses. They will pasture their pigs if there should be pannage. And then they will give for a pig over a year old 2d. and for a young 1d. And if pannage shall be lacking they will give for a pig 1d. and for a young pig ½d. They will make four seams of malt and they shall have four half loads [*carectatas*] of wood to dry this. And if they brew to sell they will give 2 pence of Gavelsester for the first second and third times, but not beyond a year.

(Extract from the Otford Custumal, c1284, Canterbury Cathedral MSE, 24, ff 69v to 74v, translated by Dennis Clarke).

CHAPTER VII

VH96/5684   A true and perfect Inventory of all the goods and chattells of Thomas Petley Junr. of Filstone in the Parish of Shoreham in the County of Kent, gent taken and apprized by us the 24th day of September in the second year of his Majesties Raigne anno domini 1686 whose names are here under written.

IN THE RED GARRETT   £   s   d

Imprimis   One feather Bedd two feather pillows
one feather boulster two blankets
one rugg one payre of red curtains   3   0   0
and valence three curtain rodds one
bedstedle matt & cords

two trunks one box two chairs
one wrought stoole one court cupboard   0   13 4
& one looking glass

IN THE STUDDY WITHIN THAT CHAMBER

Three Chaires two deale Boxes &
certain books   2   0   0

IN THE HALL CHAMBER GARRETT

one feather bed two feather boulsters
two blanketts one rugg one old couch   1   10 0
& one wrought stoole

IN THE ENTRY CHAMBER

Two feather beds two feather boulsters
three feather pillows fower blanketts
two ruggs two paire of curtains and   4   10 0
vallence six curtain rodds two joined
bedsteddles two matts and two cords

five payre of flaxen sheetes seaven sideboard clothes	5	0	0
Two dozen of Diap Napkins, three dozen of flaxen napkins four paire of pillow coates one looking glass one joined chest & two chaires	4	0	0

IN THE CHAMBER OVER THE LITTLE PARLOR

Two feather bedds two feather boulsters Two feather pillowes two blanketts one rugg one joined stoole one pair of curtains & valence one matt and one cord	3	10	0
one chest of drawers one table four chaires & two stooles	1	5	0
One truckle Bedsteddle one fire pan one paire of tonges & one pair of bellows	0	5	0
one silver hilted sword	1	0	0

IN THE WENSCOATE CHAMBER

One feather bed one Downe bed two feather boulsters two feather pillows two blanketts one green counterpaine one bedsteddle one paire green serge curtains & vallence one matt. & cord three curtaine rodds one window curtain & rodd fower white callecoe curtains one hempen sheete	10	16	6
One great chest three green chaires four little stooles three stands one couch & one looking glass	2	10	0
One pair of andirons and one pair of Bellows one fire pan and tongs	0	4	0

IN THE CLOSETT WITHIN THAT CHAMBER

One old press three wenscote Boxes & certaine earthen ware	0	4	0

IN THE KITCHEN CHAMBER

One feather bed one feather pillow one feather boulster two blanketts one rugg one bedsteddle one paire of curtains & vallance three curtain rodds, one Matt & cord one great chest One box two chaires two stooles one looking glass one window curtain & rod	2	15	0

IN THE OUTER CHAMBER

One Chest one paire of Seacole Racks one seacole firepan two tubbs and other old lumber	1	0	0

IN THE CHAMBER OVER THE BREWHOUSE

Two flock beds three flock boulsters three blanketts two bedsteddles matt & cord	1	14	0

ON THE KITCHEN STARES & HEAD

Three Chests and one box	1	14	0
One silver Tankard one silver Candlecup with a douter, one dozen of silver spoones six silver salts & two silver porringers	16	0	0
Five paire of fine sheetes & two paire of fine pillow coats	2	15	0
Eight paire of course sheetes sixteen course table clothes five towells & four dozen & an halfe of course napkins	4	6	6
Eighteen fine napkins two flaxon table-clothes & fower baskett clothes	0	10	6
One old portmantou & fower fine towells	0	2	6
Six paire of sheetes one odd sheet four dozen of Napkins three paire of pillows coates two side board clothes & two red carpets	4	5	6

Two paire of Holland Sheetes two side board clothes of Diap. seven flaxen

pillow-coates one dozen & an half of Diap. napkins nine small napkins two callecoe sideboard clothes & one Diap towell	2	2	9

IN THE MAIDS CHAMBER

One feather bed one flock bed one feather pillow two feather boulsters three Blanketts two coverletts two Bedsteddles two matts & two cords	1	5	0

IN THE KITCHEN

Five large pewter dishes eight middle pewter dishes sixteen small pewter dishes	3	19	0
Two dozen and eleaven plates of pewter Seaven pewter pye plates one pewter bason one pewter skinner & one pewter flagon	1	9	0
One dozen of small pewter plates & five pewter Chamber potts	0	7	0
Some old Broken pewter	0	10	0
One Bedpan fower pewter porringers one pewter bason & one Quart pott	0	4	0
Two brasse candlesticks	0	5	0
Two brasse kettles four brass skilletts Three brass pans two brass morters Two pestles one brasse warming pan & two brass candlesticks	1	17	0
Two iron potts with hookes & pothangers	0	18	0
Six spitts three iron drippen pans one jacks two Griddirons one iron ovenlidd one tosting irons two iron Racks one paire of iron andirons two fire ? fork & tonge	2	1	4
Fower fowling peeces & a case of pistolls	1	10	0

APPENDIXES

249

One table one form five payles two peeles (shovels) one screene with some other odd things	0	8	6

IN THE BREWHOUSE

One furnace & one fate	6	0	0
Two coolers & two tuntabbs	2	0	0
Two cooles (sic) & five keelers	0	14	4
One sheete one jett & one coper drinking pot	0	4	6
One Bucking Tubb & one pair of pothangers	5	5	6

IN THE MILKHOUSE & BUTTERY

Two dozen milketrays two charnes two old tables one old cupboard five dozen of Teuthers two dozen & an half of plaite trenchers & other odd things	1	12	0

IN THE OLD PARLOR & CLOSETT THERE

Fourteen Leather chaires two tables One joyned stoole one stone one cussion two window curtains one curtain Rodd one paire of bellows one paire of Andirons one fire pan & one payre of tonge	2	6	10

IN THE NEW PARLOR

Two tables a couch frame two formes one joyned stoole eight cushions ten Boxes two coates of Armes, two flower pats glasses & a payre of andirons	0	14	0
one clock	1	0	0

IN THE HALL

Nine teen Rushleather Chaires one table one forme one paire of andirons one paire of tongs three window curtains & rodds one pewter sill & one sideboard	2	16	0

IN THE ENTRY

One table one leather chair one iron beoane scailes & weights one spayde one mathooke & fower	1	19	0

IN THE SELLARS

Seaven scalders, twenty seaven drink tudds fower powdering tubbs one keeler one stoole one hamper	3	15	0
For his wearing apparell & money in the house	2	0	0

WITHOUT DOORES

Eight horses & one colt	22	10	0
Eight fatting Bullocks	16	0	0
Two cowes & one heifer one steer & one bull	7	10	0
Five calves	2	10	0
Sevenscoare sheepe & lambs	35	0	0
Eleaven hoggs & five piggs	6	2	6
five horses harnes	0	12	6
Six plowharnes & six halters	0	5	0
Two waggons two dung coart three plowes three harrowes two dewrakes & plowtackling	6	12	0
Wheat & Misline in the Barne	46	0	0
Barley in the Barne	18	0	0
Oates in the Barne	3	15	0
Clover & hay there in a stack	47	0	0
St foyne Seeds	5	0	0
Wood in the Yard	0	10	0

IN THE MALTHOUSE

One old Querne one Oasthaire one Iron crow one Tymber Chaine a Cheese presse a grinstone & other old lumber & things forgotten & out of sight.	1	6	8
Total	358	5	11

Robert Chapman 26 Oct 1686

CHAPTER X

SHOREHAM FARMS 1835

Farm	Acres	Landowner	Tenant Farmer	Additional Acres
Cockerhurst	481	Sir P.H. Dyke	Bartholomew Spain	V.
Filston	406	Lord Ashburton	Samuel Love, Senr.	V. + 126 part of Timberden Furze & Woodland
Castle	343	Lord Ashburton	Samuel Love, Junr.	V.
Preston	282	Lord Ashburton	Widow of Edward Green	
Sepham	278	George Polhill	William Tonge	V.
Colgates	273	P. P. Ricketts	P. P. Ricketts	V.
Dunstall	273	Capt Ryder Burton	Richard Groombridge	V.
Paine's etc.	272	George Polhill	Henry Friday	
Austin Lodge	269	Sir P.H. Dyke	Edward Coombe	
Weeks	175	John P. Vincent	John P. Vincent	
Romney Street	123	Capt. Ryder Burton	John Glover	V.
Copthall	118	Lord Ashburton	John Nash	+ 5 Two meadows
Home	41	Lord Ashburton	John Day	Publican of George Inn
Timberden (part)	69	G.T. Goodenough	John Day	
Oxbourne	67	Richard Cuthbert	J.C. Rout	+26 Bowling Alley
Timber Garden (until 1986 Oxbourne Farmstead)	59	Richard Cuthbert	J.C. Rout	
Timberden (part)	18	G.T. Goodenough	Mary Mills	65 (Lord Ashburton land etc.)
Total acres	**3547**			

V. = member of select vestry

CHAPTER XIII

Inland Revenue Duty on Land Value 1910
(KAO 1R4/135)
SHOREHAM FARMS
(The 1835 acres taken from Chap. X Appendix)

Farm (and Owner)	Acres 1910	1835	Tenant Farmer(s)
Castle (Mildmay)	316	343	R. Wilson (293a), Millar (23a)
Filston (Mildmay)	306	406	T. Dinnis (188a), A.H. Henshaw, Jnr (20a), Amos Brooks (62a), J. Walton (36a)
Oxbourne (Mildmay)	296	152*	J. Walton
Austin Lodge (Hart Dyke)	290	269	Millar
Paynes (part) (Morris Field)	286	—	(Also includes land & woods on Downs East of village)
Cockerhurst (Hart Dyke)	262	481	R. Buchanan
Sepham (Ex'ors C. Polhill)	232	278	W. Glen
Dunstall (Dunsany)	206	273	S. Carter
Preston (Mildmay)	179	282	J. Buchanan
Week (Vincent)	150	175	—
Romney Street (Dunsany)	148	123	W. Morris
Home (Mildmay)	131	41	C. Kendall
Porters & E. Down (Dunsany)	101	—	Terry
Timberden (Dunsany)	91	87	J. Rumens
Park Corner (Bowen)	90	—	—
Highfield & part Paynes (Cohen)	74	272	—
Well Hill, etc. (Waring)	57	—	—
Little Timberden (Scott)	40	—	—
Toppers (Vinson)	40	—	—
Warren (pt) & Home (pt) (Kersey)	35	—	—
Colgates (Bath)	17	273	—
Total acres	**3347**	**3455**	

* Combining acreage of Oxbourne, Timber Garden and Bowling Alley

CHAPTER XIII

Inland Revenue Duty on Land Value 1910

Principal Property Owners (land and Dwellings)
(with rateable value in excess of £100)

	Rateable Value	
	£	s
F.B. Mildmay	1552	10
Sir William Hart Dyke (Lullingstone)	750	10
Ex'ors late Charles Polhill (died 1874)	711	00
A. de Burgh Wilmot	614	00
Lady Dunsany	476	14
Ecclesiastical Commissioners: Rectorial Tithes	378	10
Charles Blundell	258	16
Lady Cohen	236	10
J.R.B. Gregory	178	5
Mrs Jessie Scott & Ex'ors Russell Scott	169	15
C.A. Morris Field (Tunbridge Wells)	149	00
B.I. Greenwood (noted as Trustee of Baptist & Weslteyan chapels)	115	10
A.T. Waring (Chelsfield)	107	3

CHAPTER XIV

TOWN PLANNING, SHOREHAM, KENT, April 1929
Extracts taken from Petition to the Ministry of Health

Road across the Darenth Valley.

The injury to the Valley
The new road 60 ft. wide involves the destruction of the unity of the Valley by a broad and solid rampart of earth and arches extending on a slanting direction across the Valley. However much such a mass of earth be made to follow the shape of the land, even a height of 10–15 feet to crest of road, cannot be beautiful in itself and must destroy the natural beauty and charm of the Valley.
Rights of Way
Moreover it would have the effect of destroying three rights of way, two on the right bank, and one on the left of the River which now offer uninterrrupted passage from one end to the other of the Valley.
These beautiful and restful walks would be taken away. They are of the utmost value, and to deprive the public of them and replace them by an ugly bank crowned with rushing, noisy mechanical vehicles, seems to your Petitioners an unnecessary interference with our rights and a loss in innocent delights whose values are beyond measurement.
Isolation Hospital
The proposal road will be within 100 yards of the Hospital, a distance which will be diminished for the reasons stated, thereby bringing the patients closer still to the noise and vibrations caused by the wheeled traffic.
That such an inhumane proposal should be made in the year 1929 astonishes your Petitioners. We think it carries its own condemnation, and therefore it is sufficient merely to call attention to it.
Agriculture
Your Petitioners are aware that the Minister has called the attention of the R.D.C. to the desirability of making provision in the scheme for the reservation of land as an open or agricultural belt, but we cannot discover that such provision has been made.
We therefore desire to call attention to the eminent suitability of the Darenth Valley from Lullingstone to Otford for this purpose.
It is one continuous belt of excellent grazing, hop and arable land, and practically devoid of building development.
Milk, hops, fruit and cereals are produced and these afford employment to many villagers as well as people from London at certain seasons, as pointed out in our last Petition.
It is unnecessary to lay stress upon the importance of agriculture merely as a source of food supply, but when as in this case it can be combined with the provision of a "lung" for congested areas as near as London and Dartford enabling the people to see and enjoy nature which is so essential especially to the country-loving people of England, it seems to us that Public Policy should be aimed at the preservation of such an area as the Valley for the purposes indicated – which it is now serving.

INDEX

Illustrations are shown in **bold** type

agriculture: *see* farming
aircraft 178–80, 201
air raids: *see under* Second World War
Alexander, James 164
Alexander, William 164–5, 200, 205, 220
Alfred, King 12
Almshouses 36, **38**, 76
'Ancients, The' 130, 133
Anglo-Saxons 6–7, 9–13
April Cottage 76, **78**
art: *see* Copping, Harold; Franklin White, Charles; Palmer, Samuel; Samuel Palmer School of Fine Art
Ashburton, Alexander Baring, Lord 129, 135, 137, 252
Ashby, Dan 210–11, 213, 215
Augustine, St 9–11

Badgers Mount 170, 202, 216
Balsattes, John 60
Balsatt(e)s: *see* Reedbeds
band: *see* Shoreham Village Band
Baptists 109–10, 139, 141–2, 158, 178, 225
Barbor, Herbert Reginald 193–4
Baring, Alexander: *see* Ashburton, Lord
Baring Brothers & Co 161–2, 173, 200
Barton, Robert 135, 139–40
Bayeux Tapestry **12**, 13
Beardsworth, William 104, 116
Bede, Venerable *quoted* 9
Bellisot/Belsote: *see* Balsattes, John
bells and bellringers 204, 219, 226
Bennett, R.G. *quoted* 39, 65, 86
Berkeley, Maud 185, 191, 201, **202**, 215, 226

Black Death 27, 44, 68
Black Eagle 87–8
Blackheath 32
Blake, William 130
Blundell, Charles 150–1, 180, 183–5, 254
Blundell, George 151
Blundell, James 150
Boakes, Frederick 184, 216
Boddy, William 170–1
Boer War: *see* South African War
bombing: *see* Second World War: air raids
Booker, Arthur G. 165
Booker, Mrs Ella 156, 164
Booker, H. and G. 183
Booker, Joseph 189, 191–3, 198–9
Booker, Mary 135
Booker, Ron 226
Booker, William 198
bordars 19–20, 23
borgha 31, 53
Borrett, (Sir) John 36, 39, 62, 111–2, **112**, 123, 140
Borrett, Thomas 110–4, 118, 138
borsholder 95, 99
Bowers, John **168**, 169–70, 188, 191–2, 197
Boy Scouts 185, 192
Bradewell(e), Thomas de 28, 44–5
British Legion 217
Bronze Age 2
Broomfield, Charles 117
Brown, Stanley (Skipper) 192
Brown, Capt W.A. 211
Browne, Revd Thomas 79, 80–1, 90, 93
Buchanan, Robert 184, 253

257

SHOREHAM

Buckland, Alice 40, **73**
Buckland, Sir Thomas 39
Buckland Chapel: *see under* St Peter and St Paul Church
Burne-Jones, Sir Edward 219
Burton, Capt (later Adm) James Ryder 135–6, 252
Butler, Mrs Margaret 212

'Cade, Jack' 31–3
Cage, The 74, 76, 159
Cameron, Revd Jonathon Henry Lovett 142–3, 154, 157, 159
Cameron, Lt (later Cdr) Verney Lovett 144, **145**, 146
Cantiaci 2
Canute 12–3
Cassam 178
Castle Farm 22, **22**, 30, 40, 67, 114, 134, 150, 164–5, 172, 195, 205, 212, 220, 223, 252–3
Catholics (Roman) 216
Causten, George 65
Causten, Robert 66–7
Causten, Thomas 66–7
Cazalet, Peter 200, 220, 222
Cedwulf 11–12, 222
Celts 2–3
cemeteries 7, 11
Cenwulf 10–11
Cep(e)ham, John (de) 23, 30–1, 36–9, 41–2; *see also* Sepham
Cep(e)ham, de (family) 26
Chadwick, Spencer 159–61, 165
Chapel Alley Cottages 33, 75, 123, 130, 142
Chapman, Robert *quoted* 246–51
Charity School 112–3, 118
Cheeseman, George 164, 171
Cheeseman, Samuel 140, 178
Cheeseman (family) 167, **171**, 185, 191, 196, 209–11
CHI RHO (monogram) 6, **6**, 11
Chillmaid, Thomas 77, 81
Christian Church
    Archbishopric 19, 51, 53, 71
    Baptists 109–10, 139, 141, 158, 178, 225
    CHI RHO (monogram) 6, **6**, 11
    compulsory attendance 55
    crucifix 201, **202**, 215, 225–6
    diocese 141
    Methodists 107–9, 141–2, 157–8, 169, 197, 225
    Parish Church: *see* St Peter and St Paul Church

Reformation 50–1, 79
registers 69
(Roman) Catholics 216
Shoreham deanery 12, 19, 43, 94
Westminster Abbey as patron 54
churches: *see* Christian Church; Romans; St Peter and St Paul Church
Church House 127, 185, 203
Church Street **179**
civil defence 207, 209–10
Civil War 89–93
Clarke, Dennis *quoted* 23–4, 245–6
Clarke, Dennis and A.J. Stoyel *quoted* 10, 19–20, 28, 66–7
Clements, Revd Robert 52
Clerk, Richard 45–6
clover 170–1
Cloveshoo, Council of 10–11
coal 151
Cobbe, Edmund and Isabelle 53–4
Cobbold, Margaret (Sister Mary) 185, 191, 201, 226
Cockerhurst 41, 53, 62, 135, 205, 209, 252–3
Codsheath 16, **17**, 18, 29–30, 32, 37, 42, 95
Cohen, Sir Benjamin Louis 16, 176, 184, 199, 213, 219, 253
coin 4, **5**
Col(e)gate (family) 18, 41, 109–10, 141
Colgates (Farm) 41, 60, 110, 135, 138, 147, 161, 252–3
Coombe Hollow 158, 209, 224
Cope, Charles 146
Copping, Harold **69**, **168**, 178, **179**, 183, 185, 191, 193–4
cottars 23–5, 31
countryside 160, 224–5, 227, 255; *see also* Shoreham Countryside Centre
courts of law 30, 71–2, 74, 85–6, 112–3, 134
cricket(t) 95, 103, 162, 176, 181, **182**
Crookfoot (Crokfot) 21–3, 62
Cross on the Hill, The 189–91, 208, 217, **218**
Crouch, Fred 172–3
Crown Inn 135, 183, 237
Crown Road 150, 192
crucifix 201, **202**, 215, 225–6
custumal 20–5, 37, 245–6

Danks, William *quoted* 99, 119–21, 132
D'Aranda, Paul 40, 64, 87, 96, 99, 100–4; notebook **101**, 102
Darent 41, 75, 192
    origin of name 2

258

INDEX

power for paper-mills 97
valley 1–2, 10, 67, 159, 198, 204–5, 224–5, 227, 255
Darent Hulme 160, 164, 178, 224
Day, William 154–5
deanery (Shoreham) 12, 19, 43, 94
De Decker, Mrs Anne 164, 185, 187, 218
de: *for other names with prefix 'de', refer to next word, e.g. Shoreham, William de*
Depeden, John 62
Depeden, Thomas 62
Diamond Jubilee (Queen Victoria) 165
Dibden 48, 62, **63**, 65, 75, 96
Didley, Joast **101**
Dinnis, Edward George 209, 215
Dinnis, Harold 208–9, 215, 220, 224
Dinnis, John 110, 184, 205, 208, 220
Dinnis, Thomas George 165, 253
Dinnis, Thomas George 215
District Council: *see* Sevenoaks (Rural) District Council
doctors 117–8, 120, 155, 180–1, 184, 211, 219
Doling Day 171
Domesday Book 15, 19–20, 23
Dowdy, Ernest 194, 219–20
Drew, Thomas 164, 187, 220
Du Boulay, Prof J.R.H. *quoted* 11, 16, 23, 38, 53
Dunsany, John William Plunkett, 17th Baron 161, 163
Dunsany, Edward John Moreton Drax Plunkett, 18th Baron 135, 161, 165–6, 174–5, **182**, 184, 186, 188–90, **190**, 194, 198, 209, 213–4, 224, 253
Dunstall Farm 170, 252–3
Dunstall Priory 135, 161, 172–4, 186, 189, 194, 209, 213–5, 224
dupondius 4, **5**
Dyke 121, 126; *see also* Hart Dyke
Dypdens: *see* Dibden

Edmund Ironside 12–13
education: *see* schools
electricity 197–8
Emerson, Revd John 78–80, 83, 89–90
Ethelbert 10, 15
Ethelred 13
evacuees
  into Shoreham 208, 212, 218
  out of Shoreham 216
Everest, Edward 91–2

fairs 181
farming 1–3, 6–7, 19–25, 29, 34, 67, 77, 114, 120, 143, 150, 160–1, 164, 170, 183–5, 195, 205, 208–9, 223, 255
farm labourers' riot 133–4
farms 34, 252–3; *see also by name*
Feldmar, Jean 224
Feldmar, Lewis 224
fêtes 207
feudal system 18–23, 29, 42, 47
Filston 2, 13, 19, 34, 36, 42, 46, 52–3, 60, 64, 76, 87, 92, 110, 129, 133, 246–51
Filston Farm 34, 67, 120, 150, 165, 195, 215, 220, 223, 241, 252–3
Filston Hall **87**, 92, 215
fire brigade 207
fire service 208–9, 211, 213, 215
First World War 184–6; 189–91 war memorials
flax 67, 209
Flower Show and Sports 181
football 181
Forge Cottage 123, 182
Fort Halstead 165, 186, 192, 207, 215
Franklin White, Charles 133, 193–5, **196**, 203
Friars and Pilgrims 76, **76**, 123, 153, 193
fruit-growing 114, 120, 150–1, 154, 172, 180, 183–4, **196**, 205
fulling-mill 38–9, 52, 76–7, 224

gardeners 172–3, 181, 200; *see also* market gardening
gavelkind 16, 23, 31
Geerings' (butchers) 183, **196**
George Inn 64, **64**, 69, 75, 117, 119, 122, 124, 134–6, 143, 167, 180–1, 187, 189, 196, 199, 212, 237, 252
Gibson, Mrs Alice 171, **171**, 172
Gilbourne, (Sir) Edward 71, 86–90, 92
Girl Guides 191
Gliddon, Revd (Cuthbert) Paul 217, 219, 226
Goddestone (Goddingston/Godyngeston(e)) 21–2, 26, 39, 59, 65, 73, 76, 85, 147, 245
Goodenough, G.T. 126, 252
Great Cockerhurst (Cokerhurst/Cockrice) 41; *see also* Cockerhurst
Great House Mead(ow) 39, 113
Greenwood, Benjamin 180, 184, 201, 209, 212, 215
Greenwood, Benjamin Isaac 158, 178, 189, 193, 201, 254
Gregory, George Burrow 136, 142, 176
Gregory, John Roger Burrow 136, 214
Gregory, John Swarbreck 136, 142
Gregory, (Sir) Roger 123, 175–6, **177**, 184,

259

192, 197, 199, 203–4
Gregory, Lady (Mary Bertine) 176, **177**, 178, 198, 212, 223
Gregory (family) 124, 141, 181, 199
Guides: *see* Girl Guides

Halstead 19, 53, 89, 138, 148, 165; *see also* Fort Halstead
Hart, Sir Percival (Percyvall) 68, 86, 88, 90
Hart Dyke, Sir Percyval 135, 150, 252–3
Hart Dyke, Sir William 183, 254
Hart Dyke, Lady (Emily Caroline) 193
Hasted, Edward 17; *quoted* 34, 37, 39–40, 111, 113, 181
health 156, 158–9, 163, 180, 218–9; *see also* doctors; nursing service
hearth tax 96–7
Heath, Revd (one-time Archbishop) Nicholas 54–5
Hengist 9
Henry VIII, King 48·50, 52–5, 68
Hesketh, Maj Charles *quoted* 53
Hewitts (Hewets) 36, 60, 64, 87, 227
Higgins, Mrs Amy 178, **188**
Highfield 161, 176, 224, 253
highways; *see* roads
Hillier, Ronald 208, 222
Hills, Robert 91–2, 97
Holly Place 34, **36**, 66, 76, 138, 213
Home Farm 20, 23, 143, 159, 252–3
Home Guard 209–10, **210**, 211–4, 216
Homewood, John 77
hops 67, 77, 114, 120, 132, 150, 154, 172, 185, 195–6, 209, 223, 241
Horsa 9
hospitals 185, 255
hundred 16–17, 18, 24
Hundred Court 16–18, 29–30
housing 181–2, 218–9, 224
hurricane 227

Ice Age 1
inns 105, 135, 183, 237; *see also by name*
Ireland, W.H. *quoted* 126
Iron Age 2, **3**
Ivy Cottage 130

James, Sir Henry 162–3, 169
James, Miss 163
Julius Caesar 3
Justices of the Peace 70–1, 100–3, 111, 113, 138

Kent
  Anglo-Saxon 9

first map **57**
first settlement 1
Iron Age 3
Kentish Men/Men of Kent 9
origin of name 2
Preservation Order 224
railways **147**
Roman 3–4, **4**
in Tudor times 67
War Agricultural Committee 208
King's Head (King's Arms) 127

Lambarde, William *quoted* 16, 55, 67, 71
lathes 16, 70
law: *see* courts of law
Le Pender, John: *see* Pender, John Le
Lewis, Revd Cadwallader 56, 58
Linnell, John 130, 132, 134, 136
livestock 77, 120
London, Edmund de 28
Longebregge 26
Love, Samuel 133, 135, 252
Lovelands: *see* Record
Lovett Cameron: *see* Cameron
Lullingstone 6–7, 9, 19, 42, 53, 91, 137, 171, 183, 254
Lullingstone Castle 40, 90
Lullingstone Park 2–3, 7, 40
Lullingstone Roman Villa 3–4, 6, **6**

M25 motorway 30, 225
McCaughen 215
McDonnell, Michael 226
MacLening 161, 178, 185, 188
Madge, Revd (Henry) David 181, 185, 187–9, 193, 197, 204
Mannering, PC Reuben 211–2, 215, 217, 219, 224
market gardening 200
Meates, G.W. *quoted* 4, 6
Medhurst, Edward 140, 198
Medhurst, George 119
Mercians 10, 13
Methodists 107–9, 141–2, 157–8, 169, 197, 225
Mildmay, Francis Bingham (Frank), 1st Baron Mildmay of Flete 156, 162–3, 166, 174, 183–4, 188–9, 193, 201, 211, 220, 254
Mildmay, Anthony Bingham, 2nd Baron Mildmay of Flete 174, 199–201, 207, 220, **221**, 222–3
Mildmay, Mrs Georgina 144
Mildmay, (Henry) Bingham 159–60, **162**, 173–4
Mildmay, Henry Francis 162

INDEX

Mildmay, Humphrey Francis 139, 143, 148
Mildmay, Humphrey St John 136–7, **138**, 139
Mildmay, Thomas 52
Mildmay, Sir Walter 52
Mildmay (family) 137, 154, 172, **175**, 199, 220–1, 227, 253
Mildmay Chapel 144, 199
Mildmay-White, Hon Mrs Helen 138, 185, 207, 211, 220, 222
militia 99, 209
Miller, Maj Joseph Charles 210, 215, 219
Mill House 26, **96**, 224
mills 20, 26, 170, 224
 fulling 38·9, 52, 76–7, 224
 paper **96**, 97, 118–9, 224
Moriston 21–3, 40, 42, 62
Morse, Jim 210, 213
motor transport 180, 197, 203, 225
Mount, The 150, 183, 209
Myrtle Cottage 130

Nash 82, 89, 91, 252
National School 139, 153, 155–6
'navvies' (railway) 148
New House 39, 62, 75, 111–2, 123, 125, 136
Normans **12**, 13, 19
North Downs 2
nursing service 163, 180, 185, 211, 219

Offa 10–11
Oliver, Revd Edward 93–4
Orchard House 211
Otford 4, 7, 11, 79
 battles 10
 Court. *see* Shoreham Place
 Manor 11, 15, 19–20, 24–5, 27–30, 39–40, 43, 53
 Palace 48, 58
 parish 2
Oxbourne (Okebourne) 22, 40–2, 161
Oxbourne Farm 34, 40, 65, 72, 76, 85, 89, 92, 138, 252–3

Paine's (Paynes) Farm 41–2, 252–3
Palmer, Samuel **80**, 129, 130–131, **131**, 132, **132**, 133–6, 195
Palsters: *see* Planers
paper-mill **96**, 97, 116–8, 127, 135, 148–50, 169, 183, 187, 191–2, 196, 224
Parish Council: *see* Shoreham Parish Council
Payn 42
Payne, Revd Augustus 199; *quoted* 27–8, 48, 147, 204
Paynes Farm: *see* Paine's Farm
Peasants' Revolt 28–9
Pemell, Peter 30, 147
Pemell, John 30, 146–7
Pender, John Le 21, 23, 245
Penile 146–7
Perronet, Revd Vincent 94, 105–6, **106**, 107–9, 112–3
Petley, Richard 91
Petley, Samuel 52
Petley, Stephen 64
Petley, Thomas 55, 64, **64**, 87, 91–2, 97, 246–51
Petley, William 64
Petley (family) 36, 41, 83
Pig and Whistle 237
Pilgrims' Way 4, 10, 13, 15
Pinnocke, William 115, **115**, 116
Pittman, Edwin 155
plague 68–9; *see also* Black Death
Planas (Planers) 30, 37–9, 48, 53, 60, 65–6, 85–7, 113
Planers, Ralph de 37–8, 113
Planers Farm 34
Players: see Shoreham Village Players
Plunkett: *see* Dunsany
Polhill, Abraham 72–4
Polhill, Charles 113–4, 254
Polhill, David 39, 65–6, 87–8, 90
Polhill, (Sir) George 86, 97, 127, 129, 133, 135
Polhill, John 40, 64–6, 73, 85–8
Polhill, Thomas 40, 65, 55–6, 64–6, 85–6
Polhill, (Sir) Thomas 55, 65, 85–6
Polhill (family) 39, 65, 72, **73**, 82, 85, 88, 90, 253
Polhill (location) 2, 30, 129, 224
Polhill Arms 237
Polhill cemetery 7, 11
Polhill (Lady) Chapel 39
Polhill Tunnel 148
police 211–2
Polley: *see* Polhill (family)
Poor Relief 103, 116–8, 157
Post Office 135, 151, 159, 183, 196, 227
Powcy 89
Powell, Anthony *quoted* 214–5
Preston 39–40, 42, 53, 64–5, 86–7, 96, 102
Preston Hill 171, 186
Preston (Hill) Farm 11–12, 111, 215, 223, 252–3
Prestwich, (Sir) Joseph 1, 160–1, 164, 219
Primary School: *see under* schools
Primrose League 176
public houses: *see* inns

261

SHOREHAM

Puxty 216
Pysden, Mrs Lyn 178, 180

Rackard, Christopher 64, 122
railways 119, 147, **147**, 148, 151, 159, 163, 227; station 147–8, 151, 161, 226
Ramblers, The 183, 203, 208
rape (crop) 67, 223
Rat and Sparrow Club 181
Record 16, 64, 115, **115**, 122, 127, 151
recreation ground 182, 193, 199
rectors: *see under* St Peter and St Paul Church
Reedbeds 34, **35**, 60, 75, 100, 123, 133, 135, 184, 195
reeves 30–1, 51, 53, 94
Repton, Canon Edward 141–2, 144
Reve 61–2
Richmond, George 130–1; *quoted* 132
Ricketts, Peter Pemell 135, 147, 252
Rifle Club: *see under* Shoreham
rifle range 210
ring *5*
Rising Sun 183
Ritchie, Kenneth 199, 203, 207, 209, 212, 214, 219, 226
Riverside House 122, **122**, 127, 178
roads 2, 75, 126–8, **128**, 129, 148, 157, 170, 197–8, 204–5, 225, 255
Romans 3–6, 9
    British Kent **4**
    coin *5*
    ring *5*
    in Shoreham 4, 6
    villas 3–4, 6, **6**
Rom(e)ney, Henry and John 18, 62
Romney, Thomas 64
Romney Street 23, 64, 86, 135, 164, 183, 210, 252–3
rood-screen 48–9, 50, **50**, 90, 140, 219
Roos, John 36–7, 46
Rose and Crown 91
Round 81–2, 88–9, 91, 119, 126
Royal Oak 180, 199
Rural District Council: *see* Sevenoaks (Rural) District Council
Russell, Alexander 97, 103, 118
Russell, Benjamin 126–7
Russell, Frank 178–9, 200, 214
Russell, John 116, 118

St Peter and St Paul Church (Shoreham parish) 11–12, 19–20, 26, 39, 45–6, **49**, 54, 79, 113, 120, 123, 140–4, 146, 158, 165, 198–9
    bells and bellringers 204, 219, 226

bombed (Second World War) 215, 219
Borrett memorial 112–3
Buckland (Gregory) Chapel 126, 199
Cameron homecoming 144, 146
Church Room 182–3, 208
lych-gate 143
Mildmay Chapel 144, 199
Mission Chapel 165
organ 141, 176, 197
'pelican' window 46, 48, 90, 219
Polhill (Lady) Chapel 39
Polhill memorials 85–6
rectors 28, 43–6, 48
rectory 93–4
registers 69, 93, **93**
rood-loft 126
rood-screen 48–9, 50, **50**, 90, 140, 219
stipends 55, 105
tithe barn 197
vicarage 51–2, 94, 141
vicars 43, 51–2, 55, 79–82, 93–4, 105–9, 126, 129, 134, 141, 146, 163, 165, 173, 178, 183, 185, 187–8, 199, 210, 216–7, 219, 226
war memorial 216–7
Saker 135, 153
Samuel Palmer School of Fine Art 133, 195
Sandys, Col Edwin 89–90
Saxons: *see* Anglo-Saxons
Saye and Sele, Lord 32
schools 58, 135, 138, **164**
    Charity School 112–3, 118
    Infant School 163
    National School 153–5, 159
    Parochial Mixed School 156, 163
    Shoreham Primary School 226–7
Scouts: *see* Boy Scouts
Second World War 207–17
    air raids 211–6, 226
    thanksgiving service 218, **218**
    Victory in Europe parade 217. **217**
    war memorials 216–7
    war savings 215
Sepham 18–9, 21–2, 26, 29, 36–7, 48, 53, 60, 62, 85; *see also* Cep(e)ham
Sepham, John 48; *see also* Cep(e)ham, John (de)
Sepham Farm 5, 34, 66, 252–3
servi: *see* slaves
Sevenoaks 31–2, 75, 89–90, 148
Sevenoaks Railway Co 147–8
Sevenoaks Rural District (later District) Council 169–70, 225
sewer 159–60
Shard, Sir Abraham 112
Shepherds Barn 2, 77, **80**, 134, 165, 193,

INDEX

209
shops 115–6, 135, 180, **196**, 227
Shoreham, Thomas de 46
Shoreham, William de 26–7
Shoreham (and district) **map facing 1**
   air raids (Second World War) 216
   Amicable Benefit Society 156–7, 180
   and Otford Nursing Association 163, 219
   Castle 40, 65, 112
   Church: *see* St Peter and St Paul Church
   Cottage: *see* Shoreham House
   Court: *see* Shoreham Place
   Countryside Centre 226
   Cricket Club 162, 176, 181, **182**
   deanery 12, 19–20, 43
   Gazette 226
   House 125, 136, 143, 175–6, **177**, 211–2, 223–4
   origin of name 1, 7
   parish 1, 12, 20, 26–7, 79, 94, 134, 156, 183
   Parish Council 156–7, 168–70, 188, 191–2, 224–5
   Place 11, 23, 75, 113, 136, 138, **138**, 162, 172, 199, 207, 211, 215, 220, 223
   population 75, 116, 134, 155, 223
   Primary School: *see under* schools
   Rifle Club 181, 189
   Society 225–6
   Street 122–3, 135, 138
   tribe 2
   Turnpike 127, **128**, 129
   United Football Club 181
   Village Band 164–5, **166**, 181–2, 187, 189, 193, 199, 203, **204**
   Village Players 193–4, 198, 203, 219
   yokes 20–1, **21**, 22–3
Silver Jubilee (King George V) 203
slaves 19, 23
Smart, Ken *quoted* 215
smugglers 104–5
Sopwith, Canon Thomas Karl 173, 178
South African War 165–7
Special Constables 209, 211–2
Stafford, Sir Humphrey 32
Steane, John Vincent 156, 163, 176, 181–2, 185, 192–3, 197
Stenton, Sir Frank *quoted* 15
Stirling, Sir Walter 125–7, **128**, 129, 136
Stone Age 1
Stoyel, A.J. 10; *quoted* 12, 48; *see also* Clarke, Dennis
Streatfield, Robert 122, **122**

sulung 20–1
Summerfield, George 196
Summerfield, Jack 212
Sutton-at-Hone 16, 70, 88
Symondson, Philip **map 57**

Tatham, Frederick 129, 131–2, 134
Teflynge 21–4, 60, 62, 245–6
Terry, Thomas 83
Testa, William de 44
Textus Roffensis 11–12
Timberden 7, 21, 60, 62, 135, 146, 191, 223, 252–3
tithes 16, 37, 45, 51, 56, 67, 79, 143, 147
Townfield Cottages 213, **213**, 214
Tudor Cottage **69**
Tudors 47–74
Turnpike: *see* Shoreham Turnpike
Two Brewers 180, 199, 220
Tyler, Wat 29, 31
Tymberden: *see* Timberden
Tymberden, Robert (de) 18, 23, 26, 29–30, 52
Tymberden, Thomas 29

vicarage: *see under* St Peter and St Paul Church
vicars: *see under* St Peter and St Paul Church
Viel: *see* Vital
Vielestun: *see* Filston
Vikings 12–13
Village Hall 189, 191, 193–4, 210
villeins 20, 23
Vital **12**, 13, 19
Voluntary Aid Detachments 185

Waldron, Sir Anthony 90–1
Wales, Edward, Prince of (later King Edward VII) 163
Wall, Revd William 94, 102, 105, 114
Walnut Tree Club 192–3, 197
Walnut Tree Cottages 76, 123, 135, **196**
Walnut Tree Trust 219
Waren, John 51
Warham, Archbishop William 48, 51–2
war memorials
   First World War 189–91
   Second World War 216–7
Warren Farm 223, 253
Wars of the Roses 47
Water House 123, 130, **132**, 133, 135, 142, 158, 161, 178
water supply 198
Wesley, Charles 105, 107, 109
Wesley, John 105–8, **108**, 109, 132

263

Westminster Abbey 54, 79, 114, 141
Wheatsheaf 237
Wheeler, Helen *quoted* 26–7
White, Alfred 153–4
Wickins, Hugh (Hugo) 43–4
William, Duke (later King William I, The Conqueror) **12**, 13, 15, 18, 34
Willmott, Thomas 118–9
Willmott, William 117–8
wills 81–3, 92, 116, 160–1
Wilmot, Albert de Burgh 178, 183, 254
Wilmot, George 135, 146, 148, **149**, 150, 176, 192
Wilmot, Henry 127
Winslade 76, 123
Women's Institute 189, 207
Women's Land Army 185, 209
Wood, Arthur 220
Wood, George 143–4
workhouse 116–8, 180
World War I: *see* First World War
World War II: *see* Second World War
Wulfred 11, 222

yokes 20–1, **21**, 22–4, 31, 36–7, 59–60, 245–6